Routledge Revivals

Block Printing & Book Illustration in Japan

Block Printing & Book Illustration in Japan (1924) was one of the first guides to Japanese illustration, and remains indispensable to this day. The author travelled widely in Japan, persuading Japanese collectors to open their archives to her for study, and here compiles a wealth of unique research.

Block Printing & Book Illustration in Japan

Louise Norton Brown

First published in 1924
by George Routledge & Sons, Ltd.

This edition first published in 2025 by Routledge
4 Park Square, Milton Park, Abingdon, Oxon, OX14 4RN

and by Routledge
605 Third Avenue, New York, NY 10017

Routledge is an imprint of the Taylor & Francis Group, an informa business

All rights reserved. No part of this book may be reprinted or reproduced or utilised in any form or by any electronic, mechanical, or other means, now known or hereafter invented, including photocopying and recording, or in any information storage or retrieval system, without permission in writing from the publishers.

Publisher's Note
The publisher has gone to great lengths to ensure the quality of this reprint but points out that some imperfections in the original copies may be apparent.

Disclaimer
The publisher has made every effort to trace copyright holders and welcomes correspondence from those they have been unable to contact.

A Library of Congress record exists under LCCN 24015879

ISBN: 978-1-032-90344-6 (hbk)
ISBN: 978-1-003-55748-7 (ebk)
ISBN: 978-1-032-90345-3 (pbk)

Book DOI 10.4324/9781003557487

LOUISE NORTON BROWN

BLOCK PRINTING
AND
BOOK ILLUSTRATION
IN JAPAN

MINKOFF REPRINT
GENÈVE
1973

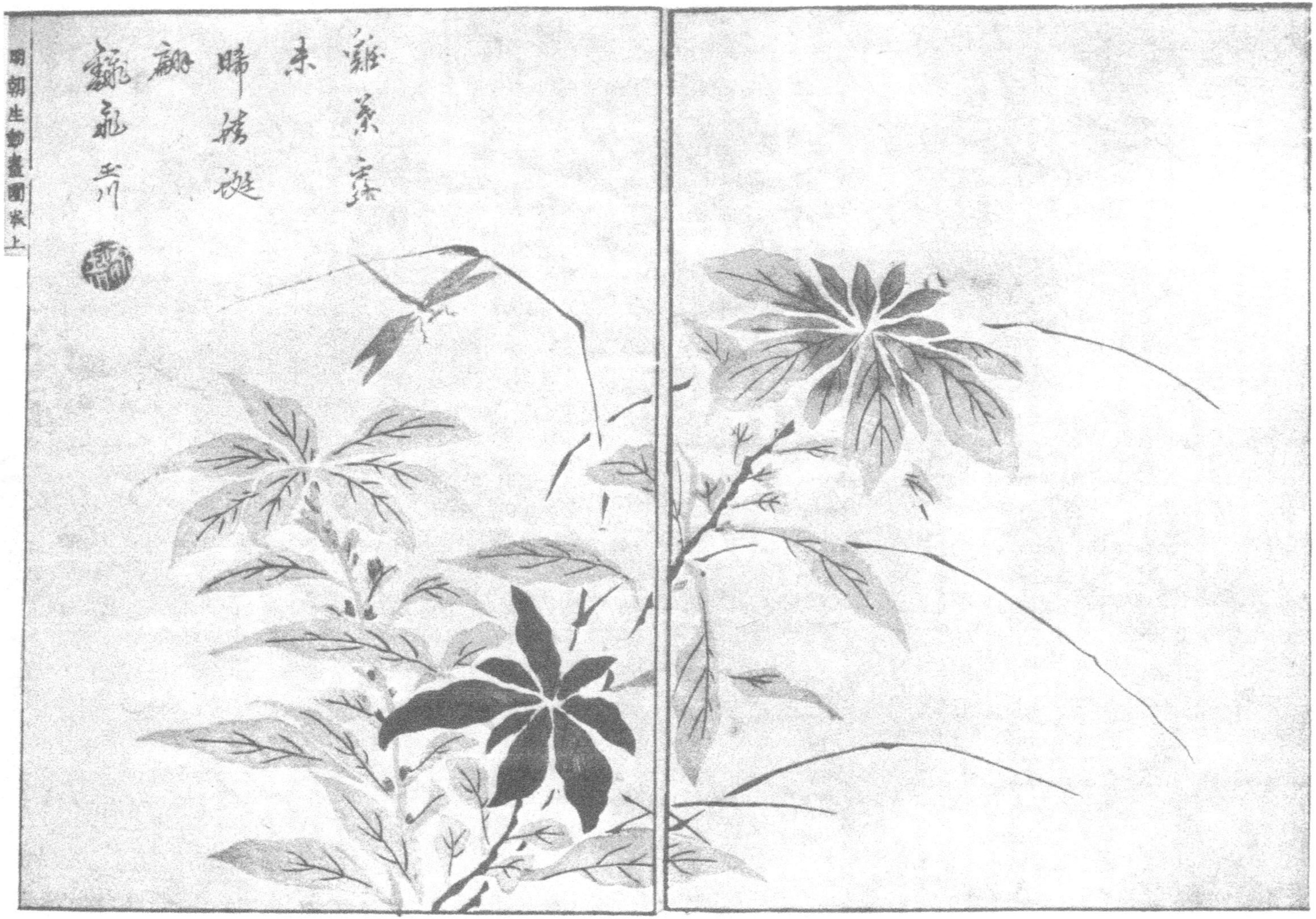

PLATE 1] From the MINCHŌ SEIDŌ GWAYEN. Vol. 1. 1746. By Ooka Shunboku (see page 110). [Front.

BLOCK PRINTING & BOOK ILLUSTRATION IN JAPAN

BY

LOUISE NORTON BROWN

WITH FORTY-THREE PLATES (EIGHTEEN IN COLOURS), AND
COPIOUS INDEXES OF TITLES AND ARTISTS

LONDON
GEORGE ROUTLEDGE & SONS, LTD.
NEW YORK: E. P. DUTTON & CO.
1924

To
Kyōto—best beloved of cities

PRELIMINARY NOTE

OOKS about Japanese life and art tend to be somewhat decorative in style; this book is written with the cold precision of an academic schedule. Let no one confuse Mrs Norton Brown's reticence with the mechanical dryness of the mere archivist or compiler. The picturesque volubility to which we are accustomed in books about the East proceeds indeed not from profoundly stirred emotion, but from superficial sentiments and impressions; whereas in the colourless severity of Mrs Brown's style there burns the white-heat of an overmastering passion.

The Japanese are in general, and with good reason, suspicious of foreign enthusiasts; but fanaticism in pursuit of a whim or a hobby has from immemorial times delighted them. How often we read of collectors who in their zest "forgot to eat or sleep". In Mrs Norton Brown her Japanese friends found not only fanatical devotion to a hobby, but also a most disarming humility. Her books were to her a sort of religion, and she (who possessed a knowledge of Japanese illustration which will never be rivalled in Europe or America) was till the last obsessed by the fear that she was not worthy to be the prophet of so glorious a cult. Thus she gained the confidence of every important collector in Japan. One by one these reputedly inaccessible gentlemen collapsed before the onslaught of so extravagant an enthusiasm, coupled with a respect for bibliographical studies so deep that it almost amounted to awe.

It was, then, partly the author's intimate relations with native students, clerics, dealers, and collectors, and partly the enormous range and extent of her own collection, that enabled her to write this unique book. At the time of her death it was already in print. But the final revision (consisting in the correction of obvious misprints, the final choice of illustrations to accompany the book, the addition of a few essential footnotes and references, and the preparation of the Indexes) had to be committed to other hands. Those who have undertaken this task are conscious that it is one which only the actual author of a book can ever properly perform.

W. S. S.

PREFACE

I HOPE, by means of this book, to hand on to other collectors information which I had to dig out, bit by bit, slowly and laboriously, and patch together. I have purposely refrained from any dissertations on style or beauty (even though sometimes sorely tempted), because I have assumed that collectors would not be collectors if they did not know beauty and good work when they found it. What I wished most, myself, when I first fell a victim to the fascinating hobby of book-collecting in Japan in 1913, was plain, hard facts, such as names, dates, and the *Where* and the *How* of things. Gradually some knowledge of this kind was garnered, and in the course of time I came to believe that it might be of a little value to others.

In addition to my indebtedness to the writers of the books listed in the Bibliography, I have to thank many Japanese friends who have been most generous, of their time as well as their knowledge, in helping me.

Among those to whom I am especially grateful for valuable help are Mr Kubota and Mr Nakamura, the Curators of the Nara and Kyōto Imperial Museums; Dr K. Hamada, Dr T. Naitō, and Mr Umehara, of the Kyōto Imperial University; Mr Ashikaga, the Librarian of the Hongwan-ji Buddhist College in South Kyōto; the Abbot and priests of Tōshōdai-ji and Mibu-dera in Nara and Kyōto, who went to great trouble in having a rare set of Buddhist rolls sent up from Nara to Kyōto, so that I might examine it at my leisure at Mibu-dera; Mr Saga, the well-known Buddhist scholar of Kennin-ji; Mr M. Wada, the Chief Librarian of the Imperial University Library in Tōkyō, who, together with Mr Bunshichi Kobayashi, was kind enough to go over my manuscript and correct it; to Dr R. Saiki, of Kyōto, who made it possible to see some valuable private collections; to Mr Y. Tanaka, who acted as my secretary; and to many other abbots, priests, artists, and collectors who helped me in many ways.

If the book wins even a few friends for Japanese thought and art, the time given to writing it will have been well spent.

L. N. BROWN.

LONDON.

CONTENTS

CHAPTER I
EARLY PRINTING AND ENGRAVING IN JAPAN - - - - - - - 1

CHAPTER II
ILLUSTRATED BOOKS OF THE SEVENTEENTH CENTURY - - - - - 23

CHAPTER III
MORONOBU, ITCHŌ, KŌRIN, AND THEIR FOLLOWERS - - - - - 41

CHAPTER IV
ŌSAKA AS AN ART AND PUBLISHING CENTRE - - - - - - 63

CHAPTER V
THE IMPRESSIONISTS: THE SHIJŌ AND MARUYAMA SCHOOLS - - - - 84

CHAPTER VI
THE IMPRESSIONISTS: THE GANKU AND THE CHINESE SCHOOLS - - - 102

CHAPTER VII
UKIYO-YE ILLUSTRATORS OF THE NISHIKAWA, OKUMURA, TORII, AND NISHIMURA GROUPS - 128

CHAPTER VIII
UKIYO-YE ILLUSTRATORS OF THE UTAGAWA, KATSUGAWA, AND KITAGAWA SCHOOLS - - 151

CHAPTER IX
LATE UKIYO-YE ILLUSTRATORS - - - - - - - - 174

CHAPTER X
MODERN ILLUSTRATORS OF JAPAN - - - - - - - - 198

CHAPTER XI
MISCELLANEOUS BOOKS - - - - - - - - - 205

CHAPTER XII
SUGGESTIONS TO COLLECTORS - - - - - - - - 218

OLD-BOOK SHOPS IN JAPAN - - - - - - - 232
GLOSSARY - - - - - - - - - 233
BIBLIOGRAPHY - - - - - - - - - 237
INDEX - - - - - - - - - - 241

LIST OF ILLUSTRATIONS

PLATE		FACING PAGE
1. Minchō Seidō Gwayen. By Ōoka Shunboku. (*Coloured*)	*Frontispiece*	
2. An Engraving of Taishaku-ten		8
3. An Engraving of Kwannon		10
4. Jūgyū-dzu		16
5 and 6. Yūdzū Nembutsu Engi		18
7. Sanjū-rok-kasen		24
8. Jinkō-ki		28
9. Kyō-Warabe. By Moronobu		34
10. Taka Byōbu Kuda Monogatari. By Moronobu		42
11. Soga Monogatari. By Moronobu		44
12. Wakoku Shōshoku Edzukushi. By Moronobu		48
13. Yamato Kosaku Eshō. By Ryūsen		52
14. Kyō Shimabara Yujo Ningyō Tsukai. By Yoshikiyo		54
15. Ehon Shahō Bukuro. By Morikuni		64
16. Onna Buyū Yosoöi Kagami. By Tsukioka Masanobu		66
17. Toba-ye Akubi-dome. By Shunchōsai		76
18. Ehon Shibai Banashi. By Shunkōsai. (*Coloured*)		78
19. Meika Gwafu. By Sosen. (*Coloured*)		82
20. Bumpō Gwafu; and a Sketch by Bruyer. (*Coloured*)		84
21. Tōkei Gwafu		88
22. Raikin Dzui. By Kitao Masayoshi. (*Coloured*)		126
23. Ehon Tokiwa-gusa. By Sukenobu		130
24. Shinsen Ō Uchiwa. By Okumura Masanobu (?)		134
25. Kokon Shi-shibai Hyakunin Isshu. By Kiyonobu		136
26. Aka-hon Sarukani Gassen. By Shigenaga		142
27. Ehon Seirō Bijin Awase. By Harunobu		142
28. Ehon Yotsu-no-Toki. By Shigemasa. (*Coloured*)		148
29. Ehon Imayō Sugata. By Toyokuni. (*Coloured*)		152
30. Ehon Azuma Warawa. By Toyohiro. (*Coloured*)		154
31. Ehon Eigadane. By Shunchō. (*Coloured*)		162
32. Shiki-no-Hana. By Utamaro. (*Coloured*)		168
33. Shinsen Kyōka Gojū-nin Isshu. By Shinsai. (*Coloured*)		174
34. Sumidagawa Ryōgan Ichiran. By Hokusai. (*Coloured*)		176
35. Hokusai Gwa shiki. By Hokusai. (*Coloured*)		180
36. Ehon Tōshisen. By Hokusai		182
37. Hokusai Gwafu. By Hokusai. (*Coloured*)		184
38. Hokkei Mangwa Shōhen. By Hokkei. (*Coloured*)		186
39. Fusō Meisho Kyōka Shū. By Hokkei. (*Coloured*)		188
40. Meishu Gwaso Shū. By Gakutei (*Coloured*)		190
41. Meiji Gwafu. By Seiko. (*Coloured*)		202
42. Kaigwai Shinwa Shūei. By Fuko		214
43. Yokohama Kaikō Kenbunshi. By Sadahide		216

BLOCK-PRINTING AND BOOK-ILLUSTRATION IN JAPAN

CHAPTER I

EARLY PRINTING AND ENGRAVING IN JAPAN

THE civilization of Japan is vaguely supposed by the inhabitants of the other side of the world to be of comparatively recent origin, dating from the time when the Meiji Tennō took his place as the real ruler of the empire and intercourse with Europe and America began. This idea is based, of course, upon the assumption that civilization can only be built on tangible and material foundations and is to be measured entirely by the utilitarian contrivances with which the Occident surrounds herself—contrivances which may or may not be means to an end, but certainly are not an end in themselves.

What really happened in 1868 was that Japan found her ancient life with its love of beauty and poetry and art to be incapable of coping with the more materialistic development of the West. She realized that unless she, also, took the path along which Occidental life was travelling, her identity as a nation was sure to be lost. It was a step on, but not necessarily a step up, for Art and Literature, the very flowers of civilization, had bloomed for Japan while Western Europe was still in her swaddling-clothes and America an unknown land.

This ancient culture was gained from China and Korea, and it is probable that intercourse between these countries and Japan commenced much earlier than is indicated by any existing records. The collection in the Shōsō-in, at Nara, of articles that had belonged to the Emperor Shōmu in the eighth century, could by no possibility have been used by people lately emerged from barbarism. The appreciation of beauty and the fine artistic feeling evidenced in those beautiful old musical instruments, *go* boards with marvellous inlaid work of pearl, ivory and coral, silver dishes and wine-cups of exquisite design and workmanship, old brocades, beautiful examples of bronze-casting, and manuscripts in such chirography, were not attained in a day. A race does not jump to æstheticism in a few generations. It requires the slow evolution of many centuries, and it is probable that soon after the beginning of the Christian era the civilization of Japan commenced to parallel that of her older neighbours.

Only traditions are left, however, of the civilization existing previous to the sixth century, and it is with the introduction of Buddhism into the country that we get our first historical facts. The missionary priests of China and Korea who appeared in Japan soon after the year 500 A.D. teaching the tenets of the Buddhist faith are the first figures to be distinctly seen through the haze which envelops the very early history of the country. These ardent pioneers brought with them copies of the Sūtras and other religious books, Buddhist statues and incense burners, and various other sacred paraphernalia, either emblematical or for use in religious services, and applied themselves with the almost superhuman zeal the Oriental nature is capable of, to winning the Imperial sanction for the propagation of the faith and its adoption by the people.

Although antagonism toward them ebbed and flowed for almost a century, it finally disappeared in the great wave of acceptance and enthusiasm which followed the conversion of the powerful Prince Shōtoku about 580 A.D. Nephew of the Empress Suiko and Regent of the Empire, his power was really supreme, and the entire Court followed its sovereign and her adviser in becoming ardent devotees of the new religion. In order that the faith might be known the length and breadth of the land, however, it was necessary to send priests with the Sūtras and other Buddhist works as well as religious emblems and images to different parts of the country. This could only be done from centres established in Japan itself, since the distance from Korea and China was too great to permit of easy and constant travel. Priestly scholars made their way, therefore, to Yamato, where they taught the reading and writing of the Chinese characters along with the principles of the cause they represented, and with artisans who understood carving, building and bronze-casting, took up their permanent abode in the new land.

At the beginning of the seventh century the Empress ordered an Imperial Rescript to be issued encouraging the spread of Buddhism, and the scholars who copied the Sūtras so beautifully, and the men who designed the temples and carved or cast the impressive Buddhist figures which were set up in them, were not only treated with the greatest reverence and consideration, but also received substantial material rewards, in the form of grants of land and rice.

The new religion, bringing in its train as it did both art and literature, must from the first have appealed strongly to the impressionable and beauty-loving nature of the Japanese, and the heart of the entire nation opened to its influence as the rain flower opens and holds up its cup for the rain. It was ready for the æstheticism and learning which were the accompaniments of the new faith, and accepted them with a passionate eagerness that knew no bounds.

As has been said, it was no primitive race who thus accepted Buddhism, and so quickly and so easily assimilated its doctrines—rather was it a people who already had achieved the spiritual and mental growth necessary for its appreciation, and had stored up a marvellous potential energy, which was ready to loosen like a spring, at the right touch, and develop in a myriad of ways. Emperors and Empresses left the throne that they might become monks and nuns, and spend their lives in studious seclusion. Princes became artists and writers. Nobles of the highest rank studied for the priesthood, and the monasteries became centres of learning where not only literature and art were taught as vehicles to bring the new faith to the people, but mathematics, geography, astronomy, and medicine as well. Silk-weaving and the manufacture of pottery, which had been known from a much earlier time, responded to the stimulus by the increased beauty of brocades, and vases and incense-burners for temple use. Paper had been introduced from Korea in the third century, and its manufacture had long been established. Nothing was lacking, therefore, for the rapid development of all the arts and crafts which could in any way foster the spread of the new doctrine, and a common tie united the men who worked at them.

Printing, as one of the most valuable agents of this kind, must have come into use in Japan to some extent almost as soon as the first Chinese and Korean priests appeared there. Its invention is attributed to the Chinese, and it is probable that it was known in some form in both Japan and China at a much more ancient time than is commonly supposed. The earliest manner of its use was by taking rubbings from texts cut in stone or metal, and this method was employed in China, according to Du Halde, a learned Jesuit priest, who travelled there extensively in the early eighteenth century, long before the Christian era.[1]

In Japan, also, this method was used at a very early period, and tombs there in the sixth and seventh centuries were marked by copper plates known as *bōshimei*, with epitaphs cut into the metal in precisely the same manner as that in which the copper plates for visiting cards are engraved to-day. There are several such grave plates in the museums in Japan, and in the Nara Museum there is also a long, narrow, gilt-bronze plate with a slender projection at one end, bearing an inscription dated Daikwa 3,

---

[1] The following is quoted by Du Halde from a Chinese book supposed to have been written in the reign of the Emperor Wu Wang about 1120 B.C. " As the stone *me* (Chinese for ' blacking ') which is used to blacken the engraved characters can never become white, so a heart blackened by vices will always retain its blackness."—(From *The Invention of Printing*, by T. L. De Vinne, p. 109.)

CHAP. I] JAPANESE BLOCK-PRINTING

or 694 A.D., commemorating the erection of a Buddhist statue at one of the Nara temples. Rubbings from this show the text in white against a black ground, and were probably made for distribution among the people who had become converts.

Wood-block printing came into use in China long after this more primitive mode, and the first record of its employment there is said to have been in 593 A.D., when the Emperor Wên-ti is supposed to have ordered certain texts and rules engraved on wood in order that they might be printed for distribution.[1]

It was wood-block printing also which became the important medium in spreading the knowledge of Buddhism in Japan, and the earliest existing examples of the art, so far as known, are four dhârani[2] from the Buddhist Sūtras ordered to be printed by the Japanese Empress Kōken, in Tempyō Hōji 8, or 764 A.D., the year in which, after having been obliged to give up her cherished dream of spending the rest of her life in a convent when she retired from the throne in 758, she again took up the reins of government and returned to the palace under the name of Shōtoku.[3] These little prayers are printed on slips of paper about 2 inches wide and 18 inches long, and are known collectively as the *Muku Jōkō Dhârani Kyō*. While the blocks for the dhârani were being engraved, other wood-carvers were busy in cutting the million small, hollow wooden pagodas which the Empress had commanded as boxes or cases, each of which was to contain one of the dhârani, tightly rolled and inserted in the tube-like receptacle under the spire.

This great work was completed in Hōki 1 or 770 A.D., and the pagodas, known as *hyakuman-tō* ("million towers"), with the prayers they contained, were distributed among the different temples throughout the country. A number of these little pagodas and dhârani are national treasures in the Kofūzō of Hōryū-ji and in the Imperial Museums of Japan. The Nara Museum has five of them, no two exactly alike, and the dhârani also differ from each other in size, printing, and paper. Two are printed on rather thin fine paper, and the others on a much heavier quality of a yellow-brown colour, that looks almost like felt or chamois skin. At the Hayashi Sale in Paris in 1902, one of these little works was listed in the catalogue[4] as the earliest example of wood-block printing in existence, and this is the generally accepted opinion of scholars in regard to them.[5]

[1] This date is probably not wholly to be depended upon. See "Note on the Invention of Printing" (*New China Review*, 1919) by Arthur Waley, of the British Museum.

[2] These dhârani are the Kompon, Jishinin, Sōrin, and Rokudo.

[3] Not to be confused with the Prince Shōtoku who lived two centuries earlier.

[4] Under the title of *Muku Jōkō Kyō*.

[5] These dhârani are just one hundred years older than the rolls discovered by Sir Aurel Stein in Western China and described in his *Ruins of Desert Cathay* (vol. ii., p. 189).

Just when the first printed pictorial work was attempted in Japan is not known. The subjects of the earliest engravings were invariably of a religious character: simple line drawings of Buddha and other Buddhist divinities at first, and then, as time passed and famous priests died and were deified, they also formed the subjects of many of these temple prints. The printing paraphernalia was all in the temples. The blocks were cut by the priests, the drawings themselves were often their work, and the printing was done by them. The sheets varied in size from mere slips of paper a few inches long to engravings a foot or more in length, and formed the precious souvenirs which the numerous pilgrims who visited the temples took away with them then, exactly as they do to-day, to be used as charms to ward off illness and misfortune.

Although there is every reason for believing that wood-engravings of this kind were made in very ancient times in Japan, and several famous priests of the seventh, eighth, and ninth centuries are credited with having carved the blocks for them,[1] the blocks in existence said to date from these early centuries are all of rather doubtful authenticity. The oldest are at Kōya-san, Nara, Shingū, and Nikkō. The Kōya-san block is supposed to have been cut by Kūkai, the Abbot of Tō-ji and Kōya-san, better known as Kōbō Daishi, who lived between 774 and 835 A.D. It is $10\frac{1}{2}$ inches wide by 26 inches long, but since the edges seem hardly sufficiently worn to indicate such extreme age, it is thought by many scholars to be of a much later period. Nevertheless it is cherished with the most extreme care by the temple, and is only taken out of its protecting covers once in fifty years, when prints are made from it for distribution among the different monasteries of the Shingon sect.[2] An engraving from this block is in the British Museum, but Dr. Anderson, in his *Japanese Wood Engraving*, says: "It can hardly be accepted as genuine." It seems, however, perfectly possible, in view of the great care taken of it, that the block may really date from the ninth century, even if the printed sheet just spoken of was made at one of the semi-centennial printings at a much later time.

In the private collection of Mr. Morita, of Nara, there is an old temple block—a *mandara*—about 18 inches wide by 3 feet long, which is thought by some Japanese antiquarians to date from the ninth or tenth century, although it is so worn that no date is discernible.

Another very ancient block, supposed to be of the eighth century, was the property of the Shingu Gongen, the collective name for the shrines of Kumano in the south-eastern part of the province of Kii. These temples,

---

[1] Shōtuku Taishi (573–621), Gyōgi Bosatsu (670–749), and Sugawara-no-Michizane (845–903) are said to have carved such blocks.

[2] See "On the Early History of Printing in Japan," by Sir Ernest Satow, in the *Transactions of the Asiatic Society of Japan* (vol. x., part 1, p. 81).

which were among the oldest in Japan, were destroyed by fire many years ago, and the block is kept in one of the other buildings in Shingu. It represents the special deities to whom the Kumano shrines were dedicated, but is so worn from the thousands of impressions that have been made from it that it is impossible to decipher any date even if it once bore one. The most that one can say of it is that it is obviously of immense antiquity.

There is a block in the Hongū shrine at Nikkō, which, at the time I write (July, 1917), is causing much discussion among Japanese antiquarians. It is 12 inches wide by 31 inches long, and bears on one side a representation of Batō Kwannon, or Kwannon with the horse's head, and on the other a figure of Benzai-ten, with a *biwa* in her hand and a group of fifteen young acolytes at her feet. Above at the right of the block is a running figure of Daikoku-ten above his two rice bales, and at the left a figure which is supposed to be Inari. The date Shōwa (承和) Kino-e-ne, Shōgwatsu, corresponding to January-February of 844 A.D., is carved on one of the long, narrow sides of the block.

The story of its discovery is as follows: Professor M. Akahori, formerly of Waseda University, Tōkyō, who has devoted much study to the Nikkō temples, found in 1911 an allusion to this block in the *Nikkō-san Shi*, a *meisho* for Nikkō, published in 1837. He instituted an unsuccessful search in the three-storied pagoda, where it was supposed to be, and again at intervals in other places, finally deciding that it must have been destroyed during the changes which followed in the wake of the Restoration. In the spring of 1915, however, it was unearthed, together with several other blocks from the old treasury of Shihonryū-ji, just west of the three-storied pagoda. At first the block was accepted as a genuine ninth-century cutting, but recently some doubt has arisen in regard to it, and art critics maintain that Daikoku was not represented with the rice bales until the Muromachi period. Anderson, in his Catalogue, says: " In the earliest Japanese representations of Daikoku, the rice bales are replaced by a lotus leaf; the hammer and bag were added in the eighth century by Kōbō Daishi in accordance with a vision in which the god appeared to him as the ' Lord of the Five Cereals.' "

The Japanese critics who have questioned the age of the block do not assert that the date was added at a later time, but think that it has some reference to the statue which the cutting represents, rather than to the time when the block was carved, although in other old blocks the dates carved upon them are invariably taken to mean the time of the cutting. It is possible that the art critics themselves may be mistaken in asserting that Daikoku was never represented with the rice bales as early as the ninth century. The style of the drawing, however, is undeniably like that of work belonging to the Muromachi period, and it is this, rather than the presence of the rice bales that would cause one to hesitate in ascribing the block to as early a time as the ninth century, although it is obviously much older than the others found with it, which date from the Shōan, Ōyei, and Kōshō periods.

The other blocks unearthed from the treasury of Shihonryū-ji include one representing Aizen-Myō-ō, a deity with a flaming halo, three eyes and six arms, who was supposed to govern the pestilences and other evils which too often visited mortals. The date on this block is Shōan 4, or 1175. In an old diary of this time written by Kujō Kanezane, an ancestor of the present Kujo family, an entry occurs which states that, in order to propitiate the deity and bring to an end a malignant fever that was raging in the country, the Imperial Household had offered prayers to Aizen-Myō-ō, and ordered three hundred sheets to be printed from this block and distributed among the people. The entry is dated the fifth day, of the ninth month, of the first year of Angen, which would have corresponded to August-September, 1175,[1] and since the fourth or last year of Shōan was the same as the first year of Angen, it forms a curious and interesting corroboration of the year in which the block was cut.

Earlier than this, however, by over a century, is a block representing Amida coming from heaven to welcome the faithful, in the temple treasury of Raigō-ji at Sakamoto, not far from Kyōto. It is said to date from Kwannin 1, or 1017,[2] and was described by Sir Ernest Satow in his "Early History of Printing in Japan," published in the *Transactions of the Asiatic Society* in 1882. A wood-engraving of the goddess Kwannon, bearing a date corresponding to 1186, mentioned in a Japanese work on the antiquities of the empire, called the *Azuma Kagami*, is also spoken of by Sir Ernest Satow.

Mr. Laurence Binyon, in his most interesting preface to the *Catalogue of Japanese and Chinese Woodcuts in the British Museum* (1916), speaks of a wood-engraving in the Petrucci collection in Brussels copied from an embroidered *mandara* of the Tempyō period. The engraving is coloured by hand, and Mr. Binyon says that M. Petrucci assigns it to the tenth or eleventh century.

A set of beautifully written Buddhist texts from the *Hokke-kyō* Sūtra was made early in the twelfth century. This is known as the *Senmen Koshakyō*, and is a national treasure. The chirography is upon fan-shaped sheets of paper, decorated with charming Tosa paintings of different subjects, the outlines for which in some of them are *printed*.[3] The use of *shikishi*, or

---

[1] At this time the Japanese chronology was slightly earlier than that of Europe, and the fifth day of the ninth month would have fallen some time before the middle of August by European reckoning.

[2] Unfortunately the block has been repaired, and braces at the back and sides hide any inscription which may be there.

[3] My attention was first called to this fact by Dr. Torajirō Naitō, of the Kyōto Imperial University.

CHAP. I]   JAPANESE BLOCK-PRINTING

decorated writing-paper, goes back many centuries,[1] and the first colour-printing in both Japan and China was probably used for this purpose, being quite incidental to the written text which overlaid the printed design and having no connection, as far as subject was concerned, with it. Although the *Senmen Kosha-kyō* belongs to Tennō-ji Temple in Ōsaka, there are twenty or thirty sheets, of the series of one hundred and thirty, in the Tōkyō Imperial Museum, twelve in the Nara Museum, one in Kyōto, and one in Hōryū-ji. The naïve and delightful practice of putting small printed sheets of a Buddhist deity inside the same deity, to make up, with the carved figure, some number like five hundred or one thousand, and thus quickly and easily propitiate the god, began probably in the late Fujiwara period and continued into Ashikaga times. Among the earliest of these printed sheets are those found in the nine statues of the Kubon Amida in Jōruri-ji Temple, near Kama Station in Yamato. These statues are attributed to Jōchō (died 1053), so that the printed sheets found inside the figure, although undated, are doubtless also of the eleventh century. They are carelessly made and were evidently printed from a block upon which a number of the drawings were carved, and then sheets of paper filled with as many impressions from the block as there was room for. Each little figure is 1¾ inches high.

In the very fine collection of Buddhist bronzes and carved figures belonging to Mr. Hashimoto Kwansetsu, the well-known Kyōto artist, there is a statue of Bishamon-ten of the early Kamakura period. While this statue was undergoing repairs Mr. Hashimoto found that the head could be removed. In doing this he discovered that the inside of the figure was crammed with printed sheets of the same deity, each engraving being about 6 inches high and numbering, in all, 999, with from three to nine prints on a sheet. Although there is no printed date, some of the sheets bear, in an ancient fashion of writing, the date Ōho 2, third month, seventh day, corresponding to a day early in the year 1162.

There is a statue of Amida, carved by Hokkyō Eiken, in the temple of Joraku-ji, near Ishibe in Omi province, inside of which Mr. T. Myōchin, a sculptor employed by the Government to keep important carvings in repair, found some months ago a number of sheets bearing little engravings of the statue, and also some of a pagoda. These date from Enkei 3 (1310).

Saeki Sōjō, the Abbot of Hōryū-ji, has a number of wood-engravings of this kind which have been found in different statues, among them some of

---

[1] See "Characteristics of Japanese Painting" (part ii.), by Sei-ichi Taki, in the *Kokka* (vol. xvi., No. 183, p. 51).

In this connection should be mentioned the well-known treasure of Daigo-ji, called the Tenchō Inshin (Buddhist teachings of the Tenchō era), originally written in the third year of Tenchō (826). The scroll owned by Daigo-ji is a copy made of the original roll at the order of the Emperor Go-Daigo (1319–1339). This fourteenth-century roll is written on paper, which, although it may be Chinese, is decorated with a heavily gaufraged and *printed* design in green and brown.

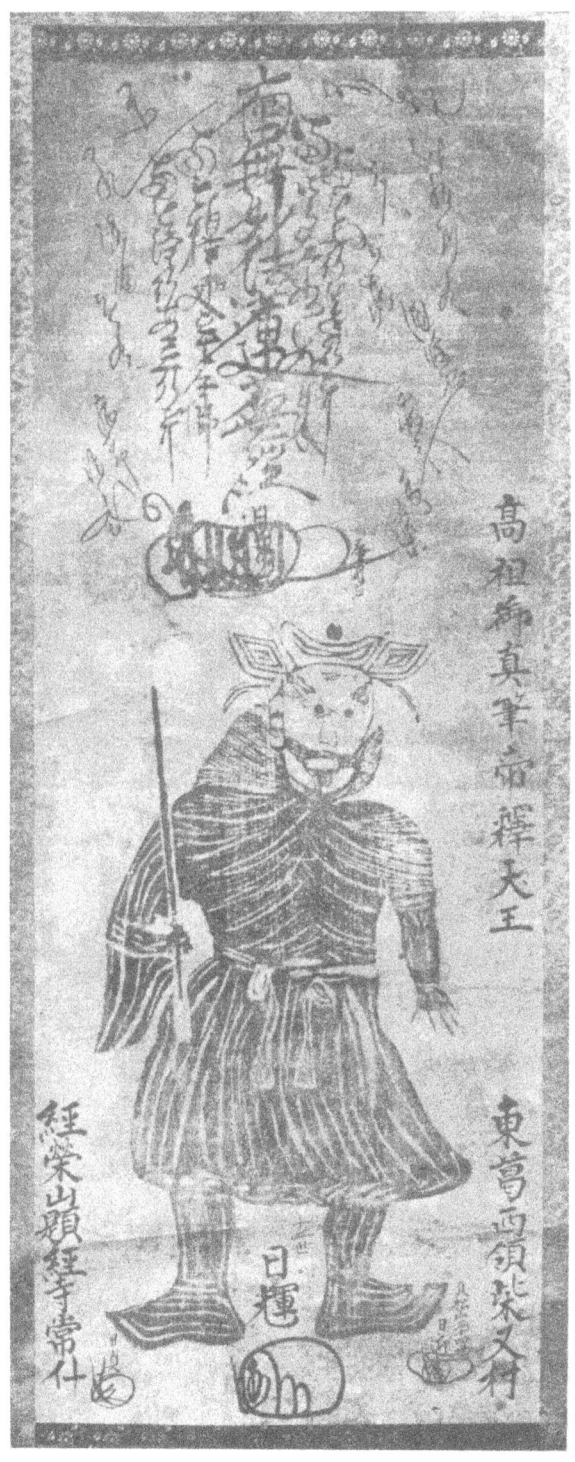

PLATE 2] An engraving of Taishaku-ten from a block cut by the priest Nichiren (1222—1282). The block is in the temple of Kyoyei-zan Daikyō-ji, in Shibamata-mura, near Tōkyō.

[Face p. 8

Amida, which were found inside of the sitting Amida at the left of the main trinity by Tori Busshi, on the altar of the Kondō of Hōryū-ji. This figure is of the early Kamakura period, a copy of a Suiko piece that once occupied the place. In Sangyō-in, one of the many buildings belonging to Hōryū-ji, the statues of Jikoku-ten, and Tamon-ten (Bishamon-ten) also of the Kamakura period, both contained small printed sheets of these deities.

Over at Hanazono, a little west of Kyōto, in the temple of Hōkongō-in, the main statue of Kwannon probably once contained such engravings, for in repairing it a few years ago Mr. Myōchin found on the base an old paper bearing an inscription, which, translated, reads: " Printed every day 333 figures of Kwannon to divide among believers. Shōwa (正和) second, ninth month, twenty-ninth day " (1313). The engravings themselves, however, had disappeared.

There is also a block of the Fujiwara period belonging to the famous Gojō-Tenjin shrine in Kyōto, representing the *Takara-bune*, and it was the custom to print at each New Year's time sheets from this block and distribute them among the people. On the night of the Setsubun festival (early in February) the engravings were put under the pillows of their possessors, and were supposed to bring dreams presaging good fortune for the coming year. Mr. Takeuchi, the editor of the Kyōto *Hinode Shimbun*, has one of these little engravings, which dates from the Kamakura period.

Although these early prints have little artistic value, and were printed from blocks that were carved with no especial care, they still are exceedingly interesting as being very early wood-block work, which European writers have, as far as I know, completely ignored.

In the thirteenth century the famous priest Nichiren (1222–1282), the leader at that time of the powerful Hokke sect of Buddhists, made some engravings of Taishaku-ten, whose spirit he believed had guarded him at times from great danger. The block from which these quaint engravings were made still exists as a treasure of Kyōyei-zan Daikyō-ji, a temple in Shibamata-mura, not far from Tōkyō. It is 4 feet 3 inches long and about 19 inches wide. Above the figure of the deity is the *Dai-moku* or prayer of the sect in Nichiren's chirography with his signature. This block is far more archaic than any of the blocks of earlier dates, suggesting that, however devout a priest Nichiren may have been, he was not gifted with striking artistic ability. The painstaking care so apparent in the other early work of this kind is absent here, for this block differs from the others in that the drawing, except of the face, is not in outline, the wood having been cut away from the edges of the figure and in lines in the clothing only, thus showing the figure as a mass of black on the printed sheet, with white lines indicating the folds of the drapery. Since one hesitates at being a heretic, perhaps if one regards this venerable work as a first experiment in impressionism, and

JAPANESE BLOCK-PRINTING

its seeming crudity as sophisticated simplicity, one may retain one's faith in the priest as an artist as well as a saint.

In the collection of Mr. Bunshichi Kobayashi of Tōkyō there are several very ancient temple prints. The most important of these represents a half-reclining figure of Kwannon most beautifully coloured by hand. The figure occupies the lower part of the sheet, while above is a Chinese poem dedicated to the goddess, with the name of the artist-priest, Dōgen Zenshi, of Ehei-ji Temple in Echizen, and the date Ninji 3 (1242). This is perhaps the most beautiful old temple print in existence. The drawing of the figure has much the feeling of that in the tenth century *mandara* painted on the walls and pillars of the pagoda of Daigo-ji, a temple some distance south-east of Kyōto.

Another extremely interesting old print in Mr. Kobayashi's collection represents twelve Buddhist divinities in four rows of three figures each, surmounted by a figure of Shaka. Back of each figure is a halo coloured by hand with vermilion. The paper is much discoloured by age, but the printing is clear and strong. This print bears no date, but is believed to be of the Kamakura period.

There is also a very interesting early fifteenth-century wood-engraving of the Jūichi-men Kwannon (eleven-faced Kwannon) belonging to Mr. Tanaka Kanbei in the Kyōto Imperial Museum. It is printed on five sheets of paper, placed one above the other, and measures 2 feet in width by about 5 feet in height. At the bottom, on the left, is the signature of the priest Sōyo, who cut the block, and on the right the date Ōyei 22, second month, which would correspond to January-February of 1415. Although brown with age, the engraving is still in a remarkable state of preservation, and as it has been mounted as a *kakemono* and is kept rolled and in its box, it will doubtless survive many more centuries.

By the beginning of the fourteenth century—over a century before the very earliest wood-engravings of Europe[1]—pictorial wood-engraving in Japan was certainly well established, and was beginning to be used in some of the *kyō-mon* or sacred Buddhist books.

There are many temple blocks of this century in existence, of which the well-known set by the priest Ryōkin, representing different Buddhist divinities, is perhaps the most interesting. These blocks bear the date Shōshu 2, or 1325. A small facsimile of one of these engravings is printed in Anderson's *Japanese Wood-Engravings*.

Chion-in Temple in Kyōto owns three fourteenth-century blocks, all

---

[1] The earliest European wood-engravings known are the *St. Christopher Print* of 1423, the *St. Bridget Print* of about the same time, and the *Brussels Print* of 1468 (some authorities give 1418). The first European book known to contain wood-engravings is the *Book of Trades* published in Frankfort-on-the-Main in 1564. See *The Invention of Printing*, by T. L. De Vinne, p. 70.

PLATE 3] Engraving of Kwannon beautifully coloured by hand. Signed Dōgen Zenshi. Dated Ninji 3 (1242). In the Bunshichi Kobayashi collection in Tōkyō.

representing Hōnen Shōnin, or Enkō Daishi, the founder of the Jōdo sect. The earliest dates from the fourth year of the second Shōwa, or 1315; the second from the fourth year of Jōji, or 1365; and the third bears an inscription stating that it was cut by the priest Seidō in the sixth year of Jōji, or 1367. The blocks are all of about the same size, and measure from 12 to 13 inches wide by 20 to 30 long.

At the time Professor Akahori discovered the blocks already described in the go-down of the Nikkō Hongū-ji, two blocks of the Ōyei and two of the Kōshō year periods came to light. These are all double-faced blocks, each cutting representing one of the eight famous priests of the Shingon sect, known collectively as the Shingon Hassō. The two Ōyei blocks represent the priests Kongōchi, Ichigyō, Zemmui and Kōbō Daishi, and bear the signature of the carver, Yukai, with the date Ōyei 33, or 1426. The Kōshō blocks represent the other four priests, Ryūmō, Ryūchi, Fukū and Ekwa, and are dated Kōshō 1, or 1455. The name of the carver is not given, but the execution is identical with that of the two Ōyei blocks.

Still another block of the Shingon Hassō bears an inscription stating that it was cut by the priest Yukai from a drawing by Hōgen Shimyōbō Shusui in *Kōshō nenshu* ("certain year of Kōshō"), and that the work was done by order of one Eikai, who furnished the funds for the cutting of the block and the printing of sheets from it for distribution among the people, in order to help the cause of Buddhism. The year-period Kōshō was very short, beginning in 1454 and ending in 1457, so that the block must have been carved in one of those three years.

At the time these blocks of the Shingon Hassō were cut, the Nikkō temples belonged to the Shingon sect, and it was not until Tenkai Jigen Daishi was appointed Abbot, in 1613, that they came under the control of the Tendai Buddhists. The blocks had doubtless been put away at that time and forgotten until discovered by Professor Akahori in 1915. There are still two great chests of old blocks in the treasury of Rinnō-ji at Nikkō which have not yet been thoroughly examined. Most of them are blocks of old *kyō-mon* and bear no pictorial work. One, however, that I was allowed to drag to the light from its dusty resting-place is a representation of Amida and bears the almost illegible inscription, "Amida Reizō Aizen Ō Sonzō," with the date Chōkō 1, fifth month, corresponding to May-June, 1487. On the other side is a carving of Shaka seated upon a lotus flower.

From this time on there were hundreds of such blocks cut and engravings printed from them, but it would be tedious to further elaborate the list. They are chiefly interesting as early examples of wood-block work, but have little individuality of drawing or technique, and are confined to a narrow range of subjects. It seems very possible, however, that other blocks as old or older than the ones found in Nikkō may still be hidden away in the go-downs of other temples where they have been lying forgotten for hundreds of years, for the Chinese and Korean priests who came to Japan in the early centuries penetrated to distant parts of the Empire, where they established many monasteries in which the various arts and crafts were taught, and it may well be that in the forests around Nikkō, Nara, and places in Yamato and Kii, there are half-forgotten buildings where old blocks cut in those remote days are lying among the mouldering rubbish of centuries. As Japanese scholars awaken to their importance as forming immensely valuable additions to the history of pictorial engraving, perhaps these deserted and half-ruined buildings will be more thoroughly searched.

ANCIENT RELIGIOUS BOOKS

Just when wood-engravings were first used in books and rolls as illustrations to the text it is impossible to say, although it is certain that it was much earlier than has been believed. Printed books without illustrations were known in Japan soon after Buddhism was introduced into the country, as the Chinese and Korean priests brought copies of the Sūtras with them which had been printed in their own lands.

One of the earliest works, the blocks for which are known to have been cut in Japan, and of which a complete set is still in existence, is the *Jō-yuishiki-ron*, published in ten rolls and beautifully printed from *movable* wooden types. This ancient work is kept in the Shōgō-zo, the detached library of the Shōsō-in, at Nara. The last roll ends with a colophon, stating that the blocks were cut by the priest Kwanzō of the Tōfuku-ji Monastery, and that the printing was finished on the twenty-sixth day of the third month of Kwanji 2, corresponding to a day in February or March of the year 1088. A box of the movable wooden types used in printing these rolls is in the treasury of Tōdai-ji in Nara.

In the first year of Chōkwan (1163) this work was published again from a written copy which had been made by Shigemori, the son of the famous Kiyomori. Still another edition was published in Kenkyū 6, or 1195. This formed the first of the *Kasuga-ban*, or Buddhist books printed in Nara and dedicated to the Kasuga-Myōjin,[1] whose shrine was upon the slopes of Kasuga-yama, the eastern hills of this beautiful district. The blocks for this edition of this noted work are still kept in the treasury of Kōfuku-ji.

These very early books were followed by a number of others printed at different monasteries at about the same time, or before the end of the

---

[1] The Kasuga-Myōjin is the collective name for the four Shintō deities, Takemikatsuchi, Futsunushi, Amenokoyane, and Hime-kami. The first two are gods of war, the third accompanied the Divine Grandson, Ninigi, on his descent to the Japanese islands, and the fourth is believed to be Jingō-Kōgō, the Empress who subjugated Korea.—*Eastern Asia Official Guide-Book*, vol. ii., p. 114.

century, and in Shōan 2 (1172) the priests of the ancient temple of Sanzen-in on the hill above the little village of Ōhara, north of Kyōto, published an edition of the *Jūshichi-Kem-pō*, or *Seventeen Laws of Shōtoku Taishi*, which had been compiled by the Prince Shōtoku in 604 A.D.

From this time on, in constantly increasing numbers, religious works, copies of Chinese and Korean books, encyclopædias, and works on morals appeared, many of which with their dates have been listed by Sir Ernest Satow in his valuable monograph.

Beautiful books known as *Nara-e-bon*, with text and pictures done by hand, were made early in the Kamakura period, and considering the alertness of the Japanese mind and the fact that wood-engraving had probably been practised to some extent, at least, as early as the ninth century, it seems certain that very early experiments must have been made in the cutting of blocks for pictorial work in printed books.

Any one who has examined many of the works of these early centuries without illustrations will remember the numerous and elaborate seals which were often engraved along with the text, the borders of the colophon, and the *hashira* on the outer edges of the pages. These in themselves practically constituted wood-engravings of a decorative character, and it would have been the easiest of easy steps to cut blocks bearing true pictorial work in addition to the text.

The fact that the first illustrated books were invariably of a religious nature, and the property of temple libraries and priests rather than the laity, would account for the slight mention of them in foreign works on Japanese engraving. They are not easily seen, at the best, for in the temples of many of the sects, especially the Zen and Shingon, which contain so much that is mystical and beneath the surface, the temple treasures, except those which are set apart to be shown, are seldom seen by visitors.

During the last few years, however, there has been an annual exhibition of old religious books in the library of the Hongwan-ji College in Kyōto, where Buddhist works dating back many centuries have been shown which are of extraordinary interest. Like the old blocks which had lain forgotten for so many centuries in the go-down at Nikkō, there are probably many very old books in temple libraries in different parts of Japan which these exhibitions may be the means of bringing to our knowledge.

Perhaps a word in regard to the form in which the old religious books were published is in place here. The *kyō-mon*, or purely sacred books, were almost invariably mounted as *ori-hon*, or long, narrow, upright folding books, the folding of the pages being symbolical of the folding of the hands in prayer, the word *ori-hon* really meaning " praying book."[1] The rolls were the old Chinese form of binding, and many of the ancient Japanese religious

[1] See *Japanese Wood Engraving*, by W. Anderson, p. 57 in small edition.

works were mounted in this way, while the *shōgyō*, or books of a more descriptive character, not scriptures intended for temple services like the *kyō-mon*, were usually, even in very ancient times, bound in true book form.

The oldest of the books exhibited at the Hongwan-ji College so far, containing anything in the way of illustration, is the *Daihan Nehan Kyō*[1] *Nyorai Seibon*, owned by Kōshō-ji in Kyōto. The wood-engraving it contains as a frontispiece was printed from a single block cut during the Ninan period (1166-1169) by a priest of the ancient Sairaku-ji Temple at Ishiyo-mura, a little village on the Hodzu River not far from Kyōto. This temple was burned many years ago, but the books and records and many of its treasures were saved and removed to Kōshō-ji, where they still are. According to the old records, the block was cut to furnish engravings to be used as frontispieces in all the books of the temple library, and also to be sold to pilgrims as charms against misfortune. The drawing is very simple, representing the nine Buddhist statues which formed the chief treasure of the ancient temple. All the books at Kōshō-ji saved from the collection of Sairaku-ji have copies of this engraving pasted into them as frontispieces. The text of the *ori-hon* containing the one from which the accompanying photograph was taken was written by hand some years after the block had been made, and ends with a colophon stating that it was the work of Shinkō, a priest of Sairaku-ji, and finished the fourth year of Jishō—corresponding to 1180. The engraving is on heavy, rather coarse paper, brown with age, and of quite a different quality from that on which the text was written. It is probable that large numbers were printed and kept at the temple to be used as required, both for the library and to be distributed to pilgrims.

An *ori-hon* of the thirteenth century containing wood-engravings as true illustrations to the printed text was among the books exhibited in 1916. It is the property of Nanzen-ji in Kyōto, and was discovered in 1914 by Mr. Saga, a well-known priest and Buddhist scholar of Kennin-ji, during the rebuilding of the Nanzen-ji library and the temporary removal of the books to other quarters. This *ori-hon* is the last volume of a set of eleven of the *Dempō Shōjū-ki*, published, according to the colophon on the last page, at Reizan-ji in Sagami province in the tenth year of Kōan (1287), in order to obtain funds for the temple. Unfortunately only two numbers of the set were found, and it is not known whether the others contained illustrations. Indeed, it was not certain, until the unearthing of these two old volumes, that this very ancient edition of the *Dempō Shōjū-ki* contained cuts at all, and that the illustrations in the three-volume edition of 1630 were not printed then for the first time. The discovery of the two *ori-hon* of this early edition sets this question at rest, therefore, and proves that the engravings in the 1630

---

[1] *Mahāparinirvāna Sūtra* ("Book of the Great Decease").

books were copied from the original work. The volume from which the photograph was taken contains forty-six of these primitive woodcuts, one at the top of nearly every fold. Most of them are much smaller than the one reproduced, and consist of a single small figure or some Buddhist emblem.

A book entitled *Sanken Itchi Shō*, written by the priest Dairen in an endeavour to harmonize the teachings of Buddha, Confucius, and Laotze, was printed in the first year of Bumpō, or 1317, which is supposed to have contained a few wood-engravings. I have not been able to see a first edition of this work, but am told by Buddhist scholars that the illustrations in an edition of 1649 were copied from engravings in the original work. An elaborate colophon in the 1649 edition explains that the original blocks were badly cut and became cracked and broken, in consequence of which new blocks were made and this seventeenth-century edition published (in Keian 2 or 1649), " in all respects like the first book except that *katakana* characters are added to the Chinese text so that people may read more easily." The wood-engravings are so exceedingly primitive in character, and resemble in such a marked degree those in the *Dempō Shōjū-ki* published only thirty years before the first edition of the *Sanken Itchi Shō*, that it seems very probable that they really are copies of extremely old originals. The subjects are religious emblems and utensils used in temple services.

Another very early work was the *Ryōgon-Kyō*,[1] published at Tenryū-ji, west of Kyōto, during the Nanboku-chō period, toward the close of the fourteenth century. It consists of ten *ori-hon*, the first of which contains an oblong wood-engraving 6 by 9 inches, as a frontispiece, representing Buddha seated upon a lotus flower before a temple gate, surrounded by other Buddhist divinities and his disciples. The printing is admirably done on smooth paper of a beautiful texture, much resembling parchment. These books belong to the library of Ryōsoku-in, one of the monasteries of the Zen group of Kennin-ji in Kyōto, which is said to contain some of the most ancient and valuable Buddhist works in Japan.

The Nara temples also own some very ancient sacred books which contain engravings. A set of six hundred *ori-hon* of the *Daihannya Haramita Kyō*[2] is probably the earliest. This rare work is the property of Saidai-ji, the chief temple of the Shingon-Ritsu sect, situated about three miles from the city of Nara. It was published in the Kamakura period, and contains a wood-engraving of Monju-Bosatsu as a frontispiece. At the end is a written inscription which translated reads:

" In thankfulness for the peace of the Imperial Court and the firm establishment of the Buddhist faith, I have read these books before the shrine of

[1] *Langkāvatāra Sūtra*. [2] *Prajnā Pāramitā Sūtra*.

Hiraoka[1] to which they have been presented, with the hope that they may long be treasured there and serve to increase the growth of our blessed religion."

(Signed) YESON, priest of Saidai-ji.[2]
Gift of the nun, NEN-A.

25th day of the third month of the second year of Kōan
(February-March, 1279).

The *Hokke-giso* is also a very early work. It consists of several rolls, the first of which contains a small frontispiece of nine Buddhist divinities, probably representing some old temple group, printed on the upper part of the first few inches of the roll. At the end is the date Einin 1, corresponding to 1293. This set of sacred books was shown at an exhibition of ancient Buddhist works held in Nara in the spring of 1916.

Another series of the *Daihannya Haramita Kyō* is a Kasuga-ban of Jōwa 1, or 1345. It contains a frontispiece of Buddha surrounded by his disciples, about 8 inches high by 23 or 24 inches wide. These *ori-hon* belong to Shin-Yakushi Temple, which also owns a later edition, probably of the Keichō period, printed from slightly larger blocks and with narrower marginal lines.

The famous Tōdai-ji Temple of Nara owns two exceedingly interesting sets of a Kasuga-ban known as the *Daihōkō Engaku Shudari Ryōgi Kyō*, one mounted in two rolls and the other bound in true book-form. They contain a double-page frontispiece representing Shaka-Sanzon and Jūroku-Zenjin surrounded by other divinities, and at the end an upright tailpiece, about $3\frac{1}{2}$ by 7 inches, of Ida-Ten, the protector of Buddhism, with a flaming halo behind his head and his hands clasped before him in prayer. Both of these engravings are from well-cut blocks and are beautifully printed. Although this work bears no precise date, it is thought by antiquarians to belong to the Meitoku period (1390–1394).

A remarkable religious book of a slightly later time is an edition of the *Myōhō Renge Kyō*[3] belonging to Tōshōdai-ji Temple in Nara. In the first edition it formed probably the earliest of all the Japanese printed books, having been published in Shōreki 4, or 1080, from the original written manuscript, by Dengyō Daishi, of the ninth century. It was printed a number of times in succeeding years, and early in the fifteenth century appeared with illustrations added to the text. This edition is in eight rolls. Seven of them contain wood-engravings as frontispieces, representing different aspects of the Buddhist paradise (really small *mandara*), and it is probable that originally they were all thus embellished, as the roll without a plate is torn at the end and part of it is missing. The pictures vary slightly

---
[1] An ancient shrine in the province of Kawachi.
[2] A famous priest who lived between 1200 and 1290.
[3] *Saddharma Pundarīka Sūtra.*

PLATE 4] From the Jūgyū-dzu, a 15th century go zan-ban.
Imperial University Library, Tōkyō.

in size, but are about 8 inches high and from 20 to 26 inches wide. Although no two are exactly alike, they all represent Buddha and his disciples seated upon a terrace, with worshippers below. In front, at the foot of the terrace steps, the various phases of earth-life, its temptations, hell, and the gradual progress of the soul, are depicted, with the narrow path leading to paradise shown where Buddhist angels await the new-comers to welcome them to their strange surroundings. At the end of the last roll there is a small wood-engraving of Zenzai-Dōji as a tailpiece, followed by a colophon stating that sixty-six sets of the work were printed by the priest Kengaku in the Plum month of the Dragon year of Ōyei, which translated into our more prosaic English corresponds to January-February of 1412.

A little earlier than this, in Kyōto, the Zen monasteries of Kennin-ji, Nanzen-ji, Tōfuku-ji, Tenryū-ji, and Shōkoku-ji, were all printing editions of religious and moral works which received the name of *go-zan-ban*, or " five-mountain blocks," from the fact that they were printed at these five famous temples under the shadows of the encircling hills.

The *Jūgyū-dzu*, literally meaning " ten pictures of the ox," was, as far as is known, the first and one of the few *go-zan-ban* to contain illustrations. This rare and most interesting work is bound in book-form and measures 7 by 9 inches. The ten wood-engravings it contains are enclosed in circles 3 inches in diameter on a black ground margined by a narrow white space. Their meaning is mystical and only to be fully comprehended by a student of Zen. The ox, however, represents Truth, and the engravings the Soul's aspirations and the ten steps in its search for Truth. The first cut is of a man carrying a rope and hurrying along a river-bordered path; the second shows him as he discovers some ox-dung on the road before him; the third represents him hurrying after the ox, which is disappearing in a tangle of trees, while in the fourth he has thrown his rope over the ox's horns and is being dragged up a hill by the animal. The fifth cut represents him leading the ox. In the sixth he is astride the back of the great animal and is playing upon his flute. (This picture is well known to everyone familiar with Japanese art, and signifies the victory over self and the harmony with Truth which this victory brings.) The seventh cut represents the man before a hut by a river's bank, engaged in meditation, the moon rising behind the mountains at the back. The eighth is simply a white disc on a black ground, signifying the spiritual calm and equilibrium which meditation brings. The ninth cut is a drawing of a landscape and flowers, typifying the appreciation of Beauty which Zen gives, and the tenth and last cut represents the searcher for Truth as reaching it through his meeting with the Buddha himself.

Even though unfamiliar with the Zen teachings, anyone with imagination may get a glimmering of what the book means. Unfortunately, like most of the *go-zan-ban* this work bears no precise year, although known to date from the Ōyei or Eikyō period.¹ The accompanying plate is from an original edition of this remarkable book owned by the Imperial University Library in Tōkyō.

Another exceedingly interesting *go-zan-ban* is the *Fukugen Koku-hon Kunshi Kōji*, a copy of a Chinese work on morals, dating from the early Muromachi period (toward the close of the fourteenth century). It consists of two volumes, 6½ inches wide by 8½ inches high, bound in true book-form, and contains an account of the creation of the world, the first kings, the duties of kings, the relation of the family to the state, children to parents, methods of instruction and government, the best means of punishment for different crimes, etc. At the top of each page is a primitive but most delightful wood-engraving illustrating the text below. This unique book is in the private collection of Dr. Torajirō Naitō, of the Imperial University, Kyōto, and is said to be the only one in Japan, although the library of Waseda University in Tōkyō possesses an old reprint.

Early in the fifteenth century a block-printed work was published in Japan which eclipses anything else known in the way of mediæval wood-engraving. This is a history of the Yūdzū Nembutsu sect of Buddhists, known as the *Yūdzū Nembutsu Engi*. It was printed from the original manuscript history of the Nembutsu sect, written by the priest Ryōnin in 1125, the year after the sect was founded by him. The work consists of two large scrolls, 11 inches wide and each 76 feet long. Interspersed with the beautiful text are twenty wood-engravings, many of which are several feet in length. The drawing is in the Tosa style, and the printing, where it shows at the edges of the colour which was applied afterwards by hand, and in the masses of black which are formed by it, is extremely well done. The paper of the rolls looks and feels like soft undressed kid. It is brown with age, but the work is nevertheless in a most remarkable state of preservation, being kept in the fine old black-and-red lacquered box which was probably made for it at the time it was published. The rolls bear three dates, Ko-ō 1, or 1389, when the cutting of the blocks for the text was begun; Meitoku 1, or 1390, when the text was finished and the blocks for the engravings were commenced; and Ōyei 21, or 1414, when the blocks for the engravings were finished and the work was published.

At the end of the second roll there is an elaborate colophon giving an account of the production, and stating that the expense of the undertaking had been borne by fifty devout adherents of the sect, whose names are printed. The chirography from which the text was cut was the work of the ex-Emperor Go-Komatsu, assisted by the Shōgun Yoshimochi and

¹ The *Daitsu Zenshi Nembutsu*, a *go-zan-ban* in my own collection without illustrations, is dated Eikyō 12 (1441), and is precisely like the *Jūgyū-dzu* in bindings, printing and paper, making the date of the latter book, within a few years, a matter of certainty.—L. N. B.

PLATES 5 and 6]   From the YŪDZU NEMBUTSU ENGI, in the collection of Mr. Bunshichi Kobayashi, Tōkyō.

several other eminent chirographers, while the drawings for the blocks were made by six artists of the Tosa school—namely, Jakusai, Takamitsu, Mitsukuni, Eishun, Yukihide, and Yukihiro. The painting, which was most wonderfully done after the rolls were printed, is, of course, attributed to the same famous masters.

These two rolls are known to every antiquarian and book-collector in Japan. They belong to Mr. Bunshichi Kobayashi of Asakusa, Tōkyō, whose superb collection of screens, *kakemono*, prints and illustrated books, is the envy and admiration of all art-lovers who have ever had the privilege of seeing it. Mr. Kobayashi found these rolls in a small curio shop in Tōkyō long after Sir Ernest Satow's monograph on early printing in Japan had been published, and had them in his possession for several years before realizing how unique and valuable they were. So far as is known there is no other set in Japan. The blocks have never been located, and it is thought that they must have been destroyed by fire.

The well-known painted scrolls of the *Yūdzū Nembutsu Engi*, which are a national treasure and usually to be seen in one of the Imperial Museums in Japan, are not, as was asserted and believed at first, the originals from which the printed rolls were copied, for, in the autumn of 1916, Mr. Kobayashi took the printed rolls to Nara and, with Mr. Kubota, the curator of the museum there, compared them inch by inch with the painted *makimono*. It was found that the latter bear the date Ōyei 30, or 1423—nine years later than the last date on the printed rolls.

After the publication of this remarkable fifteenth-century work, and until well into the sixteenth century, there was a curious lapse during which almost nothing of note in wood-engraving was produced. The country was shaken to its foundations by civil war, and Kyōto, which had been the scene of turmoil and strife in the twelfth century, again became the centre of serious disturbances between different factions of powerful local families in the fifteenth century. From 1466 to 1477, a period of eleven years, the city was little more than a huge battlefield, and during the fierce and destructive warfare hundreds of great fires occurred, the Imperial Palace, the *yashiki* of the nobles, houses, go-downs, and many of the finest temples with their priceless treasures being destroyed. Tenryū-ji, Shōkoku-ji, and other famous monasteries which had been publishing centres, were burned to the ground, and with them hundreds of ancient books and rolls and invaluable documents. The whole city and all the surrounding district was reduced to a state of desolation, and even the people of the upper classes were plunged into abject poverty.

Kyōto, as the capital, had been the centre of the art and literature of the Empire for over six hundred years, and its temples and palaces were store-houses of the most precious treasures of both Japanese and Chinese art. It was not until the time of Oda Nobunaga that peace was really restored, and the people, feeling their feet on firm ground, dared begin to build again.

The paucity of art work at this time is explained by this terrible period of conflict. It was natural that the things which could be done without should be left undone, and with the destruction of so many of the temples, where the blocks and printing paraphernalia were kept, the publishing of books necessarily received a severe check. No one will ever know the treasures in the way of ancient literature that were destroyed by these devastating conflagrations, and it is only by what is left that one feels justified in assuming that hundreds of others of equal interest once existed.

In describing these early books, therefore, one jumps from the first part of the fifteenth century to the sixteenth, for during the century which elapsed after the publication of the *Yūdzū Nembutsu Engi*, there is almost nothing to record. It is probable that some books were published during this time in other parts of Japan, if not in Kyōto, for it is most unlikely (and most unlike the Japanese) that after having achieved a work of such magnitude in the art of printing as these two rolls, there should have followed totally empty years afterwards, even if conditions were against such work. What was accomplished, however, was done at less important centres than Kyōto had been, and the output of books from these lesser monasteries was probably not very great.

One of these publications is the *Fumon-bon* of the *Hokke-kyō* Sūtra, an illustrated roll in Sir Ernest Satow's collection, bearing the date Eishō 1, or 1504.

The *Jizō-Kyō* in the Tōkyō Library, a religious work published during the Eiroku period (1558–1570), contains one primitive but interesting engraving representing the Buddhist hell.

In Eiroku 10, or 1567, a series of canonical books, called the *Daihōkō-butsu Kegon-Kyō*, was published in *ori-hon* form, and printed on the very fine Chinese paper known as *tōshi*. Each number of the series contains a frontispiece printed from the same block, representing Buddha and his disciples.

Towards the end of the sixteenth century, however, another superb work was printed at Kōya-san. This was a biography of Kōbō Daishi, called the *Kōbō Daishi Gyōjō-ki*, in ten large rolls, containing 105 spirited and beautifully printed wood-engravings, some of them over 5 feet long, interspersed with *hirakana* block-printed text. The entire life of the saint, from his birth to his death, is described and pictured in these remarkable rolls. Although there is no date or place of publication printed on the rolls themselves, I am indebted to Hōgen Toru, the Abbot of Jingō-ji, and the President of the Kōya-san Buddhist College, and to Mr. Wada, the chief librarian of the Imperial University Library in Tōkyō, for some account of them. The blocks for the rolls are said by Mr. Toru to have been ordered to be cut by Kōzan Ogo, a famous priest of Kōya-san, who lived between 1536 and 1608. Kōzan had been, before entering the priesthood, a *samurai* of high rank under the Daimyō Sazaki, the feudal lord of Ōmi. After the death of the latter in a war against Hideyoshi, Kōzan, brooding upon the loss of his master, resolved to enter the religious life. He went to Kōya-san in 1573, where for many months he is said to have lived alone and subsisted upon uncooked food. His bravery as a warrior in earlier days had won him the admiration and regard of Hideyoshi even though they had been adversaries in battle, so when that general decided to destroy the Kōya-san temples, Kōzan was sent as an envoy, representing all the monks, to negotiate with him. His efforts were successful, and the plan for razing the monasteries was abandoned. Kōzan is still called the " Saviour of Kōya-san," and his tomb is in the old cemetery on the mountain. In addition to saving the temples from Hideyoshi, he rebuilt parts of them, had roads made, irrigating ditches dug, bridges built, and book-publishing by the temples resumed.

This remarkable biography of Kōbō Daishi is said to have been printed under his direction in Bunroku 2, or 1593. The blocks for it were kept in the treasury of a temple which formerly occupied the site of the Buddhist college, and are supposed to have been destroyed in the fire which ravaged that part of the mountain early in the nineteenth century.

The account of the rolls translated from the title-slips on a set belonging to Daishō-in, a temple of the Kōya-san group, is, that the work was originally written by Goshinshin-in Kwanbaku[1] Michitsugu, the drawings were made by Echizen-no-Kami Yukimitsu, and the blocks were cut and the rolls printed at Jizō-in,[2] in the Snake year of Bunroku (1593).

It is probable that these rolls were printed with the idea of colouring them by hand afterwards, as are those of the *Yūdzū Nembutsu Engi*, and at least one set so painted is in existence. This belongs to the Imperial University Library in Tōkyō. It is very finely coloured, doubtless by Yukimitsu himself, and bears the autograph of the priest Honsai Endo, who presented it to the monastery of Saka-no-Uye, at Wasaka-mura in the province of Harima, on the twenty-first day of the third month of the first year of Kwanyei, or March-April, 1624.

There is an early Kwanyei edition of this work with slightly smaller, but exactly similar, drawings, and the text a mixture of Chinese and *katakana* characters which was published in ten large folios. Even this set is so excessively rare that few collections can boast its ownership, and as far as can be learned it has never been seen in Europe or America.

---

[1] The Kwanbaku was the head official of the Court.

[2] One of the temples of the Kōya-san group—not the better known monastery of the same name west of Kyōto.

In 1594, the year after the publication of these rolls at Kōya-san, the book was printed which foreign collectors, if they are willing to admit that anything containing illustrations preceded the *Ise Monogatari* of 1608, generally consider to be the first. This is known as the *Bussetsu Jō-Kyō*, a canonical book containing wood-engravings representing the Ten Rulers of Hell at their task of judging the dead and giving them their sentences of punishment The book was written by the Chinese priest Zosen, and, according to the colophon in the Japanese edition, was published in China in the year 1582. Afterwards drawings were made from the Chinese originals by the Japanese priest Tokusen, and the work was republished in Bunroku 3, or 1594.

Another book of about this time was the *Tengu Dairi*, a description of spirits in charge of mortal affairs, published in three rather small volumes and containing thirteen primitive woodcuts. An illustration from this rare book, in which the drawings were crudely coloured by hand, is reproduced in the Gillot Catalogue.

The foregoing list of ancient illustrated books is by no means complete, but it will serve to prove that printed pictorial work was used in books long before the *Ise Monogatari* of 1608, which for many years has been regarded as the first Japanese book to contain engravings.

In talking with Japanese book-lovers one often gets interesting bits of information in regard to ancient volumes that have disappeared or been destroyed. The old scholars are full of such delightful gossip, and although it is too vague to be of much real help or value, it nevertheless establishes a certainty in the mind of the student that these old works did once exist, and may still do so.

The difficulty of the written language in Japan is, unfortunately, a great barrier to thorough study of the subject, for, if unable to read it, the foreigner gets only a superficial and imperfect knowledge of what he may be most earnest in desiring to know. It is only the highly educated Japanese, moreover, from whom he can obtain any real help, for to master completely the Chinese characters as used in the old books is a gigantic task, requiring a knowledge, not only of obsolete words, but also of the many different readings which may be given the same characters—a knowledge by no means possessed by guides or ordinary interpreters.

The very old books were, as has been said, invariably of a religious nature and are only to be found in temple libraries and among the priests, and without special letters of introduction to abbots and prominent Buddhist scholars it is impossible to see them. At best the foreign student can do little more than make a few suggestive notes, realizing that it will not be until some Japanese scholar writes the history of early engraving in Japan that full justice can be given the subject. One hopes that this may be done before many years and the result translated into a European tongue.

CHAPTER II
ILLUSTRATED BOOKS OF THE SEVENTEENTH CENTURY

ITH the beginning of the Keichō era (1596–1615) one enters upon a most interesting period in Japanese illustration. Everything preceding this time had been more or less religious in character, but with the establishment of printing houses under private ownership, illustrated novels, poems, and other works, commenced to be issued in large numbers. Kyōto again became the centre for this work, and books were printed at presses located both in the city itself, and at Fushimi, Saga, and Takagamine villages on the outskirts.

An interesting figure in the art life of this time, and one who helped to make the possibilities of beautiful printing become realities, was Honnami Kōyetsu. This artist was born in Kyōto in 1558, the son of Honnami Kōji, a famous judge and appraiser of swords for the powerful Ieyasu. At his father's death Kōyetsu nominally followed the same profession, but his genius and versatility were too great to be limited to this work. He entered the studio of Kaihoku Yūshō, where his talent for designing and painting was quickly recognized, and encouraged by Ieyasu, who became his friend as he had been his father's, Kōyetsu soon achieved the highest rank as an artist.

While a child he had been called Jirosaburō, but later as a painter and chirographer he used the signatures Jitokusai, Tokuyūsai, Taikyō-an, Iman, Motoami, and Honnami. All the great men of the time were his friends, the Shōgun Ieyasu, and the famous general Oda Nobunaga, together with princes, court nobles, *daimyō*, scholars, poets and other artists among the number. Kanō Tanyū, although a generation younger, was of this circle, and Tawaraya Sōtatsu, the famous painter, was his pupil. Kōyetsu became known not only as a designer and painter of great originality, but ranked with Shōkwadō Shōjō and Prince Konoe Nobutada (Sammyaku-in) as one of the greatest chirographers of his time. His genius flowed through many channels, and beautiful objects in lacquer, wood, ivory, and metals, as well as paintings and some remarkable books, were produced by him. In 1605 Ieyasu abdicated as Shōgun in order that he might devote his entire time to encouraging the renaissance of Japanese art and literature, which had suffered so cruelly during the wars of the preceding centuries. One of his munificent acts was to present Kōyetsu with a large tract of land in the village of Takagamine, and give with it an annual grant of rice.

On this land, just north of Kyōto, Kōyetsu built over fifty houses, where his family, pupils, and the various artisans whom his multiform activities had by this time made necessary, lived. The place became a true arts-and-crafts village, where men could give their lives to the making of beautiful things without worrying about daily needs. Paper-makers, brush-makers, paint-mixers, printers, and workers in wood, lacquer and ivory, formed part of the little community, and small shops sprang up to supply food, fuel and everyday necessities. The swift-flowing stream at the foot of the mountain turned the rumbling wheel of a tiny mill where the exquisitely embossed paper was made which was used in the books afterward known as *Kōyetsu-bon*.

Pupils came and went, and other artists and writers as well as titled folk found their way across the sunny, southern slopes of the hills to this little settlement, which came to be called Kōyetsu-mura, and goes by that name to-day.

Among the men whom we may imagine as often visiting this busy spot was Suminokura Soan,[1] Kōyetsu's friend and his pupil in chirography, and it was largely due to their combined talents, for Suminokura was a man of fine artistic instincts as well as wealth, that book-illustrating and book-publishing received such a stimulus at this time.

Suminokura Soan was the son of Suminokura Ryōi, a well-known civil engineer, who lived in the little village of Saga, about as far west of Kyōto as Takagamine was north. The elder Suminokura had amassed a fortune by trade with Annam and the South Sea Islands, and owned a large fleet of junks and sampans engaged in carrying exports and imports to their destinations. His ability as an engineer was often called into service by the Shōgunate, and many of the canals in and around Kyōto, and the making navigable such rivers as the Hodzu, Tenryū, and others were his work.

Suminokura Soan was connected with his father in all these enterprises, and at the death of the latter, in 1614, was left a rich man. He was a man of taste and education as well, and was known as an artist and poet under the signatures Yoichi, Yoichirō, Mitsumasa, Genshi, Shigen, and Sansoan—the last name being adopted toward the latter part of his life in commemoration of three narrow escapes from death and signifies " three times risen from death." His classical studies had given him an interest in the publication of books by the different monasteries, and led him to consider the printing of other forms of literature. The result was the establishment of the famous press at Saga by Kōyetsu and himself, even before Kōyetsu had completed his hive of industry at Takagamine.

Kōyetsu had introduced a form of small movable wooden types, and these

---

[1] The family name was really Yoshida, the name Suminokura being taken from the part of Saga where they lived.

PLATE 7] The poet Taira no Kanemori. From the SANJŪ-ROK-KASEN, an excessively rare book by Honnami Kōyetsu. Undated, but believed by Japanese connoisseurs to antedate the ISE MONOGATARI. The poem inscribed is No. 40 in the HYAKUNINISSHU.

[Face p. 24

and the beautiful embossed paper designed by him were used in many of the books issued by the Saga establishment. These books became famous among book-lovers throughout Japan, and were known as *Saga-bon*, while those with the text in Kōyetsu's chirography, or printed from the movable types just spoken of, were called *Kōyetsu-bon* or *Kōyetsu-Saga-bon*. A few of these books were illustrated by Kōyetsu, and, although not dated, are thought by Japanese collectors to have been published even earlier than the *Ise Monogatari* of 1608. Among them is the *Waka Sanjū-rok-kasen*, a large folio of superb drawings of the Thirty-six Poets, beautifully printed on rich and heavy paper.

The drawings in the *Ōgi-no-Sōshi*, a book of charming designs for fans with a poem at the top of each page in Kōyetsu's chirography, are also attributed to him. This rare book was printed on paper of five tints like that used in the *Ise Monogatari*, but is supposed to have been an earlier work.

The earliest *Saga-bon* to contain illustrations, bearing a date, is the *Honchō Kokon Meijin*, a book describing the different kinds of swords used before the Keichō era. It was printed the first year of Keichō (1596) and contains simple wood-engravings representing different blades. This edition of this book is extremely rare and valuable, most collectors having to be satisfied with a reprint of Kwanyei 2 (1625) which may occasionally be found.

Another early book which may have been issued by the Saga press, although there is no colophon or date, was the *Nōka-densho*, a work on the classical *Nō* dramas which contains wood-engravings of the masks, drums, and other paraphernalia used in these plays.

The most famous of the *Saga-bon*, however, or at least the one most widely known in Europe, is the *Ise Monogatari*, published by Suminokura Soan in the thirteenth year of Keichō (1608). This book was for many years considered to be the first Japanese work to contain illustrations. It is in two volumes, $7\frac{1}{2}$ inches wide by $10\frac{1}{2}$ inches high, and printed from the Kōyetsu movable types on paper of a peculiar kid-like texture of five different tints—blue, a purple-pink, yellow, a soft brown, and a cream white. It contains forty-eight full-page wood-engravings, which Fenollosa thought might have been done by Kanō Mitsunobu,[1] but which most Japanese connoisseurs believe to have been the work of Kōyetsu. There are many things about the drawings, notably their composition and the treatment of reeds and grasses, which certainly suggest Kōyetsu, but since nothing positive is known about the artist, one can only compare and conjecture and hope that some old document will eventually turn up which will settle the question.

The text is supposed to have been copied from the original written manuscript of the poet Narihira, who lived between 825 and 880 A.D., and was

[1] See *Epochs of Chinese and Japanese Art*, vol. ii., p. 185.

collected and preserved by the poetess Ise. It records the incidents in the life of a young nobleman of Kyōto, his love affairs, travels, etc., and is interspersed with short poems.

The 1608 edition of this book was probably a small one and soon exhausted, for it was followed only two years later by a second printing. The bindings of the 1608 edition are of embossed paper, but not invariably of the same colour. I have seen undoubtedly genuine sets bound in light brown, dark brown, and dark blue covers, but always with the same design embossed upon them. Some copies have Suminokura's autograph on the last page, but this could so easily have been forged that it is not considered as giving any special extra value to the book.

During the association of Kōyetsu and Suminokura Soan, many other books were printed at the Saga press which have become very rare and valuable. They were all notable for their beautiful paper and bindings as well as the printing, and although not all were illustrated, they formed most beautiful examples of book-making and are greatly prized by Japanese collectors. The output was probably small and formed the *éditions de luxe* of feudal Japan, only to be indulged in by the upper classes, and, like modern limited editions, out of print in a short time.

The collaboration between Kōyetsu and Suminokura in the work at Saga came to an end with Kōyetsu's death in 1637. By his will the land and houses at Takagamine which Ieyasu had given him were returned to the Shōgunate. The little village has been swept by fire since that time, and the place where his houses and studios once stood is now occupied by vegetable gardens, a small temple or two, and private houses. A little to the west, however, the temple of Kōyetsu-ji still stands, its garden sloping down to sunny pine woods through which one gets a glimpse of Kyōto lying like silver in the distance, with the winding Kamo-gawa cutting the landscape. Close by, in the quiet little cemetery under the great pines, are the tombs of Kōyetsu and the members of his family, while within the temple the priests keep incense burning before the mortuary tablets not only of Kōyetsu and his son, but also that of Kōrin, who they say was the grandson of Kōyetsu's sister.

A few simple treasures there are at Kōyetsu-ji, which the pilgrim to this silent and little visited spot will be interested in seeing. An ancient map showing the location and arrangement of the houses in this seventeenth-century arts-and-crafts village is among them, and there are also several drawings and poems by the master, an incense burner of his design, and a wonderful old lacquered *hibachi*.

There were many books printed by Suminokura at the Saga press less richly embellished than those described, and at least two of them are thought to have been illustrated by him. These are an edition of the *Hyakunin Isshu* and one of the *Sanjū-rok-kasen*, the latter bearing the title *Kasen*.

Printed *Jōruri-bon* were also among the early books and probably made their appearance before the end of the sixteenth century. Their origin lay in the chanted recitatives of small companies of men who made singing and reciting their profession, but later were recited by a single man kneeling at a low table, upon which he emphasized dramatic passages, striking it with his fan or twanging a few notes on a *samisen*. The name came from the story of Yoshitsune's love for a beautiful girl named Jōruri, and the tale known as *Jōruri Jūni-dan Sōshi*, written toward the end of the Muromachi period, was the earliest of hundreds of other similar ballad dramas, composed to be chanted and recited by strolling singers.[1]

An edition of the *Jōruri Jūni-dan Sōshi* called *Jūni-dan* (Twelve Acts), although bearing no date, is thought by Midzutani Futō, the author of the *Eiri Jōruri-shi*, a recent book on the old *Jōruri-bon*, to have been published even before the Keichō era, and the drawings, paper and bindings of the book certainly have all the characteristics of very early work.

Another early book of this kind published by Suminokura Soan at the Saga press is thought by Japanese collectors also to date from the early Keichō period, although it bears no precise year. It is called the *Jōruri-Hime Monogatari*, and was issued in two volumes with paper, bindings and illustrations very similar to those in the *Ise Monogatari*.

A slightly later *Jōruri-bon* than the two already spoken of was published at the Saga press in 1617. It is called the *Satsuma Tayu* and deals with the adventures of a nobleman of Satsuma. All of these books are extremely rare, only a few copies being known in Japan, and probably no European collection boasts one of them.

Perhaps the rarest of all the *Saga-bon*, however, is the *Nijū-shi Kō*, or *Twenty-four Examples of Filial Piety*. It contains twenty-four primitive wood-engravings which are supposed to have been copied from a Chinese work, although the text is in the cursive *hirakana* characters. It is printed on white paper of the peculiar quality used in the *Ise Monogatari* and bound in covers bearing the same embossed design. No precise year of publication is given, the brief colophon only stating that it was issued in " *Saga-bon* time."

Another printing establishment which came into being early in the Keicho era was that of the monastery college of Enkō-ji at Fushimi, south of Kyōtō. It was one of the many institutions which owed its origin and support to Ieyasu, and was under the management of a priest named Sanyō Genkitsu, who had been transferred to this post by Ieyasu from the old Ashikaga school north of Kyōto, where he had been director.

[1] See *Japanese Literature*, by W. G. Aston, p. 274.

Thus, the Fushimi press under Sanyō's direction, the Saga press under the wealthy Suminokura, and the establishment at Takagamine belonging to Kōyetsu, were all printing books at about the same time, and it is interesting to imagine the rivalry between the different institutions and the meetings and discussions of the men interested in them.

The Fushimi press commenced its work in 1599 with the copy of a Korean book printed from the fonts of wooden types which Ieyasu had had made for Sanyō. In 1606 the *Seven Military Classics* was published, said to contain a few primitive drawings of the paraphernalia of war. This was followed later in the same year by the six volumes of the *Teikan Dzusetsu*, a series of biographies of famous rulers copied from a Chinese work, and containing a large number of very interesting wood-engravings.

It was not only the presses at Fushimi, Saga, and Takagamine, however, which were issuing books in Kyōto at this time, but also many smaller publishing houses which had sprung up as a result of the powerful impetus given to printing by the wise and liberal patronage of Ieyasu. In 1609 some quaint medical books were printed at one of these minor presses by a man named Baiju, and among them is a copy of a Chinese work on acupuncture, containing several wood-cuts showing where the needle should be applied to the body.

Another of these private printing establishments, belonging to Tanaka Shōzaemon, issued very early in the seventeenth century, although the exact date is not given, a book on the Chinese sages entitled *Seiken Zu*, printed from movable types and containing engravings. This book was reprinted from blocks in 1657.

Shimomura Tokifusa, a contemporary and friend of Suminokura Soan, also owned a small press in Kyōto, from which some early seventeenth-century books were issued.

Before the second quarter of the seventeenth century, book-publishing and book-illustrating had again become firmly established in Japan, and not only *shōgyō* and other religious works, but novels, *Jōruri-bon*, poems, works on divination and magic, medicine, geography, mathematics, astronomy and history, were appearing in large and constantly increasing numbers, many of them profusely illustrated.

Wood-engraving became one of the most popular and widely patronized of any of the arts, and it was used in Japan in the early centuries to a far greater extent than it has ever been used in any other country in the world. The Kwanyei period (1624–1644) was especially rich in illustrated books, for by that time peace had settled over the country again, prosperity was restored, and the results of the stimulus given to art and letters by Ieyasu were apparent everywhere. Innumerable histories and other works of an

PLATE 8] From the JINKŌ-KI (1627). Printed in beni and green.
In the Bunshichi Kobayashi collection, Tōkyō.

[Face p. 28

educational nature were printed in sets which often numbered from ten to twenty volumes, and contained a wood-engraving on every second or third page. In some of these works the drawings were coloured by hand, in a rather inartistic way, one must admit, for the colours were the most garish reds, yellows, blues and greens. These rare books are known as *edoribon* and were the precursors of the illustrated books and single sheets printed in colour in such numbers in the following century.

These books were accompanied by experiments in colour-printing much earlier than those generally known, however, for in the fourth year of Kwanyei (1627), in an educational work entitled the *Jinkō-ki*, such an experiment was made. When I first saw this remarkable book I could hardly believe my eyes, and although I examined the colour-printed page it contains with a powerful glass, I went back the next day to see it again, fearing that I had been mistaken. Even without the date in the preface to the first volume of the set of three, the book would be recognized immediately by any experienced collector as a *Kwanyei-bon*. The bindings are the embossed scarlet covers one finds on the original editions of the *Soga Monogatari*, the *Hōgen* and *Heiji Monogatari*, and many other books of that period, and the paper is the same thin, tough paper one grows to know as belonging to most of the *Kwanyei-bon*.

This excessively rare work is the property of Mr. Bunshichi Kobayashi of Asakusa, Tōkyō, whose superb collection of screens, *kakemono* and *ehon* has already been spoken of. The book was written by Yoshida Mitsuyoshi, and consists of various information on useful arts and inventions, including printing. It is illustrated by a large number of woodcuts of architectural details; river flumes and dams; irrigating devices; household utensils, such as boxes, tubs, buckets, etc.; the abacus with instructions for its use; and the tools used in agriculture, printing and other occupations, with one very simple drawing of a flowering branch in which the flowers and leaves are printed respectively in red and a greyish green. I reiterate the fact that this engraving is *printed* from two colour-blocks—*not* painted and *not* stencilled; and although undeniably crude and with a very poor register, is still colour-printing, and done almost one hundred and twenty years before the Ukiyo-ye artists of Yedo were supposed to have commenced their experiments. The fact that there is only one page printed in colours, and that the simplest of any of the illustrations, suggests that it was a novel and important innovation, attended with considerable difficulty and probably a good deal of expense, and used once simply to explain the process. Whether this very early venture was followed soon by other similar work is uncertain; a second edition of the *Jinkō-ki*, called the *Shimpen Jinkō-ki*, also a *Kwanyei-bon* with drawings similar to those in the earlier work, contains no attempt at colour-printing, and neither does a Kwanbun edition with illustrations of the Moronobu school. As far as is known at present, there is nothing between the first printing of the *Jinkō-ki* and Ōoka Shunboku's *Minchō Seidō Gwayen* of 1746 containing printed coloured cuts, although Mr. Morrison is undoubtedly right in holding to his opinion that Kiyonobu printed single sheets in colour before Shunboku's time.[1]

At any rate, if other early ventures were made in the process, the books containing them have long ago been destroyed.

Ordinary wood-block engraving, however, was, as has been said, used very largely in the Kwanyei period, and although hundreds of the Kwanyei books have been lost, there are, fortunately, a good many still in existence. Until within a few years ago they were considered of no value, and many of them have gone to the rag collectors and been made into paper. Often, also, in remounting old screens pages from some of these ancient books will be found used as backing for the screen itself.

Among other Kwanyei books containing engravings was a catalogue of the *Confucian Analects* entitled *Shinkan Shaku Kōsei Hyōrui Mokuroku*, a very rare book printed in 1625 in four long, narrow volumes with illustrations of Chinese subjects.

The *Hōgen* and *Heiji Monogatari*, of three volumes each, the former not dated and the latter published in 1626, are usually regarded as parts of the same set, and together constitute a history of the civil disturbances in Kyōto in the twelfth century; the *Hōgen Monogatari* being an account of the trouble in the year 1157 respecting the succession to the throne, and the *Heiji Monogatari* a continuation of the account of the conflict in 1159, when the Taira clan won the supremacy over the Minomotos. The *Hōgen Monogatari* contains thirty-five full-page drawings, and the *Heiji Monogatari* thirty-six. The latter occupy part of the pages only, leaving small spaces at the tops and sides for a few lines of text. The technique of the drawings in the two books is sufficiently different to indicate either great progress, if done by one man, or the work of two different illustrators. Those in the *Heiji Monogatari* were by an artist a little surer of himself, and are less coarse in line and mass than the ones in the *Hōgen Monogatari*. They have something of the vivacity of Hinaya Ryūho's work, and it is possible that they were early engravings by that artist.

[1] In connection with this example of early colour-printing, it is interesting to recall what Strange in his *Japanese Colour Prints* (p. 148) quotes in translation from the *Adzuma Nishiki-ye Yurai*. He says: "In the period Genwa (1616–1623) Katsushika Hokyūshi, a comic poet who lived in Musashi, ordered Chikamatsu Ryūsai to engrave on cherry-wood a picture of a pine branch, and this was the beginning of *surimono*. In the period of Manji (1658–1660) another man from the same district, Takekawa Minosuke, observing how impressions were rubbed off leaves, obtained the idea of making colour-prints."

Strange also mentions a set of books in the British Museum containing designs for *kimono*, published in 1667, in which each design is printed in a colour—red, blue, green, and olive being used in addition to black. (See *Japanese Colour Prints*, p. 124.)

Another book which appeared about this time was the *Soga Monogatari*. This is a history of the revenge of the Soga brothers against the man who killed their father, and the aid given them by Tora Gozen, a famous courtesan of that day, who, after the execution of the Sogas by order of the Shōgun, retired to a convent and became a nun. The work contains many extremely interesting drawings representing these different events.

One of the most interesting of the early Kwanyei books, because, so far as known, it is the first of the illustrated *meisho-ki*, is the *Kumano-no-Honji*. It is in two volumes and contains delightfully primitive drawings of temples, shrines, religious services, and festivals at different places in the province of Kii. The drawings are coloured by hand as in the *edori-bon* described. Although the books bear no precise date, they are evidently of the very early years of Kwanyei, probably about 1625 or 1626.

The *Kwanyei Gyōkō-ki*, published in two large scrolls in 1626, is a series of wood-engravings, representing the visit of the Emperor and Empress Go Mizu-no-o to the Shōgun, Hidetada, at Nijō Castle in 1624. This was a famous event, for it was the first time that an Emperor had ever so honoured a Shōgun. In this case, however, it was also the ceremonial visit which is always paid to her parents by a woman after her marriage, for the Empress was Hidetada's daughter. The pictures show the procession headed by the Court ladies of the Empress's suite and their women in waiting, followed by *daimyō*, *samurai*, and finally the imperial carts, Court musicians, etc.

In the first year of the Genroku era (1688) the blocks from which these remarkable rolls were printed were burned in one of the numerous fires which have destroyed so many art treasures in Japan, and in order to preserve a printed pictorial record of the magnificent procession, other blocks were cut from existing rolls and another edition was published in 1694, which the Preface states to be in all particulars like the earlier work.[1] The drawings are full of spirit, evidently the work of some Tosa artist of no mean ability, and give a vivid impression of the pomp and splendour of the old feudal days.

Going back to other books of the Kwanyei era, there is a curious work on divination called the *Nijū Gaku Dzusetsu*, published in two rather large folios in 1626. The illustrations show the effect upon the body of different planetary conditions, and include many diagrams for ascertaining fortunate days for special events. Other old calendars and works on magic appeared even earlier than this, and in 1635 a most remarkable work of this kind, called the *San-ze Sō*, was published by Nakano Shōzaemon of Kyōto from a

---

[1] In spite of the Preface there is much difference between the two medium-sized Genroku books and the large original rolls. The Imperial University Library of Tōkyō and the famous Nanki Bunko both possess fine examples of the original work.

Chinese original. It is in two large folios and contains many extremely curious and amusing old woodcuts.

In 1629 one of the first of the many illustrated books for girls was published. It is called the *Jokyō Hiden*, and contains maxims, instructions in etiquette, the care of clothing, and various other information supposed to be useful to women.

A book entitled *Takadachi*, an historical romance of Yoritomo and Yoshitsune, appeared in 1625 in three oblong volumes, in which the illustrations are mixed in with the text in a curious way, both being cut on the same block. A different rendering of the same subject followed in 1630 which is better known, although both works are extremely rare.

In 1631 the *Sekkyō Karukaya*, a book on the daily affairs of life containing crude but interesting drawings, was issued by the Kyūemon press in Kyōto.

A famous Life of Nichiren, called the *Nichiren Shōnin Chūgwasen*, was published in four volumes in Kwanyei 9 (1632) by Nakano Shōzaemon of Kyōto, containing a large number of wood-engravings, often five or six pages running, picturing the saint from his birth, through the many adventures and vicissitudes of his life, to his death, and ends with drawings of the funeral cortège. The drawings are primitive but of extraordinary interest, making the work one of the greatly prized treasures of any collection. The name of the artist is not given.

In 1635 a biography of Yoshitsune entitled *Gikei-ki*[1] was published in eight large volumes. The drawings, although crude, are not without a good deal of rough strength. This set of books was occasionally coloured by hand, and the colours are applied with more care than in most of the *edori-bon*, giving the effect of coarse prints. The engravings were printed from blocks $8\frac{1}{4}$ inches high by $10\frac{1}{4}$ inches wide, and were then folded in the centre, the fold being placed out and the edges brought together and sewed into the back of the book. Each illustration thus extends over two full pages, with no *hashira* or dividing line on the fold. It is one of the most interesting sets of books of this period, not only because it represents rather typical Kwanyei work in wood-engraving, but also because it shows the dress, armour, weapons, etc., of the time of Yoshitsune.

The *Genpei-Hon* is the collective title of a series of eighteen volumes on the history of the Genpei period (twelfth century), during which the Minamoto and Taira clans were at war. It appeared the twelfth year of Kwanyei (1635), and is profusely illustrated. Some sets are coloured by hand.

Other *edori-bon* of about this time, although not bearing precise dates, are *Urashima*, a very rare and curiously illustrated rendering of this old

---

[1] Gikei is the Chinese reading for Yoshitsune. The title may also be read Yoshitsune-ki.

tale; *Shuten Dōji*, a collection of old legends in two volumes; and *Shida*, a book of historical tales.

A work entitled *Moromatsu*, of which there is said to be only one copy in Japan—that in a private collection in Kyōto—was published in 1637 in one small volume, and contains very interesting engravings representing scenes from everyday life. Its great rarity gives it a rather special interest.

In 1639 the *Yashima Michiyuki*, another early *Jōruri-bon*, was printed, which contains a number of primitive engravings of considerable interest.

The *Azuma Monogatari*, published in 1642, consists of tales of "trarembo," or the foolish squandering of money. The illustrations suggest that it was a sugared pill of warning against the occupants of the Yoshiwara. The drawings are in simple outline, with here and there a note of black.

Another *Gikei-ki*, an extremely rare series of historical books on Yoshitsune and his time, profusely illustrated and with some sets coloured by hand, appeared in Shōhō 2 (1645). It is one of the most interesting works of this period, and when complete in the eight volumes in which it was issued, is very valuable.

It was toward 1640 that the illustrated *meisho-ki* commenced to be so popular, and one of the earliest after the *Kumano-no-Honji* already spoken of was the *Shiki Onron* in two volumes, published in 1643, containing simple drawings. It is a very rare and valuable book, only to be found by great good fortune.

A third edition of the *Ise Monogatari* printed from the original Saga blocks on ordinary paper appeared in 1645. This old reprint can sometimes be found, and aside from the difference in paper and bindings is exactly like the 1608 edition, which has become so rare as to practically never be seen now except in museums and valuable private collections, and for sale only when such collections are broken up.

Although the foregoing list of early seventeenth-century books is by no means complete, it brings one to the middle of that century by gentle gradations. After 1650 wood-engraving became much less archaic in character, and from having been largely the work of artisans rather than artists, it grew to be dignified by well-known painters producing drawings for the blocks. Numerous as illustrated books had been before, by the middle of the century they were appearing in such numbers that it is no longer possible to list more than a few of them. Works on history and the different *monogatari* continued among the favourites, and the illustrated *meisho-ki*, or guide-books, a few of which had appeared much earlier, jumped into an immense popularity.

The origin of these books lay, according to Aston, in very remote times, for "early in the eighth century the Japanese Government gave orders for the compilation of geographical descriptions of all the provinces. The mineral, vegetable, and animal productions were to be noted, with the quality of the soil, the origin of the names of places, and local traditions. Of these works only a few have reached us, the best known of which is the *Idzumo Fudoki*, written in 733. . . . This was the forerunner of the very considerable modern typographical literature known to us as Meisho."[1]

The *Kumano-no-Honji* and the *Shiki Onron*, already spoken of, are, as far as known, the first of these books to contain illustrations. Following them in 1658 the *Kyō Warabe*, a very famous Kyōto *meisho-ki*, appeared in six volumes, with a supplementary series, also in six volumes, issued in 1667, known as the *Kyō Warabe Atoöi*. The books were written by Nakagawa Kiun, a well-known seventeenth-century author, chirographer and physician of Kyōto. The name of the artist is not given, but there can be little doubt that it was Moronobu, since the illustrations in the *Takuan Oshō Kamakura-ki*, published in 1659, are known to be his work, and are too strikingly similar in every way not to make it practically certain that the drawings in the *Kyō Warabe* were also by him. The first series of the *Kyō Warabe* can, by diligent searching, still sometimes be found, but the second series is so rare that the gods must guide a collector if he is to obtain a set. The first series went through several editions, being published by Yamamori Rokubei of Kyōto, and later by two other publishers to whom the blocks were sold, so that the last page varies with the name of the printing house, that bearing the imprint of Rokubei seldom being found now.

The six volumes of the *Tōkaidō Meisho-ki*, written by Asai Ryōi, another popular seventeenth-century writer, were also published in 1658, and contain many illustrations representing scenes along the old Tōkaidō road. The artist is not known.

Between 1650 and 1700 there were over fifty different *meisho-ki* published, some of them comprising several volumes and nearly all profusely illustrated.

A list of the most important illustrated books of this kind includes the

Kumano-no-Honji : A guide to the temples and shrines in Kii. 2 vols. *Circa* 1625–1626.
Shiki Onron : A guide to the province of Musashi. 2 vols. 1643.
Kyō Warabe (" Kyōto Children ") : A guide for Kyōto and the environs. 6 vols. 1658. Attributed to Moronobu.
Kyō Warabe Atoöi : A supplementary series to the above. 6 vols. 1667.
Tōkaidō Meisho-ki : Scenes along the Tōkaidō. 6 vols. 1658.
Takuan Oshō Kamakura-ki : Guide to Kamakura. Illustrated by Moronobu " in his middle age." 2 vols. 1659.
Yamashiro Meisho-ki : Guide to Yamashiro. 11 vols. 1658.
Kamakura Monogatari : Guide to Kamakura. 5 vols. 1659.
Rakuyō Meisho Shū : 12 vols. 1660. A reprint in 1664.
Yedo Meisho-ki : Guide to Yedo. 7 vols. 1662.
Kyō Suzume (" Kyōto Sparrows ") : A guide to Kyōto. 7 vols. 1665.
Yoshino-yama Hitori Anai : A guide to Yoshino. 6 vols. 1671.

---

[1] From *Japanese Literature*, by W. G. Aston, pp. 22-23.

PLATE 9] From Vol. 1. of the KYŌ WARABE, a Kyōto guide-book published in 1658. Illustrated by Moronobu. Kabuki performance in the Shijō river-bed.

[Face p. 34

BOOKS OF THE SEVENTEENTH CENTURY [CHAP. II

Arima Shigure : Guide to Arima. Written by Masanaga. Illustrated by Moronobu. 5 vols. 1672.
Yamashiro Shiki Monogatari (" The Four Seasons in Yamashiro "). 6 vols. 1674.
Nanto Meisho Shū : Guide for Southern Japan. 10 vols. 1675.
Naniwa Meisho Ashiwake-bune : Ōsaka and environs. 6 vols. 1675.
Sumiyoshi Aioi Monogatari : Legends of Sumiyoshi. Illustrated by Moronobu. 4 vols. 1676.
Yedo Suzume (" Yedo Sparrows ") : A guide for Yedo. Written and illustrated by Moronobu. 12 vols. 1677.
Dekisai Kyō Miyage : Kyōto and environs. 2 series of 7 vols. each. 1678.
Santo Suzume : Kyōto, Ōsaka, and Yedo. 3 vols. 1678.
Nara Meisho-ya E-zakura : Guide to Nara. Attributed to Moronobu. 6 vols. 1678.
Kawachi Meisho Kagami : Kawachi district in Kyūshū. 6 vols. 1678.
Naniwa Suzume (" Osaka Sparrows "). 1679.
Naniwa Suzume Atoöi : Supplement to above. 2 vols. 1679.
Kyō Habutae : Guide to Kyōto. 6 vols. 1685.
Minobu-san Kongen-ki : The famous temple of Minobu. 1685.
Hokke Reijoki : 10 vols. 1686.
Kokyō-ga Eiri-no-Yedo Banashi : Tales of Yedo. 6 vols. 1687.
Yedo Kanoka : 6 vols. 1687.
Shikoku Henrei Junrei-ki : A pilgrimage to Shikoku. 7 vols. 1688.
Yedo Sō-Kanoka : A supplement to Yedo Kanoka. 7 vols. 1689.
Hitome Tamaboko (" Impressions during a Stroll "). 4 vols. 1689.
Meisho Miyako-dori : Famous dances of Kyōto. 6 vols. 1690.
Nippon Kanoka : Famous places in Japan. Illustrated by Ishikawa Ryūsen. 11 vols. 1691.
Yedo Banashi (" Tales of Yedo "). 1695.
Kokka Manyoki (" Cheerful Places "). 14 vols. 1698.
Kaisei Zōho Nippon Kanoka : Supplement to Nippon Kanoka. By Ishikawa Ryūsen. 12 vols. 1698.[1]

The illustrations in these different *meisho-ki* form a veritable epitome of seventeenth-century life with the human interest quite overshadowing that of the places the drawings are supposed to represent. All sorts and conditions of people, from lordly *daimyō* and their accompanying *samurai* to artisans, farmers, and shop-keepers at their work, are represented. Picnic parties on river banks, pilgrim bands at temples, audiences of nobles, priests, and people of the upper classes watching the performance of a *Nō* drama or a sacred dance, *geisha* singing to the *samisen*, night crowds thronging the Yoshiwara, festivals and religious processions, are a small part of the subjects depicted, which with the architecture of the buildings, the utensils in everyday use, the paraphernalia of great fêtes and the various costumes of the times make these books not only a source of never-ending interest, but extremely valuable to the student of Japanese history and customs.

It is greatly to be regretted that so few works of this period bear the names of the artists. It was not until Hinaya Ryūho[2] and Moronobu commenced occasionally to sign the books they illustrated that there is any clue to the identity of the men who added so much to their interest by the spirited and well-drawn engravings which they furnished as additions to the text.

[1] The above list is largely taken from the *Kohan Chishi Kaidai*, a late bibliographical work on the old *meisho-ki* by Wada Mankichi, the chief librarian of the Imperial University Library in Tōkyō.
[2] Better known as Rippo.

It seems strange that it was assumed the public would care more about knowing where and by whom the books were published than who the illustrators were, but the fact remains that what to us seems most important and interesting was to them of little moment. The " book " certainly was " the thing."

There are many illustrated books on an immense variety of subjects which are just as interesting as much of Moronobu's work, but because they were by obscure artists, or at least bear no signatures, they have been given scant consideration, and rats and book-worms have had their way with them on the dusty shelves of old-book shops.

The drawings in most of the works of the latter half of the seventeenth century can be classed as the productions of about four or five artists or their schools. The leaders of different groups of artists had their rigid traditions as to method, and departure from them was almost equivalent to the disloyalty of a *samurai* to his *daimyō*.[1] Hence the similarity in technique in the illustrations by men of the same school.

Moronobu's drawings even when unsigned are unmistakable, and those of his pupils are also easily recognized.

Another man of this time whose work had great individuality was Hinaya or Nonoguchi Ryūho.

Ryūho was known not only as an artist but also as a writer, a poet and a chirographer. Morrison says he made dolls, and he is also credited with having been a carver of *netsuke*. He lived in Kyōto between 1595 and 1669, and must have been a younger member of the same literary and artistic coterie to which Kōyetsu and Suminokura Soan belonged, his teachers in poetry and chirography having been Karasumaru Mitsuhiro and Prince Sonchō of Shoren-in, who had also taught these artists. He is said to have studied painting under Kanō Tanyū, who was about his own age, but his book illustrations indicate that he had also worked under some Tosa painter. In ordinary life Ryūho was known as Beniya Shoemon, but used as other artist signatures the names Nonoguchi Chikashige and Sho-o.

Ryūho wrote and illustrated a number of books, among which are the *Rekidai Kokkei-den*, a collection of humorous tales; the *Chikusai*; the *Jūjō Genji* in ten volumes; and the *Osana Genji*. The latter was his most famous work. It was published in 1661 after Ryūho had reached middle age, and consists of ten large volumes. The drawings have a distinction of their own, although it is not easy to define their charm. They are stiff and angular, and yet so brimming over with vivacity and so interesting in composition and the placing of blacks, that one always turns to them with delight, their naïve simplicity giving them an added interest. The set is extremely

---

[1] See *Ideals of the East*, by Okakura Kakuzo, p. 196.

rare, even more so than many of Moronobu's books, and is very greatly prized by Japanese collectors.

The drawings in the *Kyō Warabe* are thought by some collectors to also have been the work of Ryūho, but close comparison shows too many points of complete difference in style to make this possible. Ryūho had a manner of his own, and was one of the few illustrators of this period who was not dominated by Moronobu.

Other works which, although unsigned, are attributed to Ryūho are a small edition of the *Ise Monogatari*, published by Hayashi Izumi-no-jō of Kyōto in 1661; the *Utsubo Monogatari*, in three volumes, by the same publisher, but undated; and a book of illustrated poems entitled *Hanabi-gusa*.

A third artist of this time was Yoshida Hanbei. He also headed a school, and his drawings of crisp little trees, positive mountains and sharp-lined figures have a technique all their own, and a most interesting one. He will be spoken of later on.

In addition to the books by these men and their followers, there are a few others which contain drawings of such force and character that although unsigned they were evidently by an artist of no mean ability. Among the works containing these unidentified drawings are the two volumes of the *Musashi Abumi*, written by Asai Ryōi and published in 1661, and the *Yedo Meisho-ki* by the same author, published a year later. The engravings in these two sets were evidently by the same man, but bear no resemblance to the work of any of the other known illustrators of this time.

The *Musashi Abumi* is a description of the devastating fire of 1657 by which Yedo was almost completely destroyed and over one hundred thousand people lost their lives. The drawings are packed full of pulsing life, and those representing the crowds flying from the devouring, approaching flames, pushing before them their wheeled chests in the endeavour to save a few cherished possessions, are not easily matched in the expression of fear and horror and tumult. The technique is absolutely simple, the drawing being in outline and only relieved by well-placed spots of black representing the iron bindings and trimmings of the chests, the hinges of great gates, parts of clothing and the hair of the terrorized throng; but the sweep of everything in one direction, the flames, the rushing crowds, the trees bending in the terrific blasts of heat and the galloping horses crushing unfortunates who have fallen in the headlong flight, all unite in giving one a painfully vivid impression of the terrible calamity.

A double-page illustration in the *Yedo Meisho-ki* representing a crowded street in the Yoshiwara of Tōkyō, where people are coming and going, drinking, wrestling and playing games, displays the same splendid verve in expressing a scene of amusement and gaiety. The technique is too similar to doubt that the drawings were by the same artist, and it is a matter of regret that we know nothing in regard to him.

Another of the *meisho-ki* which contains drawings of much interest and distinction is the *Rakuyō Meisho Shū*, published in 1660 in twelve volumes. Figures are subordinated to the landscape in these books, and mountains, streams, and temples play the important parts, with convenient cloud arrangements blotting out whatever it seemed unnecessary to represent. In the ninth volume the first four pages are given up to a drawing of Inari Temple, south of Kyōto, with the many different buildings, *torii*, lanterns, etc., while in the immediate foreground diminutive figures are engaged in horse racing, which an obliging break in the clouds enables us to see.

In marked contrast to these books are a number of publications of about the same time, containing drawings of Chinese subjects in the Chinese style. One of the most important of these works was the *Ressen Zenden*, or lives of Chinese saints and hermits, published in 1650 in eight volumes, and containing 174 full-page engravings.

Another work of the same kind is the *Kumeido Seki*, a book on the Zen sect of Buddhism, published in 1655. It contains a large number of striking and beautifully printed illustrations.

Several similar works appeared from time to time after the middle of the century, but with a few exceptions are not of very great interest. The *Jūroku Rakan Shōzō*, a history of the sixteen Buddhist disciples, published in 1667 and illustrated by Kōsetsu, is a notable book however, the drawings having great force and dignity and being very finely printed on a beautiful paper.

The *Jūhachi Rakan Zusan*, or eighteen Buddhist disciples, printed in 1687, with illustrations copied from the Chinese, is also of considerable interest.

The *Chōgonka Zushō*, which might be translated rather freely as " the broken-hearted song,"[1] is the Japanese rendering of a Chinese subject, the drawings representing fair Court favourites of a Chinese Emperor, which are charmingly naïve and interesting. The work is in two large folios, published in 1677 and beautifully printed on *toshi*, a special kind of paper used only in books of value. The set is very rare and valuable, and when found in the original edition in its bindings, with the orange and silver design on a greyish white ground, is considered a great treasure by Japanese collectors. Another excessively rare and unique book copied from the Chinese is the *Shinkwan Seiseki Dzu*, a biography of Confucius with numerous illustrations printed in white on a black ground, from stone blocks. The Japanese copy of this delightful book was published in a folio by Yamaguchiya Gombei in Yedo, in Genroku 11 (1698).

[1] The poem which this book illustrates was written in 812 A.D. by the poet Po Chü-i, and is translated by Giles in his *History of Chinese Literature*.

Several biographies of famous warriors appeared soon after the middle of the century, the *Hyakushō-den*, or One Hundred Generals, published in two large folios in 1656, being the most noteworthy. These books were printed on thick paper of rich quality, and bound in heavily gaufraged covers bearing a design of dragon-flies on a ground of small intercepting circles. The illustrations represent famous military leaders of the empire, beginning with the deified Michiomi-no-Mikoto and ending with Hideyoshi, and are accompanied by descriptive text occupying the upper part of each page.

Another similar work in two smaller folios, entitled the *Hyaku Bushō-den*, got up with about the same richness of paper and bindings, was probably also of this time, although it bears no date. The illustrations are so much like those in the *Hyakushō-den* that they may be attributed to the same artist.

The historical works and various *monogatari* which became popular during the early part of the century retained their hold on the people's interest, and many others were published in succeeding years. The *Ise Monogatari* went through an immense number of renderings, and editions were issued in large, medium sized and small volumes, all containing drawings representing the same subjects but differently treated. Other *monogatari* which had appeared in illustrated form first in the Kwanyei period were republished with other cuts at this time. Among these books the *Soga Monogatari* was printed again in twelve volumes in 1663, profusely illustrated by Moronobu and Yoshida Hanbei working in collaboration.

A story of the Genji, called the *Eiri Genji Ko-Kagami*, was published by Rakuya of Kyōto in three volumes in Meireki 3 (1657). It contains numerous finely drawn engravings in the Tosa style which fill up part of the page only, the space above and at the sides being filled in with a few lines of text. The publisher refrains from telling us who the very competent illustrator was, although he gives explicit information that the " famous Rakuya printing-house is on San-jō Teramachi, Kyōto, opposite the well-known and ancient temple of Seigan-ji."

A great many profusely illustrated biographies and histories of this time were published, the drawings in which, although not signed, were evidently the work of the Moronobu school. Lives of warriors and saints predominated, and another life of Kōbō Daishi, called the *Kōbō Daishi Goden-ki*, appeared in three volumes in 1662; the *Shōtoku Taishi-den*, a life of Shōtoku Taishi in six volumes, in 1666; and the *Shaka Hassō Monogatari*, a biography of Shaka in eight volumes, the same year.

In 1664 a very voluminous series of biographies of the Shōguns, known collectively as the *Shōgun-ki*, was issued in twenty volumes. It begins with the Kamakura Regents, takes one through the Ashikaga period, and ends with the history of Hideyoshi. The illustrations are of the Moronobu school, and represent all the principal events in the lives of these men, showing the armour, costumes, etc., of the various periods, the building of the great castle at Ōsaka, and incidents in the wars which ravaged the country before peace was restored under the Tokugawas.

An exceedingly interesting work on the famous women of Japan was published in 1668. It is called the *Honchō Retsujo-den* and is in ten folios, containing on every second or third page a full-page illustration. The early history of Japan from the time of the half-mythical Queen Jingō contains the names of many women who achieved renown as sovereigns, warriors, writers, artists and poets, and these remarkable books are made up of historical sketches and anecdotes regarding them, which the striking wood-engravings illustrate. The set forms an unusually fine example of block-printing in every way, and the pages of text in Chinese characters, instead of the usual flowing *hirakana*, give it a very distinctive appearance.

In 1671 a very famous work, copied from the Chinese, was published by allied printing-houses in Yedo and Kyōto, known collectively as the *Hashu Gwafu*. It consists of eight large folios, each with a sub-title of its own, as the *Kokon Gwafu*, copies of old paintings; the *Meikō Sempu*, designs for fans; the *Gogon Tōshi Gwafu*, classical tales and poems; the *Rokugon Tōshi Gwafu*, ancient Chinese tales; the *Shichigon Tōshi Gwafu*, illustrated Chinese poems; the *Bai-Chiku-Ran-Kiku-Shifu*, plum blossoms, bamboos, orchids, and chrysanthemums; the *Sōhon Kwa Shifu*, miscellaneous drawings, and the *Mokuhon Kwachō-fu*, birds and flowers.

The collection forms a rare and beautiful example of seventeenth-century book-making, and in the edition printed on *toshi* paper and in the grey and silver bindings is a treasure greatly sought after by Japanese collectors, although hardly known in Europe and America.

The books above described form a very small part of the many which were published before the Genroku era. There were literally thousands of others, embracing collections of poems, works on military matters, books on divination, astronomy, mathematics, geography and medicine, many others on morals and etiquette, and some beautiful folios on the ceremonial tea and flower arrangement in which the wood-engravings were occasionally coloured by hand in a charming fashion.

Perhaps nothing would be more effectual in removing the doubts held by many foreigners as to the reality of the ancient culture of Japan than to thoroughly examine a large number of these old illustrated books and to remember that the very fact that such immense numbers of such books were printed presupposed a public who read them.

CHAPTER III

MORONOBU, ITCHŌ, KŌRIN AND THEIR FOLLOWERS

OME time after the advent of Hinaya RYŪHO and Hishikawa MORONOBU into the field of illustration, the artist's part in book-making seemed to acquire a greater importance, and it became more or less the custom for the illustrator's name to be given either on the last page or on the paper title-slips of the covers. Much of Moronobu's early work is unsigned, but even from the first his style had such a marked individuality that one may say with certainty that the drawings in many books were his, even though his name does not appear.

Famous as he was, comparatively little that is really definite is known in regard to his life. Even the dates for his birth and death are somewhat uncertain, being variously given as 1625 and 1638 for the former, and 1694, 1695 and 1715 for his death. Taking a clue found in the *Takuan Ōshō Kamakura-ki*, however, a *meisho-ki* illustrated by him in 1659, which a note states to have been in his "middle age," we may assume that 1625 is more nearly correct than the later year as the date of his birth.

His father, Nyūdo Kochiku, also known as Hishikawa Michishige and Kichiyemon, was a well-known embroiderer of Hota, a town in the province of Bōshū,[1] south-east of Yedo Bay and its lagoons. Here Moronobu learned something of his father's work, as well as designing for it, but finding the employment distasteful he left Hota and went to Yedo to study painting.

Although Kanō Tanyū was living in Yedo at that time, having removed his academy from Kyōto to the new capital in 1621, and established it in the buildings given him by the Shōgun Iemitsu, it is not certain that Moronobu came under his influence until much later. The conflicting stories of his life after he left his home in Bōshū may be harmonized by assuming that he did not tarry long in Yedo at that time, but went on to Kyōto and took up his studies under a master of the Tosa school. With his lessons he combined a good deal of original work, and was designing for fabrics and illustrating books in Kyōto soon after the middle of the seventeenth century.

Moronobu used as artist signatures the names Kichibei, said to have been taken in token of his admiration for Iwasa Matabei's work,[2] Hishikawa

---

[1] Also called Awa.
[2] See the Introduction to *Japanese Colour Prints*, by Edward F. Strange, p. 9.

Kichibei Moronobu, Hishikawa Uji Moronobu, Hishikawa Kichibei-no-jō, Hishikawa Tomoyuki, Yūchiku (in later years), and other variations of these names, together with the occasional use of such prefixes as Eshi, Yamato-ye, and Bōyō (referring to his native province of Bōshū).

The *Bunsho-no-Zōshi*, neither dated nor signed but perhaps of the Keian period, probably represents Moronobu's very earliest book illustrations. Although the drawing is extremely primitive, wound up in it, as it were, are all the qualities which developed in his later work, and in it he had already settled upon the type of face and drawing of hands which make all his illustrations, even if unsigned, so unmistakable.

By the Meireki period he had thrown off most of the immaturity apparent in the *Bunsho-no-Zōshi*, and the powerful drawings in the *Miura Monogatari* of 1657 easily foretell great things. Many of Moronobu's books published during the Meireki, Manji and Kwanbun year periods contain engravings which, if lacking something of the grace and beauty that characterized his later drawings of women, are still so full of splendid strength, that signed or unsigned they bear the unmistakable stamp of his genius.

After the establishment of the popular theatres in Ōsaka and Kyōto early in the seventeenth century, the *Jōruri-bon*[1] came into great demand to be used something as the *Nō* drama books were used in following the action of the play. Many heroic actions were taken as subjects for these ballad-dramas besides the story of Yoshitsune and Jōruri which had given them their name, and the term *Jōruri-bon* came to mean all the books of this kind, including the well-known *Kimpira-bon* which dealt with the favourite subject of the giant Kimpira and his deeds.

Among the *Jōruri-bon* attributed to Moronobu, the *Miura Monogatari* of 1657, with the *Honchō Buke Ō Keizu* and the *Aki-no-Yonaga Monogatari* of about the same time, are among the first. The drawings represent many phases of feudal life, usually battle scenes and acts of heroism, including representations of ceremonial visits and conferences between great *daimyō* and *samurai* in which all the pomp and rigid etiquette of mediæval Japan are portrayed. These drawings, filling the pages with big figures and packed full of superb action, emphasized by great, striking notes of black, are on an entirely different scale from those in the classical *monogatari*, histories, poems and *meisho-ki* which he also illustrated in such numbers. The latter books, however, even if less compelling, are full of fascination and charm, and form a complete epitome of Japanese life from that of the humblest peasant and artisan to the great feudal lords in their castles in the provinces, and the nobles in their *yashiki* around the Palace.

Even Moronobu's purely Ukiyo-ye work had a much earlier beginning

[1] The origin of these books has been spoken of in Chapter II.

PLATE 10]

From the TAKA BYŌBU KUDA MONOGATARI by Moronobu, 2 vols. Manji 3 (1661).
In the collection of Mr. Koyama, Kyōto.

[Face p. 42

than is generally realized, and as early as 1661 his *Taka Byōbu Kuda Monogatari* (an exceedingly rare book) appeared, containing drawings of the Yoshiwara beauties which embraced all the characteristics of his Genroku books.

Although Kanō Tanyū had moved his academy to Yedo, his affiliations with Kyōto had by no means ceased, and there are records of his having been recalled there several times to fill commissions at the Palace, and in Nijō Castle. In 1623 he returned to finish some mural work in Nijō Castle. In 1626 he went again to paint a series of pictures representing the famous procession of 1624 when the Emperor and Empress visited Hidetada there, and in 1642 he was given the order for replacing some old frescoes of the Chinese sages which had been destroyed when the Shishinden of the Palace was burned years before. Again, in 1660, work in the Palace kept him busy for over a year, and it was at that time that Moronobu seems to have come definitely under his influence and commenced to adopt something of his technique.

Everything points to his having followed Tanyū back to Yedo and to his having then entered the great academy there. He was no amateur, but had already achieved a name for himself as a designer and illustrator, and so found no difficulty in taking a place of the first rank among the other students, and becoming a competitor, as is stated in all accounts of his life, with Tsunenobu, the Shōgun's protégé and Tanyū's nephew, and who after the latter's death became the leader of the Kanō school.

It has been said[1] that it was Moronobu's admiration for Hanabusa Itchō's work that brought him under the influence of the Kanō school, but manifestly this is impossible, for Moronobu was many years Itchō's senior, and must have finished his course in Yedo, and become well settled in his method of work before Itchō ever left Ōsaka. That they became friends afterward, however, and reacted upon each other is most probable, since Moronobu was illustrating his most famous books at a time when Itchō was also a noted painter in the capital, the latter's years of banishment not beginning until the very end of the century.

It is interesting to imagine the meetings on *tatami*-covered floors of various Yedo studios, restaurants, and tea-houses of that time, and the men who forgathered there. The great Kanō Tanyū would have dominated these artistic gatherings, with his brother Yasunobu and his nephew Tsunenobu as lesser stars of the constellation. Moronobu, Tsunenobu, and Hasegawa Tōun, also known as Kanō Tōun, the adopted son of Tanyū, were almost exact contemporaries and of about equal fame. Iwasa Gembei, the second Matabei, also known as Katsushige, probably also belonged to this group, and among the younger men would have been Hanabusa

---
[1] See *Arts of Japan*, by Edward Dillon, p. 78.

Itchō and Kōrin, who came to Yedo for a brief period of study toward 1680.

There is a generally accepted idea that a change came over Moronobu's style after he left Kyōto, to be attributed to his admiration for Iwasa Matabei's pictures. Whatever change took place, however, was probably chiefly due to the greater freedom of thought and life in Yedo, and in any case it was a change in choice of subject rather than in style, for although, as has been said, in his early illustrations of classical subjects, the figures were small and the whole effect of a Tosa-ish character, his drawings in the *Jōruri-bon*, even as early as 1657–1660, were as big and commanding and as robust in technique as any of his Genroku work. The difference was chiefly that in the *Jōruri-bon* the subjects were heroic and demanded scenes of conflict and action, while in his Genroku books they were largely of beautiful women and their surroundings.

It was the tendency to use fewer and larger figures in his later work, and these chiefly of women and their lovers, that has given the impression that his technique itself underwent a radical change after he went to Yedo, but in reality the difference was rather in scale and subject, his style remaining about what he had settled upon in the early Kwanbun period.

It is not certain that even this change of subject was due in any great degree to Matabei, and although that artist's paintings doubtless had their effect upon him, the gay life of the city itself was probably the real factor in bringing about his new choice of theme, for everywhere the artist went he must have seen the living models who had inspired Matabei's work, and around whom such a large part of Yedo life flowed.

After examining a great many of Moronobu's books from the Meireki to the Genroku period, one is forced to conclude that his technique varied with the subject rather than undergoing any decided change in itself—and that he endeavoured to harmonize the style of his drawing to what it represented —as many Japanese artists profess to do, treating classical subjects in the classical Tosa style; the *Jōruri-bon* in the big, dashing manner that the subjects seemed to indicate; landscapes, rocks, trees, and waves in the Kanō manner; and drawings of women with something of the roundness and grace of the women themselves.[1]

This theory would account for the different manner of drawing found in books of the same time treating of different subjects, and not leave one wondering at the fine-lined little Tosa illustrations in the tiny book of poems called *Shōkoku Meisho Uta Suzume*, signed Hishikawa Moronobu and published in 1682; the Kanō drawings in the book of designs for screens and *kakemono* entitled *Byōbu Kakemono E-Kagami*, of the same year;

---

[1] See Morrison's *Painters of Japan*, vol. i., p. 134, and Fenollosa's *Epochs of Chinese and Japanese Art*, vol. ii., p. 120.

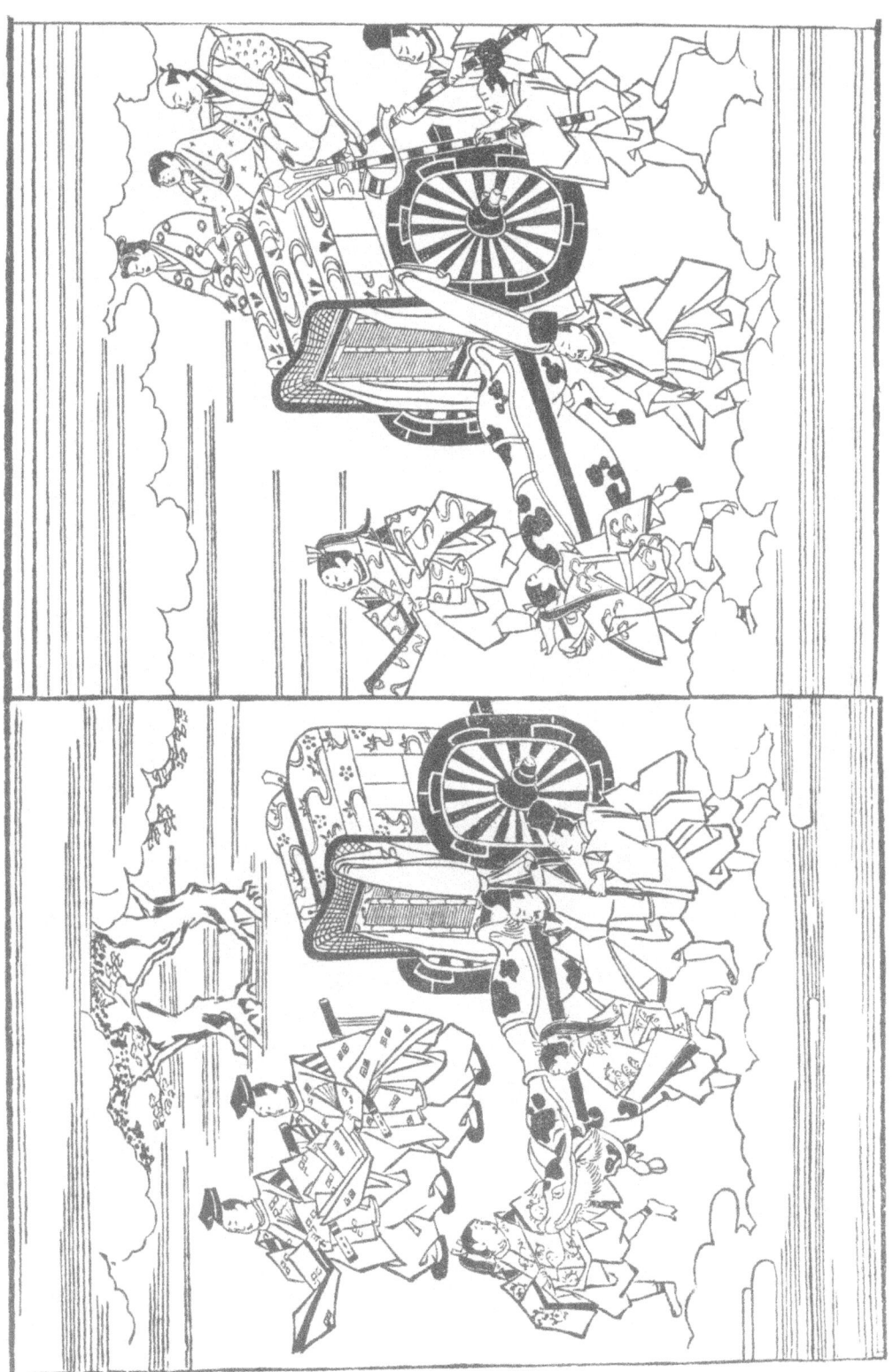

From Vol. I of the SOGA MONOGATARI (1663) by Hishikawa Moronobu.

the *Iwaki Edzukushi* of 1683 with its amazingly various drawings of exaggerated Kanō rocks and waves and charmingly graceful women, signed Hishikawa Kichibei Moronobu; and the still more various *Bijin Edzukushi* signed Yamato Eshi Hishikawa Kichibei, also published in 1683, and containing, among others, drawings representing Chinese women in the Chinese style, fascinating Japanese women, warriors in the manner of his *Jōruri-bon* of nearly thirty years earlier, and Genji playing his flute in a Kanō landscape to his lady-fair in a Tosa house.

This theoretical harmonizing of technique and subject is seen all through Japanese pictorial art, and Moronobu's eclecticism seems to have deliberately adjusted to his own strong individuality, which shone through them all, the manner of expression which he considered most suitable to the theme.

The drawings in the *Sugata-ye-Hyakunin Isshu* published in April, 1695, probably represent his last work, for in the preface the editor states that Moronobu's death occurred before the appearance of the book. As there is also a well authenticated story that a bell was presented by him in May, 1694, to a temple in his native town of Hota, it seems reasonably certain that his death occurred between May, 1694, and April, 1695, and that the story of his retirement to a monastery and his death there in 1714 or 1715 is without foundation.

It is doubtful if any other Japanese artist except Hokusai was ever equally prolific, for in addition to being a noted book illustrator, Moronobu was famous as a painter, a designer, and a single sheet artist.

Of the long list of books attributed to Moronobu[1] comparatively few of the early sets are known out of Japan, and they have never had the recognition they deserve because his signature seems to be necessary before the drawings can be valued for themselves.

This list includes the

Miura Monogatari : Historical tales. 4 vols. 1657. L.[2] A second edition in 1678. Excessively rare.
Kyō Warabe (" Kyōto Children ") : A guide for Kyōto. 6 vols. 1658. M.L.
Kamo-no-Chōmei Hōjōki-sho : 1 vol. 1658. L.
Iso-ho Monogatari : A Japanese version of Æsop's fables.[3] 1 vol. 1659. L.
Shida Monogatari : 2 vols. 1659. L.
Eiri Kamakura Monogatari : Illustrated history of Kamakura. Written by Nakagawa Kiun. 5 vols. 1659. V.S.
Onna Kagami or *Jokyō Hiden* : Instructions for women. 3 vols. 1659. M.
Hōjō Go-Daiki : 10 vols. 1659. M.
Takuan Ōshō Kamakura-ki : Guide for Kamakura. Colophon states this book to have been illustrated by Moronobu in his " middle age." 2 vols. 1659. M.
Onna Shorei-Shū : Instructive book for women. 7 vols. 1660. M. Extremely rare and charming.

---

[1] There is some dispute about a few of the early works. They were unsigned, but the style is so unmistakably Moronobu's that most Japanese collectors attribute them to him without hesitation.

[2] L.=large. M.=medium. S.=small. V.S.=very small.

[3] A copy of this rare book is in the library of Waseda University, Tōkyō.

CHAP. III] JAPANESE BLOCK-PRINTING

Jubutsu Mondō : Various drawings of people. 1 vol. 1660. M.
Yoshiwara Makura : Book of the Yoshiwara. 1 vol. 1660. S.
Taka Byōbu Kuda Monogatari : Scenes from everyday life. 2 vols. 1661. M. An excessively rare book.
Fujiwara Ishiyama Maru : 1 vol. 1661. M.
Hitachibō Kaizon : 1 vol. 1662. L.
Shi-Tennō Komyō Monogatari : Historical work. 1 vol. 1662. M.
Yuriwaka Daijin : Historical work. 1 vol. 1662. M.
Hyaku Monogatari : 1 vol. 1663. M.
Nasu-no funa-Ikon : 1 vol. 1663. M.
Kimpira Hōmon-Arasoi : Story of the giant Kimpira. 1 vol. 1663. M.
Imagawa Monogatari : 1 vol. 1663. M.
Soga Monogatari : History of the Soga brothers. 12 vols. 1663. L.
Shōgun-ki : Lives of the Shōguns. Illustrated by Moronobu and other artists. 20 vols. 1664. M.L.
Shi-Tennō Ota-gasen : Historical work. 1 vol. 1665.
Kyōgen-ki : Short comedies played in the intervals of the *Nō* drama. 2 vols. 1665. M.
Yoshiwara Sode Kagami : Book of the Yoshiwara. 1 vol. 1666. S.
Hōgen Monogatari : History of the war between the Minamoto and Taira families in the twelfth century. 3 vols. 1666. L.
Nitan-no-Shirō : 1 vol. 1667. S.
Heiji Monogatari : A continuation of the *Hōgen Monogatari*. 3 vols. 1667. L. A second edition. in 1685.
Kyō Warabe Atoöi : Supplementary series to the *Kyō Warabe*. 6 vols. 1667. M.
Mino Kagami : 3 vols. 1668. L.
Yamato Taiyō : 1 vol. 1668. M.
Ōsaka Monogatari : History of Ōsaka. 2 vols. 1668.
Shaka-Hassō-ki : 1 vol. 1669. M.
Raikō Atome-ron : 1 vol. 1669.
Ise Monogatari : 2 vols. 1669. M.
Chinzei Hachirō Tametomo : Historical work. 1 vol. 1670. M.
Genji-no-Shirahata : A romance. 1 vol. 1670.
Eiri Shikata Banashi : Tales written by Nakagawa Kiun. 4 vols. 1671. M.
Koi-no-Uwamori : 1 vol. 1671. M.
Ōjō Yōshū : Stories of the dead. 2 vols. 1671. L.
Buke Hyakunin Isshu : 100 Samurai Poets. 1 vol. 1672. L.
Sui Chōki : 3 vols. 1672. L.
Arima Shigure ("Rain in Arima"): A guide for the Arima district. Written by Masanaga. 5 vols. 1672. M.
Hamochi Shōgun : An historical work. 2 vols. 1673. L.
Nippon Ō-Daiki : Work on Japan. 1 vol. 1674. M.
Kyōgen Dzukushi : Illustrated *kyōgen*. 1 vol. 1675. L.
Shin-gaku Nannyō Kagami : 4 vols. 1675. L.
Yamato Meisho Ehon Dzukushi : Dated " a good day of the first month."
Genji Makura or *Wakan Murasaki* : 3 vols. 1676. L.
Yedo Suzume ("Yedo Swallows"): A Yedo *meisho-ki*. Written and illustrated by Moronobu. 12 vols. 1677. M.
Tamatsu-shima Honji : Temples of Tamatsu-shima. 1 vol. 1677. M.
Nasake-no-Uwamori : 3 vols. 1677. L.
Nara Meisho Yae Zakura : 2 sets of 6 vols. each. 1678. M.
Yoshiwara Koi-no-Michibiki : Book on the Yoshiwara. 1 vol. 1678. L.
Sumiyoshi Monogatari : Story of Sumiyoshi. 1 vol. 1678. L.
Ise Monogatari : 2 vols. 1678.
Genji Monogatari : 1678.
Koi-o-Tsuribari Narahira : The love songs of Narahira. 1 vol. 1678.

Moronobu, Itchō, Kōrin and Followers [Chap. III

Wakashū Asobi Makura: 2 vols. 1678. L.
Ehon Jōjō Go-no-jō: 1 vol. 1678.
Hatsuharu-no-Iwai: 1 vol. 1678. S.
Kokon Yakusha Monogatari: Stories of ancient and modern actors. 1 vol. 1678. M. Excessively rare. The first two pages give a list of principal theatres and actors, and above the text are the *mon* of the actors.
Sasa-ye-e Makura: 1 vol. 1678. L.
Jizan Kashū: 3 vols. 1678. L.
Koi-no-Mutsugoto Shijū-Hatte: 2 vols. 1679. L.
Waka Chusen-sho: 3 vols. 1680. L.
Ogura-Yama Hyakunin Isshu: 1 vol. 1680. L.
Yamato Edzukushi: 1 vol. 1680. L. Signed Hishikawa Kichibei.
Bokuyo Kyōka-shū: 2 vols. 1681. L.
Nannyō Kimmō Dzue: An encyclopædia. 5 vols. 1681. M.
Yamato Utakotoba: Poems in *uta* form. 2 vols. 1681. S.
Kōshoku Yoshiwara Harugoma: 1 vol. 1681.
Ukiyo Hyakunin Isshu Onna: One hundred Women Poets. 1 vol. 1681. L.
Shinran Shōnin-ki: Life of Shinran Shonin. 3 vols. 1681. L.
Eiri Waka-shū: 3 vols. 1681. L.
Wakoku Shōshoku Edzukushi: 4 vols. 1681. L. Artisans at work. A second edition in 1685.
Yamato-no-Oyosei: 3 vols. 1682. L.
Iwaki Edzukushi: 3 vols. 1682. L.
Saigyō Waka Shugyō: 2 vols. 1682. L.
Osana Najimi: 2 vols. 1682. L.
Onna Kasen Shinshō: Women poets. 1 vol. 1682. L.
Byōbu Kakemono Edzukushi: Designs for screens and *kakemono*. 1 vol. 1682. L.
Kokon Edzukushi: 2 vols. 1682. L.
Wakoku Meisho Kagami: 3 vols. 1682. L.
Makura Daizen: 3 vols. 1682. M.
Shiki Moyō Edzukushi: Kimono designs. 3 vols. 1682. M.
Shōkoku Meisho Uta Suzume or *Waka Rokujū Yoshū:* A poetical *meisho-ki*. 1 vol. 1682. V.S.
Hyakunin Jorō: One hundred women of the Yoshiwara. 1682.
Kyōka Tabi Makura: Humorous poems. 1 vol. 1682. M.
Uchiwa Edzukushi: Designs for fans. 1 vol. 1682. L.
Shimpan Wakoku Meisho Kagami: 3 vols. 1682. M.
Kizuden-ki Kasen Kinkyō Shō: 1 vol. 1682.
Chikusai Monogatari: 2 vols. 1683. L.
Koi-no-Tanoshimi: Love songs of Tanoshimi. 3 vols. 1683. L.
Chiyo-no-Tomozuro: 3 vols. 1683. Signed Eshi Hishikawa Fude.
Hyakunin Isshu Zō San Shō: 1 vol. 1683. L. A second edition in 1692.
Yoshiwara Daidzu Dawara Byōbu: 1 vol. 1683. M.
Eiri Nichiren Ichidai-ki: Life of Nichiren. 3 vols. 1683. L.
Sayo-goromo: 5 vols. 1683. M.
Shimpan Kwachō Edzukushi: Birds and flowers. 1 vol. 1683. L.
Kofū-tōfū Kakiwake Edzukushi: 3 vols. 1683. L.
Bijin Edzukushi: Beautiful women. 1 vol. 1683. L.
Tadanori Hyaku Shū and *Fujikawa Hyaku Shū:* 2 vols., forming one set. 1683.
Yamato Shinō Edzukushi: 1 vol. 1684. L.
Ehon Jokiwa-no-Matsu: 1684. 3 large folios.
Kazu Daizen: 1684.
Ukiyo Zoku Edzukushi: A supplementary set to the *Ukiyo Edzukushi*. 1684.
Shitaya Katsura Otoko: 1 vol. 1684.
Jūni-gatsu-no-Shinasadame: 1 vol. 1684.
Nasake-no-Yujō: A book on the Yoshiwara. 1 vol. 1685.

JAPANESE BLOCK-PRINTING

Genji Yamato E-Kagami: Romance of a Japanese prince. 2 vols. Illustrations in circular panels. 1685. M.
Nagoya Edzukushi: 2 vols. 1685. M.
Koi-no-Iki Utsushi: 1 vol. L.
Minobu Kagami: A guide for Minobu. 3 vols. 1685. M.
Kokon Bushidō Edzukushi: Famous *samurai*. 1 vol. 1685. L.
Imayō Makura Byōbu: Beautiful women. 1 vol. 1685. L.
Hyakunin Isshu Sugata: One hundred poets. 3 vols. 1685. L.
Waka-no-Tebiki: 5 vols. 1686. M. Signed Hishikawa Kichibei.
Imayō Yoshiwara Makura: Beautiful women of the Yoshiwara. 1 vol. 1686. L.
Ume-no-Kaori: 5 vols. 1687. M.
Bijin Edzukushi: A supplementary set to the earlier work of this title. 2 vols. 1687. L.
Seimei Tsuhensen Kiden: 1 vol. 1687. S.
Kōshoko Ichidai Otoko: 8 vols. 1687. M.
Ukiyo Edzukushi: A second edition. 1687.
Fuku Zasshō: 1 vol. 1687. L.
Yoshiwara Genji Gojū-shi-kun: 1 vol. 1687. M.
Onsukuki Monogatari: 2 vols. 1688.
Igyō Sennin Ehon: 3 vols. 1689. L.
Yoshitsune-ki or *Gikei-ki*: Life of Yoshitsune. 6 vols. 1689. M.
Hōgen Ikusa Monogatari: 1 vol. 1689.
Egata-Sennin Dzukushi: Figures of Sennin. 1 vol. 1689.
Genji Kumogakurei: Story of the Genji from a manuscript of 1058. 3 vols. 1690.
Musha Zakura: 2 vols. 1690.
Miyatogawa Monogatari: 5 vols. 1690.
Tōkaidō Buken Edzu: Guide to the Tōkaidō. Written by Enkindo. Drawings by Hishikawa Kichibei. Published by Hichirobei, Yedo. 5 long, narrow, upright *gwajō*: Vol. i., Yedo to Odawara; vol. ii., Odawara to Fuchu; vol. iii., Fuchu to Yoshida; vol. iv., Yoshida to Kamiyama; vol. v., Kamiyama to Kyōto. 1690. Very rare in complete set.
Tsukiyama-zu Niwa Edzukushi or *Yokei Tsukusi no Niwa no zu*: Mountainous gardens. 1 vol. 1691. L.
Tsuki-nami-no-Asobi: Months in the Eastern Capital. 1 vol. 1691. L.
Ehon Yamato-zumi: 3 vols. 1694. L.
Shōjiki Banashi O-Kagami: Old tales. Written by Ishikawa Ryūshū. 5 vols. 1694. M.
Kimono Ehon Edzukushi: Designs for *kimono*. 1 vol. 1694. L.
Wakoku Hyaku-jo: One hundred women of Japan. 3 vols. 1695. L. Signed Shigwa (Master-Painter) Hishikawa Moronobu.
Sugata-ye Hyakunin Isshu: One hundred poets. 5 vols. 1695. L.
Ko-no-Kaori: 3 vols. 1695.
Goreiko: 1 vol. 1695.
Miyagi-nō: No date. From collection belonging to Mr. Higuchi, Wakayama.

BOOKS ATTRIBUTED TO MORONOBU, BUT PUBLISHED AFTER HIS DEATH.

Sanjū-rok-kasen: Thirty-six poets. A verse in Kōyetsu's chirography above each poet and on opposite pages drawings of figures in landscapes. 2 vols. 1696.
Enroshi: 1696.

UNDATED BOOKS BY MORONOBU. (NOT ALL SIGNED.)

Bunsho-no-Zōshi: Supposed to be Moronobu's first book. Historical tales. 2 vols. L.
Bunsho Monogatari: 2 vols. Rare and charming. S.
Bushi-kun Oshiye: Teachings for *samurai* boys.
Kinsei Daizen.
Iro Zōshi.
Ama-no-hashi-date: Guide for Ama-no-hashi-date. 1 roll.
Narihira Honchō Noshinobu: 1 vol. L.

PLATE 12. From the WAKOKU SHŌSHOKU EDZUKUSHI (1681), by Hishikawa Moronobu

MORONOBU, ITCHŌ, KŌRIN AND FOLLOWERS [CHAP. III

Hana-no-Saka-dzuki: 1 vol. L.
Chiyo-no-Tomodzuru: 3 vols. L.
Uta Zakura: Illustrated poems. 5 vols.
Sewa Edzukushi: 4 vols.
Toko-no-kimono or *Shiawase-Yoshi*: 1 vol. L.
Aki-no-Yonaga Monogatari: An early *Jōruri-bon*.
Honchō Buke Ō-Keizu: Japanese *samurai*. 4 vols. L.
Mikenjyaku: A *Jōruri-bon*.
Moshiwo-gusa: 3 vols. L.
Sanze Aisho Makura: 3 vols. (Crewdson Catalogue).
Yomeiri Makura: 1 vol.

Moronobu's death left book-illustration for a time with no very great man to represent it, for his sons and pupils were much less prolific as illustrators than he had been, and with the exception of Moroshige, seldom reached his level.

Itchō and Kōrin never really worked directly for wood-engraving, the books containing their drawings being compilations made by their followers years after their deaths.

Of Moronobu's immediate pupils, his brother, Hishikawa Masanojō, and his son and son-in-law,[1] Morofusa and Moronaga, were left to carry on his teachings.

Morofusa, also known as Hishikawa Kichizaemon and Kichibei, is said to have collaborated with Moronobu to a considerable extent. He also illustrated several books himself, among which are the *Kōshoku Hitomoto Zusuki*, a love romance; the *Tsubo-no-Ishibumi*, a book of instructions for women in *koto*-playing, letter-writing, poems, etc., published in thirteen volumes in 1698, which contain some interesting drawings much in Moronobu's style; and the *Ehon Kimono-no-Moyō*, a set of books of *kimono* designs published about 1700.

Hishikawa MORONAGA, Moronobu's son-in-law, is said to have been especially noted for the beautiful colouring which he applied to the printed illustrations, not only in his own books but in many of Moronobu's. Other signatures used by him were OKINOJŌ, SAKUNOJŌ and MIKINOJŌ. He illustrated the *Yedo Kanoka*, published in 1686, and the *Yedo Zukan*.

Hishikawa MOROSHIGE, also known as Furuyama TARŌBEI, was probably a nephew of Moronobu's and was one of the very best of his pupils. Some of his work reaches Moronobu's level. The illustrations in the well-known *Kōshoku Yedo Murasaki*, an obscene book on the Yoshiwara "violets," published in five volumes in 1684, were his work. The blocks for these books were destroyed by fire in 1694, those for the edition of 1695 met the same fate in 1772, and in 1760 those for an edition of 1759 were burned.

Another notorious work illustrated by Moroshige was the *Shika-no-*

[1] From the *Kinsei-kiseki-kō*, by Santō Kyōden. 1805.

CHAP. III]   JAPANESE BLOCK-PRINTING

Makifude, which appeared in five volumes in 1692, criticizing the manners and morals of the time. Condemnation by the Government swiftly followed its appearance, and the author, Shikano Bunzaemon, was banished to a remote part of the empire, while the editor and Moroshige were obliged to leave Yedo temporarily.

Other books illustrated by Moroshige were the

Shiza (or *Yoza*) *Yakusha Edzukushi* : Favourite Yedo actors. 3 vols. Jōkyō period.
Chiwa-no-Ōyose : A romance. 2 vols. Jōkyō period.
Shikano Bunzaemon Kudan Banashi : Various tales. Written by Shikano Bunzaemon. 1685.
Harusame Goto : Jōkyō period.
Tofuon Hinagata : *Kimono* designs.

Moroshige's son, Furuyama MOROFUSA,[1] studied under Moronobu as well as with his father, and also acquired some fame as a writer. His literary name was Bunshi.

Furuyama MOROTANI, a younger son of Moroshige's, was working in Yedo late in the Kyōhō period.

Furuyama MOROMASA, also known as Bunshi SHINKURŌ and GETSUGETSUDŌ, is said to have been a pupil and possibly a son of Moroshige. He was working in the late seventeenth and early eighteenth centuries. Among the books left by him are the *Ya-egaki Kumono Tayema*, a work on puppet-shows (one volume, 1685).

MOROTSUGU was also a pupil of Moroshige.

Other pupils of the Morobonu school were Hishikawa TOMOFUSA; Hishikawa SHIMPEI; Hishikawa MOROHIRA; Hishikawa MOROMORI, also known as KATSUSHIGE; Furuyama BANSUI; Shorin MATSUNAGA, also known as KUISETSU and SEIKIN, and who illustrated a book on the Empresses of China entitled the *Meien Shisen Shū*, much in Moronobu's style, published in 1678; and Hishikawa Inshi WA-Ō.

Among the eighteenth-century followers of the Moronobu school were SHIGEYOSHI, the son of Hishikawa Morofusa, also known as SAJIBEI; and MOROHISA, the son of Shigeyoshi. No important details are available in regard to them.

Harukawa MORONOBU, also known as Hishikawa CHOBEI, was an artist of Kyōto who was working in the Hōreki period. He illustrated the *Ehon Ressen Gwaden*, a set of three books on the Chinese sages published in 1759. The drawings have considerable resemblance to Hishikawa Moronobu's work, and unscrupulous dealers sometimes sell the books as his.

Sugimura MASATAKA is also mentioned as a pupil of Moronobu, and von Seidlitz speaks of a book containing very fine illustrations by him published in 1684. The little drawings at the tops of the pages in the *Goseibai*

[1] Not to be confused with Hishikawa Morofusa, who was Moronobu's son.

Shikimoku Esho, published in one volume in 1697, signed Sugimura Jirōbei Masataka, are also very charming.

Orizomi HANA left a book of instructions for women, entitled *Onna Dōji Kyō*, in two large folios, dated 1695, containing drawings showing Moronobu's influence.

The lacquer artist, Maki-eshi GENZABURŌ, a contemporary of Moronobu, left at least one interesting book in addition to his regular work. It is entitled *Jinrin Kimmō Dzue*, an illustrated encyclopædia, and appeared in 1690.

Although little is known in regard to the life of Ōmori YOSHIKIYO, he is supposed to have been a son of Shigeyoshi. He left several very striking and rare books. The *Kyō Shimabara Yūjo Ningyō Tsukai* of 1702 being especially fine. The large, oblong double-page drawings represent scenes in the Shimabara quarter of Kyōto and compare favourably with Moronobu's best work. Other books illustrated by Yoshikiyo were the *Shin Usuyuki Monogatari*, written by Rankei, published in five volumes in 1716; and the *Shidare Yanagi* ("Weeping Willows"), a work on games made up of delightful double-page *sumi-ye* and bound in *gwajō* form.

Baikwadō YOSHIYUKI, a contemporary of Moronobu, illustrated the *Temmon Zukai*, a work on astronomy published in five volumes in 1689.

Takagi SADATAKE and Kaihoku YŪZEN, two famous dyers of the Genroku period, were also late contemporaries of Moronobu.

Sadatake, who was also known as KOSUKE and SOTENSAI, was a native of Ōsaka. He illustrated a number of delightful books, but was chiefly noted for his *kimono* designs, the *Gofuku Moyō Uta Hinagata*, published in two volumes in 1690, containing charming drawings of this kind. He also made a series of drawings from old paintings entitled *Ehon Kohitsu Gwato-Jūi*, which appeared in three volumes, beautifully printed by an Ōsaka publishing house, in 1701. His *Ehon Waka-no-Ura*, a collection of drawings much in Sukenobu's style, with a poem on each page, was published in three volumes in 1725 (a second edition in 1734). The book is rare and is sometimes sold as Sukenobu's work. Other books illustrated by Sadatake were the

Tokiwa Hinagata: A collection of *kimono* designs. Signed Takagi Kosuke. 1732.
Ehon Buyū Homare-gusa: Famous heroes. Signed Takagi Kosuke Sadatake. 3 vols. 1742.
Honchō Gwarin: Copies of old paintings. 3 vols. 1752.

Kaihoku YŪZEN, also known as MIYAZAKI and HEGI, and occasionally using the prefixes Fusō-Zenko and Some-ya ("Japanese Dyer"), although said to have been a pupil of Moronobu, was also much influenced by Kōrin's work. He evolved a style of his own in decoration eventually, which is still known by his name. Among the books illustrated by him were the

Yojo Hinagata: A delightful collection of *kimono* designs. 1 vol. Kyōto. 1691.
Ino Hagaki: Very charming landscape drawings with poems. 3 vols. 1691.
Waka-Mono-Arasoi: Signed Miyazaki Yūzensai. 2 vols. 1692.
Kaji-no-ha: Written by Kaji (a woman writer of the time) and illustrated by Yūsen. 3 vols. 1707.

Naemura JŌHAKU, a scholar and writer of Kyōto toward the end of the seventeenth century, is said to have been self-taught in drawing. He was also known as SODEN-SUNBOKUSHI. A famous set of five books, the *Onna Chohoki*, published first in Kyōto in 1692, a little later in Yedo under the title of *Onna Takara-gura*, and in Ōsaka as the *Onna Chohoki Taisei*, was written by him. The work deals with subjects of especial interest to women, and has gone through innumerable editions. The illustrations, although unsigned, are undoubtedly by Sunbokushi himself, since they are manifestly from the same brush as the drawings in the two volumes of the *Tsure-dsure-gusa Esho*, published in 1691 and signed Sodensai Sunbokushi Sankei. These charming drawings suggest Moronobu, although the figures are taller and more slender. They represent women engaged in various occupations, such as the folding and putting away of *kimono*, arranging ceremonial gifts, going through the classical rite of the *Cha-no-yu*, preparing for the advent of an heir in a great house, and finally bathing and dressing the new-born infant.

Another book attributed to Johaku is an edition of the *Ise Monogatari* with a small cut at the top of each page signed Sodenshi, and published in three volumes in 1693.

Sugimura JIHEI, a late contemporary of Moronobu, also left a few interesting books. Among them were the

Yamato Fūryū E-Kagami: Ancient customs of Japan. 1 vol. 1694. An album of landscape and other drawings. Tenwa period.
Chokei Zenta Heikei: A history of the era of peace which followed the establishment of the Tokugawa Shōgunate. 15 vols. 1716.

Torii KIYONOBU will be spoken of among the Ukiyo-ye men.

Ranking rather above the other contemporaries of Moronobu who worked for wood-engraving were Yoshida HANBEI and Ishikawa RYŪSEN.

Hanbei was illustrating books in Kyōto as early as the Empō period (1673–1681). His work has a style of its own, and is unmistakable. It is characterized by rather fine lines with few accents in the drawing of figures, but with heavier strokes of varying thickness in the landscape, while trees are invariably treated in a crisp and spiky fashion, which is distinctively his own. Although his work is stiff, it has considerable charm, and his books in complete sets are rare and valuable.

Many of the notorious books written by Ihara Saikaku, which were afterward suppressed by the Government because of their indecency, were illustrated by Yoshida Hanbei. The drawings themselves are unobjectionable, however, and many of them are of great interest. Hanbei's earliest

PLATE 13] Horse-racing at the Kamo Festival. From the YAMATO KOSAKU ESHO (1692—1696), by Ishikawa Ryūsen.

[Face p. 52]

known works are two very rare and interesting guide-books—the *Nanto Meisho Shū*, in two series of five volumes each, published in 1675, treating of places in Southern Japan; and the *Naniwa Meisho Ashiwake-bune*, on Ōsaka and its environs, in six volumes, which appeared the same year. The *Kōshoku Kimmō Dzue*, an illustrated encyclopædia published in Kyōto about 1669, was his most popular work. It was reprinted later in Yedo under the supervision of Moronobu, while Sukenobu edited it again, toward the middle of the eighteenth century, in Ōsaka.

Another extremely rare and valuable book which, although unsigned, bears the unmistakable stamp of Hanbei's manner is the *Kyō-Ōsaka Yarō Sekizumo*, published by the Shohonya Kiemon printing-house of Ōsaka in 1693. It is especially interesting as being one of the very early books devoted to actors and the stage, and consists of short biographies of famous Kyōto and Ōsaka stage favourites with text surrounding the illustrations. The exaggerated drawing of the hands in the cuts, the violent poses and the ferocious intensity of facial expression, all clearly prefigure the Torii work of Yedo in the next century. Other books attributed to Hanbei were the

Shin Otogi-bōko: Historical tales. Unsigned but attributed to Hanbei. 6 vols. 1683.
Nihon Bushi Kagami: History of famous *samurai*. 5 vols. 1683. (A second edition in 1696.)
Nyoyō Kimmō Dzue: Kimono designs and figures of beautiful women. 1685. Very rare.
Kōshoku Ise Monogatari: 1686.
Kōshoku Gonin Onna: Novel by Saikaku. 5 vols. 1686.
Nyoyō Kimmō Dzue: A supplementary set to above. 4 vols. 1688.
Wakan Fujin Yashinai-gusa: Old legends. 3 vols. 1689.
Zōho Hyakunin Isshu Esho: The Hundred Poets. 1 vol. 1693.
Tsure-dsure-gusa: 2 vols. No date.
Amayo Sanbai-kigen: Genroku period.
Honchō Ō-in Hiji: Genroku period.
Tama Ho-ōki: 1696.

Ishikawa RYŪSEN, one of the best of Moronobu's pupils, became noted not only as an illustrator and painter, but also for his fine typographical work. Other signatures used by him were Ishikawa TOMONOBU, Ishikawa IZAEMON, SHUNSHI, TOSHIYUKI, and RYŪSHŪ.

Although Ryūsen's drawing of figures and his treatment of landscape resembles that of Moronobu to a considerable extent, he was not by any means without individuality of his own. He used slightly finer lines and let his splendidly placed masses of black form the chief emphasis in his illustrations. Among the books left by him, all of which are extremely rare, are the

Eda Sangojū: Old tales. 1690.
Nippon Kanokō: Historical tales. 11 vols. 1691.
Yamato Kosaku Esho: Arts and activities of Japan. 4 vols. 1692-1696.
Kōshoku Edzukushi: 1698.

CHAP. III]   JAPANESE BLOCK-PRINTING

Kaisei Zōho Nippon Kanoko: A supplementary series to the above. 12 vols. 1698.
Yedo Murasaki: A book on the Yoshiwara.
Yedo Zukan Kōmoku.
Yedo Dzu: Pictures of Yedo life.
Yo-Banashi-gusa: Various tales.

Ishikawa RYŪSHŪ, a pupil and probably a son of Ryūsen, was a writer as well as an artist. The *Shōjiki Banashi* of 1694 is said to have been his work.

Hasegawa TŌUN, also known as MASUNOBU and, according to Anderson, as CHŌSHUN, was born in 1625, the son of Hasegawa Sōen, a well-known ornamenter of swords. He was adopted by Kanō Tanyū when eleven years old, taking the name of Kanō Tōun. He married the daughter of Kanō Yasunobu.

Tōun achieved the rank of Hōgen and established a school of his own at Suruga-dai in Yedo, where he died in 1694. Although chiefly known as a painter, he left a set of very well-known books illustrated in the Kanō style, called the *Ehon Hōkan*, published in five volumes in 1688.

His son TŌSHUN, who sometimes signed himself as YOSHINOBU, was also a painter.

Kawashima SHIGENOBU, an obscure artist of the Genroku period, illustrated the

Yononaka Hyaku-shū: One hundred aspects of the world. Published by a house in Ise in 2 vols. 1683.
Hyaku-shū Empyō.

No details are available in regard to his life.

Neither, unfortunately, is there anything known of the artist who made the drawings for a famous set of wood-engravings, published about this time, entitled *Kwaraku Saiken Dzu* (Views of the Flowery Capital), consisting of 100 large, oblong plates 8¾ inches high by 12¾ wide, representing various scenes about Kyōto. There are drawings of temples and shrines; noted historical spots; flower arrangements at Rokkakudo Temple; different festivals, including the famous Gion *matsuri* and the June horse-races at Fushimi; parts of the *geisha* quarter; picnic parties; the procession of a Korean envoy and his suite to do honour to the Emperor; a circus; and many other scenes from the everyday life of the people. The work is very rare and impossible to find now complete and in the original edition. There is considerable uncertainty as to when it was first published. Anderson gives the date as 1703.[1] The Tōkyō Imperial Museum places it between the Kwanbun and Genroku periods (1661–1681), while another Japanese authority gives Tenwa 2 (1682). The technique of the drawings is much like that in Ōmori Yoshikiyo's work, and the date given by Anderson is about

[1] See *Japanese Wood-Engraving*, p. 123 in the small edition.

PLATE 14] From the Kyō Shimabara Yujō Ningyō Tsukai, by Ōmori Yoshikiyo Genroku, 15th (1702) [Face p. 54

the time when that artist was producing his most interesting books. The *Kyō Shimabara Yūjo Ningyō Tsukai*, by Yoshikiyo, contains drawings which, although on a larger scale than those in the *Kwaraku Saiken Dzu*, are so identical in style that it seems to justify attributing the latter work to him, pending anything certain which may be discovered in regard to the artist.

Hanabusa ITCHŌ and Ogata KŌRIN, the two great contemporaries of Moronobu, never, so far as is known, worked directly for wood-engraving, although their followers compiled various collections of their drawings and published them after their deaths. Both men were about a generation later than Moronobu, and both were really far greater artists than he. We consider them here because in point of time they fall into this period.

Hanabusa Itchō was born in Ōsaka in 1652, the son of Taga Hakuan, a well-known physician of that city. At the age of fifteen Itchō went to Yedo, where he entered the great Kanō school there, studying under Kanō Yasunobu.

His ordinary name was Taga CHŌKO, but as an artist he chiefly used the signatures ITCHŌ, CHŌKO, and NOBUKA. Other names occasionally used by him were SUISA-Ō, USHIMARO, KYŪSODŌ, HOKUSŌ-Ō, IPPŌ KANJIN, RINSHŌAN, RINTŌ-AN, and as a poet WA-Ō and GYŌ-UN.

Itchō became a familiar figure in the gay Tokugawa capital, and was known not only as an artist, but as a poet and a great wit, his clever caricatures adding to his popularity there. His propensity for caricaturing the fast Yedo life brought him into serious trouble finally, and he was banished to the island of Hachijo, of the Bonin group, in 1698, for a series of drawings of the Hundred Poets, in which he caricatured the Shōgun and one of the latter's fair favourites in a shameful fashion.

During the eleven years of his exile on Hachijo he continued his work, the pictures done during this time being known as *Shima-Itchi-ye*, or " island pictures," and usually signed Hokusō-ō (" the old man of the northern window "), signifying his constant gazing toward the north, where his widowed mother was living alone in Yedo and getting on as best she could by selling the paintings which Itchō sent her by every boat.

In 1709, when he was fifty-seven years old, he was pardoned. It is said that the news was brought to him as he was sketching a butterfly hovering near a flower by his window, and in remembrance of the two events, he took the name Hanabusa Itchō—Hanabusa meaning the corolla of a flower, and Itchō a butterfly. He returned to Yedo, where he rejoined his mother, living in the Fukagawa district until his death in 1724. His tomb is in the cemetery of Kenjo-in in Tōkyō.

Most of the books containing his drawings were published many years after his death, being made up of work collected by Hanabusa Ippō, an adopted son and pupil. They include the

Ehon Juga: Reproductions of Itchō's work by Ippō. 3 vols. 1731.
Ehon Juhen: A supplementary series. 3 vols. 1751.
Eishi Gwahen: Various drawings. 3 vols. 1751.
Gwashu Dzue: Copies of Itchō's work by Ippō. 3 vols. 1751.
Gwahon Jihen: Reproductions of paintings by Itchō. 3 vols. 1752.
Eihitsu Hyaku Gwa: One hundred sketches by Hanabusa Itchō, with a poem on each page. 5 vols. Tiger year of Hōreki (1758). Rare and charming.
Itchō Gwafu: Various sketches. Compiled by Suzuki Rinsho. 3 vols. 1770. (A second edition in 1773.)
Gunchō Gwayei: Various sketches. 3 vols. 1772. (A second edition in 1778.)
Eirin Gwakyō: Copies of Hanabusa Itchō's drawings by Shunsō-ō Ippō. 3 vols. 1773. Rare.
Gwato Zetsumyō: Various drawings. 3 vols. 1774.
Gwato Zetsumyō: A supplementary set. 3 vols. 1779.
Zoku Kinsei Ki-jin-den: Lives of eccentric characters.
Fusō Gwasen-den: Historical tales.
Hanabusa Itchō Kyōgwa: A nineteenth-century compilation of coloured drawings. 1 vol.

In addition to the above, the following works containing drawings by Itchō are listed in various Japanese books and magazines, none of which, however, have been available for a detailed description:

Kaga-bike.
Shoho Yaraku.
Hairin Shōden.
Kokon Kōsaku.
Sekitei Gwaden.
Bashō Ichiren: Poems by Bashō illustrated by Itchō.
Sanko Zake.
Fūzoku Ewaki.

Many of Itchō's books have a grey tone added to the black and white which almost gives the effect of colour. This additional block was used with especial success in the *Itchō Gwafu* and the *Gunchō Gwayei*. Itchō's books are all very popular among the Japanese, and have become difficult to find in good condition and in complete sets, although modern copies of some of them may be obtained.

Itchō was survived by two sons and his adopted son, Ippō. The oldest, Taga Chōhachi, also known as Chōhachirō, Nobukatsu and Hanabusa Itchō II., died in 1737.

Itchō,[1] the second son, also signed himself Hyakumatsu, Gennai, and Kōun. No details are available in regard to their lives.

His adopted son, Hanabusa Ippō, seems to have been the one to inherit Itchō's mantle. Ippō lived between 1687 and 1774 and used the name Shunsō-ō Ippō as another signature. While chiefly known for his reproductions of Itchō's work, he also left a number of books containing very original drawings, as well as some very early illustrations printed in colours.

[1] Written with different characters than those used in Hanabusa Itchō's name.

The latter are in the *Hokku Chō*, a volume of seventeen-syllable poems by Takarai Kikaku, a famous poet of the Genroku period and a friend of Hanabusa Itchō's. The book was compiled by the poet Gyokuga, who owned the manuscript copy of the verses, and illustrated by Ippō and Katsuma Ryūsui. The preface was written by Shiyuan Gisho, and the blocks cut by Komei,[1] all friends of Gyokuga.

The first drawing is by Ippō and is a portrait of Kikaku copied from a painting in Gyokuga's possession. Nine of the plates are printed in colours. The first represents two princesses standing together, one holding a fan, and is printed from five blocks, the colours being a brownish pink, blue, green, yellow, and black. Four of the plates are of flowers, one of cherry blossoms, one of peonies, one of *fleurs-de-lys*, and one of morning glories, each printed in three colours; one of two stags standing among bushes, in three colours; and three landscapes, each in three colours; while two of the plates have a grey tone added to the black.

This rare book was a *kubari-hon*, or gift book, and was published in Hōreki 6 (1756), thus taking its place among the early works containing colour-printing.

Among other followers of Itchō were ISSHŪ, also known as NOBUTANI, TOSŌ-Ō, and YASABURŌ, who lived until 1768; SAWAKI; SUSHI; SŪSETSU or KŌ SŪKOKU (1730–1804), who was one of the foremost of Itchō's followers; Hanabusa SŪGETSU; Hanabusa IKKYŌ; Hanabusa IKKEI; and KŌ SŪKEI, the son of Sūkoku.

Suisatei ITTEISEI, who is also said to have been a pupil of Itchō's, left a book containing drawings of warriors and battle scenes much in Tsukioka Masanobu's style, entitled *Bumbu Chiyo-no-Ume*, published in 1774.

Katsuma RYŪSUI, who collaborated with Ippō in the *Hokku Chō* of 1756, was a pupil of Ikenaga Dōun, and became especially well known for his seventeen-syllable poems called *hokku* or *haikai*. He lived at Izumichō, Yedo, and used as other signatures the names Sadayasu, Shinsen, Sekiju-kwan, Hidekuni, and Katsu. He illustrated two other very beautiful books, both of which are excessively rare. These are the *Umi-no-Sachi* ("Fortune of the Sea") and the *Yama-no-Sachi* ("Fortune of the Mountains"), both containing early and remarkably fine colour-printed work.

The *Umi-no-Sachi* consists of two large folios of ninety colour plates representing various forms of sea life, including drawings of shells, fishes, prawns, crabs, tortoises, etc., with poems in very fine chirography above. The preface is signed by Ryūsui and dated Hōreki, Horse year, autumn, corresponding to the autumn of 1762. The post-face states that the drawings were the work of Sekiju-kwan Hidekuni Katsu Ryūsui. The blocks were

---

[1] The foregoing description is translated from the preface of the book.

cut by Sekiguchi Jinshirō. According to the Hayashi Catalogue this book was published by Iseya Yamazaki of Yedo in 1762.[1] A later edition was issued by Noda Shichibei and Nishimuraya Yohachi of Yedo in Anyei 7 (1778). The drawings are beautifully printed in colours on rich and heavy paper, which is decorated with a tinted design across the tops of the pages. The books are so exceedingly rare that there has been a good deal of confusion about them, and it is even sometimes asserted that Ryūsui was another name for Keisai Masayoshi. This mistake probably arose from the similarity of the drawings in the *Umi-no-Sachi* to those in Keisai's well-known *Gyodai-fu* of 1802, but if nothing were known in detail of Ryūsui, the preface and the date of the *Hokku Chō* would prove him to have been an earlier man.

The *Yama-no-Sachi*, the companion set to the *Umi-no-Sachi*, consists of two folios of the same size as those of the latter work and contain very beautiful colour plates of flowers and insects. It was published by Motozaemon Kyūchi of Yedo and the allied printing-house of Heizaburō in Ōsaka, in Meiwa 2 (1765). This book is even more rare than the *Umi-no-Sachi*, and it is only by the greatest good fortune that a collector may obtain a set.

Ogata KŌRIN, whose work, like Itchō's, was reproduced by his followers and published after his death, is said by the chief priest of the little temple of Kōyetsu-ji, up in the hills north of Kyōto, to have been the grandson of Kōyetsu's sister.[2] Kōrin was born in Kyōto in 1658, the son of Ogata Sōken.[3] Sōken in turn was the son of Ogata Dōhaku, who, in early life, had been a priest in the province of Bungo, afterward going to Kyōto, where he married Kōyetsu's sister. The Ogata family became wealthy silk manufacturers in the old capital, and at his father's death Kōrin was left a rich man. His talent seems also to have been an inheritance from his father, who was an artist of some ability and had studied under Kojima Sōshin, a pupil of Kōyetsu.

Kōrin's ordinary name was Ogata KORETOMI. He studied first under the Tosa painter Sumiyoshi Gukei and later went to Yedo, where he worked under Tsunenobu in the Kanō school for a brief period. It is said that Kōyetsu's work was too powerful an attraction, however, and he returned to Kyōto, where he put himself under the instruction of Kojima Sōshin and Tawaraya Sōtatsu, the best living pupils of that master, Kōyetsu himself having died in 1637.

Kōrin was almost as versatile as Kōyetsu had been, and there is much more of his work to judge him by. Although he is chiefly known outside of

---

[1] The Bermond Catalogue gives the publishers as Iseya Jiemon, and Yamazaki Kimbei.
[2] See also *Painters of Japan*, by Arthur Morrison.
[3] Also known as Kenichi, Soho, and Shihaku. Lived between 1620 and 1687.

Japan as a lacquer artist, his fame in his own country rests largely upon his paintings, the magnificent screens left by him testifying to his genius in this direction. He also occasionally made pottery, but in this work his younger brother Kenzan excelled, and the two men together with Honnami Kōho (Kūchūsai), their cousin, united in producing marvellously beautiful things in many mediums.

Kōrin used as other signatures the names Hōshuku, Chōkōken, Dōsō, Kansei, Seiseisai, and in lacquer painting Tōjirō. Although he was left a comparatively rich man at his father's death, his utter carelessness in regard to the practical side of life resulted in the loss of much of his property. He is even said to have incurred a severe reprimand from the Kyōto city authorities at one time for having thrown away a gold-lacquered picnic box at Arashiyama one spring, the gold dust used by artists being valuable and its distribution subject to strict surveillance.

Kōrin is said to have entered the priesthood early in the eighteenth century under the name of Nichijin. His death occurred in 1715 and his tomb is in the temple cemetery of Myōkenji in Kyōto.[1]

He was survived by two sons, the elder of whom was adopted into the Konishi family and became known as Hōshoku.

The first collection of drawings by Kōrin to be printed was a set of two volumes of charming designs for *kimono* entitled *Kōrin Hinagata Suso Moyō*, compiled by Rakuyō Chozōshi. This work appeared in Kyōhō 12 (1727).

In 1732 Nonomura Chūbei, a well-known artist and designer of the early eighteenth century and a devoted follower of Kōrin's style, compiled the *Hinagata Some-iro-no-Yama*, another set of books of *kimono* designs, from Kōrin's drawings, which was published in three volumes. This was followed by a supplementary set, called the *Hinagata Mamiya-no-Yama*, issued in three volumes in 1754. All of these works are rare and valuable and greatly prized by both collectors and the modern artists and designers of Japan.

Chūbei also compiled the *Kōrin Ehon Michi Shirube*, a well-known set of three volumes of simple drawings of flowers and plant-forms, showing the charming use of such motifs made by Kōrin. This work appeared in 1735.

The *Kōrin Gwafu*, a delightful collection of Kōrin's drawings reproduced by Yoshinaka from originals owned by Kagei, one of Kōrin's pupils, was published in two *gwajo* in Kyōto in 1802. It contains twenty-five double-page plates of delicately coloured flowers, landscapes, figures, etc. In the original edition it is extremely rare and valuable and even the later reprint is not easily found.

The *Kōrin Hyaku Dzu* was published in two volumes in Yedo in 1815.

[1] Taken from post-face of the *Kenzan Iboku* (1823).

This collection was made up of reproductions of Kōrin's work by Sakai Hōitsu, who will be spoken of later. The books were published as a memorial of the hundredth anniversary of Kōrin's death, and in the preface Hōitsu says: " This second day of the sixth month of Bunkwa (June 2nd, 1815), being the hundredth anniversary of Kōrin's death, I have collected certain of his works and have reproduced one hundred of them in his honour and have had them printed as souvenirs." The first pulls of this edition bear Hōitsu's seal and are greatly prized by collectors. After Hōitsu's death the blocks for this book came into the possession of Suzuki Ki-itsu (1796–1858), a talented follower of Hōitsu, and the Bunsei edition (1826) bears his seal. The prefaces to this edition were written by Kameda Hōsai (first volume) and Tani Bunchō. A second series of this delightful work, called the *Kōrin Hyaku Dzu Kōhen*, compiled by Fujiwara Mitsunobu, another of Hōitsu's pupils, appeared in 1864. Both of these supplementary works are of two volumes each with the drawings in black and white.

The *Ogata-ryū Gwafu* is a collection of designs in black and white for boxes, fans, screens, etc. It was published in two volumes in 1815.

The *Ōson Gwafu*, also called the *Bansho Sokugoshi*, was published in one volume in 1817. It contains twenty-five double-page colour plates reproduced by Hōitsu from Kōrin's work.

The *Kōrin Mangwa* of 1817 is made up of drawings of plants, flowers, grasses, etc., much like those in the *Michi Shirube*.

Another very rare book by Kōrin which is not to be confused with either the *Michi Shirube* or the *Kōrin Mangwa*, although with the exception of the first few pages the drawings are much like those in these two books, is the *Gwahon Kōrin*. This book is a small folio containing drawings in black and white, and was published by Kikuya Kihei and allied houses in Bunkwa 15 (1818).

The *Kōrin Gwashiki*, published simultaneously in Kyōto and Ōsaka in 1818, is a folio of fifty-six double-page colour plates reproduced by Aikawa Minwa, a well-known Ōsaka artist. It is one of the most charming and rare of all of Kōrin's books, Louis Gonze, in his *Le Japon Artistique*, speaking of it as " un des chefs-d'œuvre de la librarie japonaise." Among the drawings is the one of the dumpling puppies which has so often been reproduced.

A modern collection of Kōrin's work entitled the *Ogata-ryū Hyaku Dzu*, containing some beautiful drawings printed in black and white and grey, appeared in three volumes in 1889, and the *Bansho Zukan*, an oblong volume of some of Kōrin's most famous screens, was published by Bunshichi Kobayashi in 1901. There are several quite modern books containing reproductions of Kōrin's work, all charming and well worth having. Among them is the beautiful large oblong folio called the *Kōron Gwafu*, with designs for fans, *fusuka*, etc., printed in colours, gold and gaufrage, and published by Yamada Unsoda of Kyōto in Meiji 34 (1901). Yamada also published in Meiji 27 (1904) a set of twelve coloured plates from Kōrin's work called the *Kōrin Jūni Shu*.

The Bermond Catalogue lists an *Ogata-ryū Hyaken Dzu*, a very rare work in two volumes containing designs for lacquer painting from Kōrin's drawings, compiled by Kimei, which was published as a *kubari-hon* and of which only thirty copies were printed.

Ogata KENZAN, Kōrin's younger brother, lived between 1661 and 1742. His true name was Ogata KOREMOTO, the name Kenzan ("North Hill") being taken from the locality where the kilns for firing his pottery were established. Kenzan, although chiefly noted as a potter, was also a great designer and painter. Other signatures used by him were Shinsei, Shisui, Shuseidō, Shōko, and Tozen. A book of his drawings in colours was compiled by Hōitsu and privately printed in Bunsei 6 (1823). In the postface Hōitsu says that the collection was made eighty-one years after Kenzan's death, and during its compilation, in searching for Kōrin's grave, which he found in Myōken-ji, he afterwards found that of Kenzan in the cemetery of Zengō-ji, a temple near Hiei-zan in Kyōto, and that he wrote the inscription near Kenzan's grave.

Another book containing drawings reproduced from Kenzan's work was the *Kenzan Gwafu* (listed in the Duret Catalogue, p. 254).

Sakai HŌITSU, to whom we are indebted for most of the collections of Kōrin and Kenzan's work, was born in 1761 in Yedo, the son of Sakai Uta-no-Kami, the Daimyō of Himeji in Harima province. He became high priest of the Nishi Hongwan-ji Temple in Kyōto toward the close of the eighteenth century. Although an artist of great ability himself, Hōitsu's passionate admiration for the work of Kōyetsu and Kōrin caused him to leave the priesthood and in 1808 build himself a house, where he established a school in which the styles of these two artists were carefully conserved and taught.

Hōitsu used as other signatures the names ŌSON, MONSEN, BUNSEN, KISHIN, and TŌGAKU-IN. His death occurred in 1828. In addition to the collections of Kōrin and Kenzan's work which he edited, Hōitsu made the drawings in the *Hōitsu Shonin Shinseki Kagami*, which were collected and edited by his pupil Ikeda Kōson.

OHŌ, Hōitsu's son; Suzuki KI-ITSU (1796–1858); and Ikeda KŌSON, together with KŌITSU, SHŪ-ITSU, KI-ITCHI (who illustrated the *Seiro Manroku*, containing reproductions of paintings, art treasures, etc., two volumes 1825), Tanaka HŌNI, and other followers, continued to uphold the Kōyetsu-Kōrin methods in the school established by Hōitsu, well into the nineteenth century. Plates by these men are often found in albums of contemporary work, and Ki-itsu left a book of illustrated poems entitled *Ryū Kwashu*, published in one volume in 1837.

There were many other artists of lesser fame who were contemporaries, early and late, of Moronobu, Itchō, and Kōrin, about whom no information is available. We know them chiefly through their books, but that they have made the history of Japan familiar by their interesting and often charming drawings representing the customs of the country, the etiquette and dress in vogue at different periods, the legends, the festivals, and the great religious ceremonies at temples and shrines which long ago were swept away by fire, is perhaps fame enough, and they have done their part in preserving pictorial records of these things for us.

There are literally thousands of these illustrated books by means of which the Japanese historian can reconstruct the past life of the country. It would require a large volume merely to list such as are easily available, and even a superficial acquaintance with them is enough to give the foreign student an immense respect for a people who so manifestly for hundreds of years have been book-lovers and seekers after knowledge.

CHAPTER IV
ŌSAKA AS AN ART AND PUBLISHING CENTRE

OMMERCIAL city that it is in these days, Osaka in earlier times was never without a distinctive art life of its own, and it was the Ōsaka artists who chiefly bridged the gap between the Moronobu school of the seventeenth century and the eighteenth and early nineteenth century Ukiyo-ye movement of Yedo.

Hanabusa Itchō, Torii Kiyonobu, Tachibana Morikuni and Oöka Shunboku were all born in Ōsaka, and Sukenobu spent the last twenty years of his life there. The city vied with Kyōto and Yedo as a publishing centre, and its printing-houses were noted for the beauty and technical excellence of their work, even the debased Ukiyo-ye sheets and books issued by them in the mid-nineteenth century being redeemed from utter worthlessness by the wonderful printing, in which not only colour, but gold, silver, and gaufrage were freely used.

Although the Ukiyo-ye movement is associated almost exclusively with Yedo, its roots stretched west to Ōsaka and Kyōto, where Moronobu had first made wood-engravings of beautiful women popular and where Sukenobu followed in his footsteps a generation later.

The Torii school also had its real beginnings in the west, for the artist-actor Kondō Shoshichi of Ōsaka, the father of Kiyonobu, was devoting his spare time to designing advertising posters for the playhouses there, and Ōsaka publishers were printing books on actors and the drama soon after the middle of the seventeenth century.

One of the earliest of these theatrical books was a collection of *kyōgen*, or the short comedies which are performed in the intervals of the *Nō* drama. It is entitled *Kyōgen-ki* and was published in two volumes in 1665. The illustrations are of the Moronobu school and represent the stage, the theatre, and the actors in costume in their rôles, while part of the text has musical annotations added to indicate the rise and fall of the voice in chanting.

In 1678 the *Kokon Yakusha Monogatari*, stories of ancient and modern actors, appeared with extremely interesting wood-engravings by Moronobu.

At the time these books were in circulation Torii Kiyonobu was about fourteen years old and still living in Ōsaka. His father's profession doubtless brought him into frequent contact with the actors of the city, who probably often discussed such drawings, and this may have had a part in determining the channel his own work was to follow later in Yedo.

Perhaps the most remarkable of all the early books on actors, however, was the *Kyō Ōsaka Yarō Sekizumō*, issued in ten medium-sized volumes by the Shōhonya Kiemon publishing house in 1693. The drawings represent the stage favourites of Kyōto and Ōsaka in their most famous rôles, each being surrounded with descriptive text. Although not signed, the illustrations are attributed to Yoshida Hanbei, and the set is excessively rare, commanding a high price when offered for sale.

The gentler form of Ukiyo-ye art at this time was represented by SUKENOBU, whose drawings of beautiful women became famous throughout Japan, but since Sukenobu is so entirely of the Ukiyo-ye school, and this school is so much more closely connected with Yedo than Kyōto or Ōsaka, it seems better to consider him with the Yedo artists, although his work was really done in these older cities.

Tachibana MORIKUNI, however, who was a contemporary of Sukenobu, did not belong to the Ukiyo-ye group and stood rather apart even in Ōsaka, where he lived between 1670 and 1748. He is said to have been a well-educated man, and endeavoured to popularize again the old classic art by publishing copies of ancient work by the Chinese masters and the painters of the Ashikaga period. He studied under artists of both the Kanō and the Tosa schools, Tsuruzawa Tanzan having been one of his masters. His ordinary name was Narahara Arichika, but he used as artist signatures the names YŪSEI, YŪYETSU, KŌSOKEN, and Tachibana CHIKARA.

At one time in his career he came into disgrace by publishing as his own drawings some copies of old Kanō and Tosa pictures which were treasured private possessions of the descendants of these families. This was in the *Tōdo Kimmō Dzue*, an illustrated encyclopædia issued in fourteen volumes in 1719. It resulted in his ostracism from their houses and in his leaving Ōsaka for a time.

Most of Morikuni's drawings have far less charm than Sukenobu's or Masanobu's work, although some of them show a good deal of virility. Those in the *Umpitsu Sogwa*, published in 1749, the year after his death, have much more freedom and breadth than most of his work. They show the Kanō technique rather than the severely academic manner which characterized so much that he did.

Morikuni's tendency to plagiarize is seen again in his books of *kimono* patterns, for if not exact copies of Kōrin's designs, many of them so closely resemble that artist's work that they might easily be taken as his without Morikuni's signature. Some of his best work was in his drawings of animals, and these have hardly been surpassed. He illustrated a

PLATE 15] From the 5th Vol. of the EHON SHAHŌ BUKURO,
by Tachibana Morikuni. 1720.

number of books, of which the following list embraces the most important.

Ehon Kojidan: Various drawings illustrating old legends. Signed Kōsoken Tachibana Yūsei. 9 vols. 1714.
Wachō Meisho Gwadzu: 10 vols. 1717. (A second edition in 1732.)
Tōdo Kimmō Dzue: An illustrated encyclopædia. Signed Tachibana Chikara. 14 vols. 1719.
Ehon Shahō Bukuro: Various drawings. 9 vols. 1720.
Shasei Kedamono Dzue: Drawings of animals. Unsigned but attributed to Morikuni. 3 vols. 1720.
Ehon Tsūhōshi: Signed Tachibana Yūsei Morikuni. 10 vols. 1721.
Gwaten Tsūkō: Old legends. Signed Kōsoken Tachibana Morikuni. 10 vols. 1727.
Hinagata Akebono Zakura: Designs for *kimono*. In collaboration with Hasegawa Mitsunobu. 3 vols. 1727. Very rare.
Ehon Ō-Shuku-bai: Celebrated poets. Written and illustrated by Morikuni. Signed Kōsoken Tachibana Morikuni. 7 vols. 1730. (A second edition in 1740.)
Yōkyoku Gwashi: Origin and history of the *Nō* drama. 10 vols. 1732. (A second edition in 1735.)
Fusō Gwafu: Celebrated places in Japan and China. 5 vols. 1735.
Wakan Gorui Ehon Kagami: Drawings of Sennin.
Jikishikō: Drawing book. 3 vols. 1745.
Umpitsu Sogwa: Rapid sketches. 3 vols. 1749.
Ryaku-gwa: Various sketches. 3 vols. 1750.
Honchō Gwayen: 6 vols.
Nanto Meisho Dzue: Places in Southern Japan.
Shōshoku Edehon: Unsigned, but attributed to Morikuni.
Arima Shokei-zu: Pictorial map of Arima. 1 *gwajo*. 1760.

A son and pupil of Morikuni, Hōkoku or Tachibana YASUKUNI also left a few books, among which is the well-known and charming series of studies of plants and flowers called the *Ehon Noyama-gusa*, signed Hokkyō Tachibana Yasukuni, published in five volumes in 1755; the *Ehon Yeibutsu-sen*, historical poems, five volumes in 1778; and a very rare set of books of caricatures entitled *Bahōsai Zatsuga*, in which a grey tone is added to the black (three volumes, 1785).

Sekichūsai MORINORI, an early follower of Morikuni, illustrated the *Gwato Hyak-kwachō*, published in five volumes in 1730. The drawings are fine-lined, exquisite representations of birds and flowers, and form excellent examples of academic work, relieved from too great monotony by their wonderful delicacy. The *Gwato Shūyei*, a collection of copies of old paintings in three volumes, published about 1740, signed Sekichūsai, is also Morinori's work.

Some early colour-printing as applied to books was done in Ōsaka, and Ōoka Shunboku, who will be spoken of later, Sukenobu, and pupils of Morikuni, illustrated books in colours.

A posthumous work by Sukenobu, the *Onna Imagawa*, on the occupations of women, was published there in Hōreki 13 (1763), which contains a frontispiece printed in three colours—pink, green and yellow—representing a princess kneeling before her mirror with an attendant near by bearing a black lacquered box tied with a pink cord.

Tachibana MINKŌ was another Ōsaka artist who used colour in some early work. He was known as a writer, a designer, and a block-cutter, as well as an artist, and is credited with having perfected a process of his own in colour-printing. His early training was obtained under Tachibana Morikuni, but in 1760 Minkō left Ōsaka and went to Yedo. It was here that his famous *Saigwa Shokunin Burui* was published, representing in a series of delicately coloured illustrations different artisans at their work. By several Japanese authorities he is credited with having produced coloured book illustrations in the Hōreki period, but this book was first published in 1770 by a Yedo printing-house belonging to Uemura Tozaburō and Sawa Itsuki. In any case it is among the early works to contain coloured wood-engravings. The first edition is extremely rare, and the preface to the second issue, published in 1784, written by Shokusan, explains that the original blocks were destroyed by the great fire of 1772 which devastated the whole city and which the Hayashi Catalogue gives as the reason for the scarcity of Yedo books published before that time. The differences in the two editions are of course due to the use of new blocks.

Minkō also illustrated an edition of the *Sanjū Rok-kasen*, or Thirty-six Poets, published about 1765; and the *Kakuchū Kidan*, containing drawings in black and white enclosed in circles, published in 1769.

Kitao SEKKŌSAI also made a few book illustrations in colour. His work somewhat resembles that of Tsukioka Masanobu, although his drawing of faces is easily distinguished. He is said to have studied in Yedo under Ippitsusai Bunchō and was illustrating books before the middle of the eighteenth century. Kitao Tatsunobu was another signature used by him. Among his books were the

Fumi Kotoba: A small oblong volume of black-and-white drawings of beautiful women, everyday scenes, etc. 1749.
Onna Shorei Aya-nishiki: Occupations of women. 1 vol. About 1754. Black and white.
Ehon Kusa (or *Sōkin*) *Nishiki*: Various black-and-white drawings. Signed Sekkōsai Kitao Tatsunobu. 3 vols. 1764.
Onna Geibun Sansai Dzue: Landscapes, sea and fishing scenes, and other drawings. Horeki period. Colours. A very rare book.
Saishiki Gwaden: Various sketches, in some of which a grey tone is used. 3 vols. 1767.
Ehon Iro Arasoi: A curious book representing battles in which the weapons are household and toilet utensils. One cut shows women fighting with combs, hairpins, etc. Signed Kitao Tatsunobu. 1769. Black and white.
Ehon Shinobu-zuri: A charming little set of two volumes of poems illustrated in colours. About 1770.
Nyoyō Bunshō Ito Guruma: A book of instruction in letter-writing for women. Frontispiece in colours representing a woman bearing a scroll, with her left hand on a Korean dog, and a phœnix in the upper left-hand corner. 1 large volume. 1772.
Onna Imagawa: Instructions in letter-writing for women. Written by Genkai. Illustrated by Kitao Tatsunobu. 1778.

PLATE 16

Kamada Masakiyo's Wife. From the ONNA BUYŪ YOSOŌI KAGAMI (1757), by Tsukioka Masanobu.

Kitao Tokinobu, a somewhat obscure follower of this school, left a book entitled *Ehon Kakure-gusa*, published about 1772–1780.

Among the other members of this Ōsaka colony was Tsukioka Masanobu, about whom there has always been more or less confusion. He signed his work Tsukioka Tange, Tsukioka Tange Masanobu, Tsukioka Masanobu Settei, Kindo, Shinten-ō, and Tankōsai, adding occasionally the title Hokkyō which had been conferred upon him by the Shōgunate. Little is known of him except that he was born in the province of Ōmi in 1717 of a family named Honda, spent the greater part of his life in Ōsaka, where he studied under Takata Keiho, and died there in 1786.

He illustrated a number of books, chiefly on historical subjects, which contain extremely spirited drawings of warriors and battle scenes, and in a few works dealing with heroines and occupations of women, the drawings of women compare with the Yedo Masanobu's work, being characterized by a robust and noble dignity that Sukenobu, famous as he was for depicting beautiful women, never entirely reached.

Among the books illustrated by Tsukioka Masanobu were the

Yojo Gojū-nin Isshu: Poems on fifty noted courtesans. 2 vols. 1753.
Onna Buyū Yosoöi or *Kurabe Kagami*: Anecdotes of famous women. Signed Rojinsai Tange Tsukioka Masanobu. 3 large folios. 1757.
Ehon Musha Tadzuna: History of Yoritomo and Yoshitsune. 3 vols. 1759.
Ehon Kōmyō Futaba-gusa: Historical tales. Signed Tsukioka Rojinsai Masanobu. 3 vols. 1759.
Onna Bunshō Shinan-shō: Instructions for women. With a coloured frontispiece of chrysanthemums. 1 vol. 1759.
Ehon Hime Bunko: Book for women. 1 vol. 1760.
Ehon Fukami-gusa: Anecdotes of celebrated heroines. Signed Tsukioka Tange Masanobu. 2 vols. 1761.
Tōgoku Meisho-ki: Guide book. Signed Tsukioka Tange. 5 vols. 1762.
Ehon Ranjatai: Anecdotes of ancient poets with their poems. 5 vols. 1764.
Ehon Shorei-kun: Work on etiquette. Signed Tsukioka Tange. 3 vols. Ōsaka, 1758.
Onna Buyū Kehai Kurabe: Anecdotes of heroic women. 3 vols. 1766.
Ehon Yeiyū Retsujō-den: Women heroes. Signed Rojinsai Tsukioka Masanobu. 3 vols. 1766.
Sōhitsu Boku-gwa:[1] Various drawings. Signed Ōsaka Tankōsai. 3 vols. 1766. Rare and delightful.
Wakan Meihitsu Kingyoku Gwafu: Copies of old Chinese and Japanese paintings. Signed Tsukioka Masanobu Settei. 6 vols. 1771.
Ehon Yūmō Sanryaku-no-Maki: Old legends and historical tales. 3 vols.
Nippon Kōdan Bokuga Meika:[2] Signed Getsuoka Rojinsai Masanobu. A series of double-page sumi-ye.

Tsukioka Masanobu left two sons, Sekkei and Sessai (or Shūyei), who achieved some fame, and was awarded the title of Hōgen.

Terai Naofusa, a pupil of Tsukioka Masanobu's, left the *Ehon Yumei-gusa* in three volumes, published in 1752, containing work very similar to

---
[1] There is some dispute as to whether this book was really the work of Tsukioka Masanobu, and whether the signature Tankōsai was used by him.
[2] Listed in the Bermond Catalogue.

that of the latter artist, and the *Ehon Isa-na-gusa*, drawings of heroes, in three volumes, 1752. The *Ehon Senga-no-Ura*, a collection of old proverbs in three volumes, signed Terai, is also probably his work.

Tsukioka SETTEI, a famous artist who lived between 1759 and 1835, may have been a son or nephew of Tsukioka Masanobu, since he, too, went to Ōsaka from Ōmi, where he was born in the little town of Gōshun. He also used the signatures SHINTEN-Ō and Honda MASANOBU as well as Tsukioka SETSUTEI. He studied under Takada Keiho as Tsukioka Masanobu had done earlier, and became almost as well known for his paintings of fish as the famous Okyo of Kyōto. The last years of his life were spent in Yedo, where the title of Hōgen was conferred upon him.

Hasegawa SETTAN (1778–1843) was a contemporary of Tsukioka Masanobu, but belonged to Yedo, where he was given the title of Hokkyō. He was a well-known illustrator of *meisho-ki* and left a son who has sometimes been confused with Tsukioka Settei. The latter was known as Hasegawa Settei and lived between 1818 and 1882. There was in reality no family or artistic connection between these two artists, and Tsukioka Masanobu and Tsukioka Settei.

Settan used the names MUNEHIDE and Gangakusai SETTAN as other signatures, and he and his son Settei collaborated in considerable work. Among the books illustrated by these artists were the

Yedo Meisho Hanagoyomi: The flower seasons of Yedo. 3 vols. 1827.
Yedo Meisho Dzue: Description of Yedo and its famous places. 20 vols. 1833. Signed Hasegawa Settan. Black and white.
Tōto Saijiki: Annual fêtes of Yedo. 5 vols. 1838.
Seiroku Ruisan: A history of music, drama, and puppet shows. 5 vols. Illustrated by Hasegawa Settei.

Shitomi KWANGETSU, a well-known artist who studied under Tsukioka Masanobu, lived well into the nineteenth century. He also used the signature TEIYŌSAI, and was known in ordinary life as Genji Tokuki. He illustrated the

Ise Sangu Meisho Dzue: Description of Ise and places on the road from Kyōto. Two series of three volumes each. 1797.
Nippon Sankai Meisan Dzue: Wealth of the mountains and sea. Signed Hokkyō Kwangetsu. 5 vols. 1799.

Hanbei SHŌKŌSAI, also known as Shoyōsai, was an early nineteenth-century artist of Ōsaka whose work was chiefly devoted to actors and the theatre. He left the

Ehon Futaba Ao-ye: Theatre scenes. 1 vol. 1798.
Gekkei-jō Gakuya Dzue: A work on the theatre. Two small oblong drawings on each page. 2 vols. 1800.
Gakuya Dzue Shū: Supplement to foregoing. The first few pages in colours. 2 vols.
Shibai Gakuya Dzue: Actors and their surroundings. 4 vols. 1800.

Okada GYOKUZAN, who lived in Ōsaka between 1736 and 1812, was one of Tsukioka Masanobu's most famous pupils. He was known in ordinary life as Naotomo and used as other signatures the names ISHIDA, SHŌ, SHŪTOKU, and SHISHŪ, and occasionally added the title Hokkyō which the Government had conferred upon him. His most important work was the *Ehon Taikō-ki*, a biography of Hideyoshi in eighty-four volumes, published in 1798, done in collaboration with Toyokuni, Hokusai, Utamaro, and several other well-known artists. Other books illustrated by him were the

Raikwō Ichidai-ki: Life of Raikwō (Yorimitsu). 1 vol. 1796.
Ehon Tsukinu Idzumi: "The inexhaustible Fountain." Signed Hokkyō Gyokuzan. 2 vols. 1797.
Sumiyoshi Meisho Dzue: Description of Sumiyoshi. 5 vols. 1797. (A second edition in 1801.)
Ehon Kusunoki Nidai Gunki: History of Kusunoki Masashige and Masatsura. 1800.
Ehon Kan-so Gundan: History of the war between Kan and So. 1802.
Tōto Meisho Dzue: Celebrated places in China. Signed Hokkyō Okada Gyokuzan. 6 vols. 1805.
Ehon Tamamo Monogatari: Story of a "fox woman." The first few pages are made up of very curious coloured cuts. 5 vols. 1805.
Ehon Dōji Kyō: Moral instructions for children. 1806.
Ogasawara Shōrei Daizen: Ceremonial etiquette of the Ogasawara family. 2 vols. 1809.

Ishida GYOKUZAN was probably the pupil of Okada Gyokuzan, although some critics believe him to have been identical with the latter artist. He was also known as GYOKUHO. He illustrated the

Kiyomasa Shinden-ki: Life of Kato Kiyomasa.
Shiranui Sōshi: Story of Shiranui.
Nagara Chōja Uguisu-dzuke.
Otoshi Banashi Saru-no-Hitomane: Old tales. Kwansei period.

A well-known Ōsaka artist of this time, and a man of really great ability, was Hayami SHUNGYŌSAI. He studied under Okada Gyokuzan and used as other signatures the names RYŪKOKU, HAZAMIZU, and HIKOSABURŌ. He died in 1823. Among the books illustrated by him, some of which he also wrote, were the

Ehon Asakusa Reigen-ki: The Divine Power of the Asakusa Kwannon. 10 vols. 1806.
Nenjū Gyōji Taisei: Famous festivals of Japan. 5 vols. 1806. Rare and delightful.
Ehon Nankō-ki: Life of Kusunoki Masashige. 30 vols. 1809.
Miyako Fūzoku Keshō-den: Miyako (Kyōto) fashions for women. Printed on *toshi* paper. 3 vols. 1813. (An edition on ordinary paper in 1851.) Extremely rare in first edition.
Otoko-Yama Hōjoye Dzuroku: Description of an Imperial visit and procession to Hachiman Temple on Otoko-Yama, south of Kyōto. 1 vol. 1821.
Korobanu-Saki-no-Dzue: Various scenes. 3 vols.

The illustrations in the *Nenjū Gyōji Taisei* and the *Miyako Fūzoku Keshō-den*, if they had been printed in colours, would have placed these books among the most famous of the Japanese *ehon*, for both in composition and drawing they are beyond praise, quite equalling anything ever done by the Yedo contemporaries of Shungyōsai.

Chap. IV] JAPANESE BLOCK-PRINTING

The most famous and really the greatest of all the Ōsaka artists, however, was Ōoka Shunboku, whom we have left until now because he headed a school (the Dokuritsu, or Independent) rather peculiar to Ōsaka and which lasted through several generations.

Collections of drawings copied from old Chinese and Japanese masterpieces formed a large part of the work of this group, and together with the dashing, impressionistic work which it became noted for, embraces some of the most striking black-and-white sketches which perhaps have ever been done for wood-engraving. Ōoka Shunboku himself was self-taught, forming his style upon close study of old Kanō paintings. Little is known of his life, even the dates of his birth and death being rather uncertain.

According to the preface of the *Wakan Meigwayen*, however, which is dated Kwan-en 2 (1749) and which states that it was written in Shunboku's sixty-first year, he was born in 1688. The date for his death is generally given as 1768.[1] He used as other signatures the names Aiyoku, Aito, Haito (his ordinary name), Sha, Jukushi, Jakuta, and Ichi Shunboku, to which he sometimes added the title Hōgen which had been conferred upon him by the Shōgunate. His books are of the greatest interest. Except in the copies of the old academic paintings, the Kanō manner is manifest, his own work being characterized by a dash and freedom combined with an absolute certainty of brush stroke that stamp him as a really notable man.

Shunboku was one of the very early Japanese artists to use colour-printing, and his *Minchō Seidō Gwayen*, published in two volumes in Enkyō 3 (1746), is made up of thirty-six double-page colour-plates of flowers, with an occasional insect, printed from five, six, and sometimes even seven blocks. These charming and exquisitely printed drawings are copies of work by famous Chinese painters of the Ming dynasty—Kokkō, Bunchōmei, Tai Bunshin, Tei Gyokusen,[2] and others—which appeared in a Chinese work of three volumes in 1702. The date of Shunboku's copy (1746) is only three years later than the date at which Fenollosa puts the two-block work. This publication is so excessively rare that it has been entirely overlooked by collectors, who have placed the earliest coloured book illustrations in the years between 1760 and 1770.[3]

[1] According to the *Fusō Gwajinden*, Shunboku's death occurred in 1763 at the age of eighty-four.

[2] I.e., Sun K'o-hung, Wēn Chēng-ming, Tai Chin, Ting Yū-ch'uan.

[3] A set of the original edition of this rare book was in the collection of Mr. Arthur Morrison (presented by him to the British Museum in 1920), and he says of it: " The colour-printing is of a very fine, delicate and advanced sort—in imitation, in fact, of the Chinese colour-printing of the previous century and onwards. The plum branch by Kokkō is in no way adequately represented in the photograph. The branch itself, for instance, is printed in warm greyish-yellow into which the black spots at the elbows and forks gradate, the main colour being far paler than the photograph shows, and the contrast with and grading into the black being much more pronounced and striking.

Single copies of most of Shunboku's other books are not difficult to find, but clean, complete sets of the original editions are now rarely obtainable. All his works are very popular with the Japanese, and have gone through innumerable printings; of late years, also, modern copies bearing the original dates have been published. These are so cleverly done that it is difficult to be certain about them without original books with which to compare them. The difference is chiefly in the paper and the stiffness of the covers. In every other respect they are almost precisely like the first issues.

A list of Shunboku's books includes the

Gwashi Kwaiyō: Copies of old paintings. (His most famous work in illustration.) Signed Hōgen Shunboku. 6 vols. 1707.
Wakan Meihitsu Ehon Te-Kagami: Copies of old paintings and original work. Signed Hōgen Ichio Shunboku. 6 vols. 1720.
Ramma Dzushiki: Designs for *ramma*. Signed Oöka Haito. 3 oblong volumes. 1734.
Ehon Hissei Musha Suzuri: Illustrated legends and historical tales. Compiled by a pupil of Shunboku's. 5 vols. 1736. (A second edition in 1742.)
Gwakō Senran: Various drawings. 6 vols. 1740.
Minchō Seidō Gwayen: Drawings of flowers and insects from a Chinese work of 1702. 2 vols. 1746. Colours.
Wakan Meigwayen: Copies of famous paintings by Chinese and Japanese artists. Signed Hōgen Shunboku Ichio. 6 vols. 1750.
Wakan Koji Bukuyo Shingwa: Old legends. 5 vols. 1751. (A second edition in 1753.)
Tansei Kimmō: Signed Oöka Hōgen Shunboku. 6 vols. 1753.
Kōshū Nijūshi Shō Dzue: Twenty-four Generals of Koshu under Takeda Shingen.
Meika Jūni Shū: Twelve varieties of flowers.
Seki Gwa: Rapid sketches made before an audience. Signed Hōgen Shunboku Ichio. Collected by his son Hokkyō Shunsen. No date. A rare *kubari-hon*.
Gwahin Hippo: Copies of famous paintings. Signed Hōgen Shunboku. Preface by Kyō Tatsu. 6 vols. 1761.
Sogwa Benran: Sketches from old paintings. Signed Oöka Shunboku. 3 vols. 1761.

The gradation in the buds and petals also is extremely delicate, in a dusky pink. There are no black outlines in this print, nothing but the edges of the tints, and this is the case in many of the others, and in parts of nearly all. The whole book, indeed, is equal to the finest books of the late eighteenth century—indeed, superior to most. Of the Chinese original, which consisted of three volumes, Shunboku apparently possessed only the first two, so that his book ended with the colophon at the end of volume ii. There were later editions—the British Museum has one of the end of the eighteenth century in which a copy of the third Chinese volume was added. These, however, were far inferior in printing and finish and only contained Shunboku's name at the end of the preface to the first volume, not at the end of the added third. Each volume contains beside an ornamental title-page, with the characters *Sei-dō*, eighteen double-page pictures of flowers, sometimes with an insect or two. The paper is thin, smooth, and delicate, either Chinese or specially made in imitation of Chinese. . . . It is a little difficult to be sure of the number of blocks used in each case, as the gradations sometimes suggest a doubt as to whether one or two blocks should be counted, but six blocks seem to be used in most cases, seven in some, and five in some, apart from the red used in reproducing the painters' seals. It would seem that a blue of extreme delicacy has been used on many pages to get a green by superposition of yellow, but this blue has wholly vanished, whether from damp or other causes, leaving the leaves and stems yellow instead of green. I am speaking, of course, of my own copy, which is the only one of the first edition I have seen or heard of. Nishimura Genroku was the publisher, and Murakami Genyemon the engraver, as you will see from the colophon."

CHAP. IV]   JAPANESE BLOCK-PRINTING

Minchō Shiken: A copy of the *Minchō Seidō Gwayen*. 3 vols. Hōreki period and again in 1812. Colours.
Toba-ye Daizan: Complete collection of drawings in the style of Toba. 3 vols. No date. (Gillot Catalogue.)

UNSIGNED.

Keihitsu Toba Guruma: Caricatures. 3 vols. 1720. (A second edition in 1752 and a third in 1788.)
Toba-ye Sango Kushi: Comical sketches of three cities: Spring in Kyōto, Evening in Yedo, and Autumn in Ōsaka. 3 vols. 1752. (Another edition in 1788.)
Toba-ye Ōgi-no-Mato: Comical drawings of different pastimes. 3 vols. Horeki period (?) and again in 1772 and 1788.

Among Shunboku's books the three oblong volumes of the *Ramma Dzushiki*, made up of designs for the wooden panels called *ramma* used above the *fusuma* in Japanese houses, are as rare as they are charming, and afford one of the many instances where a famous artist has made designs for the use of artisans.

The *Wakan Meihitsu Ehon Te-Kagami* is not only delightful as a collection of reproductions of old paintings, but it contains some original and extremely clever caricatures on pages 13, 14, and 15 of the last volume, which go toward proving that Shunboku was the artist who made the drawings in three sets of books of *Toba-ye* which are generally attributed to Hasegawa Mitsunobu or Nichōsai. These books are the *Keihitsu Toba Guruma*, the *Toba-ye Sango Kushi*, and the *Toba-ye Ōgi-no-Mato*. The caricatures just spoken of in the *Wakan Meihitsu Ehon Te-Kagami* are manifestly from the same brush as those in these three sets of books, and moreover, in the advertising pages of the 1788 edition of the *Keihitsu Toba Guruma*, published only a few years after Shunboku's death, these works are all listed as his. It is difficult to understand why such confusion has persisted in regard to them, for although not signed they are entirely different from Nichōsai's work and have little resemblance to that of Mitsunobu. Even in the Hayashi Catalogue two of them are listed as by Nichōsai, the only possible reason for which could have been the fact that Nichōsai was a famous caricaturist and these books are books of caricatures. Comparison of them with Nichōsai's signed work shows plainly that they were by another artist. The advertisements alluded to, together with the absolute identity in drawing and style of the cuts in the *Ehon Te-Kagami*, seem sufficient to warrant our including them among Shunboku's books. The explanation for their anonymous appearance may be that they were regarded by Shunboku as rather beneath the dignity of an artist who had achieved his position and rank. Whether at the time they were published they were attributed to Mitsunobu, who seems to have illustrated a somewhat similar set of books in the Kyōhō period, we have no means of knowing, but if not, the secret was out after the Temmei edition was issued.

ŌSAKA AS AN ART AND PUBLISHING CENTRE [CHAP. IV

Shunboku left a number of followers who adopted parts of his name. Among these men Ōōka SHUNSEN, who lived between 1718 and 1773, was his son and pupil, and won in his turn considerable distinction, especially in lacquer painting. He was awarded the rank of Hokkyō, and used this word and sometimes the name Hosei (Yasumasa) as part of his signature. Shunsen acquired a famous collection of lacquer and toward the close of his life wrote a history of the art. He illustrated a number of books, chiefly of design. They include the following:

Ehon Fukujūsō: Charming designs from plants and flowers. Signed Hokkyō Shunsen Hosai. 3 vols. 1737.
Dzushiki Hinagata Maki-ye Daizen: Designs for lacquer work. Signed Shunsen Hosai. 5 vols. 1759.
Seki Gwa: Reproductions of quick sketches done by Shunboku before an audience. Signed by Shunboku aud Dan (Son) Hokkyō Shunsen. 1 vol. No date. A rare *kubari-hon*.

Yoshimura SHŪZAN, also known as MITSUOKI and TANSEN, was an Ōsaka artist whose work closely resembles that of Shunboku, of whom he was a contemporary. He studied under Kanō Mitsunobu, a master of the Kanō school, and was known as a fine engraver and *netsuke* carver in addition to being a painter.[1] He attained the rank of Hōgen and is said to have died about 1776. Books by him were the

Wakan Meihitsu Gwayei: Copies of celebrated Chinese and Japanese paintings. Signed Hōgen Mitsuoki Shūzan. 1749.
Shūzan Gwayei: Signed Hōgen Shūzan. 6 vols. 1750.
Wakan Meihitsu Gwahō: A similar series. 1764.
Wakan Meihitsu Kingyoku Gwafu:[2] Various drawings. 1771.
Gwasoku: 1777.

Ōōka MICHINOBU was another pupil of Shunboku's who was working in Ōsaka during the Kyōhō period. He illustrated the

Banzai Buyū E-Kagami: A book on celebrated warriors. Signed Ōōka Denai Michinobu. 3 vols. 1721.
Oshi-ye Te-Kagami: Various drawings. Signed Ōōka Michinobu. 3 vols. 1736.

Ichiō SESSHŌSAI was an Ōsaka artist who has sometimes been confused with Shunboku. He was known in ordinary life as Otani Takuma, and used as other artist signatures the names YUKIAKI and SHINSAI. His work is much like that of Shunboku, the technique being simple and strong and emphasized by striking masses of black. Among his books were the

---

[1] See *Arts of Japan*, by Edward Dillon, p. 160.

[2] I list this book here because Anderson attributes it to Shūzan, although giving the latter's name as Sakurai Shūzan. I believe two mistakes are involved, however: one in attributing the book to Shūzan instead of to Tsukioka Tange Masanobu (although there are reproductions of some of Shūzan's work in it) and the other in the name of Sakurai. Sakurai Shūzan was a woman artist of Yedo in the Kwansei period, the daughter of Sakurai Sekkwan, who also signed herself Seppō and Keigetsu.

Ehon Jūyō: Copies of famous paintings. Signed Ichiō Sesshō. Two series of three volumes each. 1751.
Ehon Heroika: Various drawings. Signed Sesshōsai. 3 vols. 1751.
Gwahin: Copies of old paintings. 3 vols. 1760.

Since it is easier to consider books of the same kind together even if they are not of precisely the same period, this seems the place to devote to the two other artists to whom the three sets of Toba-ye (about which there has been so much confusion) have been attributed.

Hasegawa MITSUNOBU, one of these men, was living in Ōsaka in the Kyōhō period—a contemporary and doubtless a friend of Shunboku's, and possibly the willing scapegoat whom that artist chose to bear the responsibility for his caricatures. Mitsunobu himself is credited with a set of such books—the *Toba-ye Fude Byōshi*, published in three volumes in 1724. It has been impossible to see an original edition of this work and make certain that it was really signed by Mitsunobu. It has been generally attributed to him, however, which was probably the reason for assuming that he was the artist of the other three sets.

Almost no details that one can be certain of are available in regard to Mitsunobu's life, except that he used as other signatures the names NAGAHARU or EISHUN, BAIŌKEN, BAIHŌKEN, and Hasegawa SHŌSUIKEN.

It is probable that there were two men, father and son perhaps, both known as Hasegawa Mitsunobu, since in no other way can the dates of the earliest and latest books signed Mitsunobu be reconciled. The list of books illustrated by him includes the

Toba-ye Fude Byōshi: Caricatures. 3 vols. 1724.
Hinagata Akebono Zakura: Designs for *kimono* for courtesans, by Hasegawa Mitsunobu and Morikuni. 3 vols. 1727. Very rare.
Nihon Sankai Meibutsu Dzue: Chief products of Japan. Compiled by Hirase Tessai. Illustrations signed Shōsuiken Hasegawa Mitsunobu. 5 vols. 1730. (A second edition in 1797.)
Ehon Fudzi-no-Yukari or *Eneshi*: Commentary on the *Genji-Monogatari*. 3 vols. 1751. (Much like Sukenobu's work.)
Onna Yōsō Bunko: Instruction for women. Frontispiece in 2 colours and black. 1 large folio. Woman admiring a potted plant. 1752.
Miwaka: Poems on the twelve months. 2 vols.
Mitsunobu Gwafu: 2 vols.
Misao: Moral teachings for girls. Colours.
Tori Kabu-ki, Tomatsuri, and *Toba-ye Musha*: Three parts of one book. Signed Hasegawa Mitsunobu. 1823. (This may be a late edition of the *Fude Byōshi*.)
Eiyū Gwafu: Book on warriors. 1 vol. 1836.
Haikai Futawarai: One hundred poems on artisans with Toba-ye illustrations. 1 folio. No date or signature, but probably of about 1740. Excessively rare.

In addition to the foregoing books there is a very rare set of drawings, of beautiful women signed Hasegawa Mitsunobu, much in Sukenobu's style.

Hasegawa Rōshu, who may have been a pupil of Mitsunobu's, left a book of humorous poems entitled *Kyōka Tsuki-no-Kage* with some Toba-ye cuts. The book is dated 1784.

Nichōsai,[1] the other artist to whom the three sets of Toba-ye drawings, about which there has been so much confusion, have been attributed, was a *sake* brewer of Ōsaka about the middle of the eighteenth century. Other signatures used by him were Matsuya Heitazaemon, Matsuhei, and Heizaburō. He seems to have been a versatile and changeful soul, for later in life he became a curio dealer, given in his idle hours to writing novels, reciting *Jōruri* ballads, and making comical drawings. He is said to have drawn actors and wrestlers especially well but caricatures best of all, and became so famous for them as well as for his witty sayings and queer ways that he was known by a nickname which might be translated as the " crank of Ōsaka."

All of Nichōsai's books are rare, and although he illustrated a considerable number, few of them have found their way into European collections. Perhaps nothing in the way of caricature has ever been done more clever than the drawings they contain. The technique is original and distinctive, but not by any means similar to that in the books attributed to him in the Hayashi Catalogue.

A list of his books includes the

Yabo-no-Shiori: 4 vols. 1774.
Ehon Mizu-ka Sora: Caricatures of actors. 2 vols. 1780.
Tsure-dzure Suigwa-kawa: 5 vols. 1782 (?).
E-banashi Nichōsai: Humorous stories and drawings of authors and artists during the four seasons. Each volume named for the season it describes. 4 vols. 1782.
Gikun Daijo-bu: 5 vols. 1794.
Arashi Koroku Kwako Monogatari: 3 vols. 1797.
Ongyōku Hanage Nuki: 1 vol. 1797.
Kotsu Jikai: 2 vols. 1802.
Katsura Kasane: Caricatures by Nichōsai with text by Toba-ye Furai Sanjin.[2] Published by Shioya, Ōsaka. 1 folio. Colours. Kyōwa 3, eighth month (August, 1803).
Saji Mepokai: A later edition of the *Katsura Kasane*.
Ehon Kotori Dzukai: 3 folios. 1805.
Toba-ye Edehon: 2 vols. No date.
Ehon Kotsu Dzue.[3] Caricatures of Japanese customs. 3 vols. 1805. Possibly another reading for the *Ehon Kotori Dzukai*.

The most famous of these books, and one almost impossible to find now in the edition listed, is the *Katsura Kasane*. In the whole range of caricature it is doubtful if anything with more clever technique exists. The drawings are slightly coloured but the background is left white. The

---
[1] Jichōsai is the reading frequently given the characters. The Gillot Catalogue makes the mistake of listing Nichōsai and Jichōsai as different men.
[2] Possibly a literary name used by Nichōsai himself.
[3] Listed in the Gillot Catalogue as the *Kotu Dzukai*.

subjects are taken from the everyday life of the people: street scenes, the festivals of the New Year, women at work, and religious processions—all depicted with inimitable wit and drawing. The book was issued in a folio 7 inches wide by 10 inches high and bound in a blue cover bearing an indistinct design of waves. Copies of the first edition are dated Kyōwa 3, Nenju (certain day), eighth month, with Nichōsai's seal in the form of a goblet to the left of the name of the publisher. Some years later the book was reprinted under the title of *Saji Mepokai*, but even in this form it is exceedingly rare.

Takahara SHUNCHŌSAI, although much better known as an illustrator of *meisho-ki* than as a caricaturist, left one set of books containing clever *Toba-ye*. This was the *Toba-ye Akubi-dome* ("Comical sketches to prevent yawning"), published in three volumes in 1793.

He was illustrating much earlier than this however, some of his work having been done in Kyōto, where he lived before going to Ōsaka. Other signatures used by him were MATSUMOTO and NOBUSHIGE. Among the books illustrated by him were the

Jishei (?) *Banashi*: 1777.
Naniwa-no-Kagami: Guide for Ōsaka. 3 vols. 1778.
Miyako Meisho Dzue: Guide for Kyōto. 6 vols. 1780.
Miyako Meisho Dzue: Supplement to foregoing. 6 vols. 1781.
Ehon Hatsu Kasei-me: Guide to the mushroom fields. 3 vols. 1787.
Yamato Meisho Dzue: Description of the province of Yamato. 7 vols. 1791.
Toba-ye Akubi-dome: Caricatures. 3 vols. 1793.
Izumi Meisho Dzue: Description of Izumi. 4 vols. 1793–1795. Signed Shunchōsai Takehara Nobushige.
Settsu Meisho Dzue: Description of Settsu. 8 vols. 1796–1798. Signed Takehara Shunchōsai.
Ehon Yōkyoku Gwashi:
Manzai Musha E-Kagami:
Gwasan Tsune-no-Yama: Poetical praise of pictures. 3 vols. About 1800. Black and white.

Jippensha IKKU, an eccentric artist and writer who was born in Ōsaka, was the son of a government official of Suruga by the name of Shigeta. Ikku himself held small offices in Ōsaka and later in Yedo, where he lived after 1796. His earliest work was a drama written in collaboration with two other writers for the Ōsaka theatres. His later works were published in Yedo, where he died in 1831. Aston, in *Japanese Literature*, gives a very amusing account of his life and the pranks he was fond of playing upon his friends.

Although chiefly known as a writer, Ikku also illustrated a number of books, among which were the

Zenaku Futatsu-no-Ryō-yaku: Charms against ill-fortune.
Ikyoku Tomawari Matsu: Poems illustrated by Ikku. 2 vols. 1799.
Ehon Yedo Sakura: Written and illustrated by Ikku. 2 vols. 1803.
Bakemono Kataki-Uchi: Vengeance among monsters. 2 vols. 1804.

PLATE 17] From the Toba-ye Akubi-dome, caricatures by Takahara Shunchōsai. 3 vols. 1793.

[Face p. 76

Hizakurige: His most important work, which he both wrote and illustrated.
Ehon Yedo Meisho: Description of Yedo. 2 vols. 1813.
Nenshi: Novel. Written and illustrated by Ikku. No date.
Tōkaidō-chū Hizakurige: Stories of the Tōkaidō. Written by Ikku. 18 vols. 1814. Illustrated by different artists.

In addition to the foregoing there were many *ki-byōshi* (yellow-covered novelettes) which Ikku both wrote and illustrated, some of the drawings being extremely clever and amusing.

Another early caricaturist, who was a contemporary of Shunboku and the originator of a style of his own, was a Buddhist priest named Meiyo[1] KOKAN. He lived between 1653 and 1717 and was High Priest of Saigan-ji, a temple of Koriyama near Nara, afterwards going to Ōsaka, and finally to Kyōto, where he became abbot of Hō-onji.[2] He studied under Kanō Einō and used as another signature the name KYOSHŪ. As an artist his fame rested chiefly upon the gigantic paintings he had made of the woman demon Hannya, the Seven Gods of Happiness, and one of Daikoku, the god of Wealth, while the Treasury of Tōdai-ji in Nara owns a very fine roll depicting the rebuilding of Daibutsu-den.

After his death his friends collected many of his drawings, which were reproduced in books. The earliest of these was the *Ruise Sogwa*, printed on fine *tōshi* paper in three volumes in 1724. In this edition Kokan's name does not appear. Perhaps his followers thought the rather broad caricatures it contained were not suitably dignified work for an abbot; the secret must have gotten out however, for in an edition of 1735, under the title of *Jimbutsu Sogwa*, Kokan is described as the artist.

Other books containing reproductions of drawings by him were the

Jimbutsu Kuse Dzukushi: Various humorous drawings. 3 vols. 1784.
Yakushi Engi: 4 vols.
Hōnen Shōnin Shijūhachi-kwan-den: The biography of Hōnen Shōnin. 48 vols.

Takata KEIHO, one of Kokan's few pupils, was born in 1674 in Hino, Ōmi province, where his father was an apothecary. He followed this work himself until the Daimyō of Omi, recognizing his talent as an artist, sent him to Kyōto to study. He entered Kanō Eishin's studio, but afterwards came under the influence of Kokan.

He became a well-known teacher in Ōsaka and Kyōto and numbered among his pupils Tsukioka Masanobu and Tsukioka Settei. His death occurred in Kyōto in 1755. Other signatures used by him were CHIKUINSAI, CHIKURIN, Kiken Gō-ō, BIKAN and HAKUŌ. Books illustrated by him were the *Keiho Gwafu* and the *Chikurin Gwafu*, the latter in collaboration with some of his pupils.

---

[1] The characters used in this name may be read also as Minyo.
[2] M. Revon says of Tofuku-ji. See *Hoksai*, p. 76.

CHAP. IV]   JAPANESE BLOCK-PRINTING

Aoi Sōkyū, who went to Kyōto from Sendai in the early part of the nineteenth century, is said to have been a follower of the Maruyama school. Later he lived in Ōsaka, and was working there until about 1840. Other names used by him were Sudo Kishi, Sōkyūshi, Kyōsho and Koemon. He left a series of extraordinary double-page caricatures of the Ōsaka courtesans, published in three volumes and printed in rich colours. The first edition was entitled the *Kishi Empu* and appeared in 1803.[1] It was reprinted in 1815, and in 1903 Yamada of Kyōto printed twelve of the plates and published them in a *gwajo* under the title *Kakuchu Empu*. In both the original edition and that of 1815 it is excessively rare. The drawings are much like Soken's work, suggesting that Sōkyō may have been his pupil.

In addition to this book he left a plate signed Sudo Kishi in the *Meika Gwafu* of 1815. The very useful index to this well-known work contains a few brief notes in regard to him.

After the decline of the Ukiyo-ye began, the Ōsaka work deteriorated even more rapidly than that of Yedo. There were an immense number of Ōsaka print designers who were influenced by Shunshō and Toyokuni, most of whom also illustrated books. With few exceptions, however, their work had become so exaggerated in both line and colour that it has little interest or value, and their books seem hardly worth listing. Edward Strange, in *Japanese Illustration*, devotes a chapter to these men from which, one who is interested may gain considerable information. Among the degenerate followers of these Yedo artists one should except Shunkōsai Hokuyei and one or two others.

Shunkōsai was a pupil of both Shunshō and Hokusai and used as other signatures the names Naniwa (Ōsaka) Shunkōsai, Shunbaitei, Shunbaisei, and Sekkwaro. He left a few illustrated books of decided merit. The *Ehon San Katsu-gushi Akebono Iro Gōshi* or the *Ehon Shibai Banashi* (one title appearing on the title-slips of the covers and the other on the first page of the book) consists of stories from the drama with a preface by Bakin. It was published in two series of three volumes each in 1811, and contains both black-and-white and coloured drawings. The latter compare favourably with some of Toyokuni's best illustrations of actors, and like most of the Ōsaka work was beautifully printed.

Shunkōsai also illustrated the *Irohata Yotsuya Kwaidan*, a collection of ghost stories with very curious illustrations (both coloured and black and white), which was published in five volumes in 1836. H. L. Joly, in *Legend in Japanese Art*, reproduces a few plates from this book.

Hokusai's fame was too great not to have had other followers in Ōsaka, and there were several artists there who left work closely resembling his.

[1] In the Gillot Catalogue the mistake is made of attributing this book to Kishi Chikudo.

PLATE 18]   From the EHON SHIBAI BANASHI, by Naniwa Shunkōsai, 1811.

[Face p. 78

Akatsuki KANENARI was one of these men, and his work deserves far greater recognition than it has ever received. He was born in Ōsaka in 1792, his father, Izumiya Tohei, being a soy manufacturer there. It is not known whether he studied directly under Hokusai or not, although when that artist was in Ōsaka in 1818 or 1820 this would have been possible even if he had not done so in Yedo. His work is so strikingly like that of Hokusai, that one might be tempted to attribute it to that master. Kanenari had a very definite history as an artist himself, however, and was known also as a dramatist and writer, using the signature Kimura KENKADŌ in this work. As other artist signatures he used the names KEIMEISHA, KYŌSHO, YASHIRO, MEIKEI, SHIKANOYA, MAHAGI, SEIYO, MISO-SHIRABO, ICHIZEN, and MANGIDŌ.

Toward 1850 he became mixed up in political matters, and was finally convicted of complicity in an attempt against the life of the Governor of Tamba province. He was put into the Fukuchiyama prison, where he died in 1860. He wrote and illustrated a number of books, among which were the

Ogura Hyaku-shū Ruidai Banashi: One hundred famous poems. Signed Kyōsho. 3 vols. 1823. Colours.
Yodagawa Ryōgan Shōkei Dzue: Views along the banks of the Yoda River. The preface states this work to have been in imitation of Hokusai's Sumidagawa set. 3 folios. 1824. Colours. Rare and charming.
Komochi Nezumi Hana-no-Yama-uba: Stories of a fortunate rat. Written by Urabe Ryōsai. Illustrated by Akatsuki Kanenari. 2 vols. 1827. Colours.
Ibuki Monogatari: Signed Keimeisha Akatsuki Kanenari. 5 vols.
Kokkei Mangwa.
Temman-gū Goshin-ji Omukai-bune Ningyō Dzu: Drawings of the figures carried at the Tenjin Matsuri. In collaboration with Matsukawa Hanzan. 1 *gwajo*. Colours.
Sato-no-Hatsuhana: Collection of poems and drawings in honour of Hatsuhana. In collaboration with Matsukawa Hanzan. 1 vol. 1859.

Another Ōsaka artist who showed Hokusai's influence strongly was Hishikawa KIYOHARU, not to be confused, as von Seidlitz and other writers have confused him, with the earlier Kondō Sukegorō Kiyoharu. Hishikawa Kiyoharu was a nineteenth-century artist, perhaps a grandson of the early Kondō Shoshichi who was the Ōsaka founder of the famous Torii school. He illustrated the

Kwannon Gyō Dzue: A book on Kwannon. 3 vols. 1833.
Ginka Zōshi: Poems on the Tanabata Festival. Illustrations much in Hokusai's style. 3 vols. 1835. Colours.

The latter book has been called a second edition of a work by Kondō Sukegoro, but this is a mistake. The drawings are of the nineteenth century. The work is rare and a lack of familiarity with it would account for this error.

Togetsu HOKUMEI, a talented woman artist, also known as Kyūkyūshin HOKUMEI and Kyūkyūshin TŌSHI, is said by Strange to have been an Ōsaka follower of Hokusai. No details are available in regard to her life, but the

CHAP. IV]　　JAPANESE BLOCK-PRINTING

charming drawings she left in a few books indicate a training in the Hōitsu school, where Kōyetsu's and Kōrin's styles were fostered and taught, rather than under Hokusai. Her books are excessively rare, but contain some delightful colour-printed work. Among them are the

Hokumei Mangwa: Sketches in colour. 1 vol. Signed Kamuri Hokumei Shi. 1818.
Hokumei Gwahin: Coloured sketches. 1 vol. 1818.
Hokumei Gwafu: Various sketches. 1 vol. 1830. Colours.
Tsuruga-Oka Yahazu Daimon: Episodes in the life of Kajiwara Kagetoki. 6 vols.

Urakawa KOSA, also known as Urakawa KIMISUKE, ISSENSAI, KOSEN, and KOSA, was a contemporary of Akatsuki Kanenari and Matsukawa Hanzen and collaborated with both of these men in different books. Little is known of his life, except that he was both an artist and a writer. He illustrated the

Fūryū Niwaka Tengu: Old tales. Contains very amusing and excellently drawn illustrations. In two editions, one printed in black and white and one in colours. 5 vols. 1841.
Ehon Hana Manabi: Lessons for children about fishes. 3 vols. 1847. Colours.
Kompira Sankei Meisho Dzue: Guide to the temple of Kompira. Written by Akatsuki Kanenari. 6 vols. 1847.
Saikoku Sanjūsan-Shō Meisho Dzue: Thirty-three famous pilgrimages in Western Japan. 10 vols. 1853.

Matsukara HANZAN was one of the best of the Ōsaka illustrators of the years just before the Restoration. His work bears some resemblance to that of Hiroshige, although more cramped and mechanical. Other signatures used by him were YASUNOBU, GIKYŌ, SUIYEIDŌ, and Kakyō HANZAN. He left a large number of *surimono* and some interesting books, among which are several small *meisho-ki* containing coloured drawings of considerable charm. A list of his books includes the

Kyōka Yagyō Hyaku-dai: One hundred poems on the monsters of the night. 1 vol. 1839.
Kyōka Naniwa Meisho Shū: Humorous poems on places in Ōsaka. 1 vol. 1844. Colours.
Temman-gū Goshin-ji Omukai-bune Ningyō Dzu: Drawings of the images carried in the Tenjin matsuri. Written by Akatsuki Kanenari. 1 gwajō. 1846. Colours.
Nakatomi Ō Harai Dzue: A Shinto prayer. 3 vols. 1851.
Ekuchiai Hisago-no-Tsuru: "The Gourd Vine of Kuchi-an." Written by Unwatei Koryu. 3 vols. 1851. Colours. Interesting and somewhat rare.
Naniwa Meisho: Views in Ōsaka. 3 small vols. 1855. Colours.
Dōmō Mitsu-no-Oshie: Duties of children to parents. 3 vols. 1855.
Yodogawa Ryōgan Ichiran: Views along the Yodo River. 2 series of 2 small vols. each. 1861. Colours.
Higashiyama Meisho Dzue: Views in the mountains east of Kyōto. 2 small vols. 1863.
Dai-fuku Setsuyō Mujin-Zosen: Places and customs in the province of Ōmi. First fourteen pages in colours. 1 vol. 1863.
Kwaraku Meisho Dzue: Description of Kyōto. 8 vols. 1859–1864.
Kyō Miyage:[1] Souvenir of Kyōto. In collaboration with Nishikawa Sukeharu. 2 vols. 1866.

Also of this group was Seki BUNSEN, a native of Yedo, who signed himself GYOKUZAN, KWANSAI, and GYOKURANDO. He was working during

---
[1] Not to be confused with Hiroshige's famous set of same title.

the Tempō and Kōkwa periods and left several books containing illustrations something in Hokusai's manner. Among them are the

Bunsen Gwafu: Birds, flowers, mythological characters, etc. 1 vol. 1848. Colours.
Gwashiki Shishō Shōken: Drawing book. 1 vol. 1849.
Bunsen Gwafu: Second series. 1 vol. 1854–1860. Tints.

Among the Ōsaka followers of Toyokuni and Kunisada, Hasegawa SADANOBU deserves mention. He was a fellow-pupil with Sadahide of Yedo in the Utagawa school, but much of his work closely resembles that of Hiroshige. There is in particular a small set of views of the Tōkaidō which is much like Hiroshige in both composition and the rich colouring; and still another little set copied from the famous Tōkaidō series by that artist. Sadanobu used as other signatures the names HISHIKAWA, SEIKWAEN, KINKWADŌ, TAMURA, Nanso TOKUBEI, and Nanso-rō SADANOBU. Among the books illustrated by him were the

Meihitsu Gwafu: In imitation of Hiroshige's well-known book. Preface by Ikado Kunimaro. Drawings signed Seikwaen Sadanobu. 2 small vols. 1823. Colours.
Oyose Hanashi-no-Shiriuma: Comical stories. Sadanobu and other artists. No date.
Yakusha Ehon: Actors' heads. Very beautifully printed with gold, silver, and *gaufrage* added to the colour. Variously signed Nanso-ro Sadanobu, Nanso Tokubei, and Hasegawa Tokubei, but with identical seal on each plate. No date.
Yoshikono Gyokuyō Shū: Geisha songs. 1 small vol. 1852.

Ryūtei SHIGEHARU, also known as GYOKURYŪTEI, RYŪSAI, YAMAGUCHI, and Yamamoto Heishichirō SHIGEHARU, illustrated the

Yakusha Sango Kushi: Actors of three cities. Contains a page by Tani Bunchō and one by Kosa. 3 vols. 1831. Colours.

Utagawa SADAHIRO, another Ōsaka artist of the group to which Sadanobu and Shigeharu belonged, also signed himself Gorakutei, Gochotei, and Shokwotei. He left a well-known book entitled

Naka-no-Yume: Queer dreams. Preface by Ichikawa Hakuyen (Danjuro III). The illustrations represent a "picture meeting" which was held the 25th of each month. The names of the artists appear printed in small characters by their sides. 3 vols. 1836. Colours.

Utagawa Sadashige, also known as Okada Tōshiro, and later as Kuniteru, lived between 1829 and 1874. Among the books left by him was a *hōsō-ye-bon* entitled *Hōsō Anzen Kodomo Karuwaza* (Tempō period).

Nakai RANKŌ was a well-known Ōsaka artist who lived between 1766 and 1831. He used as other signatures the names NAOSHI, CHOKU, HAKUYŌ, SHIN, SHIKO, and YOSEI. His training had been under Shitomi Kwangetsu. Although chiefly famous as a painter he did some work for wood-engraving, among which is a charming little set of colour prints of the Fifty-three Stations along the Tōkaidō. Plates by him are often found in collections of contemporaneous work, and he illustrated the *Banshū Meisho Junran*

Dzue, a guide to Harima province, which his friend Murakami had written (1803).

An earlier Rankō, who sometimes signed himself Yoshida, left a book of designs for fans published by his pupils in three volumes in 1783.

Branches of the impressionistic schools of Kyōto were established in Ōsaka early in the nineteenth century. Among these studios that of Mori Sosen, the famous painter of monkeys, was known all over Japan.

Sosen was born in Nagasaki in 1746. He lived for a time at Nishinomiya, near Kobe, and afterwards went to Kyōto, where he studied under Maruyama Ōkyo. Eventually he went to Ōsaka and opened a school of his own founded on Ōkyo's methods. Other signatures used by him were Morikata, Tōshinshō, Jokansai, and Reimeian.

Although seldom working for wood-engraving, there are several compilations of contemporary work which contain plates by Sosen. Among these books the well-known *Meika Gwafu* contains an extremely interesting double-page plate of a monkey clinging to the branches of a tree, which is his work. Sosen died in 1821, leaving many followers to carry on his methods. Among these men was Mori Tessan, the son of his elder brother Mori Shūhō (1737-1823).

Tessan lived between 1775 and 1841. He was adopted by Sosen and made the school established by him an affiliated school with the Kyōto Maruyama academy. Other signatures used by him were Tetsuzan, Morimasa, Shigen and Shushin. Some of his latest work shows European influence. Drawings by him are occasionally found in albums of contemporary work, although he did not often work for wood-engraving.

Mori Ippō, also known as Keishi, the son of Tessan, achieved considerable fame as a painter, and left a few book illustrations. He worked in Ōsaka until about 1820, leaving two sons who were also artists. Mori Bunrei, the elder of the two, also known as Shikan, Hanko, and Sanpei, was working until after the middle of the nineteenth century.

Mori Nihō, Mori Ippō's second son, also worked to some extent for wood-engraving, and the *Naniwa Kippo Fu*, a rare and charming collection of tinted drawings in illustration of poems, published in two volumes in 1856, contains work by all of these men.

Mori Kwanzan (1844- ?), the son of Mori Nihō, was also a painter.

Mori Kansai, also known as Shiyu and Kōshuku, lived between 1814 and 1894. He was born in Kyōto of a family named Ishida, but after some

Also, possibly, Mayekawa. There is a set of two volumes of coloured plates of birds and flowers, entitled the *Bunrei Gwafu*, by Mayekawa Bunrei, published in 1885, but this artist may have been a Yedo man, a follower of the Bunrin Bunchō teachings.

PLATE 19] By Mori Sosen. Taken from the last volume of the MEIKA GWAFU (1815)

study there went to Ōsaka, where he entered Mori Tessan's studio and was finally adopted by that artist. Later he returned to Kyōto, where he became a teacher in the new art school there. A book of reproductions of the paintings by him exhibited at the thirteenth anniversary of his death, called the *Kansai Gwafu* (two volumes), was published about 1909. The *Kansai Shūbi Gwafu* (one volume, colours) is another late collection of his work.

Mori SHUNKEI, also of this group, left an album of flowers and birds in the Chinese style, called the *Shunkei Gwafu*, published about 1820, and the *Chūka Senchū*, a book of insects, one volume, in colours, 1820.

Mori SHUNKYŌ left a striking flower plate in the *Yume-no-Yokozuchi*, an album of contemporary work published in 1817.

Nishiyama HŌYEN was a follower of Keibun in the Shijo school in Kyōto and established a branch of this famous studio in Ōsaka, where he was working until about 1865. His work consisted chiefly of paintings of birds, flowers, and landscapes, some of which have been reproduced in albums of contemporary work.

This résumé of Ōsaka work in illustration covers but a small part of what was accomplished there, and there were hundreds of other books which have not been listed because wood-engraving had become so universally used in Japanese books that it would require a work of encyclopædic size to enumerate them all.

In prowling around the old-book shops one often discovers interesting volumes published in Ōsaka in the eighteenth century, the drawings in which are signed by men of whom one can learn nothing. Many of these unknown artists were evidently followers of Shunboku, and their work has a breadth and dignity entirely lacking in the prints and books of the Ōsaka Ukiyo-ye group.

CHAPTER V

THE IMPRESSIONISTS: THE SHIJŌ AND MARUYAMA SCHOOLS

HE early years of the eighteenth century witnessed the beginnings of a rather special school of illustration in Japan, in which the work, although representing scenes from the everyday life of the people, like the Ukiyo-ye pictures of Yedo, was done with something of the old Kanō manner. It was a combination of genre subject and aristocratic technique, and the result was a great number of books of extraordinary interest.

It is a question whether the impressionism in modern French illustration did not have its origin in this movement. Some of the books of which this chapter treats found their way to Europe in the early seventies of the last century, and both the Duret and Burty collections in Paris possessed copies of works by Okyo, Bumpō, Suiseki, Nantei, and others of the men who belonged to this new-old art movement. The similarity in technique between the drawings of some of the modern European illustrators and that in these Japanese books is too marked not to cause comparison, and the juxtaposition of the accompanying sketches by Bruyer done in 1915 and Kawamura Bumpō a century earlier, shows this amazing likeness very plainly.

Impressionism in art even a hundred years ago was no new thing in Japan, however, for the school founded by Toba Sōjō toward the end of the eleventh century was characterized as much by the impressionistic technique of its work as the humorous nature of the subjects it dealt with.

Since Toba Sōjō may be considered as one of the far-off sources from which this really great eighteenth and early nineteenth century school of illustration sprang, it may not be out of place to give here the few details which are known of his life. Born in 1053, the son of Minamoto Takakuni, while still a boy he became the disciple of Kakuyen, a high-priest of the Tendai sect. Toba was known in his priestly work as Kakuyu, taking the name Toba Sōjō as a painter—Toba from the little village near Kyōto where he once lived, and Sōjō, his priest's rank. The Emperor Sutoku made him his special protégé, and under his patronage Toba Sōjō achieved a name both as an artist and a priest, being made shortly before his death in 1140 the chief abbot of the entire Tendai sect. His fame rests on his paintings, however, which are national treasures, to be seen from time to time in the Imperial Museums in Tōkyō, Kyōto, and Nara.

It is said that these famous rolls were intended by the artist to amuse

"Waiting," by Bruyer.

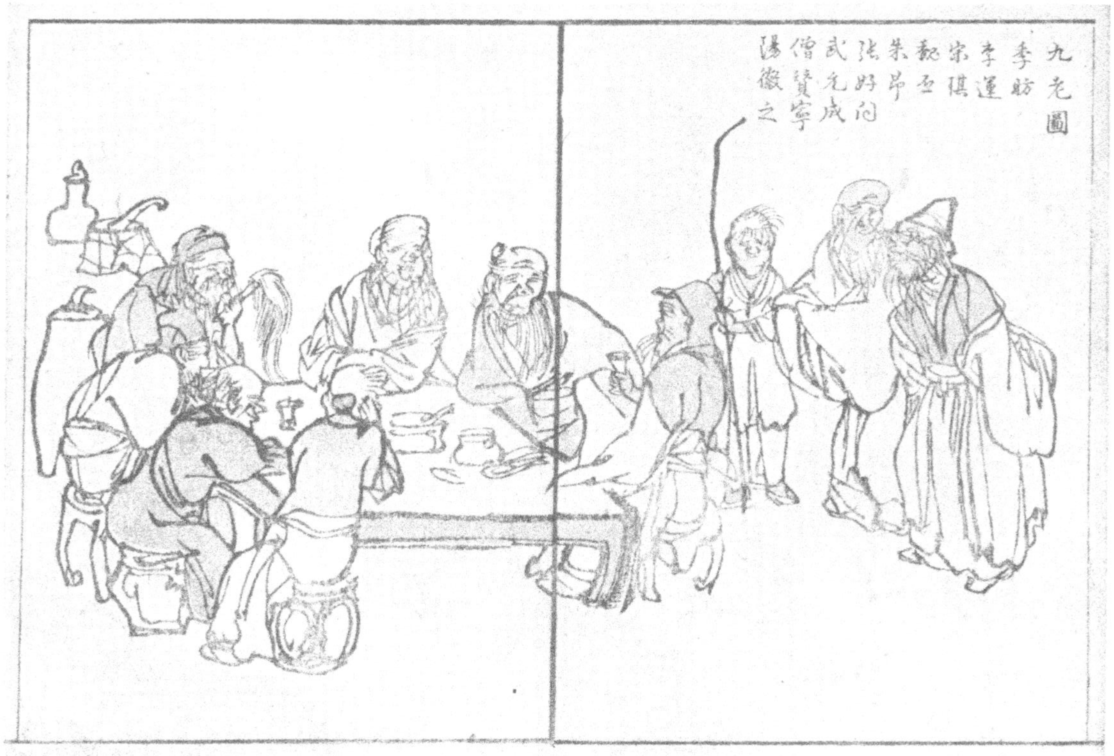

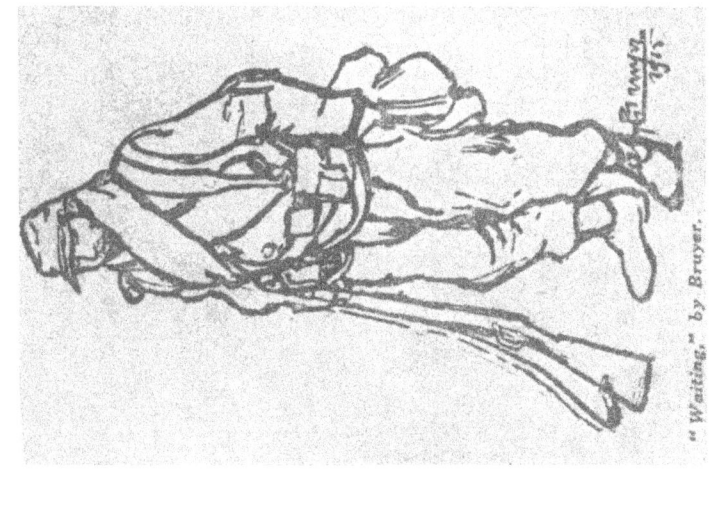

PLATE 20] The nine Ancients' and a page from the 3rd volume of the Bumpō Gwafu (1813); and sketch by Bruyer (1915).

[Face p. 84

and lighten the depression of the Emperor, who, unhappy at the extravagance and decadence of the Court, and the growing insubordination of the priests of Hiei-zan, finally abandoned the Throne, taking the name of Toba-no-in.

Most of the work in painting up to this time had been stiffly classical both in treatment and subject, and these rolls of comical pictures and grotesque caricatures struck an entirely new note. In them the artist-priest satirized the life he saw around him, and represented people at their daily occupations and pastimes by the most astonishingly precocious animals, great and small—horses, cows, dogs, rabbits, mice, frogs, and lizards, all representing men and women and impersonating warriors, courtiers, and Court beauties. The technique was as original as the subjects, and the dashing impulsiveness of the drawings is so astonishingly similar to that in European work of eight hundred years later, that the venerable assurance that there is nothing new under the sun becomes once again true—even if trite. Perhaps if the Emperor had not given his friendship and support to Toba Sōjō such a departure from all accepted standards would have been impossible, or so frowned upon by the artificial Court with its rigid and fixed traditions, that the painter's name would have been lost to coming generations. The patronage of his sovereign, however, made his work popular, and to-day in Japan there is not a street coolie who does not know who Toba Sōjō was. His name became associated with all humorous drawings and caricatures, and this class of work has been known as Toba-ye, or Toba pictures, ever since.

The influence of this early artist trickling through the intervening centuries and uniting with that of the Kanō school had its part in the new movement. Other rills springing from the realistic school which the Chinese artist Chin Nampin had established in Nagasaki in 1730 united with the *bunjingwa* stream, which was turned toward Japan during the turmoil which accompanied the downfall of the Ming dynasty in China in the seventeenth century, when Chinese refugees introduced their beloved Confucian scholarship and art to their eastern neighbours, and together gave impetus to what is known as the Shijō movement in Japanese painting—an art movement which has enriched the world not only by paintings of great beauty, but by some of the most delightful illustrated books that have ever been printed.

These books have always been especially popular with the Japanese. The foreigner did not have to teach them their value. The technique in them, impulsive and expressing much in little, was the technique they had been familiar with for generations—the technique which in superb *hakemono* and screens depicted with a few rapid strokes of the brush a snowy landscape that made one shiver with the chill, or a rain-swept river where a dim brown spot or two became broad-hatted boatmen sculling their sampans to the sea.

CHAP. V] JAPANESE BLOCK-PRINTING

The men who made these charming drawings were famous in their own generation and occupied a far higher place in the estimation of artistic circles of the time than the print designers of Yedo, whose fame is so largely posthumous.

This impressionistic movement separates itself into several groups under the leadership of different men. The earliest was in reality the Chinese school, but we will consider that later since it never merged into other academies, although its followers passed on its teachings through schools of their own. After the Chinese school the earliest was the circle dominated by the poet-artist Buson, who established a studio in Kyōto about 1750, and whose work was of the pure *bunjingwa* order. The Maruyama school under the great Ōkyo was founded some years later, but became so much the most famous of them all that eventually it rather overshadowed the other groups. Nevertheless, the Shijō studio under the direction of Goshun which was established by him after Buson's death, whose pupil he had been, was a great force in Japanese art and existed in friendly rivalry with Ōkyo's school, the manner of work being sufficiently similar so that the " Shijō school " has become a term meaning both of these art centres. Lastly there was the school founded by Utanosuke Ganku, known as the Ganku *Ryū*, where the style of the Chinese artist Chin Nampin[1] was taught to a large and aristocratic following.

These five Kyōto schools were thus the five springs the confluence of which formed the great stream of Impressionism to which we owe so much that is unique and delightful in Japanese illustration as well as in printing. In speaking of the individual artists it seems best to consider them as members of the groups to which they belonged, since each of these famous studios had a more or less distinctive technique of its own.

BUSON, who established his art school in Kyōto about the middle of the eighteenth century, was already well known both as a poet and an artist. He was born in 1716 at Tennō-ji, near Ōsaka, of a family named Taniguchi, but later lived in Yosa, a district near Kyōto, which had been his mother's home and from which he took one of his names. He studied painting under Sakaki Hyakusen and poetry from Uchida Tenzan, becoming under the latter's tutelage the originator of a new school of *haikai* (seventeen-syllable poems), called the Tenmei-chō, which attained such a popularity that it resulted in his establishing a school of this kind of verse, which became almost as well known as his art academy.

Buson's true name was Taniguchi Chōko, but he used as artist and poet signatures the names TORA, YOSA, SHUNSEI, BUSEI, TŌSEI, YAHANTEI, SHIKOAN, HAKUSETSUDŌ, KANAN, and RŌUN. He died in 1783, and is to-day

[1] Shēn Nan-p'in.

ranked very highly by the best Japanese critics both as a poet and as a painter.

Although Buson never worked directly for wood-engraving, the *Haikai Sanjū Rok-kasen* contains drawings by him of the Thirty-six Poets which were collected and published by his followers in 1799, sixteen years after his death. The poems above the drawings are in his chirography. The first printing was on the soft Chinese paper called *tōshi*, and the book was bound in covers bearing a design of a stag standing in autumn leaves, on a greyish-brown background. This was followed later the same year by a reprint on ordinary paper in plain yellow covers. Both editions are rare and valuable, and a late nineteenth-century copy printed in soft colours is hardly less interesting. The first drawing of the series is signed Yahantei Buson.

In 1832 the *Zoku Haigwa Kijin-den*, a work on old books, pictures, etc., was published containing coloured reproductions of another set of drawings by Buson of the Thirty-six Poets said to have been taken from a *gwajō* of the Kyōhō period.

Both of these sets of the *Sanjū Rok-kasen* are very characteristic of Buson, the technique being absolutely simple, with not one touch more than was necessary to express what the artist wished. The result is a series of illustrations which in every particular stands as far from the print designers' work as imagination can conceive.

Living in Kyōto at the same time as Buson was Ikeno TAIGADŌ, who was also a leader in the *bunjingwa* style of painting.

Taigadō (1723-1775) was the son of Ikeno Kayemon, who owned a fan shop on Nijō-dori just west of Nijō bridge. He manifested talent while still a child, but when only twelve years old his father died, leaving the business to be carried on by his mother and himself. It is said that he was so fond of exercising his ability in chirography that he kept the fan shop books in writing which his mother was obliged to take to the priest to decipher, and when the lure of the outdoor world became too great to resist he escaped from the shop with his sketching materials. A fanciful anecdote is told of him which reads almost like a little drama.

It is said that, being dissatisfied with the fans which the professional designers furnished the shop, he painted one hundred himself and took them to Nagoya to sell. Unsuccessful in disposing of them he started back to Kyōto. On Seta bridge, as he approached the village of Ōtsu, he lingered watching the sun go down in lurid splendour behind the western hills. Not wishing to be burdened in his enjoyment of it by the load of fans, he threw them into the river which leaves Lake Biwa at this point and flows down through Uji and Fushimi. At Fushimi a *daimyō* lived who was an artist himself as well as a famous connoisseur. As the *daimyō* walked by the river two or three of Taigadō's fans came floating down the current. He caught them, and upon inspection immediately recognized them as the work of a genius. The next day he went to Kyōto and hunted up the man who had painted them. He found Taigadō with his wife and mother in a poor little house[1] up near Chion-in where they had gone some time before, after having been obliged to sell the fan shop to pay their debts. In spite of the difference in their stations, the two men agreed so well upon art that they soon became great friends. The patronage of the *daimyō* made it possible for Taigadō to devote himself exclusively to painting, and he soon became very famous. The story tapers off at the end without any startling climax, but is interesting and pleasantly possible.

Among this artist's many signatures were MUMEI, KASHŌ, YŪKASANSHŌ, TAIGA, TAISEI, SANGAKUDŌSHA, CHIKUKYŌ, and FUKO-CHŌSŌ. Like many of the men who illustrated books, Taigadō was far better known as a painter than as an illustrator, although there are several books containing drawings by him which were compiled by his students after his death. Perhaps the rarest is the *Taigadō Gwafu*, a *gwajō* chiefly made up of landscapes in pronounced *bunjingwa* style, printed in colours and published in *gwajō* form in Kyōwa 3 (1803). Another very rare work is the *Taigadō Gwaho*, in three large folios, published in 1808. The drawings are in black and white, with here and there a wash of grey or a slight note or two of soft colour. They represent rocks, trees, and landscapes, and are extremes of impressionistic work. Both of these sets are extremely valuable and command high prices if they can ever be found. They are sumptuously gotten up, the paper being rich and heavy, and the printing beyond praise.

Taigadō and Buson collaborated in an interesting series of drawings known as the *Jūben Jūgi*, and Taigadō with I-fukyū illustrated the *I-fukyū Gwafu* of 1803; whilst the *Sansui Jūseki Gwafu* contains copies of some of Taigadō's work drawn by Yanagisawa Kien. Occasionally also in books of illustrated poems and in collections of drawings by different artists of the time one finds a plate by Taigadō.

Fenollosa, in his *Epochs of Chinese and Japanese Art*, condemns utterly the work of both Buson and Taigadō, and calls them "*bunjingwa* fanatics," (see vol. ii., p. 165). Nevertheless their work is extremely fascinating and grows upon one as familiarity with it increases. It is very highly thought of by Japanese critics, and to all lovers of impressionism it must appeal strongly. It has nothing of the obvious in it. A sketch by Buson or

[1] On the site of this house is a building made of the materials which formerly were in the house belonging to the famous scholar Kinoshita Choshoshi, put up by Taigadō's pupils in his memory. It is known as the Taiga-dō and back of it is a monument bearing an inscription from Tagaidō's writings.

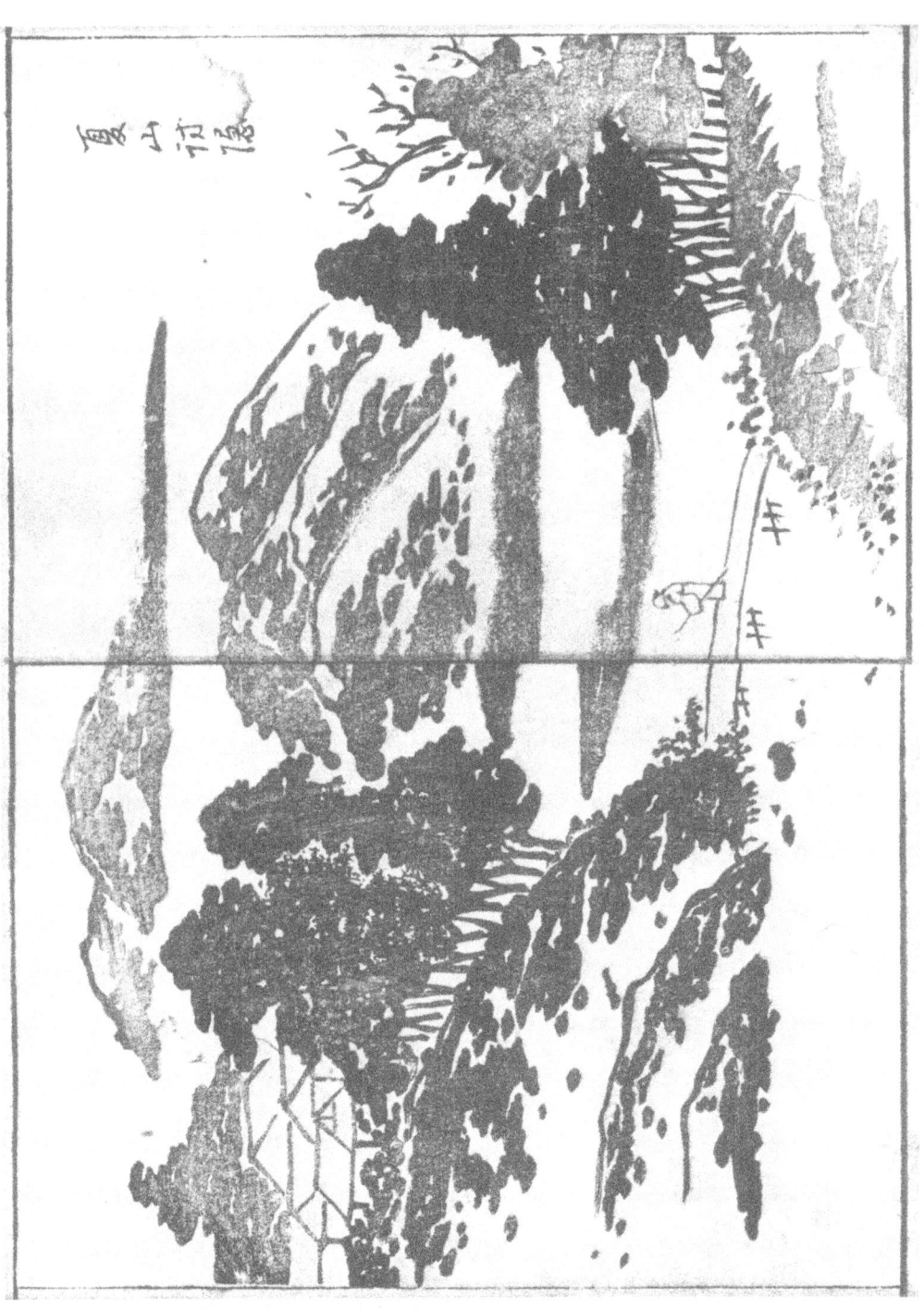

PLATE 21] From the rare TŌKEI GWAFU, by Ogura Tōkei. 2nd. series, 1809.

Taigadō or Goshun is a hint—a suggestion more than a sketch—and its admirer instantly leaps mentally to fill it in and give it completion with his own understanding. Certainly it is far more than " an awkward joke."[1]

Ogura Tōkei, whom Fenollosa calls the " arch-impressionist," was born in Sanuki in the island of Shikoku. Although a follower of the *bunjingwa* school, he had also studied in Nagasaki and was a great admirer of Chin Nampin's work, numbering among his friends many of the Chinese painters who had come to Japan in the wake of that famous painter.

Tōkei used as other signatures the names Fujū, Kirei, and Hakuō Inso, and sometimes appended to these names the word Rō-gyo (" old fisherman "). He was chiefly noted for his paintings in black and white and grey, and left one remarkable set of books illustrated in this manner. This is the *Tōkei Gwafu*, the first series of which appeared in two volumes in 1787, containing drawings of birds, flowers, etc., much in Chin Nampin's style, although printed without colour. The second series, published in 1809, consists of plates in black and white and grey of landscapes, figures, designs for fans, etc., in the most pronounced *bunjingwa* manner, the masses of soft grey added to the black giving a wonderful richness of effect. The first edition of this rare book was printed on the fine *tōshi* paper, but was reissued the same year printed on an ordinary quality. In either form it is a treasure greatly to be prized. It is signed Tōkei Rō-gyo.

A pupil of Taigadō's, Aoki Shikuya of Kyōto, also known as Shunmei, Shunto, and Hachigaku, although chiefly noted for his landscape paintings, left a remarkable book containing architectural drawings, published in 1790. One of the plates is a bird's-eye view of a temple, showing the different buildings, surrounding walls, etc., which is as precise and exact as if the artist had had the most academic training.

Geppo, another follower of Taigadō, who was sometimes called Taiga II., was born in 1759. He entered the priesthood when a young

---

[1] Arthur Morrison is one of the few European art critics who has the inner understanding of *bunjingwa* painting. He says (*Painters of Japan*, vol. ii., p. 75): " This is the style absolutely last to be comprehended by the European student, and very frequently it is never comprehended at all. It arose in a reaction against the finished technique, often concealing poverty of inspiration, of professional painters. ... The coming of professionalism brought a danger of loss of spirituality, such as it brought to the art of Europe after the passing of the early religious painters. Recoiling from this danger ... the painters of the literary style deliberately threw overboard the *bravura*, polish, and obvious power of technique which were the mark of the trained professional, and sought to convey their ' shadowed lessons of the whole world ' by lines and touches of unstudied and child-like simplicity, with no preoccupation but purity and elevation of thought. The pictures thus painted do not commend themselves at first sight to Western students. Many indeed declare the whole thing a fad and an affectation off-hand. But the amateur whose will is to take all from the East that its art has to give will make no such error, but will familiarize himself with the best examples and see them as far as he may with the painters' own eyes; and in this, as I may testify, he will not waste his sympathies."

man, becoming toward the latter part of the century the Abbot of Sorin-ji, a temple of Kyōto near Maruyama Park. Geppo was known as a poet, a chirographer, and an artist, as well as a priest. Other signatures used by him were SHINRYŌ, KIKAN, TATSUSUKI, and GETSU-Ō. His death occurred in 1839. Two sons, Giryō and Seiryō, survived him, both of whom became painters.

Although Geppo did not work to any extent for wood-engraving, a few albums of contemporary work contain plates by him much in Taigadō's style, as in the *Keijō Gwayen*, made up of coloured drawings by Hakuyei, Gito, Shiba Kōkan, Minwa, Toyohiko, Tōsen, and other artists, and published in 1814; and the *Shiki ku-awase*, verses on the four seasons, illustrated by Geppo and Hokkei in collaboration.

Asai TONAN, a *bunjingwa* painter of this time and a follower of Buson and Taigadō, was of *samurai* rank and a physician in addition to being an artist. Other signatures used by him were CHŌJIN and KANTEI. Coloured plates are sometimes found by him in the popular albums of the early nineteenth century, and he left a number of very interesting *surimono*, done in the most impressionistic style and beautifully printed.

Matsumura GOSHUN, the talented and famous pupil of Buson, is said to have been born in 1742 in Kureha, a little village of Tamba province near Kyōto. He studied for a time under Onishi Suigetsu and then entered Buson's studio. Other names used by him were Matsumura KAYEMON, GEKKEI (his poet's name), SHUN, HAKUBŌ, INHAKU, IMPAKU, and SOMPAKU. The signature he chiefly used as a painter, however, was Goshun, a combination of the first syllable of Gofukumura and *shun* (spring), recalling a visit he had made one spring season in his youth to the village of Gofukumura in the province of Settsu.

Goshun was not only the disciple of Buson in art, but also in poetry, and achieved a name as a poet hardly less well known than that of his master. He is said to have been greatly addicted to drink and careless as to whether he earned money or not, frequently giving away paintings which he might easily have sold for large sums, and never working at all unless in the mood for it, although his family was often in need. He seems to have been a versatile genius and was known as a chirographer and writer of *Jōruri-bon* as well as an artist and a poet. After Buson's death Goshun would have entered Ōkyo's famous Maruyama school, but the latter refused to take him, assuring him that he had sufficient ability and had studied long enough to continue his work by himself. It resulted in Goshun and his younger brother Keibun establishing what became the famous Shijō studio, near Shijō bridge—the two academies, Ōkyo's and Goshun's, working along nearly parallel lines and apparently in perfect harmony.

Goshun's work is not often found in books, for he was known as a painter rather than an illustrator. The *Shin Hana-tsumi*, a poetical diary written by Buson, was illustrated by him, however. This book was published in 1784, probably in two volumes, since the original wrapper which has been pasted on the fly-leaf of my copy states this to be so. No collector, as far as can be ascertained, however, has ever seen the other volume, and it is possible that the blocks were destroyed by fire before many sets had been printed. This book is one of those extremely rare works which is immensely prized by Japanese collectors, and hardly known to foreigners. In five years' collecting in Japan I found only two copies. The illustrations show plainly the influence of Buson. They are of the simplest technique and are printed in soft tints. These drawings are not by any means intended as caricatures, as one might at first suppose, but are instances of a style of the greatest simplicity used to fit simple subjects. It is perhaps to the lack of understanding of this application of a technique to the underlying meaning of a subject, as the artist feels it, that the foreign denunciation of *bunjingwa* art is to be attributed.

A modern collection of landscape drawings by Goshun, called the *Goshun Sansui Gwafu*, is published by Yamada of Kyōto, and the *Nihon Meigwa Kagami*, copied from an old *makimono* by Goshun, was printed by Tanaka Moitsu, Tōkyō, in 1899, in colours.

Goshun died in 1811, leaving his younger brother, Matsumura Keibun, to carry on the Shijō school.

KEIBUN (1799–1843), also known as KWAKEI, was chiefly noted for his paintings of flowers and birds and his beautiful work in black and white. He illustrated the *Keibun Gwafu*, and the drawings in the *Go-Keibun Gwafu* of 1839 are partly his own work and partly reproductions of drawings by Goshun. Plates by him are also occasionally found in compilations of contemporary work.

Okamoto TOYOHIKO (1778–1845) is sometimes spoken of as a younger brother of Goshun and Keibun. This is a mistake. He and Gitō were pupils only of the Shijō school. Toyohiko achieved considerable fame as a painter and was given the title of Hōgen by the Government. Other signatures used by him were RIKYŌ, CHŌSHINSAI, and KŌSON. Although he did not often work for wood-engraving, he illustrated the *Toyohiko Kwachō Gwafu*, a charming collection of drawings of birds and flowers; and there are plates by him in the *Ariwara Bunko* of 1802, the *Keijō Gwayen* of 1814, and the *Meika Gwafu* of 1815.

Shibata GITŌ (1779–1819), who followed Toyohiko to Kyōto from their native town in Bizen, entered the Shijō school while Goshun was still its master, continuing his work under Keibun. He was also known as KITARO, KINCHŌ, and KINKAI. Drawings by him appear in the *Keijō Gwayen* and other similar compilations.

Gitō left a son, Gihō, and Mayegawa Gorei and Shiogawa Unsho, both of whom attained considerable popularity as painters, were his pupils.

Kino BAITEI (1743-1816-17) was an almost exact contemporary of Goshun's, and was the latter's fellow-pupil in the famous *bunjingwa* school established by Buson. Little is known of Baitei's life except that he was a native of Ōmi province and that he returned there in his old age, spending his last years at Ōtsu. According to one account he was a servant in the employ of Wakaki Randen, a scholar and *samurai* of rank, living in Ōtsu, who, recognizing his talent, sent him to Kyōto to study at Buson's academy. In another short sketch of his life he is said to have been a physician and poet as well as an artist.

Baitei used many different signatures, among which were the names KYŪRŌ, Baiju ITSUJIN, SUIGETSU-AN, Baikei ITSUJIN, Baitei KAHEI, Ki BAITEI, BAIKIKEN, KINRO, RYŪTEI, HŌ-KWAYEN, and HAKURYO, and sometimes a seal bearing the name OSO.

His work is very well known by lovers of *bunjingwa* art, and although it includes only a few books they are of great originality and interest. They are also all extremely rare, the collector only finding them by great good fortune. Among them are the

Sanuki Buri: A collection of humorous poems and drawings. 1 vol. 1798.
Kyūrō Gwafu: A collection of various drawings in extreme *bunjingwa* style. 2 vols. 1799. Black and white. (A second edition in 1824.)
Hitomane-Saru Shiri Warai (" Monkey tricks ") : A novel written by Nakagawa Kotei, containing very interesting illustrations by Baitei, one or two of which have a slight note of colour introduced. 4 vols. 1806.
Suigetsu Shū: A collection of charmingly illustrated poems. Signed Baikiku Itsujin. 5 vols. 1813.
Ho-ru Shū: Poems and drawings. Signed Itsujin. 1 vol. 1813. Published by Kwanzendo in Owari.
Ginga or *Mushi-no-Koye* (" Silver River " or " Singing Insects "): An astonishing and extremely rare little volume containing richly coloured drawings of the most pronounced *bunjingwa* type in illustration of poems on the Tanabata festival. 1 vol. 1813.

Baitei's drawings show that the teachings of Buson had sunk deep, but added to a style which is undeniably that of the master, is something which belongs to Baitei in an especial degree among the Japanese artists—a brutal strength which even though it is repellent and often grotesque, commands one's instant attention.

Satō SUISEKI, also known as MASUYUKI (EKISHI), MASUO, Hotei KEIKWA, GYŌDAI, RANDOMEI and Tokuyen GYŌKA, was a native of Ōsaka, but spent much of his life in Kyōto. He was a pupil of the Shijō school, and since he was a contemporary of Baitei's it is probable that he was one of Buson's pupils, continuing his work under Goshun when the older master died. Little is known in regard to his life. In the preface to the *Suiseki Gwafu* his friend Hayano Masami writes that Suiseki was so devoted to his work that he often forgot to eat, and sometimes only slept an hour or two at night. He is also said to have had brain trouble at one time from overwork.

He illustrated a number of books, among which are the

Roku-Roku-sen: A collection of poems the preface to which says that the originals of the illustrations formed a series of large paintings which were presented by Suiseki to a Shinto shrine near Ōsaka. 1 vol. 1807. Colours.
Tokiwa-gusa: Illustrated poems. Signed Masayuki. 1 vol. 1808. Colours.
Yanagi Musubi: Illustrated poems. Signed Masayuki. 1 vol. No date. Colours.
Suiseki Gwafu: Sketches of everyday life. Signed Suiseki Satō Masayuki. 1 vol. Ōsaka. 1814. Colours. Rare and interesting.
Yume-no-Yoko Dzushi: A collection of poems and sketches, containing a very striking landscape signed Randomei. 1 gwajo. 1817. Colours.
Hōrai-zan: Poems illustrated by Suiseki and other artists. 1 vol. 1818. Colours.
Suzuri-no-Chiri: "Blots from the brush of Hotei Keikwa." Signed Masayuki. 1 vol. 1819. Colours. A rare and charming book.
Suiseki Gwafu Nihen: A supplement to the *Suiseki Gwafu*. Delicately tinted drawings of birds and flowers. 1 vol. 1820. Extremely rare.

Suiseki's early work had something of the same brutality that marked that of Baitei. Both men flung rules utterly aside and expressed what they wanted to convey in the baldest and most abrupt fashion. Nothing could be further removed from the work of the artists who were illustrating books in Yedo at this time than the impressionism of these Kyōto men. One must be in entirely different moods for the two kinds of drawings. Comparisons are utterly impossible. If one admires the beauty and flowing lines of a print by Utamaro, he may also have moods when the tremendous daring and strength of the rebellious souls of the *bunjingwa* school who created such work as Buson's, Taigadō's, Baitei's, and Suiseki's appeals powerfully to him, and seems, for the time being at least, the very essence of art, in which the artist, despising any sensuous appeal of beauty, endeavours to express his ideas by the simplest and ruggedest truth.

In addition to book illustrations, Suiseki designed many *surimono* in his characteristic style. These are usually signed Gyōdai, and are among the best examples of the work of the impressionistic school. They show also a technical excellence of printing which is beyond praise.

Although there are no details available in regard to Tsuji Hozan, the excessively rare set of four books known as the *Bitchū Meisho-ko*, published in 1822, bears this signature. Many Japanese collectors believe this to have been another of Satō Suiseki's artist names. Mr. Hosogawa, one of the well-known dealers in old books in Kyōto, whose constant handling, for over twenty-five years, of these volumes has made him one of the best judges in

Japan, thinks the illustrations were by Suiseki. The set is practically extinct in the first edition, and in the modern copy no colours are used in the plates.

Of about the same time as Suiseki was an artist by the name of Yoshida GETCHO, whose work is so plainly of the Shijō school that we must assume he studied there, although there are no details available in regard to his life, except that he is supposed to have come from Ōmi province and was also known as HAKUSHU, SHISAI, and Taniguchi SUKENEGA. Many of the collections of drawings made up of work by different contemporary artists of much greater fame include work by Getcho, indicating that he belonged to their circle. He illustrated the

Chūkō Michi-no-Shiori: Talks on filial piety, duty of servants to masters, etc. 3 vols. 1819. Kyōto, Ōsaka, and Yedo. Black and white.
Tatsu-no-toshi: Poems on the festival of the New Year. 1 small vol. 1820. Colours.
Sankyō Dōyu: A book of instructions for boys on various subjects. 4 vols. 1820. Ōsaka. Black and white.

Ueda KŌCHŌ of Ōsaka, also known as YUSHU, YOSHO, and JUNZO, was a late pupil of the Shijō school. More or less confusion has existed about Kōchō and Satō Suiseki, some collectors maintaining that these were merely different names for the same artist. This is an absurd mistake, for, although their work is somewhat similar, as seems to have been inevitably the case with students of the same master, there is sufficient difference to mark the individuality of two men. Suiseki was an earlier artist, probably one of the students of Buson himself during his later years, and of Goshun after the leadership of the famous school fell to him. Kōchō was of the next generation and worked under Keibun. Strange in *Japanese Illustration* also confuses Oishi Matora with Kōchō, although there is no great similarity in their styles, the illustration given as Kōchō's in that work really being taken from the *Songwa Hyaku-butsu* of 1833, by Matora.

Kōchō illustrated at least three very delightful books. They are the

Kōchō Gwafu: Sketches of many subjects. 2 vols. 1834. Colours.
Kōchō Gwafu Nihen: Supplement to above. 2 vols. 1849. Colours. Rare.
Suiun Gwafu: Various sketches. 1 vol. 1850. Colours.
Kōchō Ryakugwa: Various sketches. 2 vols. 1863. Colours.

Of these books the *Kōchō Gwafu* may occasionally be found, but the others in the original editions are rare and seldom in good condition if discovered; as for the *Kōchō Gwafu Nihen*, one has to see it to believe in its existence, it is so rare. Plates by Kōchō are also sometimes found in compilations of work by different artists of the time and in books of illustrated poems.

Kōchō left a son, Ueda KŌKEI, also known as SHŌFU, BAKU, and MORI-ICHI, who was working in Ōsaka toward the middle of the nineteenth century. Drawings by him are found in the *Osaka-Kippō Fu*, a collection of delightful coloured drawings by different Ōsaka artists published in 1856.

Nishiyama HŌYEN, who lived until 1865, received his training under Keibun, and then went to Ōsaka, where he established a branch of the Shijō school. He left a son, Shukei, of Ōsaka.

Two other artists trained in the Shijō school were Ōhara DONSHŪ and Tanaka NIKKWA. Both men were chiefly known as painters. Donshū was the son of Ōhara Donkyō of Kyōto, and a student of Shibata Gitō, working during the Tempō period. He was also known as Hi.

Tanaka NIKKWA, also known as BENJI, HAKKI, GETCHO, and FUMEI, received his training under Okamoto Toyohiko. He was well known in Kyōto for his landscapes and paintings of flowers and birds. He died in 1844. Donshū and Nikkwa together illustrated the *Kaikaku Kongen Roku*, a collection of poems on a temple festival. The drawings are very clever impressionistic sketches in black and white. The book was published in 1831.

These artists also made the plates in the *Ake Yasuke*, a *gwajo* of poems celebrating the erection of a Buddhist temple in Kyōto, the preface to which was written by Kitamura-an Tōshu, an artist and teacher of that city. The first plate is by Donshū and represents a picnic crowd on the banks of the river at Arashiyama after the " roof ceremony." The second plate by Nikkwa is a very clever drawing of the crowd toward evening with a storm approaching. The wind is swinging the lanterns and the people in the middle distance have become mere grey silhouettes showing through the dust. The plates are full-sized oblongs, and beautifully printed in colours. The book was published in 1831. After Nikkwa's death a most beautiful *kubari-hon* was printed by Ikkyūsai in Kaga, containing colour-plates from his work. This is the *Kyūhōdō Gwafu* and is made up of two rather large *gwajo* beautifully printed on rich and heavy paper. It is dated the Dragon Year of Ansei (1856).

Oda KAISEN (1785-1862), also called HYAKKOKU, was born at Akamagaseki in Nagato province. He studied in the Shijō academy and also under an artist of the Chinese school. He became very well known in the early nineteenth century.

Of all the artists of the eighteenth century who founded schools of their own, Maruyama ŌKYO was probably the most influential and popular. Although his academy in Kyōto was not the first one established there when this new-old art movement commenced to bubble and simmer, it became so much the most famous that in time it rather overshadowed the other studios.

Ōkyo was born in 1733, the son of a farmer who lived at Anada-mura in Tamba province. He was adopted in his boyhood by a *samurai* of the Minamoto clan, who, recognizing his unusual talent, called the attention of the *daimyō* of the province to some of the boy's work. Realizing that this young retainer had exceptional ability, the *daimyō* paid his expenses for a period of study in Kyōto under Ishida Yutei, who had been bred through several generations to the traditions of the Kanō school. At the time Ōkyo commenced his studies, the effects of Chin Nampin's teachings had reached Kyōto, and the *bunjingwa* movement had come to full tide there in Buson's and Taigadō's work; so that, influenced by both the realism of Chin Nampin and the impressionism of these two men, as well as by the teachings of Yutei, Ōkyo finally evolved a style of his own, and became, as other really great artists had become before him, an eclectic and the leader in a method of his own. This evolution was gradual and his work is classified by Japanese connoisseurs into the three styles which marked the halting-stations in it—the Kamigata-ye, the Shijō, and the Maruyama. He used different signatures during these periods, and was known as CHŪSEN, CHUKIN, SEIJUKWAN, SENSAI, ŌSUI GYŌFU, MONDO, KA-UN, ISSHŌ, TANSAI, and SENREI—the name Maruyama Ōkyo not being assumed until 1766, after he had become well settled in his Maruyama manner. His ordinary name was Kunii Ōkyo. The greater part of his life was spent in Kyōto, where he died in 1795, his tomb being in the little cemetery of Gōshin-ji temple.

The charm and beauty of Ōkyo's paintings are well known to every one who takes any interest in Japanese art. His books are less well known. They were, like those containing Kōrin's and Itchō's work, compilations made by students and published after his death. Among them are the

Yennō Gwafu: A collection of Ōkyo's drawings reproduced by Soken, one of his most famous pupils. Sixty-five coloured plates of flowers, birds, Chinese subjects, etc. 2 vols. 1837.
Ōkyo Gwaden: 2 vols.
Ōkyo Gwafu: Various drawings. 1 folio. 1850. Tints.
Shichi-nan Shichi-fuku Dzue: A rare and beautiful work made up of drawings copied from his famous paintings of the gods of happiness and misfortune. 3 *gwajō*. Colours.

Work by Ōkyo is also found in the collections of drawings so popular with the Japanese, as in the rare and valuable *gwajō* entitled *Shōshun Hōjō*, published in 1782.[1] This book consists of poems and drawings made by a party of celebrated poets and artists of the time, who met at the house of Emi Chokei at Kamigamo, Kyōto, on " a spring day of Anyei 6 " (1778), in celebration of his birthday. The gathering lasted several days, during which the poems were written and the sketches made which were after-

---

[1] A plate from this work is reproduced in Edward Dillon's *Arts of Japan*, p. 105.

wards published in this unique book. They were printed from stone blocks, the drawings being in white on a black ground and are heavily retouched with Chinese white. The last drawing in the collection is a spray of cherry blossoms by Ōkyo illustrating a poem by his host—thus evidently filling the place of honour.

Ōkyo left a son, Maruyama Ōzui (1765–1829), also known as GIHŌ and TAISHINDŌ. There is a plate by him in the *Meika Gwafu* of 1815; and the *Ōzui Gwafu*, a modern work published in 1880, contains reproductions of his drawings.

Ōju (1776–1815), an adopted son of Ōkyo's, and ŌSHIN (1789–1838), the son-in-law of Ōju, were also followers. Ōshin left a book entitled the *Kimbō Gwafu* published in 1839.

A large number of Ōkyo's pupils worked for wood-engraving and many beautiful books were produced by them.

Shaku GESSEN was among the earliest of these men, being only eight years younger than Ōkyo himself. He was born in Nagoya in 1741 and when only ten years old became an acolyte in a Buddhist temple of the Jōdo sect. It is said that his fondness for drawing often incurred the displeasure of his abbot, who advised him to spend his time in studying the Buddhist doctrines. He went to Yedo later, where he studied painting under Sakurai Sekkwan, and after this to Kyōto, becoming a student in the Maruyama academy. He worked also for a time with Buson and was associated with Goshun, Buson's pupil, in the painting of some screens ordered by a member of the Imperial Family in Kyōto. In 1774 Gessen was made high priest of the Jakushō temple in Yamada in Ise province. This temple had become very dilapidated, but by painting almost constantly and selling his pictures, which by this time commanded high prices, Gessen was able in a few years not only to completely repair it, but to build a new treasury where the valuable Buddhist manuscripts, old books, and pictures belonging to the temple could be stored. Gessen also gave large sums of money to the poor, and in 1805 he deposited with the Government several thousand yen, the yearly interest on which was to be used in the relief of the helpless and needy. He divided the remainder of his property a year or two later and died in 1809.

Gessen's ordinary name was Genzui, but as artist signatures he used the names TANYA, GYOKUSEI, Sorio SANJIN, and Jakushō Shujin GESSEN. His work shows little of Ōkyo's influence, his admiration of Chinese masters being much more evident both in his paintings and book illustrations. Gessen was especially remarkable in his drawing of faces, the individuality and marvellous intensity of expression which he was able to convey giving his work a distinction which is unmistakable. Although a painter rather than an illustrator, he made the drawings in a few books. These include the

Gessen Gwafu.
Gessen Dzusan: Chinese sages. 3 vols. 1784.

and a plate in the *Gusai Shachu Gwafu*, a collection of drawings by artists of the Chinese school (1 vol., 1798).

Taniguchi GESSŌ (1773–1865), a pupil who carried on Gessen's teachings, came to Kyōto from Ise. He was also known as SETATSU, MOSEN, and CHIZETSUAN. A book illustrated by him called the *Haikai Hyaku Gwasan*, a version of the Hundred Poets, appeared in two volumes in 1814, published by a house in Wakayama.

Komai GENKI (1746–1797) is ranked by Fenollosa as one of the greatest of Ōkyo's pupils. He was born in Kyōto and used as other signatures the names KONOSUKE, MINAMOTO, and SHION.

Nagasawa ROSETSU, one of the ten famous pupils of Ōkyo, was born in 1754 of a *samurai* family of Yodo in Yamashiro province, south of Kyōto. It is said that his unwillingness to be completely dominated by Ōkyo's teachings, and his propensity for following his own ideas as to technique, led to such friction in the school that he was finally expelled. Rosetsu used as other signatures the names HYŌKEI and GYO—the last from a slight episode in his student days under Ōkyo, when passing a frozen pool one winter morning on his way to the studio, he saw a fish struggling to free itself from the encircling ice. Speaking of it to Ōkyo, the latter replied that his own struggles in art were on a parallel and that he must emulate the fish in his endeavours to reach the great sea of art. The signature Gyo (fish) was adopted from this incident.

After his years of study, Rosetsu became painter to the feudal lord of Yodo. His sudden and mysterious death in 1799 followed his having been loaned by his own lord to the *daimyō* of Aki to do some work in the latter's castle, thereby causing intense jealousy among the own followers of that noblemen. The suspicion that he was poisoned, although never verified, has never died out.

The *fusuma* by Rosetsu at the Summer Palace in Kyōto are very famous, and his paintings are highly valued by Japanese connoisseurs. His style was simple and highly impressionistic, resembling Goshun's manner rather than Ōkyo's. His work for wood-engraving was incidental to his painting, and there are but few books by him. Among them the *Daimon Koshinden* contains drawings of the Bon festival of mid-August in Kyōto. It appeared in one slender volume in 1786 and is a very rare book. The *Rosetsu Gwafu* consists of various sketches printed in colours. There is also a *Rosetsu Gwafu* which is a late work containing coloured plates from his paintings, published a few years ago by Yamada of Kyōto.

Rosetsu left an adopted son, Nagasawa ROSHŪ, also known as DONKŌ and NANKYO, who lived between 1766 and 1847; and Tsuruoka ROSUI may have been an early pupil. The latter artist left a rather remarkable and very rare work published in two large rolls, entitled *Sumidagawa Ryōgan Ichiran*, with the date of Temmei 1st, or 1781. The drawings are in black and white and form long, connected panoramic views of the river, bridges, and towns along the Sumida river. Colouring applied by hand has been used in some sets.

ROHŌ and ROGETSU, the son and pupil of Roshū, were late followers of Rosetsu's style.

Nishimura NANTEI, also known as YOSHO and Kawamura NANTEI, was born in Ōsaka in 1754. He studied under Ōkyo in the Maruyama school and finally established a studio of his own at Shijō-Muromachi in Kyōto. He died in 1834. He was a painter, a designer of *surimono*, and an illustrator. The *Nantei Gwafu* of three volumes, published in Kyōto in 1804, contains fifty-one double-page drawings of so clever and amusing a character that one can look at them by the hour with pleasure. They really have more of the Shijō school technique than Ōkyo's, although there is no record of his having studied there. A supplementary volume to the foregoing work containing slightly coloured sketches was published in one volume in 1823, called the *Nantei Gwafu Kohen*. It is a trifle smaller than the books of the first series. Drawings by Nantei are also occasionally found in collections of illustrated poems, and albums of drawings by contemporary artists.

Although little is known in regard to his life, Yamaguchi SOKEN is ranked among Ōkyo's ten great pupils. He was born in Kyōto in 1758 and died there in 1818. Other signatures used by him were SANSAI and HAKUGO.

Soken illustrated several very interesting books which of late years have become extremely difficult to find in the first editions. Among them are the

Kyō Gwayen: Copies from Kanō Tanyū and other artists. 3 vols. 1775.
Yamato Jimbutsu Gwafu: Humorous drawings of everyday scenes. 1st series. 3 vols. 1799.
Yamato Jimbutsu Gwafu: 2nd series. 3 vols. 1804.
Soken Gwafu Sogwa-no-bu: Flowers and plants. 3 vols. 1804.
Soken Gwafu: Unsigned. 3 vols. 1806.
Soken Sansui Gwafu: Landscapes. Black and white and grey. 2 vols. 1918. Rare and beautiful.

The clever and delightful *Yamato Jimbutsu Gwafu* is Soken's best-known book. The black-and-white drawings are excellent examples of the contemporary Kyōto work. The original edition of the first series is rarely found now, although one may sometimes pick up odd volumes and so in time form a complete set.

In the *Sansui Gwafu* the grey tone added to the black and white gives a richness of effect almost incredible, while the superb composition and placing of masses produces the effect of great pictures rather than book illustrations.

Hatta KOSHŪ became a follower of Maruyama Ōkyo after having studied for a time under Murakami Tōshu. His style bears considerable resemblance to Ōkyo's. He lived between 1759 and 1822 and was also known as SHI-EI, HACHIDA, and KIKEN. His principal work for wood-engraving was in the *Koshū Gwafu*, published in one volume in 1812—one of the most charming and characteristic books printed in Kyōto at this time. It consists of delicately coloured landscapes, flowers, people, etc., in which both the drawing and composition are beyond praise. The plate representing fishing nets hung to dry on a beach, with its receding perspective and simple colouring, and the one of an arching snow-covered bridge through which is seen a winter landscape, are delightful examples of impressionistic work.

A pupil of Koshū's, Fukuchi or Keichūrō HAKUYEI, also illustrated a few delightful books. The *Ena-oshi*[1] *Gwafu* is a little volume of extremely interesting sketches made by taking meaningless blots and masses of black, and by adding a few touches making them into intelligible pictures. The book is signed Keichuro Hakuyei, and was first published in 1808 with the drawings in black and white. In this form it is exceedingly rare. Another edition containing about half of the drawings was printed in colours in 1852 under the title of *Sokuseki Gwafu*.

The *Roku-roku Kyōka Sen*, a collection of humorous poems illustrated by Hakuyei, appeared in 1814.

In 1834 the *Kyōka Riren Gwafu* was published in two *gwajo* with a preface by Maruyama Oshin. It contains thirty-seven delicately coloured double-page plates of landscapes and figures in landscape settings which are very charming. In them Hakuyei used an entirely different style, and the work suggests Hokusai so strongly that it is probable he came under that famous artist's influence toward the latter part of his life. The set is excessively rare.

Kikuchi YŌSAI, whose ordinary name was Takeyasu, was born in Kyōto in 1787, of a family of wealth and position. He was a scholar and writer in addition to being an artist, and although a follower of the Shijō school, it was his aim to bring back to popularity the classical Tosa work. He

[1] M. Revon (*Hoksai*, p. 103) speaks of the game of " *éna-oshi*, qu'on ne pratique plus guère aujourd'hui; a tort peut-être, car, au dire des artistes, il constituait un merveilleux exercice de la main."

was given the title of Hōgen by the Government before his death in 1878 and is ranked very highly by the Japanese both as a writer and an artist. His life work was the *Zenken Kojitsu*, commenced in 1836 and completed in 1868. It consists of twenty volumes of biographies of famous men illustrated by line drawings of great force. The series forms a striking work and deals with a dignified subject in a noble and dignified manner. Yōsai also illustrated an historical work known as the *Yōsai Rekishi Gwafu*, and copies of some of his paintings made by his pupil Matsumoto Fuko are found in the *Kikuchi Yōsai Gwafu*, published a few years ago.

Seiyo GASSO, also known as Seiyoshi Seiyo SANJIN, and SUI-EN, was a follower of the Shijō school, who is said to have come to Kyōto from Inaba province. He was a contemporary of Hokusai and some of his work suggests that he may also have come under that master's influence. He illustrated the

Yoitoyu Hyakunin Isshu: Fantastic drawings of the Hundred Poets. 1 vol. 1803. Colours.
Kyōyei Miyako Meibutsu Shū: Poems on celebrated places in Kyōto. 3 vols. 1829. Colours.
Kyōka Hyakki Yakyō: Humorous poems on the " Monsters of the Night." Illustrated by Seiyo and Kogaku. 1 vol. 1829. Colours.
Kyōka Rantei Jo: Poems in the style of Rantei Kyokusui. 1 vol. 1831. Colours.
Bijin Ryōkwa Shū or *Bijin Hishikwa Shū:* " Beauties of the *hishi*-flower collection." A book on the Yoshiwara. 1 vol. 1831. Colours.
Kyōka Tagoto-no-hana: Humorous poems. Illustrated by Seiyo in collaboration with Gyokuto, Hakuyei, Baitei, and other artists. 1 small vol. 1834. Colours.
Seiyo Nampitsu: Various sketches. 1 folio in colours. Published in 1834. Charming and rare.
Kyōka Fusō Meisho Dzue: Humorous verses on famous places. Compiled by Kwaiyen. Illustrated by Seiyo. 1 vol. 1836. Colours.
Ryakugwa Hyakunin Isshu: The Hundred Poets. 1 vol. 1851. Colours.

Niwa TŌKEI (not to be confused with Tōkei the *bunjingwa* painter) was working in Kyōto a little later in the century. He was a native of Owari and used as other signatures the names MAYA, KYO, SHIKEN, KO-IN, and KANSHIRŌ. Among the books illustrated by him are the

Settsu Meisho Shū: Description of the province of Settsu. 1798.
Kawachi Meisho Dzue: Description of the province of Kawachi. 6 vols. 1801.
Honchō Meika Gwafu: 1 vol. 1812.
Meika Gwafu: Collection of coloured drawings compiled by Niwa Tōkei from work by many artists of the impressionistic schools. Originally published in three volumes, of which the middle volume is rarely found. 1815. Rare and delightful.
Asagao Hinrui Dzuko: Different varieties of morning glories. 1 vol. 1815. Rare. Colours.

Nakajima Raishō (1796–1871), also known as Jinzūdō, was a well-known artist and teacher toward the middle of the nineteenth century. Many of the famous modern artists were his pupils.

CHAPTER VI

THE IMPRESSIONISTS: THE GANKU AND THE CHINESE SCHOOLS

HE Ganku school, founded by Utanosuke Ganku, was another of the famous Kyōto centres where the impressionistic movement flourished. The technique of this school was founded upon the teachings of Chin Nampin, the noted Chinese master, who established a studio in Nagasaki about 1730. Originally the work was confined to pictures of flowers and birds, but eventually it broadened in scope, and as the Japanese artists passed on its teachings, other subjects—figures, landscapes, and animals—also came to be used.

GANKU, who became one of the most renowned exponents of Chin Nampin's style, was born in 1748 in the old city of Kanazawa, where his father, Kishi Michihisa, had retired after his service as a *samurai* under the Daimyō of Toyama in Etchū province. Ganku himself was in the service of Prince Arisugawa of the Imperial Household, and is said to have taken up the study of painting at first as an amusement, making what must have been a long journey in those days to Nagasaki, where he entered the famous Chinese school presided over at that time by Kumashiro Yūhi, one of Chin Nampin's early pupils. After a period of study there Ganku returned to Kyōto, where he opened a studio of his own, taking students who admired and wished to study the method of the famous Chinese master.

Ganku's real name was Kishi Masa-aki. He used as artist signatures the names SAIKI or Saihakki MASA-AKI, RANSAI, KYOSEN, KWAYŌ, DŌKŌKWAN, KAKWANDŌ, KYŪSŌRŌ, KOTŌKWAN, TENKAIKUTSU, and FUNZEN. Toward the close of his life he was given the title of Lord of Echizen. He received a number of commissions from the Court and some of his most famous screens are in the imperial collection. His pictures of tigers became especially renowned, and it is said that the first of these animals ever brought to Japan was one which a wealthy Chinese (for whom he had painted a set of screens) sent to a distant province of China for, as a gift to the artist in special appreciation of his work.

Ganku died in 1838, leaving a son, Uchida Gantai (1784–1865), also known as Takudō, Kuniaki, and Dōkōkwan; a son-in-law, Aoki Renzan, (died in 1859) who took the name of Kishi after entering Ganku's family, and also signed himself Gantoku; and an adopted son, Kishi Ganryō (1798–1852). All of these artists collaborated with Ganku in much of his work.

Ganku himself was a painter rather than an illustrator, and the delightful and very rare *Ransai Gwafu* or the *Nampin, Sensei Gwafu*, containing drawings in both black and white and colours after Chin Nampin, published in eight folios in 1772, is one of the few books left by him.[1] Many of his pupils, however, some of whom became very famous, illustrated charming books.

Kishi Chikudō (1825–1897), also known as Ganki, the adopted son of Kishi Renzan and the grandson of Ganku, became one of the most noted pupils of the latter artist. He lived in Kyōto and illustrated the *Chikudō Kwachō Gwafu*, birds and flowers; and made the drawings which were eventually edited by Gen-Chikudō in the beautiful *Chikudō Iboku* (2 *gwajō*, 1903). He was survived by a son, Kinsui.

An earlier CHIKUDŌ (Kino) was a pupil of Murakami Tōshu. A remarkable book by him entitled the *Chikudō Gwafu* is in some of the French catalogues attributed to Kishi Chikudō. This may be because the edition usually found, although even this is extremely rare, was published about the time that Kishi Chikudō was working. The original *Chikudō Gwafu* contains a preface by Minagawa Gen, a writer and artist of the Chinese school, and was first published in Kwansei 12 (1800). It contains eleven double-page colour-plates mounted in *gwajō* form. In 1815 another volume was added and a second edition issued, while a third edition appeared still later but with much poorer colour. Both of the early editions are almost impossible to obtain now. The drawings are of the most pronounced *bunjingwa* type and most beautifully printed on very fine paper. It forms a very great treasure in any collection of the Kyōto work, and is a fine example of the books of the impressionist schools.

Among Ganku's followers who worked for wood-engraving, Kawamura BUMPŌ takes high rank. Little is known in regard to his life, even the dates for his birth and death remaining uncertain. He is said to have been a native of Kyōto, however, and used as other signatures the names KI, SHUNSEI, BASEI, GOYU, SHUYOKWAN, CHIKURIKWAN, KIMPAYEN, and HAKURYŪDŌ. His work indicates that he was familiar with many styles and had studied the ultra-impressionism of Buson and the classic Chinese work, as well as Ganku's transmission of Chin Nampin's method. Hi-Kangen,[2] a Chinese artist, also had his influence upon Bumpō, and the drawings in the *Bumpō Sogwa* and the *Bumpō Kangwa* bear much resemblance to some of the sketches in the *Hi-Kangen Sansui Gwashiki* (1787). Bumpō's books, although little known in Europe and America, are among the most delightful

---

[1] There is a later edition of 1802.   [2] *I.e.*, Fei Han-yüan. He came to Japan in 1734.

CHAP. VI] JAPANESE BLOCK-PRINTING

and typical examples of the work done by the men of these Kyōto schools. A list of them includes the following:

Bumpō Sogwa: Wonderful little sketches of people at various occupations. 1 medium vol. 1800. Slightly coloured.
Bumpō Sogwa: Same as foregoing, but without colour. Rare.
Ariwara Bunko: A collection of poems illustrated by many artists of the Shijō schools. Last volume given up to drawings by Bumpō of famous poets, many of whom were his contemporaries. 4 vols. 1802. Black and white. Extremely rare.
Bumpō Kangwa: A companion volume to the *Bumpō Sogwa.* 1 vol. 1803. Slightly coloured.
Kōko-Shōkei Ichiran: Drawings of figures, landscapes, houses, etc. No date.
Shunkyō ("Spring Thoughts"): Poems illustrated by Bumpō in collaboration with Goshun, Keibun, Kiho, Watanabe Kwazan, and other artists. No date. A *kubari-hon.*
Kikido-kuri: Poems illustrated by Bumpō and other Kyōto artists. 1 vol. 1804.
Teito Gakei Ichiran: Famous temples and scenes in Kyōto. 4 vols., marked North, South, East and West. 1st vol. published in 1807; last in 1809. (A second edition about 1813.) Colours.
Teito Gakei Ichiran: On *tōshi* paper. In black and white. Rare.
Kangwa Shinan: Drawings of trees, grasses, buildings, bridges, and figures in the first volume; rocks and landscapes in the second; and people and landscapes in the third. 3 vols. 1811. Colours. (A second edition in 1813.) One of Bumpō's most charming books.
Bumpō Gwafu: Various sketches. According to the advertising pages in the first edition this work was intended to be issued in ten volumes. For some reason this remained an unfinished undertaking, and is considered complete in three volumes, the first of which, however, is much rarer than the other two. 1st vol. dated 1811; last 1814. Colours.
Kimpayen Gwafu: Flowers and plants. 1 vol. 1820. Colours without contours. Rare.
Bumpō Sansui Gwafu: Landscapes. 1 vol. 1824. Colours.

In 1811 a delightful work which was the joint undertaking of Bumpō and Watanabe Nangaku appeared. The original edition, which is so rare as practically never to be found, consisted of two volumes, the first containing poems with the title *Kaidō Kyōka Awase,* and the second, called the *Kaidō Sogwa,* made up of thirty-six drawings alternately by Bumpō and Nangaku, representing incidents in a journey made by them along the Tōkaidō road. In this edition of this work the second volume contains a preface by Fumiya Shigetaka giving a short description of the book, and a list and description of the sketches; the first drawing being a double-page plate of a coolie in a straw raincoat leading a horse bearing great bundles of charcoal, signed Nangaku. Just what happened to cause the next edition of this book to appear in only one volume, retaining the name of the first book, although the *kyōka* or poems are omitted and the preface, list of sketches, and first page of the first cut lacking, is not known. It is supposed that part of the blocks were destroyed by fire, and an edition—the one usually found, although even this also is extremely rare—was printed from those saved, which fortunately were the ones for the drawings instead of the poems.

This rare book not only contains some of Bumpō's best and most characteristic work, but almost the only drawings done by Nangaku especially intended for wood-engraving. The plates are printed in black, grey, and a yellow-pink, which very curiously give the effect of full and rich colour, and it is not until one has counted the colours used that he realizes that this effect was gained with such a minimum of effort.

Work by Bumpō is also found in a delightful compilation of drawings, called the *Keijō Gwayen*, published in Kyōto in 1814.

The *Kimpayen Gwafu*, containing drawings of flowers and printed in colours, without the use of lines to any extent, which appeared in 1820, is one of Bumpō's rarest books and is seldom found now in the first edition. It resembles considerably the *Kwa Ryakugwa-shiki* by Keisai Masayoshi, which was published seven years earlier, and which although a much more famous book than the *Kimpayen Gwafu* is no more delightful.

Bumpō left three sons, Kawamura Ippō,[1] Kawamura Nihō,[1] and Kawamura Kihō (an adopted son). Ippō was also known as Bumpei. He illustrated the *Haikai Ogura Hyaku Shū*, a collection of poems with a dashing little black-and-white sketch on each page, signed Kawamura Ippō (1 vol. 1708).

Kawamura Nihō left several plates in albums of the time and many very impressionistic and charming *surimono*.

Kawamura Kihō lived in Kyōto between 1781 and 1852, and was also known as Shun, Goitsu, and Chikurikwan. He illustrated the *Kwafuku Nimpitsu*, a volume of humorous coloured sketches representing lucky and unlucky days, which appeared in 1809. It is rarer than any of Bumpō's books, and is seldom found now in the first edition. The drawings rival that artist's work in spontaneity, and are of the most extreme impressionism. Kihō also illustrated the *Kyōka Kotori Zugai*, poems with a small ink sketch on each page (1 vol. 1809), and the *Kihō Gwafu*, delightful coloured sketches of everyday life (1 vol. 1824).

Some of the best work done by Kihō for wood-engraving was in his numerous *surimono*, which are very characteristic of the Kyōto schools of this time and are beautifully printed.

Oku BUMMEI was a Kyōto artist who is said to have been a pupil of both Ōkyo and Bumpō. His name suggests Bumpō, but the dates of his books are earlier than any by that artist. It seems more probable, therefore, that whatever connection there may have been between the two men would have been one in which Bummei took precedence.

Other names used by him were SADA-AKIRA, MANKI, SEIKA, and RIKU-CHINSAI. Among the books containing illustrations by him are the following:

Tōkaidō Meisho Dzue: A description of the Tōkaidō road. Bummei with Mitsusada, Soken, Shunsensai, Ishida, Yutei, Soyen, Nagatoshi, and Keisai Masayoshi. 6 vols. 1797. Rare.
Miyako Rinsen Dzue: A Kyōto guide-book. Bummei with other artists. 5 vols. 1799.

And a book of coloured drawings of fishes, birds, etc., with Bunko and Geppo.

[1] Not to be confused, of course, with Mori Ippō and Mori Nihō of Ōsaka.

Watanabe NANGAKU is usually spoken of as one of Maruyama Ōkyo's pupils, but he also certainly studied at the Ganku school, and is placed by Burty[1] as a follower of that artist. He lived in Kyōto between 1766 and 1813 and used as other signatures the names IWAO, ISEKI, TSABURA, and GAN. He was a contemporary and friend of Kawamura Bumpō and the teacher of Ōnishi Chinnen.

Nangaku's collaboration with Bumpō in the *Kaidō Kyōka Awase* and the *Kaidō Sogwa* has already been mentioned. With the exception of the *Hokku Shita-ye*, a *kubari-hon* of striking and highly impressionistic illustrations of poems, published in 1810 (slightly coloured), and some illustrated poems and plates in certain albums of work by different artists of the Kyōto schools, Nangaku is not known to have done other work for wood-engraving.

KŌGAKU, also known as SENSHŪ, was the son of Watanabe Nangaku and a pupil of Toyohiko. Work by him is found in the *Ginyei Bokuseki*, a compilation of poems and drawings by different artists published in 1837.

Suzuki NANREI, also known as JUN and KWANSUIKEN, is said to have been a Yedo artist who first studied under Toyo and then came to Kyōto and worked with Nangaku. He lived until about 1844, and was chiefly famous for his pictures of birds, flowers, and landscapes. Plates by him are found in several albums.

Of all the disciples of Ganku, however, Ōnishi CHINNEN (1791–1851) has, perhaps, left the most interesting and characteristic books. He was keeper of one of the Government rice warehouses in Yedo, where he studied under Tani Bunchō, later going to Kyōto and entering Nangaku's studio. He is said to have been a pupil of Soken's also for a time. His work shows allegiance to both Nangaku and Bunchō, and some of his drawings of flowers and grasses indicate that Kōrin's work had had its influence upon him, as earlier it had had upon Nangaku. Other names used by Chinnen were SONAN, DAIJU, UNKADŌ and KINCHŌ (?). He illustrated the

Ehon Azuma-no-Teburi: A charming collection of drawings. 1 folio. 1829. Colours.
Taihei Yusho: The second edition of the *Ehon Azuma Teburi*. 1830. Colours.
Sonan Gwafu: Drawings of figures, flowers, fruit, birds, etc. 1 folio. 1835. Colours.
Kinchō Gwafu: Various sketches. Listed in the Gillot Catalogue as by Chinnen. 2 vols. 1834.
Seika Jō: A very rare work made up of coloured plates by a number of artists of the impressionistic schools. In it is a superb double-page plate of a peacock by Chinnen. Privately published in two large *gwajo* by a printing house at Ueno, a little place south of Kyōto in Iga province. 1848. Colours.
Shin Gyoku Jō: A collection of drawings by different artists, including a double-page plate of a flowering branch and a butterfly, the former signed Chinnen and the latter Tani Bunchō. No date. Colours. Rare.

---

[1] See *Collection Ph. Burty* (*Catalogue de Peintures et d'Estampes Japonaises*), p. 45.

The technique in Chinnen's work is amazingly like that in the drawings of some of the modern French artists. It has a dash and spontaneity in the drawing and a richness of colour which gives his books a high rank among the Japanese *ehon*. The *Sonan Gwafu* has become very difficult to find of late years and all of his books are increasing rapidly in value.

Although few details in regard to the life of Aikawa MINWA are available, the technique of his work makes it seem probable that he too was a follower of Ganku. He was an Ōsaka man and used as other signatures the names HIDENARI, SETSUZAN, AIKATEI, and GŌSENTEI. He made the charming reproductions of Kōrin's work in the *Kōrin Gwashiki* of 1818, and left original and very interesting drawings in the *Onna Hyaku-fu*, a book on the occupations of women, printed in colours and published in 1813. Other books illustrated by him were the *Mangwa Hyaku Jō*, tinted sketches of one hundred women, published in 1809 and again in 1814; the *Hen-gaku Kihan* (in collaboration with Kitagawa Harunari), a work devoted to the votive tablets belonging to Kiyomidzu Temple and the Gion shrine of Kyōto, written by Hayami Shungyosai, and published in two volumes in 1819; and the *Sōgwa Tsushin Gwafu*, containing drawings of animals, landscapes, birds, flowers, etc., in one volume, also in 1819.

Nakabayashi CHIKUTŌ, who lived between 1775 and 1853, was a native of Owari, but spent most of his life in Kyōto, where he studied under Miyazaki Impo. He was known for his rather peculiar technique, using his paint as dry as possible. His work was chiefly in landscape painting, although some of the pictures of bamboos left by him are very fine. Other signatures used by him were SEISHŌ (NARIMASA), HAKUMEI, TAIGEN-AN, YUSAI, and TŌZAN INSHI. Among the books illustrated by him were the

Chikutō Gwafu: Landscapes. 1 vol. 1812. Slightly coloured.
Yūsai Gwafu: A large folio of charming colour-plates in the Chinese style. On *tōshi*. Privately printed in Tempo 2 (1831).
Chikutō Sansui Gwakō: Landscapes. 1813.
Chikutō Shikunshi Gwafu: Flowers, fruit, birds, etc. Two large *gwajō*. 1831. Black and grey.
Chikutō Sanjin Jimbutsu: 1852.

Shiokawa BUNRIN was a landscape painter of Kyōto who lived between 1814 and 1877. He studied under Tani Bunchō of Yedo and also with Ganku, and worked for a time under Toyohiko of the Shijō school. He left a well-known set of folios of birds and flowers in colours.

Kondō ARIYOSHI, a descendant of the Ōsaka Kondō family, whose Yedo branch formed the famous Torii school of artists, was a pupil of Ganku's about 1834. He lived in Kyōto, and although he worked to some extent for wood-engraving, he was chiefly known as a painter. The

Taisei Shin-Shafu is a collection of his drawings reproduced by Nambara Keisho. It contains coloured plates of flowers, birds, insects, fishes, etc., and was published in two volumes in 1888.

Although Kyōto is regarded as the centre of the impressionistic movement, there were several noted Nagoya men who belonged to it. Chō GESSHŌ was the foremost of these artists. He was born in Hikone in 1771, the son of a bookbinder and mounter of *kakemono*. Disliking his father's work, he finally obtained permission to study painting, and entered the studio of Ichikawa Kunkei, who had gone to Kyōto from Nagoya some years earlier. This artist was quick to recognize Gesshō's unusual ability, and helped him to establish a studio in Nagoya after his work in Kyōto was completed.

A painting of peacocks and chrysanthemums which Gesshō painted for the Daimyō of Owari was considered so remarkable that the latter sent it as a gift to the Shōgun in Yedo. Here it came under the notice of Tani Bunchō, who was private instructor in painting to the Shōgun's family and at the height of his popularity in the capital. It is said that he was much struck with the picture and greatly astonished to find that an artist of such pronounced talent was content to remain in Nagoya. Every inducement was used to persuade Gesshō to come to Yedo and open a studio there, but without avail. His indifference to fame and money was as great as his carelessness in regard to the rules and customs of ordinary life. He even refused to be adopted as the heir of a wealthy artist friend of Nagoya, fearing that this might cripple his freedom. Marriage was finally forced upon him, the story being that his pupils and friends conspired against him one spring day when he was away on a sketching trip, and moved all his things into a clean new house, and upon his return insisted that he must marry and have a wife to keep things in order. Whether the prospective bride was also chosen and in the house, the story does not tell. One hopes that the collection of rare birds and orchids and other precious plants which Gesshō had made was well cared for by the woman who was in this business-like way selected to superintend the new *ménage*.

Gesshō used as other signatures the names YUKISADA, SUIKADŌ, GENKAI, HARI, GENKEI, GYŌTEI, and KAISUKE. He became especially noted for his charming and original drawings in interpretation of a kind of poem which was very popular, and these books, called *haigwa*, are greatly prized by Japanese collectors. His death occurred in 1832 and his tomb is in the cemetery of Chōyei-ji Temple, south of Nagoya Castle.

Gesshō's earliest work for wood-engraving was in the rare little *gwajo* called *Meitoku Saya*, published in 1790 when he was nineteen years old. It contains coloured plates illustrating poems on the classical Chinese garden party of the Meitoku period, when verses in teacups were floated down the stream to be caught and added to by other guests. Other works illustrated by him were the

Zōku Hakoya Bunko: A collection of poems with illustrations in black and white, in imitation of those in the *Hakoya Bunko* of 1768, a work greatly admired by Gesshō. 5 vols. 1798. Rare and charming.
Shin Hakoya Bunko: A supplementary set to the foregoing. 2 vols. 1818. Also extremely rare.
To-jō: Drawings by Gesshō and his pupils. 1 vol. 1811.
Fugyō or *Fukei Gwasō*, or sometimes listed as *Fukei Gwafu:* Various delightful drawings illustrating old legends. 1 folio. 1817. Rare in this edition, but can sometimes be found in a reprint of a few years later in which the title-page and preface are missing. Colours.
Gesshō Sogwa: Sketches much in the style of the *Keisai Sogwa*. 1 vol. No date. Colours. Rare and delightful.
Jimbutsu Gwayen: Very clever and amusing drawings of people. In two series of one and two volumes.
Kwashi Bukuro: Various drawings by Gesshō and other artists. 1 vol. 1818.

The advertising pages of the *Fugyō Gwasō* list the *Kanko Shogwa*, published in two series of three volumes each. It is not certain that this work was ever issued, however, and as far as I can learn no Japanese collector, all of whom are very keen about Gesshō's work, has ever found a copy.

Although Gesshō is not known to have illustrated any other books than those listed, one often finds a plate by him in albums of contemporary work and in collections of illustrated poems.

Gesshō left a pupil, Ōishi MATORA, who worked in very much his style. Matora was born in 1792, the son of Koizumi Ryūsuke, a physician of Nagoya, but later was adopted into the Ōishi family. He first studied under an artist of the Tosa school, but afterwards entered Gesshō's studio and quickly became the best of all that artist's pupils. In much of his work the technique is so similar to that of Gesshō that if it were not signed a picture by him might easily be taken as that artist's work.

Matora is said to have had a vast store of the most accurate historical knowledge, and became very proficient in painting historical scenes and war pictures in which every detail of the armour, weapons, and setting was of absolute accuracy. He was as eccentric as he was talented, however, and unfortunately given to drink. After a disturbance in a Nagoya teahouse, he left that city and took up his work in Ōsaka. He is also said to have been insane for a time.

Although much better known as an artist than a poet, Matora was nevertheless very clever at the composition of the little seventeen-syllable poems so popular among the Japanese. He died in 1833, a comparatively young man, and his tomb is in the cemetery of Shinpuku-ji Temple in Nagoya.

His work for wood-engraving was done almost entirely during the last five years of his life, the *Sogwa Kokufū* of 1828 being, as far as is known, his first book. This illustrates in a series of extremely interesting coloured drawings various Japanese festivals, customs, etc., and was published in two beautifully printed folios,[1] which have become excessively rare.

In the following year, 1829, the first volume of the five composing the *Jin-ji Andon* appeared. This was also by Matora and consists of spirited sketches printed in colours to be used as designs on the paper lanterns used at the Bon festival.

The *Itsukushima Dzue* is a description of Itsukushima and its famous Shinto shrine, illustrated by numerous drawings, and published in Hiroshima in 1832. This was followed by a supplementary series in five volumes entitled the *Itsukushima Ema-Kagami*, containing drawings of the *ema* or votive tablets, antique manuscripts, and other treasures belonging to this renowned shrine. The bindings of these books are embossed with the temple *mon*.

The *Hyakunin Isshu Issekwa* consists of stories of the Hundred Poets, and is illustrated with numerous drawings in black and white. It was published in nine volumes in 1833.

A work on the occupations and etiquette for women, called the *Onna Shōgaku*, appeared in one large volume in 1833. This contains illustrations printed in black. It is not of very great interest, although somewhat rare.

A book called the *Eireki-Dai-Zassho* is listed in the advertising pages of one of Matora's other books, but has not been available for a detailed description.

The *Sogwa Hyaku-Butsu*, literally "sketches of one hundred things," was issued in two medium-sized volumes in 1833, and was probably Matora's last work for wood-engraving. It is also among the most interesting, and contains humorous sketches printed in colours representing various episodes of everyday life. Strange in his *Japanese Illustration* gives a reproduction from this work of Matora's, but calls it a drawing from the *Kōchō Gwafu*, although it bears no great resemblance to Kōchō's work.

Numada GESSAI was another Nagoya artist of this time whom Revon places as a pupil of Bokusen. He was also a follower of Gesshō. The dates for his birth and death are given as 1787 and 1864, but the first must be several years too late, as books illustrated by him appeared in 1798. He used as other signatures the names HANZAEMON, HANSHIRŌ, and Utamasa GESSAI. Drawings by him are found in the

Eigyoku Gwakan: A collection of spirited impressionistic sketches in black and white. 3 vols. 1798.
Gwako Hikketsu: Drawing book attributed to Gessai. 1 vol. 1799.
Ehon Imagawa Jō: Etiquette for women. 2 vols. 1824.

Yorita (?) KUHO of Nagoya was also of this group of artists, but he did little work for wood-engraving. He was chiefly known for his paintings of

[1] There is also an edition of same year in which no colour blocks were used.

bamboos. One beautiful folio was left by him, however, entitled the *Shinkoku Kinshi Gwafu*, containing drawings in black and white and grey of orchids and bamboos, which was published in 1813.

THE CHINESE SCHOOL

The Chinese school was another strong influence in Japanese art of this time, and its followers left many beautiful books. Its origin may be traced to the downfall of the Ming dynasty in China (1662), which was both preceded and followed by periods of unrest and turmoil that caused many Chinese artists and writers to seek refuge in Japan.

Among these men were Shinyetsu Tōkō or Kōchū (1639–1695), a priest who settled in the province of Mita; Ingen, Sokuhi, Kō Unkaku, Itsunen, Moku-an, and I-fukyū,[1] all artists of the " southern school " who brought with them their *bunjingwa* art and Confucian ethics and scholarship, and settled in and around Kyōto and Yedo, while Chin Nampin, Sō-Shigan, and Hōsaiyen represented the realistic Ming school, and established studios in Nagasaki, Kyōto, and Yedo respectively.

It is probably to some of these Chinese refugees rather than to the print designers of Yedo that colour-printing in Japan should be attributed, for books and pictures printed in colours were brought by them from China early in the seventeenth century, and it is certain that their introduction into Japan would have been followed by experiments there in the colour process as soon as the work became known.

The *Jinkō-ki* of 1627 belonging to Mr. Kobayashi of Tōkyō has already been spoken of, and the page printed in colours which it contains resembles the angular Chinese drawings sufficiently to suggest Chinese influence.

Many Japanese collectors say that a Japanese reproduction of the charming Chinese book, the *Kaishiyen Gwafu*, in colours, was published in Yedo in the first year of Enkyō (1744). I have never seen this edition, but there was a very delightful copy printed by Nakagawa Tōshirō and Hishiya Magobei (Yedo) in 1817. The drawings are of orchids, bamboos, landscapes, etc., and are very beautiful and printed in a superb fashion.

Ōoka Shunboku, whose reproductions from ancient masterpieces are so well known, also gained the idea of colour work from these Chinese refugees, and his *Minchō Seidō Gwayen* of 1746 is in pure Ming style, the drawings of flowers, plants, insects, etc., being printed in colours in imitation of Chinese books of the same kind. (See Chapter IV., p. 70.)

Hōsaiyen,[2] one of the Chinese teachers in Yedo, himself illustrated

---

[1] One of Taigadō's teachers. The drawings in the two volumes of the *I-fukyū Gwafu* (1803) are by I-fukyū and Taigadō working in collaboration. I-fukyū was known in China as I Hai; he settled at Nagasaki in 1727.

[2] Known in China as Fang Chi; he settled at Nagasaki in 1772.

a work on drawing entitled the *Saiseiyen Gwaden*[1] published in Japan in 1748 in six volumes, in which some of the plates are said to have been printed in colours. We hear also of the *Ling Mao Hua Hui*,[2] a book containing coloured drawings of birds and flowers published in China in 1701, being reproduced in Japan by Yamamoto Kihei in 1748.

That these early attempts at colour-printing were doubtless attended by considerable difficulty and expense is indicated by the fact that but a single page of the *Jinkō-ki* was so printed and this in a very crude manner. Also the editions of such books were small, so that to-day copies of them are exceedingly rare and only to be found by miraculous good fortune. The mastery of the art seems to have been attained slowly, and it was not until almost the middle of the eighteenth century that it came to be used to any extent. That examples of colour-printed work appeared fitfully at first and with long intervals between them may be explained both by the cost and the difficulty there must have been in getting block-cutters who understood this special kind of printing; for the first Japanese workmen could only have learned from the Chinese artists or possibly from a few Chinese block-cutters who had followed in their wake, and the knowledge would necessarily have spread slowly.

It is certain, however, that the Ukiyo-ye men of Yedo did not invent the process or even use it first in Japan, and 1743, the date at which Fenollosa places the first use of the two-colour blocks,[3] is 116 years later than the attempt made in the *Jinkō-ki* and only three years earlier than Shunboku's book, in which five, six, and even seven blocks were used.

In view of the date of the *Jinkō-ki*, there seems no longer to be any good reason for doubting Sakakibara Yoshino, Sir Ernest Satow's authority for the story that printed sheets in colours of the actor Danjūrō were sold in 1695 in the streets of Yedo, nor that Arthur Morrison is correct in adhering to his belief that Kiyonobu (1664–1729) understood the process of colour-printing.[4]

The early use of colour from one block is shown in the set of books of *kimono* designs which appeared in 1667, spoken of by Edward Strange in *Japanese Colour Prints* (p. 124); and Anderson in *Japanese Wood Engraving* (p. 67) says that the colour process was used by Idzumiya Gonshirō, who

---

[1] See Burty Catalogue, p. 35. Hōsaiyen also illustrated the *Kyō Kaku-Shu*, drawings of Japanese scenery, 1789.

[2] See Anderson's *Japanese Wood-Engraving*, p. 25 in small edition.

[3] See the Ketchum Catalogue, by Fenollosa.

[4] See *Painters of Japan*, vol. ii., p. 33.

In my own collection I have a brown and weather-beaten engraving of a statue supposed to have been carved by Dengyō Daishi. The figure is in black, but the halo is printed in red. It is very crude in workmanship and has no artistic value. The officials at the Kyōto Imperial Museum say that it cannot be less than three hundred years old at the least. It is not dated, however.—L. N. B.

lived at the end of the seventeenth century, and who made use of a second block to stamp certain parts of his designs with *beni*.

There is also a well-known set of books on military tactics entitled *Gunpō Goku-Hiden-sho*, published in the Manji period, in which the drawings of fortresses and moats contain lines of direction for certain walls, roads, etc., printed in red.

To go back to the Chinese artists, however, we find that both the *bunjingwa* and Ming styles which were introduced by them into Japan were soon being taught by Japanese painters.

Buson, the leader of the native *bunjingwa* school, who has already been spoken of, became the founder of the group which eventually melted into the Shijō academy. Chin Nampin in Nagasaki was followed by Kumashiro Yūhi, Shūzan, and the Ganku school of Kyōto, while in Yedo book illustration was almost entirely in the hands of either the Ukiyo-ye artists or followers of the Chinese method—Bunrin, Bunchō, Ōnishi Keisai, and Tsutsumi Tōrin all adopting the impressionistic Chinese technique and teaching it in their studios.

Of the Japanese artists who followed the more delicate Ming style, Yanagisawa Kien (1701–1758) was one of the first. Kien was the principal retainer of the powerful Daimyō of Koriyama in Yamato province and studied in Kyōto under Sō-Shigan. He used his wealth and influence in helping other artists who were less fortunate, among whom Ikeno Taigadō is said to have numbered. Other signatures used by Kien were Ryūrikyō, Kōbi Chikkei, and Gyokkei. Although chiefly known as a painter, Kien worked to some extent for wood-engraving, and there is a most interesting and rare print by him representing a Chinese mountain scene, in which a stream flows down from the high horizon through a cleft in the rocks with garden parties of mandarins and poets on the bordering sward. At the top of the sheet are poems in beautiful and finely printed text by Hokuzen Shochu and Minagawa Gen, which the drawing is supposed to interpret. It is a wonderful example of colour-printing and looks like a small painted *kakemono*. It bears no date, but must have appeared before 1760.

Another follower of Sō-Shigan was Kusumoto SHISEKI, or, as he was afterwards called, Kusumoto Sō-SHISEKI, who illustrated a number of charming books, some of which contain drawings printed in colours. Sō-Shiseki lived between 1711 and 1786. He studied first under Kumashiro Yūhi of Nagasaki, who followd Chin Nampin as leader of the Chin Nampin school there, and later returned to Kyōto, where he put himself under Sō-Shigan's instruction. His name indicates allegiance to both of these masters, Kusumoto being taken from Yūhi's name, and the first syllable of Sō-Shiseki from that of Sō-Shigan. Other signatures used by him were Sō-Gaku, Sō-Hansei, Kunkaku, Kōun, Katei, and Sekkei.

Sō-Shiseki illustrated a number of books which contain some very charming colour-work printed from several blocks. Even when colour was not introduced the printing was peculiar and interesting, emphasis of tone being obtained by holding a part of the paper much more closely to the inked block than the rest, thus gaining a sharpness and definiteness where these qualities were desired and a more or less misty effect where distance was expressed or too great clearness not wished.

The first editions of Sō-Shiseki's books were all printed on the fine cream-white *tōshi* which lends itself so beautifully to colour, and although not all the illustrations are tinted, most of his books contain many with a grey tone added to the black and white and accented by one or two slight touches of colour. Among the works illustrated by him were the

Shuko Meiken Gwashiki: Reproductions of work by Sōhei, a Chinese artist. Signed Katei. In collaboration with Shunkoku. 5 vols. Kyōto. Koshin year.
Sō-Shiseki Gwafu: Sketches of landscapes, birds, flowers, buildings, etc., in the style of Chin Nampin. 3 long, narrow volumes. 1765. Second volume printed in colours.
Genji Ike-bana-no-ki: A work on flower arrangement. 3 vols. 1765. Black and white and grey.
Sō-Shiseki Sansui-fu: Landscape drawings. 3 vols. 1770. Some colour.
Kokon Gwasō: Various drawings. 7 vols. 1770. Soft tints and black and white.
Kokon Gwasō Kōhen: A supplementary series to the foregoing. 8 vols. 1771. Colours and black and white. Both of these sets are rare and charming.
Sō-Shiseki Gwaso Sansui: Landscapes and figures. 3 vols. 1772. Tints and black and white.

The subjects in Sō-Shiseki's books range from house interiors and drawings of gates, trellises, and bridges, to charming soft-coloured landscapes and flowers, birds, figures, and designs for fans and trays. Sō-Shiseki's books are not well known in Europe and America, and even in Japan complete sets in good condition are very difficult to obtain, especially those printed on the Chinese paper, Japanese collectors prizing them too highly to leave many to the Europeans who have fallen under the spell of the old *ehon*.

A son of Sō-Shiseki, Sō-Shizan, was working in Yedo in the latter part of the eighteenth century. The *Yomo-no-Haru*, an album published in 1796, contains a plate by him of a bird on a flowering branch.

Another famous artist of about this time was Kaidō or Mikuma Shikō. He was of the *bunjingwa* school and especially well known for his pictures of cherry-blossoms. Although working very little for wood-engraving, he left one book entitled *Tōtōmi Dzufu Seiki* made up of poems written by himself on the famous Hamana-bashi (bridge) between Yedo and Kyōto. This slender volume with its tinted *bunjingwa* landscapes was printed on a beautiful quality of *tōshi* in 1786. It is excessively rare, having been published as a *kubari-hon*.

A contemporary of Sō-Shiseki's, and a fellow-student with him for a time under Kumashiro Yūhi in the Nagasaki school, was Takebe KANYŌSAI.

Kanyōsai was born in 1712, the son of a *samurai* family of Hirosaki, in the province of Mutsu, but went to Yedo while still a boy, where he lived in Asakusa and studied for the priesthood. He became noted as a poet and chirographer early in life, but upon going to Kyōto as a priest of the famous Zen monastery of Tōfuku-ji, he entered into the artistic life of the old city to such an extent that he finally decided to leave his religious surroundings and take up painting as a profession. He went to Nagasaki for a period of study, and upon returning to Kyōto worked for a time under Moku-an, finally opening a studio of his own and spending the remainder of his life in the old capital, leaving a reputation behind him after his death, in 1774, as a poet, a writer, a chirographer, and an artist.

Kanyōsai used as other signatures the names RYŌSOKU, CHŌKŌ, RYŌTAI, and MŌKYŌ. He left a number of books containing superb drawings in black and white. Among his contemporaries there was not one who was his peer as a draughtsman. Curiously, however, his work is not well known outside of Japan, and has never had anything like its due recognition.

The first editions of his books, like most of those illustrated by men of the Chinese school, were printed on the Chinese *tōshi* paper, and are not often found now. One of his early works was the *Kanyōsai Gwafu*. It appeared first in 1762 in two series, one of three volumes and one of two, printed on *tōshi*. Later in the same year it was printed again in one set of five volumes on ordinary paper, but bound in wider books. In either of these editions it is valuable. The drawings comprise landscapes, birds, fishes, and animals, done with magnificent sweep and certainty of brush, and in the first volume a preface in his remarkable chirography. Some of the drawings have a grey tone added which gives an extraordinary richness of effect. Other works by him were the

Riyōun Chikufu: Drawings of bamboos. 1 vol. 1771.
Kenshi Gwayen: Landscapes, flowers, birds, animals, etc. 3 vols. 1771. Black and white and grey and one plate in colours.
Mōkyō Wakan Zatsuga: Various drawings in black and white and grey. Signed Mōkyō Takebe Ryōtai. 5 vols. 1772.
Kangwa Shinan Susumi-gusa.
Kaisaku Dzue: Drawings of fishes. First edition on *tōshi*. 1 vol. 1775. Rare.
Kangwa Shinan: Drawings in the Chinese style. 2 vols. 1779.

Itō JAKUCHŪ, also known as Jokin and Tobei-an, lived between 1716 and 1800, and became one of the most famous Kyōto painters of his time. It is said that as a boy he sold vegetables in the streets there. He received his early training from an obscure artist of the Kanō school, but later in life devoted himself to realistic work in the style of the Ming paintings. His paintings of cocks and hens are very famous, and he is said to have kept a

CHAP. VI]   JAPANESE BLOCK-PRINTING

number of fowls in his garden for subjects of study. Shōkoku-ji temple in Kyōto owns many beautiful screens by him, and some of his early Kanō work is found on the *fusuma* at Kinkaku-ji. Jakuchū never married, and after the death of an adopted son entered the priesthood and became a monk of Sekihō-ji.

Although known chiefly as a great painter, there are a few books containing reproductions of his work. The *Jakuchū Gwajō*, two *gwajō* of superb drawings of flowers, plants, etc., in white on a black ground, was printed from stone blocks and retouched with Chinese white. Copies of the first edition are immensely valuable, and even Yamada's modern reprint is an expensive book.

Other publications printed by Yamada containing reproductions of Jakuchū's work are the *Jakuchū Gwafu* in four volumes, and the *Gempo Yokwa*, both beautiful late books.

Another noted follower of the Chinese school of about a generation later was Niwa KAGEN, who was born in Nagoya in 1741. Although he formed his style chiefly on the realistic Ming paintings, some of his work shows the influence of the Japanese *bunjingwa* school, and it is possible that he studied for a time under Buson. He was a friend of Ikeno Taigadō of Kyōto and of Hokusai in Yedo. The latter artist was a great admirer of the sketches done with one stroke of the brush which Kagen became so noted for, and the *Ippitsu Gwafu* of 1823, although attributed to Hokusai, is really made up from work of this kind left by Kagen under the name of Fukuzensai, some forty years earlier.

Kagen's work is all of great originality and interest and comprises many *surimono* and drawings, often of a humorous nature, in the albums of contemporary work which were so popular, in addition to his book illustrations. Other signatures used by him were SHŌHO, SHŪCHINDŌ, FUKUZENSAI, TOHIKKIDŌ, and Niwa SHAAN.

His death is said to have occurred in 1786. If this is correct, all but one of the books containing illustrations by him must have been compiled by his followers. They include the

Kwachō Koretsu: Birds and flowers. 1781.
Fukuzensai Gwafu: Very charming drawings of flowers, landscapes, etc., copied from work by Kono Shuho, an artist of the Chinese school, who, according to the preface, died in 1786. Signed Fukuzensai Tohikkido. 6 long, narrow vols. 1814. Colours. Rare and charming.
Fukuzensai Seishi Roku: 2 vols.
Fukuzensai Jibyō Rutoku-no-Zu.
Ogasawara Dai Shorei-shu Daizen: A work on the etiquette and ceremonies of the great Ogasawara house. Illustrations show *bunjingwa* influence. Signed Kagen. 3 folios. 1826.
Hakuso Sodan: Historical tales. Signed Kagen. 5 vols. 1829.
Onna Shisho Geimon Dzue: Women heroes of Japan. First few plates in colours. 4 vols. 1835.

THE GANKU AND THE CHINESE SCHOOLS [CHAP. VI

Yamamoto BAI-ITSU was also a Nagoya painter who joined the artists of the Chinese school. He lived between 1784 and 1857 and used as other signatures the names RYŌ, BAIKWA-ITSUJIN, GYOKUZEN-KOJI, and MEIKEI. He attained considerable fame and was the friendly rival of Chikuden. Although not working to any extent for wood-engraving, he left several interesting drawings much in Baitei's style, in compilations of sketches by contemporary men and as illustrations of poems.

Bai-itsu was survived by a son, Yamamoto Bai-oku, who lived in Kyōto about the middle of the nineteenth century, and who left a rather striking book, entitled *Bai-oku Gwafu* (1 vol. 1865), containing drawings of flowers, which was printed in two editions, one in black and white and one in colours.

A great art movement like the Impressionism which centred in Kyōto was bound to have followers in many other cities, since it was largely a matter of temperament that a man expressed himself in that particular manner. Yedo, therefore, as well as Nagoya and Ōsaka, had its supporters of the movement, and among them were some of the greatest artists of the entire school.

Katō Iyo-no-Kami BUNREI (1705–1782), the Daimyō of Ōzu in Iyo province, was one of the earliest Yedo followers of the Chinese impressionistic school. He was almost an exact contemporary of Yosa Buson of Kyōto, and commenced his work in Yedo at about the same time that Buson established his famous *bunjingwa* studio in the older city. Bunrei used as other signatures the names YOSAI and TAITO (or YASUSATO). Although chiefly famous as a painter, he left a few very beautiful books, all of which are excessively rare in the first editions. Many of the drawings have a grey tone added and occasionally a note or two of soft colour is introduced. Among the books left by him are the following:

Rei Gwasen: Various sketches. 3 vols. 1777.
Ehon Bunrei: Flowers, birds, landscapes, etc. 3 vols. 1778.
Bunrei Gwasen: Drawings by Bunrei (vols. i. and ii.) and his students (vol. iii.). 3 vols. 1778.
Rei-ye Gwayen: Sketches in black and white and grey, with an occasional note of soft colour. 3 vols. 1779.
Kogwa Yōran: Copies of pictures by different artists, including work by Bunrei. Compiled by Takado Enjo. 3 vols. 1812. Black and white and grey.

Tani BUNCHŌ, a pupil of Bunrei's, became one of the foremost artists of his time. He was born in 1761,[1] the son of Tani Rokkoku, a well-known poet, and after studying with Bunrei, whose page he had been, he worked for a time under Kitayama Kangan and Suzuki Fuyō, painters of the Chinese school. He also devoted much study to the classical paintings by Sesshū, Kanō Tanyū, and to the work of the famous Chinese artist-priest Bokkei.[2]

Bunchō became painter to the Tokugawa Court and was private instructor

---
[1] Translated from a book of 1836 containing a sketch by Bunchō "when seventy-five years old."   [2] In Chinese, Mu Ch'i; thirteenth century.

in the Tokugawa and Tayasu families. His paintings have become great treasures and are immensely valuable.

In ordinary life Bunchō was known as Tani Bungorō, but he used as artist signatures the names SHAZANRŌ, SHŌSŌ, MUNI, GWAGAKUSAI, and ICHIJO. He came of a family of artists and poets, and his two sisters, Shūko and Kōran, were well-known painters, the latter's work being especially fine. His wife, Hayashi Kangan, also achieved considerable fame as a painter, and his daughter Kitsukitsu followed the same profession and finally married the artist Bunichi, who had been adopted into Bunchō's family as a son.

Although Bunchō's death is said to have occurred in 1841, there is a little book in existence called the *Enshū Gwafu* describing the visit of Bunchō and some other artists and poets to Enshū near Nagoya, where they went for the autumn moon-lit views in September of Kōkwa 3, or 1846. This charming book is made up of poems, and drawings of the scenery near Enshū by members of the party, which the preface states was composed of Tani Bunchō; Bunji, his son; Bunichi, his son-in-law; Kitsukitsu, the latter's wife; Kōran, his sister; and Takekiyo, Ryōko, Tokuho, and other of his pupils. The drawings are in black and white and printed on a peculiar and beautiful paper, the book being intended for a *kubari-hon* to be given to friends as a souvenir.

Although Bunchō's work for wood-engraving was entirely incidental to his painting, he nevertheless left a few very interesting books and, as might have been expected of so prominent an artist as he, several other *kubari-hon*. The list of his books includes the

Hyōkakku Kisho-no-dzu: Containing fine line drawings of landscapes in the Chinese style. 1 vol. Kwansei 2 (1790). Rare.
Honchō Gwayei: A very extensive compilation of copies of old Japanese paintings and other works of art.
Shūko Jisshu: A similar work done by order of Matsudaira Rakuō. 2 vols.
Tani Bunchō Honchō Gwasen Daizen: Copies of old paintings. 4 vols.
Shazanrō Gwahon: Delightful sketches of fruit, flowers, bamboos, etc. 1 vol. Printed on *tōshi*. Colours. Rare.
Nippon Meizan Dzue: Mountains of Japan. 3 vols. 1810.
Bunchō Gwafu: Various sketches. 2 vols. 1811.
Tani Bunchō Gwafu: Reproductions of Bunchō's work by his students. 2 vols. 1862.
Toba Meihitsu Gwafu: Comic drawings. Compiled by his followers. 1 vol. 1869.
Kogwa-Jō: Poems illustrated by Tani Bunchō and his pupils, Bunji, Nammei, Komei, Unkoku, Settan, Bunshin, Umpō, Tamaichi, Bunnō, Chinnen, Teisai, Kwazan, and Nanrei. No date.

The drawings in the *Bunchō Gwafu* and the *Shazanrō Gwahon* are very characteristic of Bunchō's style and have a superb daring and sweep. Both books are exceedingly rare and valuable in the first editions.

Bunchō left a large number of followers, and there are several compilations of drawings containing work by Bunchō and these artists. Among these books is the *Kwachō Gwafu*, made up of coloured drawings of birds and flowers by Bunchō, Hasegawa Settan, Kita Takekiyo, Hōshu, and others, published in one volume in 1819.

Among Bunchō's pupils, Tanomura CHIKUDEN achieved considerable fame as a painter, but worked only occasionally for wood-engraving. Chikuden was born in 1775 in Takeda in the province of Bungo, where he afterwards became private physician to the *daimyō* there. He showed so much skill in drawing, however, that when he was twenty-three his *daimyō* sent him to Yedo to study art and Chinese literature. After some time spent in the study of the old Chinese masterpieces, he entered Bunchō's studio. Later he lived in Ōsaka and Kyōto. Chikuden used as other signatures the names KŌKEN (or TAKANORI), KOSETSU, Kwachiku Yūsō, SETSUGETSUSHODŌ, and HŌSETSURŌ. His death occurred in 1835. Tinted reproductions of work by him are found in the *Tenshi Zufu*; the *Chikuden Gwafu*, copies of Chikuden's work by To-ō, two small volumes, 1879; and the *Chikuden Gwafu Kōhen*, compiled by Najima Kyo-ō, two small volumes, 1880.

Chikuden's most famous follower was Chokunyu (1814-1908). By some authorities he is said to have been Chikuden's son.

Kita TAKEKIYO (or Busei) lived between 1775 and 1856. He was a contemporary and friend of Hokusai's, but a follower of Tani Bunchō in painting. In his later life he devoted himself to the masterpieces left by Kanō Tanyū and finally became an adherent of the Kanō school. Although chiefly known as a painter, he worked to some extent for wood-engraving, and left a few illustrated books as well as some very rare prints. Other signatures used by him were KA-AN, GOSEIDŌ, and KAKUŌ. Among the books left by him were the

Kinseikiseki-kō: A work on ancient customs, old Japanese books, fans, utensils, etc. Written by Santō Kyōden. Preface by Kameda Bōsai. 2 vols. 1805.
Kasen Kashū: Poems by thirty-four poets. 1 folio. Signed Kita Takekiyo. 1810. Colours.
Kottō Shū: Curious ancient utensils and works of art. Written by Santō Kyōden. Illustrated by Takekiyo in collaboration with other artists. 4 vols. 1814.
Ehon Isaoshi-no-gusa: Anecdotes of celebrated heroes. 10 vols. 1838. Signed Ka-an Busei.
Zōho Isaoshi-gusa: A supplementary series of the foregoing. 5 vols. 1839. Colours.
Ka-an Gwafu: Reproductions of Takekiyo's work by his son Tansai. 1 vol. 1859.

Watanabe KWAZAN, the most famous of Tani Bunchō's followers, was born in 1793 of a *samurai* family of Tawara in the province of Mikawa. Their poverty is said to have been so great that he had difficulty in getting even the paper, brushes, and paints necessary for his work. About 1830 his *daimyō* increased the family's pension and this, together with help from Kaneko Kinryo, who introduced him to Tani Bunchō and the latter's son-in-law Bunichi, smoothed away his difficulties as far as painting was concerned. Politics engrossed much of his attention also, however, and at the time the first foreign gunboats appeared in Japanese waters he made great efforts to persuade the authorities to strengthen the coast defences. Nevertheless, he advocated the admission of foreigners into the country, and wrote several books on affairs in Europe and America and the superiority of Western civilization.

Although he rendered loyal and important service to the Government, Kwazan became unpopular with the Shōgunate, and for an imaginary offence he was condemned in 1842 to death by his own hand.

It is said that before he carried out the sentence he gathered his painting materials about him, painted one of the best pictures that ever came from his brush, and then with all the traditional ceremony, and before the appointed witnesses, he performed the tragic *seppuku* and fell dead before them.

Kwazan has come to be ranked not only as an artist of originality and unusual talent, but also as a great patriot, and his memory is cherished as that of a popular hero. Among other signatures used by him were TEISEI, HAKUTO, NOBORU, GŪKWAIDŌ, ZENRAKUDŌ, SAKUHI-KOJI, and ZUIAN-KOJI. He worked very little for wood-engraving, but left the following books:

Kwazan Gwafu Issō Hyaku-tai: One hundred drawings from everyday life. 1 vol. Colours.
Kwazan Gwafu: Various sketches. 2 vols.

Kwazan was survived by a son, Watanabe SHŌKWA (1833–1887), who was also a painter of note.

Tsubaki CHINZAN (1801–1854), also known as HITSU, TAKUKWADŌ, and KYŪAN, was of *samurai* descent and first studied under Kaneko Kinryō, afterwards working in the Chinese style with Watanabe Kwazan. It is said that Kwazan's last letter, written just before his death, was to Chinzan, to whom he left the instruction of his son, Watanabe Shōkwa. Chinzan worked little for wood-engraving and the *Chinzan Gwafu* (2 vols.) was one of his few books.

Watanabe GENTAI (1748–1822), also known as Uchida GENTAI, Hen GENTAI, YEISHŌDAI, HENYEI, and RINROKU-SODŌ, became a well-known painter of birds, flowers, and landscapes in Yedo toward the close of the eighteenth century. Among the books containing illustrations by him were the

Yomo-no-Haru (" Spring in the Country "): Contains seven double-page colour-plates. No. 1, Princesses looking at pictures, by Yujitei Tsunezune; No. 2, A ferry boat, by Hokusai Sōri; No. 3, A bachelor in the Yoshiwara, by Kitao Masanobu; No. 4, Butterflies, by Hen Gentai; No. 5, Seven gods of Happiness, by seven artists; No. 6, Lady and *samurai*, by Kitao Masanobu; No. 7, Bird on a flowering branch, by Sō-Shizan. 1 *gwajō*. 1796. Rare.
Henshi Gwafu: 2 vols.
Gentai Sensei Gwafu: Various sketches—birds, flowers, plants, etc. Signed Henyei. 5 vols. 1806. Black and white.
Gentai Gwafu: Reproductions of Gentai's work by his son. 1834.

Gentai was survived by a son, Watanabe SEKISUI (1775–1833), also known as Hakuga, who was also an artist.

The Ganku and the Chinese Schools [Chap. VI

Kameda Bōsai,[1] who lived between 1753 and 1826, was a friend of Sakai Hōitsu, and, although chiefly famous as a scholar and poet, studied painting late in life and left one utterly charming book—perhaps the most so of any produced by the artists of the impressionistic movement. It is entitled *Kyōchūzan*[2] (" Mountains of the Heart ") and was published in one slender volume in 1809. It is made up of softly coloured sketches of mountainous landscapes printed on a beautiful quality of paper, each signed with a fanciful name. Among the signatures used are Chōkō, Kō, Chiryō, Zenshindō, Sairyō, and others.

Bōsai also collaborated with other artists in the illustrations in the *Imayō Genji* (2 vols.).

Other followers of the impressionistic Chinese method were Ōnishi Keisai, a small official of the Tokugawa Government and the keeper of one of the rice-warehouses in Yedo, who studied under Bunrei and became noted for his pictures of flowers and birds in the late eighteenth century; Okamoto Shūki (died 1861), a follower of Ōnishi Keisai and Watanabe Kwazan; Sō-Shikō, the son of Sō-Shizan, also known as Rekisentei and Sō-Rin, who was a Yedo painter of flowers, birds, and landscapes in the early nineteenth century; Ōoka Umpō, a follower of Tani Bunchō's and later a teacher of Hiroshige; Haruki Nanko, also known as Kon, Yusekitei, Enka-Chōsō, and Domboku-ō, who was a pupil of Tani Bunchō's; Haruki Nammei, the son of Nanko, who also signed himself Ryō and Kōun-gyosha, a painter of landscapes, flowers, and birds, and who lived until 1878; Okada Hankō (1782–1846) also known as Shuku, Kanzan, Dokushōrō, and Fukuda, who was the son Okada Beisanjin, also an artist; and Okada Kanrin, (1780–1849), also known as Tōren, Ren, and Bukō, and who became famous for his charming pictures of birds and flowers. Kanrin left a rare and very beautiful set of books, called the *Kanrin Gwafu*, made up of tinted drawings of flowers and birds, signed Tōren. (2 vols., 1832. A reprint in 1849.)

Among the books containing work by the men of the Chinese school were the following:

Hi-Kangen Sansui Gwashiki: Copies of drawings by the Chinese artist Hi-Kangen. 3 vols. 1787. Black and white. Charming and rare.
Tozan Ran-jō: Copy of a Chinese work on orchids. White on a black ground. 1 gwajo. Rare.
Sogwa-Ho: Various sketches by Kakuzan and other artists. 1 vol. 1807.
Meisū Gwafu: Various drawings by Japanese artists of the Chinese school. 4 vols. 1810. Black and white and tints.
Sakura : Poems on fans, with alternating coloured drawings by Kinseki, Shoto, Tani Bunchō, Hōshu, Seiko, Chikusa, Gessō, Nanko, Kinryō, Shūzan, Untan, Joshin, Bunichi, Shunyei, Hōitsu, Ōnishi Keisai, and Takekiyo. 1 *gwajō*. No date.

---

[1] May also be read Hōsai.
[2] May be read *Kyōchū-no-Yama*. The Duret Catalogue lists an edition of 1817.

CHAP. VI] JAPANESE BLOCK-PRINTING

Kyokun Kokon Michi Shirube: Various drawings by Umpō, Kobayashi, Torei, Moriyoshi, Genseki, Hozan, Shutoku, and Sekkio. 1 vol. 1837.

Keisai MASAYOSHI, whose name is probably the most familiar to foreign collectors of any of the artists of the impressionistic schools, stands by himself, for although most of his work is in the highest degree impressionistic, it is a decorative impressionism which has little resemblance to the impressionism in the drawings of the other followers of this movement. Where he learned it does not appear. It has no affinity with the style of his teacher Shigemasa, and little, except in the breadth of technique, with the paintings of Kanō Tanyū which he admired so ardently. Here and there, however, suggestions of Kōyetsu and Kōrin are caught as well as indications that the Shijō and Maruyama schools of Kyōto were not without their influence upon him.

Keisai, or, to give him his full name, Kitao Keisai Masayoshi, was born in Yedo between 1750 and 1760 and lived there until well into the next century, when he was taken into the Matsudaira family as one of their retainers, and left the capital for their great place in the north, returning only a year or two before his death in 1824. He was a friend of Hokusai's, who was greatly influenced by him, and an early pupil of Kitao Shigemasa, from whom he took one of his names. Other signatures used by him were Kitao MASAYOSHI, in early years, Kitao SANJIRŌ, Kuwagata KEISAI, Kuwagata JŌSHIN rather late in life, Seibi KITAO, GENSEI, Sanko SANJIN, SANSUI, and AKABA, while Keisai was a *nom de plume* used throughout his working years.

From a manner which was entirely of the Ukiyo-ye and much like Shigemasa's, Keisai's style gradually developed into the delightful impressionism which is so generally associated with his work. It was well into the nineties of the eighteenth century, however, before he reached this freedom, his early work showing the Ukiyo-ye influence exclusively. Early drawings by him, in which Shigemasa's influence is paramount, are found in the

Nami-no-Sachi: Fishes, shells, etc. 2 vols. 1775. Colours. (Listed in the Happer Catalogue.)
    I should like to be certain that this *Nami-no-Sachi* is not the *Umi-no-sachi*, an excessively rare book, in 2 vols., by Sekijukwan Hidekuni Katsu-Ryūsui.
Saru Hodoni Satemo Sono-nochi: Tales of ancient and modern times. Signed Kitao Masayoshi. No date. Black-and-white drawings in the Ukiyo-ye manner.
Kumempeki Daruma Daitsū: The temptations of beauty. Very curious drawings, one of which represents Daruma leaning out of the *kakemono* upon which he is painted to watch some beautiful women in the room. Signed Kitao Masayoshi. 1 vol. No date. Black and white.
Kyōka Yedo Meisho Torikumi: Poems, and drawings of famous places in Yedo. Much in Shigemasa's style. Signed Kitao Sanji Masayoshi. 1 vol. No date. Black and white and grey.
Michinoku Matsushima Hakkei: A series of eight medium-sized upright colour-plates of views of Matsushima. Printed in green, pink, yellow, grey and black. Signed Kitao Masayoshi. 1 *gwajo*. No date, but evidently very early work.

THE GANKU AND THE CHINESE SCHOOLS [CHAP. VI

Yedo Meisho Kinryūzan: A series of upright colour-plates 8 by 11 inches, representing views in Yedo, with figures. In Shigemasa's manner. 1 *gwajō*. No date.
Ehon Soga Monogatari: No date. Colours.
Yedo Meisho Dzukai: Fifty scenes in and about Yedo. Postscript by Mobutsu-an Shujin. Drawings by Kitao Keisai Masayoshi. Blocks cut by Kobayashi Mohei. Published by Noda Shichibei, Yedo, 1785. (Rare work, in Masayoshi's early manner. Delicate colours.)

The difference in style which is so apparent in Keisai's later work should probably be attributed to a visit paid by him to Kyōto about 1786. Here he met all the famous painters of the impressionistic schools, and their work was bound to have its effect upon him. It was certainly soon after this visit that his technique underwent a complete change, the beginnings of which may be traced in the *Ehon Miyako-no-Nishiki*, a rare and beautiful folio of twelve upright colour-plates of scenes in and about Kyōto, signed Kitao Keisai Masayoshi and dated Temmei 7 (1787).

In this book the figures retain a resemblance to Shigemasa's work, but here and there in the landscape there are many suggestions of Ōkyo's manner. The change progresses and almost under our eyes develops into something of the Maruyama impressionism in the *Haikai Kato Manshu*, an excessively rare *kubari-hon* of about 1787–1788. This little known folio is a collection of *haikai*, or seventeen-syllable poems, on the Four Seasons by a poem club of Kyōto. The drawings are four double-page colour-plates by Keisai Masayoshi representing Arashiyama in spring, the river-bed in Kyōto with its summer night picnic parties, the Bon Odori of August, and the preparations for the New Year festivities. The preface was written by Shinratei (or Banshōtei), who also wrote that in the *Miyako-no-Nishiki*. In it he says that the poems and drawings in the book were made at the request of Maruyama Mondo (one of Ōkyo's names), " in his old age," who desired to have the book printed as a souvenir to give to his friends. We may suppose it was also done as a compliment to Keisai, and suggests meetings and talks between him and the Kyōto artists which finally won him to their looser technique. The drawing of the river and hills at Arashiyama in this book are much in the style of those in the *Miyako-no-Nishiki*, but the groups of dancing figures representing the Bon fête, and the drawing of the river-bed of Kyōto, except that they have not wholly reached the freedom of his later work, might be taken from his *Jimbutsu Ryakugwa-shiki*. Unfortunately it bears no date of publication, but the facts that the preface is by the same writer as that in the *Miyako-no-Nishiki* and that the book was printed in Ōkyo's " old age," as well as the increased impressionism of the drawings, all indicate a date slightly later than 1787.

Following these books there appeared the

Ehon Kwachō Kagami: Drawings of birds and flowers in the Chinese manner. 1 vol. 1789.
Yedo Ichiran Dzue: Glimpses of Yedo. In imitation of Kō (Yokoyama) Kwazan's *Karaku Ichiran Dzue*. Signed Kitao Sebi (Masayoshi) Jōshin. 1 vol.

Shoshoku E-Kagami (or *Gwakyō*): Designs for artisans. 1 vol. 1794. Black and white.
Ryūzoku Kyōkasen: Humorous poems illustrated by Keisai. 1 vol. 1794. Black and white.

Beginning with 1795 we have Keisai's well-known and delightful books of sketches, in which the technique has lost every trace of Ukiyo-ye influence and has become wholly impressionistic in style. These include the

Ryakugwa-shiki: Various sketches. 1 vol. 1795. Colours. Rare.
Jimbutsu Ryakugwa-shiki: A set of books of which the first volume is made up of the sketches which originally appeared in the *Ryakugwa-shiki.* 3 vols. 1795-1799. Colours, and also an edition in black and white.
Chōjū Ryakugwa-shiki: Birds, animals, fishes, etc. 1 vol. 1797. Colours.
Sansui Ryakugwa-shiki: Landscapes. 1 vol. 1800. Colours. Rare and charming. A second edition in 1813.
Shinki Ipputsu: Rapid sketches " to drive away sadness." 1 vol. 1800. Colours.
Gyokai-fu: Fishes, shells, etc. The Hayashi Catalogue states that in this edition of this book there are poems on each page which in subsequent printings under the title of *Gyokai Ryakugwa-shiki* were omitted.[1] 1 vol. 1802. Colours.
Shinki Isso: A supplementary series to the *Shinki Ipputsu.* Signed Keisai. Sealed Joshin. 3 vols. 1804. Black and white.
Gengwa-yen: Various drawings. 1 vol. 1808.
Keisai Ryakugwa-shiki: Various sketches. 2 small volumes. No date, but about 1809-1810. Colours.
Ryakugwa-yen: Various sketches. Signed Keisai. Sealed Jōshin. 1 vol. 1809. A second edition in 1823.
Sōkwa Ryakugwa-shiki: Various sketches. Signed Keisai Jōshin. 1 vol. 1813. Colours.
Kwa Ryakugwa-shiki: Drawings of flowers and plants without outlines. 1 vol. 1813. Colours. Rare.
Hyakunin Isshu: Humorous and highly impressionistic drawings of the Hundred Poets. Signed Keisai. 1 vol. No date. Black and white.

After 1813 there seems to have been a pause in Keisai's work. He was probably in the retinue of his *daimyō* in the north, and published nothing more, so far as is known, until his return to Yedo some ten years later. His last books were the

Kyōka Kinyō Shū: Humorous illustrated poems. Signed Jōshin. 1822.
Imayō Shokunin Dzukushi Uta-awase: Poems on artisans and their work. 2 vols. 1823.
Shokunin Dzukushi: Artisans at work. Curious distorted illustrations. Signed Jōshin. 3 vols. 1825. Colours. Excessively rare.
Keisai Sogwa: Various sketches. Preface signed Gensei. The first edition of this book appeared about 1824-1825, bound in red covers bearing a design of tortoises and waves in heavy gaufrage. Afterwards it was added to four other volumes by Baitei Kahei, Keisai Eisen, Rai-an Genki, and Keisai Eisen respectively, under the collective title of *Saryō Togwa Keisai Sogwa,* and bound as a set in plain scarlet covers. The last volume was published in 1832 and the set is usually attributed to Keisai Eisen. 5 vols. Colours. Rare in the first edition.

Plates by Keisai are also occasionally found in compilations of drawings; as in the *Shitori Haiku* (2 vols.), a rare *kubari-hon* containing work by many

[1] I have seen several copies of this early edition, but never with the poems, and I think it possible that the *Umi-no-Sachi,* a rare book illustrated by Katsuma Ryūsui, with poems above the drawings, may have been confused with this much better known book by Keisai.—L. N. B.

celebrated artists of the time; the *Tōkaidō Meisho Dzue* (5 vols.), with illustrations by Tosa Mitsusada, Soken, Shunsensai, Bummei, Ishida Yūtei, and Nagatoshi, and one or two less important works.

There is one other very important and excessively rare book by Masayoshi. This is the *Raikin Dzui*, a very beautiful *gwajō* of twelve oblong colour-plates, 8 by 14½ inches in size. The first two plates represent Chinese men with their luggage, including a bird in a cage, waiting on the sea-shore for a boat. In one of these plates one of the men is represented as seated upon a red-lacquered box. The first plate bears, in the upper left-hand corner, the inscription, *Nankin Hito-no-tsu* (meaning, loosely translated, " Chinese men at the harbour "). The second plate bears an inscription in Dutch, in the upper right-hand corner. The men are supposed to be bringing singing birds from China to Japan and the following ten plates represent the different varieties of birds. The drawings are enclosed in black-line borders and are most beautifully printed, delicate gaufrage being used in addition to the charming colour. The book is even more beautiful, and very much rarer, than Utamaro's famous *Momo-chidori*. It has been printed at least twice. The first and by far the more beautiful edition has no artist's signature whatever on any of the plates. A later issue was printed from more coarsely cut blocks and in far cruder colours, but bears Masayoshi's signature and seal on each plate.

There has been great confusion about this book because it is almost impossible to see a complete first edition, with the colophon, the dealers only occasionally getting in single sheets from it and usually selling them as the work of Utamaro, probably not knowing themselves where they come from.

The book is listed in the Duret Catalogue as in one volume illustrated by Seki Eibun. In the Hayashi Catalogue it is listed as in one volume *edited* by Seki Eibun. De Goncourt, in his book on Utamaro (p. 184), only speaks of it as " un livre à joindre aux *Cent Crieurs*, et dont on n'est pas sûr, que le nombre de dix planches sont le nombre des planches de l'ouvrage complet. Il porte pour titre *Copies d'Oiseaux Etrangers* par un fonctionnaire de Nagasaki, pour être presentées au Shōgun." Nothing is said of Utamaro's signature on any of the plates nor of the volume of text, which Mr. Happer lists in his catalogue as being part of the work.

In Julius Kurth's exhaustive work on Utamaro, this book is only listed from Gonze, who in his turn took it from de Goncourt, as a series of ten pictures of birds to be taken as a gift to the Shōgun. Mr. Happer believes the book to have been by Utamaro, and describes it in the catalogue[1] of his collection as being made up of two volumes, one containing twelve colour-plates, the first of which is signed by Utamaro; and the second volume,

[1] See *Catalogue of the Happer Collection of Japanese Prints and Illustrated Books.* London, 1909. P. 56.

which is of text, also bearing Utamaro's signature and the date 1793. He says of it: " What has hitherto been seen of this work has nearly always been attributed to Keisai Masayoshi, and it is thought that probably owing to some dispute with the publishers who held the blocks when Utamaro was imprisoned in 1804 for his print aimed at the Shōgun, a fresh issue was put before the public signed Keisai."[1]

In addition to the foregoing, Mr. Happer says in a letter in reply to one in which I asked for further information about his copy of this book: " I regret that I can give you very little further information regarding the two-volume edition of the *Rai Hin Dzu I*, as sold in London. . . . The preface was translated by me and it distinctly stated that the originals were paintings in the possession of some official in Nagasaki, and in order that they might be more widely known Utamaro was asked to make the designs for the blocks. The letterpress gave details as to the habits of the birds and the date when they were first brought to Japan, on the — sailing of — year. There were so many sailings a year allowed from China. Personally, I am sure they were by Utamaro. I have had many arguments about the book. Many [collectors] still maintain that it was Masayoshi's, but Masayoshi never did any work comparable to this, and Utamaro did in his *Momo-chidori* and the *Mushi-erabi*. This fine first edition is almost extinct, most collectors having seen only the Masayoshi edition."

Fortunately, in the collection of Japanese books in the British Museum (No. 76 in the Catalogue) there is an undoubtedly genuine first edition of this extremely rare work. It is in one volume (a *gwajō*) and the two colophon pages name Kitao Masayoshi as the artist and the *first* year of Kwansei (1789) as the date. Two other series are advertised to appear later, and although it is possible that the set Mr. Happer describes may be a continuation of this work carried on by Utamaro four years later, nothing of this sort is said in the advertisement.

In addition to the books spoken of by the various artists of the impressionistic movement, there were a number of charming albums made up of drawings by these men. Many of these books are extremely rare, and form valuable additions to a collection. Among these works are the

Kikido-kuri: Drawings by Bumpō and other Kyōto artists. 1804.
Kyōka Tagoto-no-Hana : Poems illustrated by Chiharu, Hakuyei, Ōshin, Minwa, and other artists. 1 vol. 1811. Colours.
Keijō Gwayen: Double-page plates by Hakuyei, Geppo, Gitō, Shiba Kōkan, Minwa, Toyohiko, and Tōsen. 1 *gwajō*. 1814. Colours. Rare and charming.

Of these works, however, the *Meika Gwafu* is perhaps the most noted. Every collector is familiar with it. It was compiled by Niwa Tōkei and

[1] See *Catalogue of the Happer Collection of Japanese Prints and Illustrated Books.* London, 1909. P. 56.

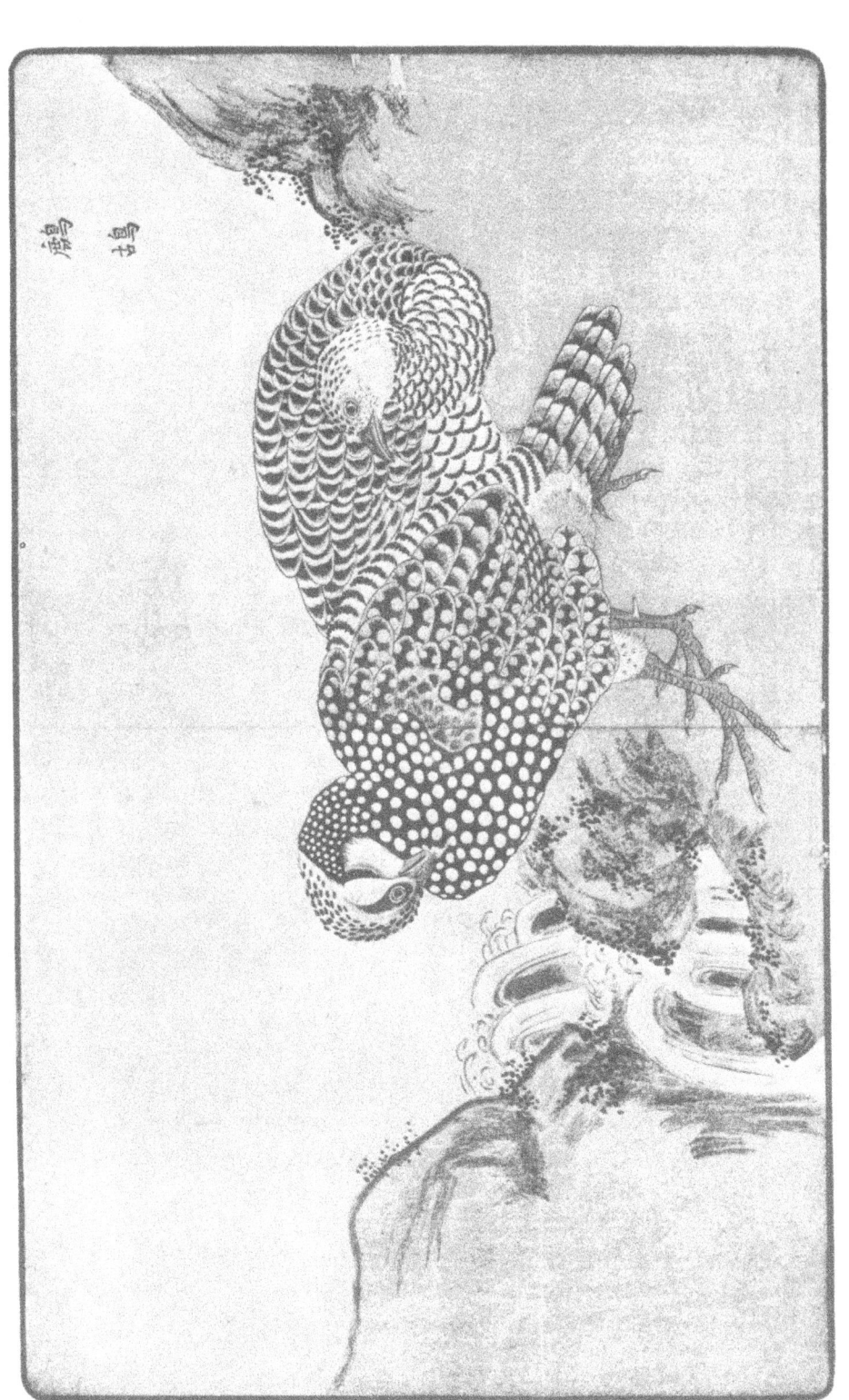

From the RAIKIN DZUI (1789), by Kitao Masayoshi.

PLATE 22

published in three folios (Ten, Chi, and Jin) in the Boar Year of Bunkwa (1815). The set is rarely found complete, the middle volume almost invariably being gone. It is said that the blocks for it were destroyed by fire soon after the first few sets had been printed, making the series as originally issued well-nigh impossible to obtain. The index of this book is very useful as it gives the various signatures used by the artists represented in it, and a word or two of a biographical character in regard to them. The coloured plates it contains represent flowers, birds, animals, landscapes, figures, everyday scenes, etc., etc. Perhaps no one book would give a better understanding of the work in illustration by the Kyōto schools than this charming and famous collection. Of late years it has become rare and a set, even of the first and last volumes, which are all one ever finds, is difficult to obtain in good condition. Other compilations were the

Yume-no-Yokozuchi: Poems illustrated by Kakusen, Gekko, Mori Shunkyo, Randomei (Suiseki), and Kaishō. 1 *gwajō*. 1817. Colours.
Sekkei Gwafu: Edited by Sekkei (Sō-Shiseki). Contains work by Kunkei, Goshun, Shūhō, Takata, Sōyen, Nantei, Kishi Takudō, Tōkei, Sekisui, Hōdai, Tōyei, Futei, and Shingaku Kunsen.
Kinaga Gwafu: Various drawings by artists of the impressionistic schools. 3 vols. 1835. Colours.
Seikwa Jō: A very rare and beautiful set of two *gwajō* containing work by the Kyōto men. 1848. Colours.
Tama Hiroi: Poems and sketches on Kyōto and its environs. 4 vols. 1860. Colours.

Other earlier books by Kyōto men who were followers of the Kanō school, and who worked very little for wood-engraving, were the

Ehon Ritsuo (Hitsuyo ?): Various ink drawings of decided merit. Signed Nakaji Sadatoshi (also known as Unshū). 3 vols. 1752.
Saishiki Gwasen: An excessively rare book of very striking drawings of flowers, plants, fruit, a lobster, shells, fish, toys, etc., printed in colours without outlines and with gold, silver, and gaufrage used. One of the earliest books in which these additions to colour have been employed. 3 folios. 1770.
Ehon Tanoshimi-gusa: Poems on the moon, snow, flowers, etc. Illustrated by Ratcho. 3 vols. 1796.
Gosen Hyakunin Isshu: The Hundred Poets. Illustrated by Fuchigami Kyokuko. 1 vol. 1807.
Kaitaro: By Wakabayashi Shōkei (Sekiryo). Bunkwa period, an excessively rare *kubari-hon* with *bunjingwa* drawings illustrating poems. In Awaki Collection, Ōsaka.

One might go on almost indefinitely listing these delightful impressionistic books, for there are an immense number by little known men, many containing remarkable work.

In my numerous trips after books into remote parts of Japan, I never failed to find something beautiful or interesting of which I had never heard before, and which I had never seen listed in any catalogue. It is probable that important and rare books were illustrated by many of the well-known men, especially the gift books known as *kubari-hon*, which were published in small editions and never reprinted. I feel certain, also, that very early works printed in colours existed as well, of which now there is no record, but which patient searching may yet unearth.

CHAPTER VII

UKIYO-YE ILLUSTRATORS OF THE NISHIKAWA, OKUMURA, TORII, AND NISHIMURA GROUPS

WITH the beginning of the eighteenth century, the famous Ukiyo-ye school of Japanese art commenced to assume form. Despised and rejected of the aristocrats, the work found its welcome among the masses of the Shōgun's capital, gaining a constantly increasing popularity there for over a century. Kyōto and Ōsaka had, as has been said, however, an early share in this movement, for Moronobu had lived for many years in Kyōto, and Sukenobu spent his entire life between the two western cities.

The work of these early men and their pupils was the light that followed in the train of Iwasa Matabei, who had discovered before the middle of the preceding century the wealth of material for painting which lay in the everyday life of the people. It was a fund hitherto not drawn upon to any extent, for the classical traditions which held both the Tosa and Kanō art in the moulds long usage had prescribed for them were difficult to break through. Now, however, artists began to see that other subjects had possibilities and the decorative aspect of life itself commenced to be revealed to them, as long, long before the decorative possibilities of small things—flowers, grasses, insects, and birds—had been perceived and used by them as no other artists in the world had ever used them. Women and children in their beautiful *kimono* and *obi* were found as interesting for subjects of pictures as they were in everyday life, and the primrose path of naughtiness not without its lovely colour and graceful composition. Actors proved themselves as startling and wonderful on the painted or printed sheet as in the theatre; festival scenes with their gay colours and groupings; summer night fêtes on the river lighted by thousands of wind-tossed, glowing lanterns; arching bridges bearing picturesque processions, all lent themselves to art, until finally every aspect of the humblest work-a-day affair yielded a measure of beauty to the man who apprehended and reached out for it.

Still, it was not by any means the subjects alone which differentiated the Ukiyo-ye work from everything that had gone before or made it so strikingly different from contemporary Kyōto art. It was as much the peculiar technique that characterized it, and this technique had really formed as great a part of Matabei's legacy as the subjects themselves. In it the drawing was purely decorative. It had nothing of realism about it, and in the earlier Ukiyo-ye productions was full of dignity and charm. It increased in beauty until about 1780, reaching its height in Kiyonaga's work, and then slowly but certainly losing all restraint in both line and colour, and becoming, toward the time of the Restoration, offensively grotesque and exaggerated.

When the sincere lover of Japanese life and art has pessimistic notions about the real value of foreign intercourse to Japan, he may comfort himself with the reflection that the excitement and changes of 1868 at least interrupted the output of these atrocious later prints, and that the study of Occidental art might after all have proved a wholesome change at that time, since European painting in 1870 was at least innocuous and not yet suffering from aberrations of its own in the form of cubist extravagances and other strange afflictions.

From the beginning of the Ukiyo-ye movement its artists illustrated books in addition to designing the prints which are so much more widely known. In fact, the early Ukiyo-ye work was chiefly found in books, and Moronobu and all of his followers, as well as Sukenobu two generations later, devoted almost their entire energies to illustration.

Like many movements which begin and then seem to recede for a second and more impelling start, the *ehon* pure and simple suffered something of a decline after Moronobu's death, and although the publication of books on a multitude of subjects continued in constantly increasing numbers, it was well into the eighteenth century before the purely Ukiyo-ye work was revived, and in the drawings of Kiyonobu, Sukenobu, and Okumura Masanobu, appeared again in its full promise. With this second beginning, however, the Ukiyo-ye movement was really launched and books, as well as the more popular prints, were produced in great numbers for the next century and more.

Kiyonobu, although in point of time preceding any of the other Ukiyo-ye men of the second generation, belongs to the Torii group to be considered together, so it is with Nishikawa SUKENOBU that we come back to the form of art which Moronobu had brought to such a height—and with him take farewell of the more ancient works.

One leaves the early books with regret—they were our first loves, never to be quite replaced in our affections and always retaining the charm of slight mystery. They baffle our eagerness for a complete understanding by seldom fully revealing themselves, retaining reserves of uncertainty as to time and place which bring us back to them at the slightest beckoning—away from those of later years which, beautiful and interesting though they may be, lack the indefinable charm of these earlier volumes.

Large giving, however, is an attractive quality and Sukenobu gives much.

He was one of the most prolific of all the illustrators, and it is doubtful if anything like a complete list of his works has ever been made.

He was born in Kyōto in 1671, studied under Kanō Einō Sukenori for a time, from whom he took the first syllable of his name, and then abandoned this teaching for the Ukiyo-ye art. His name in ordinary life was Nishikawa Ukyō, but as artist signatures he used the names BUNKWADŌ, YŪSUKE, JITOKUSAI, FUJI, and NANSEI.

It was Sukenobu's ambition to found a school of purely Japanese art, and the great popularity of the Chinese paintings was always a source of the keenest dissatisfaction to him. He speaks of this in the preface to one of his books, calling it a shame that people should laud the work of another country and despise that of their own. In a measure his efforts to establish a wholly native art had their reward, and his work achieved a widespread popularity, becoming as well known in Yedo as in Kyōto and Ōsaka, many of his books being published simultaneously in the three cities.

Although his drawings are less virile than Moronobu's, Sukenobu occupied about the same place in Kyōto art of the eighteenth century that Moronobu had filled in the seventeenth, and like the latter artist had a large number of followers. Toward 1730 he moved to Ōsaka, where several noted publishing houses had arisen which were issuing great numbers of books and rivalling the work of the Kyōto printers. Here he became one of a colony of famous artists who had maintained an individuality of their own—neither producing work in the Kyōto or the Ukiyo-ye manner, but travelling their own interesting paths. Sukenobu remained loyal to the Ukiyo-ye, however, and continued in this manner in Ōsaka, where he spent the remainder of his life.

His death occurred in 1751. He was brought back to Kyōto for burial, and his tomb is in the cemetery of Myōshin-ji, west of the city.

The following list embraces the most important of Sukenobu's books, although it is probably incomplete. Many of them appeared after his death, his son Suketada publishing them during the Hōreki and Temmei periods (1751–1764).

His earliest work, as far as known, was the *Shōtoku Hinagata*, kimono designs for the Shōtoku period (1713). There followed the

Shibai Hare Kosode: 1716.
Kyōhō Hinagata: Designs for *kimono*. 1 vol. 1716. Excessively rare.
Ehon Hiji Bukuro: Witty sayings of the time. 1716. A later edition in 1776.
Ehon Yamato Hiji: A work on drawing with instructions in regard to brushes, colours, etc., and model drawings of landscapes, people, historical scenes and others. 10 vols. 1716. A later edition in 1742.
Fukusa Hinagata: Designs for *fukusa*, the square cloths used to carry parcels in, with a double-page frontispiece of three women looking at *fukusa*. Signed Nishikawa Sukenobu. Published Kyōho 3 (1718). An excessively rare book.
Hyakunin Jorō Shina Sadame: Lives of one hundred courtesans. 2 vols. 1723.

PLATE 23] From the EHON TOKIWA-GUSA (1730), by Nishikawa Sukenobu.

NISHIKAWA, OKUMURA, AND TORII GROUPS [CHAP. VII

Onna Manyō Keiko Zōshi: Letter-writing for women. Written by Hayashi Uji Ranko. 3 vols. 1728.
Ehon Towa Kagami: 2 vols. 1729.
Genji-no-Yesho: History of the Genji. 1730.
Ehon Tsukuba Yama: Poems by famous poets with illustrations. 3 vols. 1730.
Ehon Shō-Chiku-Bai: The New Year festivities. 3 vols. 1731.
Ehon Tokiwa-gusa: Scenes in the lives of women. 3 vols. 1731.
Jo-chū Fūzoku Tsuya Kagami: Occupations of middle-class women. 2 vols. 1732.
Shimidzu-no-Ike: Poems on morals. 3 vols. 1734.
Ehon Chiyomi-gusa: Scenes in the lives of women. 3 vols. 1735. Kyōto. Published again in Ōsaka in 1740 and 1741.
Ehon Tama-Kazura: Occupations of women. " Pictures of Tama-Kazura " (a spring flower) 3 vols. 1736. Signed Kwaraku Bunkwadō Nishikawa Sukenobu.
Ehon Kawana-gusa: Kimono designs. 3 vols. 1736.
Ehon Sonare-matsu: Poems by Ono-no-Komachi illustrated by Sukenobu. 3 vols. 1736.
Ehon Asaka-yama: Drawings of single figures of women. 1 vol. 1739. Extremely rare.
Ehon Kagami Hyaku-shu (" Mirror of a Hundred Things "): 3 vols. 1739.
Zoku Hyaku-shū: Supplementary series to foregoing. 3 vols. 1739.
Hana Musubi Nishiki-ye Awase: Directions for making the stuffed silk pictures called *oshi-e*. Written by Karaku Hori. Illustrated by Sukenobu. 2 vols. 1739. Rare.
Ehon Chitose-yama: Beautiful women. 3 vols. 1740.
Ehon Tsure-dzure-gusa: Stories for humdrum hours. Signed Bunkwadō Nishikawa Sukenobu. 3 vols. 1740.
Ehon Nazame-gusa: Illustrated poems. Signed Bunkwadō Nishikawa Jitokuso Sukenobu. 3 vols. 1744.
Ehon Hime Tsubaki (" Princess of the Camelia Tree "): Historical work. 1 vol. 1745.
Ehon Miyako Zōshi: Customs of Kyōto. 3 vols. 1746. Signed Kwaraku Bunkwadō Nishikawa Jitokuso Sukenobu.
Heigo Waka Ehon Kame-no-yama: Poems by warriors, nobles, and ladies, and stories from the Heike Monogatari. 2 vols. 1747.
Ehon Fude Tsubana: 1747.
Ehon Yotsugi-gusa: Kimono designs. 3 vols. 1747.
Ehon Kawa-no-gusa: Beautiful women. 2 vols. 1747.
Goryū Ehon Zoroe: Various drawings. 1748.
Ehon Kawa-no-gusa: Second series. Kimono designs and drawings of beautiful women. 2 vols. 1748.
Ehon Matsu Kagami: 1 vol. 1748.
Ehon Fukuro-no-Kujō (" Pictures of Ninety Owls "): 3 vols. 1749.
Hina Asobi-no-Ki and *Hina Awase-no-Ki:* 2 vols. 1749. Forms one work.
Ise Monogatari: 2 vols. 1749.
Ehon Shinobu-gusa: Legends of the fifteenth century. 3 vols. 1750.

The following books, although signed Sukenobu, may have been the work of his son, since Sukenobu died in 1751:

Ehon Hime-Kagami: Historical tales. 1755.
Joyō Bunshō: Book of instruction for women. Colour-printed frontispiece of two pheasants on a flowering branch printed in pink and green. Signed Nishikawa Jitokusai Sukenobu. 1 vol. 1755.
Ehon Miyako Zōshi: 3 vols. 1756. Second edition.
Ehon Mitsuwa-gusa: Scenes in the lives of women. In the preface Suketada, who edited this book, says that it was intended as a continuation of the *Tokiwa-gusa* and the *Chiyomi-gusa*, the title being adopted because of its similarity to those of these two famous and popular works. 3 vols. 1758.
Ehon Yoshino-gusa: Scenes from Japanese life. 3 vols. 1759.

CHAP. VII] JAPANESE BLOCK-PRINTING

Onna Imagawa Hemei Kagami: Occupations of women. Contains a frontispiece printed in pink, yellow, and a greyish-green representing a princess kneeling before a mirror with her attendant waiting near by bearing a black lacquered box tied with a pink cord. 1 large vol. 1763.
Ehon Ike-no-Kawa den: Scenes from everyday life. 3 vols. 1768.
Onna Fūzoku Tama Kagami: Book on etiquette. 2 vols. 1782.
Ehon Ogura-Yama: Illustrated poems. 3 vols. Signed Nishikawa Jitokusō Sukenobu.

Other books attributed to Sukenobu, but bearing no dates, were the

Fūryū Yamato Edzukushi Nishikawa Fude-no-Yama: An excessively rare *gwajō* of ten (?) full-sized oblong *sumi-ye*, representing women and their lovers. One of Sukenobu's strongest works. Probably about 1730.
Wakoku Hyaku-jo: One hundred beautiful women.
Fūryū Bijin-no-gusa: Famous women of Japan. 1 vol.
Fūzoku Kagami Yama: Women of the *geisha* class. 2 vols.
Ehon Komatsu Hara: 1 vol.

Sukenobu's most famous books are the *Hyakunin Joro Shina Sadame*, the *Ehon Tokiwa-gusa*, the *Ehon Chiyomi-gusa*, and the *Ehon Mitsuwa-gusa*. They represent women of different classes at their various occupations. The drawings are graceful and pleasing, but of considerable similarity and not to be compared with either the best work of Moronobu of the preceding century or with that of Okumura Masanobu, the Yedo contemporary of Sukenobu. While these books are Sukenobu's best-known works, there are others which are very much rarer, as the *Fūryū Yamato Edzukushi*, made up of full-sized oblong *sumi-ye*, which is so rare as practically never to be found complete and which is in Sukenobu's early manner, resembling Moronobu's work sufficiently so that one might easily be deceived as to the artist; the *Fūryū Bijin-no-gusa*, containing drawings of single figures of women; the *Ehon Kawa-no-gusa*, a similar work, both extremely rare; all of his books of *kimono* designs; and the *Hana Musube Nishiki-ye Awase*, a very curious set of books with directions for making the stuffed silk pictures known as *oshi*, or *oshi-ye*, in which the drawings show the way the patterns are to be cut and put together, the tools for the work, and several complete drawings, with colour applied by hand, to indicate the shades of silk to be used.

Sukenobu's most popular books have been printed many times, and it is the issues of the Hōreki and Temmei periods which are usually found and often sold by unscrupulous dealers to collectors as first editions. The books which appeared after 1754 are supposed to have been largely the work of Suketada, the son of Sukenobu, who retained his father's signature because of the latter's fame and whose name had become known all over Japan.

SUKETADA was also known as TOKUYŪSAI, and lived from 1706 till 1762. He illustrated a number of books much in Sukenobu's manner. Among them were the *Ehon Hime Kagami*, a collection of ancient poems published in one volume in 1748; the *Ehon Uta Bunko*, also a collection of poems, published in 1750; and the *Ehon Kagami Hyaku-shu*, issued in three volumes in 1752 (not to be confused with Sukenobu's book of the same title of 1739). The latter is a collection of poems of an instructive character, the illustrations representing people at various tasks, each drawing pointing the moral to the little verse at the top of the page. The books are of medium size, in the well-known covers bearing a design in blue on a greyish-white ground. Other books illustrated by Suketada were the

Ehon Fuji-no-Yukari: Poems on the Genji. 3 vols. 1750.
Ehon Hibiki-no-Taki: Interiors and street scenes. 3 vols. 1753.
Mikawa: Poems on the twelve months. 1 vol. No date.
Ehon Toki Dzukase: 1777.
Joyō Hana-no-Yu: Instructious for women. 2 vols.
Mina-no-gawa: Everyday scenes. 3 vols.
Ehon Kagami Hyaku-shu: Various drawings. 3 vols. 1752.

A pupil of Sukenobu's, Yūkōken SUKEYO, also known as KWAGETSUTEI and Nishikawa SUKEYO, left a few books, among which were the

Ehon Karu-kuchi Eho Nadzo: 1760.
Ega-no-gusa: Old legends. 1 vol. 1761.
Chi-ye-no-Umi: Puzzle pictures. 1 vol. 1761.
Ehon Miyo-no-Haru: Humorous tales. 5 vols. 1763. Rare.

Nishikawa SUKENARI, who was also an early pupil of Sukenobu's, illustrated the *Ehon Homare-no-Taki*, published in 1753.

It is with Okumura MASANOBU, however, who a little later in the century occupied about the same place in Yedo art that Sukenobu had filled in Kyōto, that we at last find ourselves in the midst of the Ukiyo-ye movement, for although the roots of this school stretched west to Kyōto and Ōsaka, Yedo was the real place of its blooming, and it was there that all its most important artists lived.

As an artist, Masanobu should be ranked much higher than Sukenobu, for his work not only has far greater variety, but it combines the qualities of beauty and strength in much greater degree. He did not confine himself to book illustration, but became noted as a painter also, and was one of the first of the print designers, using lacquer colouring and gold dust in some of his prints with an extraordinary richness of effect. Although he is said to have been a pupil of Moronobu, this is hardly possible in view of the fact that he was only ten years old at the time of Moronobu's death. The work of the older artist, however, was manifestly a great inspiration to him, and an important factor in the formation of his own style as well as that of the Okumura school, which continued in the art life of Yedo parallel with the school of the Torii artists.

To the influence of Moronobu's work upon him was added that of

Miyagawa Chōshun and the latter's pupil, Yasutomo Andō Kwaigetsudō, who was working in the first quarter of the eighteenth century. Sukenobu's books probably also had a large part in determining his choice of subject, for they had become as great favourites in Yedo as in Kyōto, many of them having been printed simultaneously in the two capitals.

Masanobu lived between 1685 and 1768. He became a publisher and the owner of a book-shop, using as one of his artist signatures the name Honya Genroku, meaning "Genroku Book-shop." Other signatures used by him were BAI-Ō, BUNKAKU, KWAMMYŌ, TANCHŌSAI, GENZOKU, SHŌMEI, HŌGETSUDŌ, O-GENROKU, and GEMPACHI. He also sometimes added to his name the words *Yamato Eshi*, meaning " Japanese painter." Masanobu is said to have experimented with foreign drawing to some extent, and painted a few bridge and pontoon pictures in what he conceived to be the European manner. His book illustrations and prints are his best-known work, however, and with the productions of the two first Torii artists, Kiyonobu and his brother Kiyomasu, constitute the early Ukiyo-ye work of Yedo, upon which the coloured prints and illustrated books which have since become so famous were grounded.

Masanobu commenced illustrating and designing prints toward the beginning of the eighteenth century, and a book called *Kyōtarō*, a theatre piece in one volume which appeared in 1703 containing a note explaining that this was in the artist's eighteenth year, was probably his earliest work. After colour-blocks came to be used Masanobu devoted himself to this work and produced some very beautiful and graceful sheets in which gaufrage was used to a considerable extent in the printing.

Although prints and drawings of actors were the rather special work of the Torii men, Masanobu also designed some of these sheets much in the Torii manner, and was one of the group of artists who gathered in the Torii studios to experiment with the colour process. After his death in 1768 a number of pupils carried on their work in his style, among whom were Okumura Bunshi Masafusa; Okumura Toshinobu, who may have been his son; Kishigawa Katsumasa; and the famous Nishimura Shigenaga.

The following list embraces most of the books illustrated by Masanobu:

Kyōtaro : A theatre book. 1 vol. 1703.
Yorō-no-Daki: 2 vols. 1704.
Waka-no-ura Kabuto: The helmet of Waka-no-ura. An historical tale. 5 vols. 1706.
Danshōku Hiyoku-dori: 6 vols. 1706. L.
Buke Chōku Genchō: Duties of military families. 2 vols. 1706.
Wakakusa Genji Monogatari: History of the Princess Wakakusa and the Genji. Written by Yoshitsuken. 6 vols. 1707. M.L.
Gensan Daishi Ōmi Kūji Shō: 1 vol. 1708. S.
Kanto Nagori-no-Tamoto: 5 vols. 1708.
Togen-sō: A *Jōruri-bon*. 1 vol. 1708.
Kohaku Genji Monogatari: 5 vols. 1709.

PLATE 24] From the SHINSEN Ō UCHWA (Old and New Ghost Stories), a rare book attributed to Okumura Masanobu.

[Face p. 134

Fūryū Kagami Ga-Ike: 6 vols. 1709. L.
Miyoshi Gun-ki: A *Jōruri-bon*. 1 vol. 1710.
Sanshō Tayū: 1 vol. 1711.
Buke Shōkugen-sho: Military ethics. 2 vols. 1716. S.
Kōbō Daishi-ki: Life of Kōbō Daishi. 1 vol. 1719.
Zokukai Genji Monogatari: 6 vols. 1721.
Hina Zuru Genji: 6 vols. 1721.
Raiko Yama Eiri: A *Jōruri-bon*. 1 vol. 1721.
Ehon Fuga Nana Komachi: 1723.
Teikwa: 1 vol. 1724.
Hyakunin Ikku: A version of the Hundred Poets. 1 vol. 1727. L.
Ehon Sembon Sakura: Scenes in the lives of women. 2 vols. 1734.
Ukiyo Ehon Tsuru-no-Kuchi Bashi : 2 vols. 1752.

Other books by Masanobu and some attributed to him which are not dated are the

Shinsen O Uchiwa: Old and new ghost stories. *Attributed* to Masanobu. 8 vols. Exceedingly interesting and rare.
Ehon Ogura-no-Nishiki: One hundred poems on beautiful women. Signed Tanchōsai. 5 vols. About 1740.
Yukiyo Ehon Nukumei-dori: 2 vols.
Yedo-ye Sudare Byōbu: 2 vols.
Musha Ehon Yedo Shisōkon: 2 vols.
Musha Ehon Kongō Rikishi: Biographies of famous warriors. 2 vols.
Musha Ehon Tsunamono Yushi-kana Meishi: 2 vols.
Yedo O Yama Ehon Bijin Fukutoku: Beautiful women of Yedo. 2 vols. S.
Genji Hyakunin Isshu.
Ehon Tenjin Goichi Dai-ki: Fifty-one stories of Tenjin. 2 vols.
Hokuri Yugi-jō: Amusements of the North Quarter (the Yoshiwara). Oblong *gwajō* containing fifteen full-size *sumi-ye* and one single page. On the first page Masanobu is represented as signing a picture. L.
Yoshiwara Yukun Sugatami : Book on the Yoshiwara. 1 vol. L.
Ehon Musha Byōshi Yoseki: Book on warriors, heroes, etc. 2 vols. of large double-page *sumi-ye*. (Gillot Catalogue.)
Senzai Waka-shū.
Shitsuken Yume Monogatari.
Oboko Narihira Kyōdo-ji.
Saru Genji.
Aikei Sannen Daikoku Musozukin: 3 vols.
Onna Shuten Dōji Makura Kotoba : Occupations of women. 3 vols.
Jenaku Jimi Shikata Dōjō-ji: 3 vols.
Kai Awase Hamaguri Genji Kasen Gai : 3 vols.
Fūryū Tamare-gusa: 1 vol.
Jūgo Hiden Nanmai Shō: 1 vol.
Kiyo-ye Sakura : Signed Okumura Gempachi Masanobu. 1 vol.
Shido-ken Yumi Monogatari.
Ehon Fukutoku Sanjūni-sō: Thirty-two types of faces. 2 vols. M.
Hana-saki Jiji Tano-shimi-no-Eiga: A " small-pox book." 2 vols.
Mamei Maki Otoko: 1 vol.
Ehon Hitsusei Otogi Zōshi: 5 vols.
Ehon Kinichō.
Jūni Kwagetsu.
Yu Gwa-shiki: 1 vol.
Kōshoku Tamago Zake.

Ori Ehon.
Fukujō Sō.
Momoyo-gusa.
Ehon Shin Yoshiwara Sembon Sakura: New book on the Yoshiwara.
Okumura Musashi-ye: Pictures from Musashi.
Yoroi Sakura: 1 vol.
Fude-no-Yama: Humorous drawings of different deities. 1 vol.
Matsuri-no-ye: The Inari festival. 1 vol.
Musashi-no-Tsuki: Drawings of single figures of women.

It is extremely interesting to trace the change in Masanobu's style through his books. His early work was much like Morofusa's, showing Moronobu's influence plainly. The drawings in the *Wakakusa Genji Monogatari* of 1707, done in his twenty-second year, are perhaps the best examples of these early illustrations. In them, although the resemblance to Moronobu's work is marked, the broad and rather thick shoulders of the women are peculiarly characteristic of Masanobu. This is one of the few distinguishing marks of his early unsigned work, for at this period his faces were of the Moronobu type. Later, between 1730 and 1740, his drawing is finer lined, the noses become slightly aquiline, and the figures are taller; his style maturing into a robust dignity which is considerably like that in Kwaigetsudō's work.

An illustrated book by Okumura Bunshi MASAFUSA, published in Yedo in 1747, is listed in the Hayashi Catalogue (No. 1463). Other books by this artist were the

Ega Yoshitsune Ezo Nishiki: About 1744.
Tsuru-take Nasakeno Akibito: 2 vols. 1747.

Okumura Toshinobu illustrated a book entitled

Takasago Tokai-eiri: About 1748.

Yoshimura Katsumasa, a contemporary of Masanobu, left the

Taisei Shuchō : Drawings of animals, plants, shells, etc. 3 vols. About 1720. This has been reprinted a number of times.

THE TORII SCHOOL

The famous Torii branch of the Ukiyo-ye school also had its beginnings in the West, for KIYONOBU I. was born in Ōsaka, his father, Kondō Shōshichi Kiyomoto (1645–1702) having been an actor, famous for taking female parts, and who in his leisure hours painted theatrical posters for the Ōsaka playhouses. One of these posters, done in 1687, is among the early examples of theatrical work.

Kiyonobu, who was born in 1663, studied first under his father, then went to Kyōto, where he lived for a time, and finally in 1687 both father and son migrated to Yedo, where they established a studio and taught a large number of pupils, as well as painting, designing theatre posters and prints, and making book illustrations.

PLATE 25] From the KOKON SHI-SHIBAI HYAKUNIN ISSHU, illustrated by Torii Kiyonobu. Published Genroku 6 (1693). This book was one of the famous works written by Saikaku. Exposing certain customs of the day, it was pronounced indecent by the Government and the blocks for it were confiscated and destroyed. The book is sometimes mistakenly attributed to Moronobu.

[Face p. 136

Kiyonobu was also known as Torii Shōbei and is considered as the founder of the Torii group. His younger brother, Kiyomasu, was associated with him, and Okumura Masanobu, although the leader of a school of his own, worked along considerably the same lines, even producing the actor prints occasionally which had become so popular.

Kiyonobu is said to have made the advertising posters which were placed outside the principal theatres in Yedo, and to him also have been attributed the portraits of the actor Ishikawa Danjūrō, which were printed in colours and sold in the streets there for 5 *cash* each. Although Fenollosa puts the date for the first colour printing at about 1740, this is certainly much too late, and Mr. Morrison is undoubtedly right in maintaining that Kiyonobu understood and practised the art.[1]

Kiyonobu died in 1729, leaving a number of pupils who became famous. As a book illustrator he was not very prolific, this work being rather incidental to his print designing, painting, and teaching. It is probable that the following list of his books is incomplete and that other works were illustrated by him.

Among the books which he is known to have left are the

Ukiyo Zōshi: Illustrated legends. Signed Yamato Eshi Shōbei. 4 vols. 1687. Excessively rare.
Amida-no-Munewarai: The heart of Amida. A drama. 1 vol. About 1690.
Kokonshi Shibai Hyakunin Isshu: Written by Saikaku. Illustrated by Torii Kiyonobu. This book was considered so disgraceful that it was condemned by the Government and the blocks for it destroyed. 1 vol. 1693.
Ko Atsumori: A tragedy in six acts. 1 vol. Late seventeenth century.
Taichōku Yugao Rechō-gusa: Miraculous statue of Kwannon in Kiyomizu Temple. Text by Matsuno Midori. 5 vols. 1704.
Budo Iro Hakkei: Eight aspects of love. 5 vols. 1705.
Sadato Ikusa Edzukushi: Historical events, drawings of warriors, battle scenes, etc. Early Kyōhō period.
Shibai Iro Kurabi.
Ryōha Shigen: Fashions among women. Signed Torii Kiyonobu. 1728.
Tsumawa Morokuchi Yawaragi Sogwa: Fantastic tale in which a Japanese explorer visits Formosa. 1 vol.

Among Kiyonobu's pupils were KIYOMASU, KIYOTADA, Hanegawa CHINCHŌ, Katsukawa TERUSHIGE, and Kondō KIYOHARU.

KIYOMASU lived between 1679 and 1764. Authorities differ as to the relationship between him and Kiyonobu. Morrison says that he was the eldest of Kiyonobu's three sons. Other writers maintain that he was Kiyonobu's younger brother. His work was very similar to that of Kiyonobu and consisted of *sumi-ye* and two-colour prints, theatre programmes and posters, and book illustrations. There is great virility in his drawings and always a marvellously fine placing of blacks.

---

[1] At the sale of the Wilson Crewdson collection at Sotheby's in London, 1919, there was a print (No. 14) signed Torii Kiyonobu, printed in *beni* and green.

Among the books illustrated by him were the

Santo Yakusha-no-Sugata-ye: Silhouettes of actors of three cities (Yedo, Ōsaka, and Kyōto). Signed Torii. 1 vol. 1703.
Fukura Yanzei Yorimasa: Historical tales. Signed Torii. 1 vol. 1712.
Fuji-no-Yuki Mitsugi Soga: 1746.
Theatre programmes of plays acted by Danjūrō and other actors. 1729–1747.

Hanegawa CHINCHŌ, who lived between 1679 and 1754, was also a pupil of Kiyonobu. He was born in Kawaguchi, Musashi province, the son of a well-known *samurai* family. His true name was Ota Bengorō, but he was also known as Manaka, Ota Benjirō, and as an artist signed himself Hanegawa OKINOBU, and Hagawa and Hanegawa Chinchō. His work is exceedingly rare. He illustrated the

Kokusenya Senri-no-Hayashi Ninomaki: A history of the drama. 1 vol. About 1720.
Maru Kagami or *Impon:* 1720.
Bankai Setsu Yōshū.
Geki-jō Ehon.
Yoshiwara Saiken-ki.

Kondō KIYOHARU, also known as Kondō SUKEGORŌ and JITSUDŌ, and his son and pupil, Kondō Katsunobu, were offshoots of the Ōsaka Torii family, and may have been the grandson and great-grandson of the seventeenth-century actor-artist Kondō Shōshichi of that city, who, although not generally placed in the Torii group, was in reality the founder of it. Kiyoharu may thus have been the younger brother or nephew of Kiyonobu. Strange says he was his pupil. He was working early in the eighteenth century and left the

Hakuyen Ichidai-ki: A biography of Hakuyen, the third Danjūrō. 3 vols. 1713.
Yukun Ōmi Daishi: Autumn pilgrimages to Ōmi. Shōtoku period.
Eiri Doke Hyakunin Isshu: A humorous version of the Hundred Poets. Published by Murata Jirobei of Yedo. 1720.

Hishikawa KIYOHARU and Kondō ARIYOSHI were nineteenth-century descendants of the Kondō family, who lived in Ōsaka, and are mentioned in Chapter IV.

Torii KIYOMITSU, also known as Hanzō, the son of Kiyomasu and the nephew of Kiyonobu I., was born in Yedo in 1735, and lived with other members of the family in Naniwa-chō. At his father's death in 1763 he became the third master of the Torii group, working in much the same style that his father had adopted. In his colour-prints he limited himself to soft pinks and greens, although occasionally using a beautiful soft grey and brown. He left many prints, theatre programmes, and a few illustrated books. His death occurred in 1785. Among the books illustrated by him were the

Ehon Nintoku Tennō: Story of the Emperor Nintoku. 2 vols. About 1748.
Daruma Chishōki: History of the birth of Daruma. 3 vols. 1760.
Jōruri Naga-uta: Illustrated poems. 1 vol. 1769.
Naga-uta Jōruri Shū: Illustrated poems. 1 vol. 1750.
Naga-uta-Shū: Illustrated poems. 1 vol. 1759.

With Torii KIYONAGA we come to the fourth and by far the greatest master of the Torii group, as well as one of the greatest of all the Ukiyo-ye artists.

Kiyonaga was born in 1742, the son of Shirōkiya Ichibei, a publisher of Yedo. He was adopted by Torii Kiyomitsu, who recognized his talent while he was still a boy in his father's shop. Although he studied under Kiyomitsu, he originated a style of his own, and it was only after Kiyomitsu's death in 1785, when he found himself at the head of the famous school, that he gave up his own method for a time, to resume that which tradition through four generations had associated with the Torii work. He adopted young Kiyomine, the grandson of Kiyomitsu, trained him in the Torii manner, and then went back to the style he had originated and abandoned.

Kiyonaga used as other signatures the names SHIRŌ, SEKI, SEKIGUCHI, ICHIBEI, and SHINSUKE.

Among all the artists of the Torii group Kiyonaga was by far the most versatile both in subjects and treatment, and left book illustrations and prints not only of actors, which were the special subjects of the Torii men, but of warriors, beautiful women, house interiors, street scenes, festivals, etc. All the foremost print designers of the next generation were influenced by him; Shunchō, who had been Shunshō's pupil, Kitao Shigemasa, Toyoharu, and Utamaro, all showing the effect of his work in their own productions. Kiyonaga died in 1815, leaving many followers not only among the artists of the Torii group, but in nearly all the other Ukiyo-ye studios. All of his books are extremely rare and valuable. They include the

Temare Uta: Illustrated poems. 3 vols. 1777.
Imamu-kachi Bakemono Oyadama ("The Greatest of Monsters"): The story of the birth of a normal child into the world of monsters, where he is regarded as abnormal and a being apart. His sorrows and loneliness finally force him into the Buddhist priesthood, where he at last finds peace. 2 vols. 1780.
Kamikuzu Minu-ye Banashi: 3 vols. 1780.
Bakemono Yutsu-nino Hachi-noki: Book on ghosts and monsters. 3 vols. 1780.
Asahina Karaku Asobi: 3 vols. 1781.
Ehon Mushi Bukuro: Anecdotes of brave and unselfish men. 2 vols. 1782. Colours.
Ehon Buyū Kongō Rishiki: Heroes and warriors. 1785.
Ehon Yedo Monomi-ga-oka: Pleasure parties of the four seasons. Signed Seki Kiyonaga. 2 medium-sized vols. 1785. Black and white. Also an edition in colours.
Mitsu-no-Asa: The festival mornings of the first three days of the New Year. Seven plates in colours. No. 1, Young princesses writing. No. 2, Promenade on New Year's Day in the Yoshiwara. No. 3, Young princes shooting with bows and arrows. No. 4, Opening of a merchant's go-down. No. 5, First riding lesson of young *samurai*. No. 6, First bath and toilet of the New Year. No. 7, Publishing house of Yeijudō Nishimura, the publisher of the book, with a notice advertising the *Mitsu-no-Asa*, with Kiyonaga's signature. A most beautiful and excessively rare book. 1 vol. 1787.

Saishiki Mitsu-no-Ashita: Three mornings of the New Year. Signed Torii Kiyonaga. 1 vol. Colours. (Listed in the Duret Catalogue, p. 96. Possibly the same as the *Mitsu-no-Asa*.)

Monomo-dori Hyakunin Isshu: One hundred humorous poems on the New Year. Unsigned. 1 vol. 1793.

Ehon Tachi Bukuro: Wise men of the past.

Jikun Kaga-ye-no-Tato-ye: Allegories for children. Written by Santō Kyōden. Illustrations signed Seki Kiyonaga. 3 vols. 1798.

Ehon Yōyō-no-Matsu: Beautiful women at different occupations. 1 vol. No date. Colours.

Torii KIYOMINE, also known as Shōnosuke, the fifth master of the Torii group, really took his place as the leader of the Torii school before Kiyonaga died, the latter retiring and going back to his chosen manner of work toward the close of the eighteenth century. Kiyomine lived between 1786 and 1868, and was probably the grandson rather than the son of Kiyomitsu.[1] At the death of the latter artist he was adopted by Kiyonaga and trained for the leadership of the Torii studios.

Kiyomine made many prints and illustrated a few books, as well as having the work which some Torii artist was always given—that of supplying the theatre posters to the principal playhouses of Yedo. Although his training had been in the traditional Torii manner, he was much more influenced by Kiyonaga's work than by his teaching, and many of his own prints and book illustrations show almost nothing of the Torii manner.

In 1815, the year Kiyonaga died, Kiyomine took the name of Kiyomitsu II. With Kiyomine the Torii school, which had lasted for over a century, lost its character as a separate group, and although followers continued in its methods for a time, the early force and vigour had departed and other forms of Ukiyo-ye art were supplanting it in the affections of the people.

Few books by Kiyomine are known. The *Ito Sakura Honchō Monzui*, written by Santō Kyōden, is said to have been illustrated by him, although the drawings are not signed. It was published in 1810.

Torii KIYOFUSA, also known as Kiyomitsu III., was the son of Kiyomine, and is sometimes called the sixth master of the Torii group. He lived between 1832 and 1892, but long before his time the work of the school had degenerated to such an extent that the group had lost all importance.

In addition to the five great leaders of this famous branch of the Ukiyo-ye school, there were many lesser Torii artists, some of whom did rather notable work. Many of the old theatre programmes consisting of a title-page in colours and other pages of *sumi-ye* were by these men.

Among these artists were KIYOTADA, KIYOSOMO, KIYOAKI, and Kondō KIYOHARU, who were pupils of Kiyonobu; KIYOSHIGE, who was working between 1725 and 1759, and Tanaka MASUNOBU (also known as SANSEIDŌ),

---

[1] Von Seidlitz says this was by marriage.

who made actor prints in two colours about 1750, both of whom were pupils of Kiyomasu; KIYOTSUNE, KIYOTOSHI, KIYOHIDE I., KIYOHIDE II., and KIYOSATO, pupils of Kiyomitsu; KIYOHIRO, a pupil of Shirō Kiyonobu; KIYOKUNI, KIYOMATSU, KIYOMASA (also known as TORII SHIRŌ),[1] a son of Kiyonaga's, and KIYOMOTO, who was working about 1788–1794, all of whom were followers of Kiyonaga; and KIYOYASU and KIYOSADA, pupils of Kiyomine.

Books illustrated by these men were

Theatre programmes: Illustrated by Torii Kiyohiro. 1 vol. 1738.
Seri-fu: Dramatic dialogue. Signed Torii Kiyohiro. 1 vol. 1738.
Songs of Tomimoto: By Torii Kiyohiro. 1 vol. 1754.
Tosei Onna Danshishi: By Torii Kiyoshige. 2 vols. 1754.
Theatre programme: By Torii Kiyohide. 1 vol. 1772.
Naga Uta: Poems, illustrated by Torii Kiyohide. 1 vol. 1775.
Theatre programme: By Torii Kiyomoto. 1 vol. No date.
Ishikawa Mimasu Haikai: Poems, illustrated by Torii Kiyomoto. 1 vol. 1824.

Torii KIYOTSUNE, one of the best pupils of Kiyomitsu, left several interesting books, among which were the

Doji ga Matsu: History of the child Maruko. No date.
Naga-Uta: Poems. 1 vol. 1767.
Ehon Nijūshi-kō: Twenty-four examples of filial piety. 2 rather small vols. A well-known book. 1774. Colours.
Koi-no-Yumihari Dzuki ("The Bow of Love"): 3 vols. 1777.
Haru Bukuro ("The Bag of Spring"): 3 vols. 1777. S.
Kiso-Kaidō Futari Yoshinaka: 3 vols. 1777.
Tomodachi Banashi: Meiwa period.
Yomei Iri Fukuroku: Illustrations of the marriage ceremony. No date. S.

THE NISHIMURA GROUP OF UKIYO-YE ILLUSTRATORS

A fourth group of artists, eventually numbering among its members some of the most famous men of the entire Ukiyo-ye movement, may be called the Nishimura group. It is believed by many collectors to have originated with Nishimura Shigenobu, who, it is said, was making prints in the Torii style and drawings of women something in the manner of Kwaigetsudō, before the middle of the eighteenth century. Major J. J. O'Brien Sexton, however, believes,[2] and with very good reasons, that Nishimura Shigenobu was one of the early brush names used by Ishikawa Toyonobu, and that Shigenaga should be considered as the head of the Nishimura group.

Nishimura SHIGENAGA was born in Yedo in 1697 of a family named Suzuki. Strange says that he lived at Torii Abura-chō in Yedo, where

[1] According to the Gillot Catalogue Torii Shirō was the third son of Kiyonobu and was also called Torii Kiyonobu the younger.

[2] See article entitled "Illustrated Books of Japan" in the November (1917) number of the *Burlington Magazine*.

he kept a tea-house, and afterwards in Kanda, going into the book-publishing business there. He seems to have had a varied instruction in art, and probably studied for a time with Torii Kiyonobu before coming under the influence of Okumura Masanobu.

Shigenaga was among the most versatile of all his contemporaries, making prints in the Torii manner, drawings of women much in the manner of Masanobu, and figures in landscape settings. His first work for wood-engraving was devoted to the *sumi-ye* sheets, but when the interest in colour-printing was aroused, Shigenaga joined the group of artists that gathered in the Torii studios to experiment with the process. This circle was made up of Kiyomasu (well on in years at that time) and his followers, Kiyotada, Toshinobu, Kiyohiro, and Kiyomitsu; with whom Okumura Masanobu, Toyonobu (at that time known as Nishimura Shigenobu), and Shigenaga joined. Thus the heads of the principal Ukiyo-ye groups all joined forces to see what they could do in applying colours to printing.

It is not known who originated the idea or who made the first prints. Experiments in this work were certainly made as early as the Kwanyei period by followers of the Chinese masters who had come to Japan after the downfall of the Ming dynasty, so that at best the work of the Ukiyo-ye men was but the perfecting of a process which was already known, even though it had not been practised to any extent. Only two blocks were used in the first Yedo experiments, one for a soft pink and the other for a greyish-green, and variations of these tones placed in telling juxtapositions with black formed, with the luminous cream ground of the paper, the notes with which these early print artists composed their charming colour-harmonies.

Kiyonobu, Okumura Masanobu, and Shigenaga, are generally assumed to have been the leaders in the Ukiyo-ye colour work, and the earliest sheets are attributed to them. After the two-colour process had been brought to perfection, it was natural that experiments should follow with three blocks, and Kiyomitsu, Toyonobu, and Harunobu, the two latter Shigenaga's pupils, joined the older men, all vying with each other in this interesting work.

Shigenaga died in 1765, but his studio remained one of the chief centres of the Ukiyo-ye movement for many years after. Although book illustration was rather incidental to his other work, he left the following:

Nobunaga-ki: Life of the General Oda Nobunaga. 1 vol. About 1735.
Ehon Kokinran: Various drawings. First volume by Shigenaga. Last two by Harunobu. 3 vols. 1763.
Ehon Yedo Miyage: Souvenir of Yedo. Undated, but known to have been published in the Hōreki period. 3 vols. Rare and charming.
Aka-hon Sarukani Gasen: A " small-pox book." Signed Nishimura Shigenaga. No date.

The *Yedo Miyage* by Shigenaga was one of the first sets of books to bear this title, although other artists in later years appropriated it for similar

PLATE 26] From the AKA-HON SARUKANI GASSEN, an aka-hon or "small-pox book", illustrated by Nishimura Shigenaga. Printed entirely in red. No date.

PLATE 27] From the EHON SEIRŌ BIJIN AWASE, by Suzuki Harunobu. 1770.

[Face p. 142

works of their own. The drawings are very naïve and delightful, consisting of tiny figures coming and going in landscape settings. The books are of medium size and bound in the well-known greyish-white covers with a design in blue.

Of Shigenaga's pupils, the senior of the school was Ishikawa TOYONOBU, also known (in early work) as Nishimura SHIGENOBU, Nishimura MAGOSABURŌ, and later as TANSENDŌ, TANJŌDŌ, Ishikawa SHŪYEN, SHŪHA, and KAWAYEDO. He lived between 1711 and 1785 and formed a link between the Torii work and that of the Nishimura studio, for his early study, under Kiyomasu, had given him something of the Torii manner. His work shows the influence of both schools, however, as well as that of Okumura Masanobu.

Toyonobu was among the first of the Ukiyo-ye men to practise full polychrome printing, and with Kiyomitsu and Harunobu led in this work after it had become fully established. He left the following books, the illustrations in which are considerably like Masanobu's later work (in the faces and figures of women) while men are represented with the peculiar faces so characteristic of the Torii work. His books include the

Ehon Azuma-no-Mori: Old legends. Signed Ishikawa Shuyen Toyonobu. 2 vols. 1752.
Ehon Kotowaza-gusa: 3 vols. 1752.
Ehon Dzue Tsumo-gusa.
Kyōka Manzai-shū: 2 vols. No date.
Suetsumuhana (?): 2 vols. 1757.
Ehon Musha Tazuma: 2 vols. No date.
Ehon Shimeshi Ai-kagami: 4 vols. 1762.
Ehon Hana-no-Midori: Illustrated proverbs. 3 vols. 1763.
Ehon Azuma Asobi: 3 vols. 1763.
Ehon Yedo Murasaki: Book on the Yoshiwara. 3 vols. 1763. A second edition in 1765.
Hana-no-Yukari: 2 vols. No date.
Ehon Satoshi Mondō: Instructive dialogues. 3 vols. No date.
Ro-ye Kyō Butai: Signed Kawayedo Toyonobu.
Shiki Go-shō-Sakura: 2 vols. No date.
Ehon Chiyo-no-Haru: 3 vols. 1769.
Oshi-ye-gusa: Occupations of women. 3 vols. 1779.

In Major O'Brien Sexton's article in the *Burlington Magazine*, spoken of on page 141, there is a book listed, published in 1737, containing a large frontispiece, entitled *Mo Ba Dan Ki*, signed Nishimura Magosaburō Shigenobu. In the second edition of this book (in 1762) this same frontispiece is signed Ishikawa Toyonobu, proving Major O'Brien Sexton's belief that Nishimura Shigenobu was an early signature used by Toyonobu.

Suzuki HARUNOBU, a pupil of Shigenaga, who became one of the foremost print designers of the Ukiyo-ye school, was born in 1724. He was also known as MATABE, CHŌYEIKEN, and SEISENKWAN, and sometimes signed himself KORYŪ, which had also been one of the artist names used by Shigenaga.

Strange says that Kyosen was a signature occasionally used by him. His true name was Hozami Jihei. Few details are known in regard to his life except that he is said to have been a vendor of brushes when a boy. It is probable that he did not come under Shigenaga's instruction until well on in years, as nothing is said of him in connection with the early experiments in colour-printing, when if he had been in that artist's studio he would in all probability have been one of the group to carry on this work. A little later, however, after the three-block process had been perfected, he and Kiyomitsu and Toyonobu all took it up eagerly, Harunobu especially, for he seems to have jumped to full polychrome printing almost with his first work, and by 1765 was designing prints of several colours, as well as charming *surimono* printed from five or six blocks.

To Harunobu has mistakenly been attributed the first book containing coloured illustrations. This was the *Ehon Haru-no-Nishiki*, the preface to which says: " Suzuki is one to whom the coloured pictures at present in vogue appeal. He has illustrated this book at my request in imitation of the popular colour-prints called *nishiki-ye* which are so constantly sold in the streets at present. I have given the title of *Haru-no-Nishiki* to the book, and shall be happy if it serves to interest one during the long spring days." Signed Hekigyokudō, first month, the year *Kano-to U*, which corresponds to 1771. It was thus considerably later than several other books illustrated by Ukiyo-ye artists, not to speak of those by the followers of the Chinese school of a much earlier time.

Harunobu's book illustrations, as well as his prints, are chiefly of beautiful women and their lovers, and to the background of those printed in colours he usually added a tone of soft grey or green, thus differentiating them from the earlier work in which the background was left white. Most of the books illustrated by him in colours were also published in editions printed in black and white and grey. His early books contained simple line drawings only. As far as known his earliest work in illustration was done in collaboration with Shigenaga in the *Ehon Kokinran*, a series of three medium-sized books, the first of which was by Shigenaga and the remaining two by Harunobu. This set of books appeared in 1763 and contains a few lines of text at the side of each drawing.

Other books illustrated by him were the

Ehon Chōnai-no-Nishiki: Street scenes. 3 vols. 1763.
Ehon Shogei Nishiki: Scenes of everyday life. 3 vols. 1763.
Ehon Hana Katzura: Illustrated poems. 3 vols. Signed Suzuki Harunobu. 1764.
Buyū Nishiki-no-Tamoto: Famous warriors. 1764.
Ehon Kotowaza-gusa: Illustrated proverbs. Signed Suzuki. 3 vols. 1765.
Ehon Sazare Ishi: Illustrated poems. 3 vols. 1766.
Ehon Chiyo-no-Matsu: Illustrated poems. 3 vols. 1767.
Ehon Warabe-no-Moto: 3 vols. 1767.

Ehon Yachiyo-gusa: Illustrated poems. 3 vols. 1768.
Ameuri Dohei-den: Illustrated anecdotes. 1769.
Ehon Seirō Bijin Awase: Beautiful women. Printed in two editions, one in black and white and one in colours. One of Harunobu's most famous and beautiful books. 5 vols. 1770.
Yoshiwara Bijin Awase: Beautiful women of the Yoshiwara. 1 vol. 1770. Colours.
Ehon Haru-no-Nishiki: Spring scenes in Yedo. 2 vols. About 1770. Colours.
Ehon Misao-gusa: Virtuous women. Published after Harunobu's death. 2 vols. 1778.
Ehon Iroha Uta: Illustrated poems. 1788.
Haikai Yogoshi-no-Mono Kurabe: Illustrated poems. Signed Seisenkwan. 1 vol. 1793.

Other books illustrated by Harunobu, but not dated, are the

Tōto Meisho: Twenty-four views of Yedo. Colours.
Ehon Ukiyo-ye Bukuro: 3 vols. About 1770.
Haru-no-Uki ("Snow in the Spring-Time"): 3 vols.
Take-no-Hayashi: 3 vols.
Yoshiwara Daizen: Famous women of the Yoshiwara.
Haru-no-Tomo ("Comrades of Spring"): 3 vols.
Yedo Miyage: Souvenir of Yedo. 3 vols.
Zoku Yedo Miyage: These sets formed a supplement to Shigenaga's earlier work of the same title. 3 vols. About 1779.
Fūryū Enshōku Maneyemon: Album of twelve plates.
Shungwa Shohon Haru-no-Ashita: Unsigned, but attributed by Kurth to Harunobu.

Yamamoto FUSANOBU, also known as Tomikawa and Ginsetsu, is said by Fenollosa to have been a pupil of Shigenaga. No details are available in regard to his life. He illustrated the

Seimei Uta Uranai: Poems on fortune-telling. 1 vol. About 1762.
Ehon Hana Asobi ("Walks among the Flowers"): Portraits of the Yoshiwara women. Signed Tomikawa Fusanobu. 1765.
Tōbō-Saku Ku-Sensai: Strategy in war. Signed Tomikawa Ginsetsu. 3 vols. 1770.
Fuji Asama Monogatari: A romance. 3 vols. 1777.

A contemporary of Harunobu's and his fellow-pupil under Shigenaga was Isoda KORYŪSAI, who, although chiefly known for his delightful prints, also left a few very interesting books. The dates of Koryūsai's birth and death remain unknown. It is only recorded of him that he belonged to a *samurai* family of Yedo and had his studio at Yagenbori, near Nihon-bashi, from which district he took one of the names he occasionally used—Tōto Yagenbori Inshi ("The lazy man of Yagenbori"). Other names by which he was known were SHŌBEI and Masakatsu HARUHIRO, to which the title of Hokkyō, conferred upon him by the Shōgunate, was sometimes added.

Koryūsai's prints are of great variety and beauty, and represent not only beautiful women, but landscapes, birds, flowers, insects, and animals. Among the books illustrated by him, all of which are extremely rare, were the

Azuma-no-Nishiki Matsu-no-Kurai: Famous courtesans of Yedo with name and *mon* above each figure. Perhaps the rarest and most beautiful of all the Japanese colour-printed books. 1777.
Tayu Kurabe: Colours.

CHAP. VII] **JAPANESE BLOCK-PRINTING**

Hokuri-no-Uta: Poems on the " Villas of the North." By Gemichi. Plates by Koryūsai. 1 vol. About 1779. Colours and black and white.
Konzatsu Yamato Sōgwa: Sketch book. 3 vols. 1781. Black and white. A later edition has a blue tone added.

Another famous pupil of Shigenaga's, Utagawa TOYOHARU, was born in the province of Bungo in 1735. He is supposed to have been a younger brother of the Utagawa Toyonobu, who died when a young man, and who had been such a promising follower of Ishikawa Toyonobu.

Toyoharu's true name was Tajima Chōsaburō Shuyemon. He was working in the Nishimura studio while Ishikawa Toyonobu, Harunobu, and Koryūsai were still students there, and after Shigenaga gave up teaching, studied under Toyonobu and Harunobu, taking the first syllables of their names for his own signature. He is said to have studied in Nagasaki and Kyōto before going to Yedo, and it is certain that he painted in oils at one time, and made drawings and prints in which perspective was introduced. His fame as a painter won him the recognition of the Shōgunate, and in 1789 he was selected as one of the artists to help in the restoration of the Nikkō temples. This work kept him busy for some years, and probably accounts for the comparative rarity of his prints and books.

Toyoharu used as other signatures the names ICHIRYŪSAI, ICHIYŪSAI, SENZŌ, and SENRYŪSAI. He died about 1814, leaving a school of his own which became known as the Utagawa *Ryu*. Among the few books illustrated by him was the *Ehon Yedo Nishiki-ye*, published in two volumes in 1803. According to the preface by Sakuragawa Jishinari, the work was in imitation of Harunobu's book of the same title. The drawings are much in Harunobu's style and represent temples, streets, bridges, and the bay of Yedo, with numerous tiny figures in these settings. The book first appeared printed in black and white and grey, but later the same year was issued in colours. Both editions are charming and rare.

Of this generation of artists, although slightly younger than any of them, was the queer genius, Shiba KŌKAN. He lived between 1746 and 1818 and was a young contemporary of Utagawa Toyoharu and interested with him, but to a much greater extent, in the foreign method of painting. His true name was Andō Kichijirō. He was a pupil and possibly an adopted son of Harunobu, calling himself for a time Harunobu II., and confessing to having forged a number of the true Harunobu's prints as well as signing that artist's name to work of his own.

Either his inability to keep up with the other students in the Yedo school or a genuine interest in Occidental art finally drove him to Nagasaki, where the few Dutch who were still allowed to remain in the country were segregated. Here he studied the European method of drawing, including perspective and copper-plate engraving. The works he left of this period in his career are among the curiosities of Japanese art.

He is said to have stolen an oil painting which he found among the votive offerings of Kitano Temple, Kyōto, at one time, and upon being charged with the theft affirmed that the gods had given it to him in order that he might learn from it the European manner of painting.

Among the signatures used by him were HARUSHIGE, SHUN, SHUMPO, SHUNPARŌ, KUNGAKU, KATSUSABURŌ, MA, and MAGODAYU, to which he sometimes added the words Fugen Dōjin, meaning " rich old man."

In addition to a number of prints done much in Harunobu's style, and many of them signed Harunobu, Kōkan left a few very curious and interesting books and maps. Among these works were the

Gwato Saiyudan: A book of travels. 2 vols. 1781.
Saiyu Ryōdan: Incidents in a trip from Yedo to Nagasaki. 5 vols. 1790.
Seiyo Gwaden.
Taisei Shōkoku Senko.
Nagasaki Kunmonshi.
Saiyu Tabi Banashi.
Orando Kiko: A book on Dutch customs, furniture, utensils, etc.
Tōto Hakkei: Eight copper-plate engravings of Yedo.
Chiku Ryaku Setsu: An atlas and an accompanying map in copper-plate engraving called the *Dohan Chikuzan Dzue.*
Bankoku Fudoku: Customs in foreign countries. 1 vol., and an accompanying large copper-plate map called the *Dohan Chiku Daizen Dzue.*
Temmon Ryakugwa: Drawings of birds and insects. 1 vol., and an appendix in a copper-plate engraving called *Dohan Tenkyū-no-Dzue.*
Shunparō Gwafu: Drawings of mountains, rivers, flowers, birds, people, etc.

The *Saiyu Ryōdan* contains some very amusing drawings of foreigners, their clothes, houses, furniture, etc. This book and the *Shunparō Gwafu* are rare and command absurdly high prices among Japanese collectors. They are devoid of the slightest beauty and are prized only as curious souvenirs of the Dutch influence and the Dutch settlement at Nagasaki.

In addition to the books mentioned there are several interesting plates by Shiba Kōkan in various collections of drawings by contemporary men as in the *Keijō Gwayen* of 1814, the *Shitori Haiku*, a *kubari-hon* of about the same time, and others.

Kitao SHIGEMASA, who lived in Yedo between 1738 and 1819, was, as his name indicates, a pupil of both Kiyomasa and Shigenaga. In ordinary life he was known as Sasuke Kitabatake. While a boy he worked in a bookshop belonging to the well-known publisher Sawaraya Mohei, who afterwards published some of his books. In after life Shigemasa owned a book-shop himself and divided his time between writing and print-designing. He was also well known as a calligrapher and used in this work the signature Ichiyōsai. Other artist names used by him were TAROKICHI, TAIREI,

Kakan, Kwaran, Kwaransai, Suiho Itsujin, Saihoko, Sekkōsai, Kyūgorō, Kōsuifu, and Kōsuisai.

He illustrated a number of books and occasionally collaborated with Shunshō and his pupil Kitao Masanobu.

A list of his books includes the

Ehon Sakaye-gusa: Illustrations of theatre life in Yedo. 3 vols. About 1765–1767. Signed Kitao Shigemasa.
Ehon Biwako: Pictures of women. 1775.
Ehon Yotsu-no-Toki: 3 vols. 1775.
Seirō Bijin Awase Sugata Kagami (" Beauties of the Green House "): In collaboration with Shunshō. 3 vols. 1776. Colours. Very rare.
Ehon Biwa-no-Umi: 3 vols. 1778.
Ehon Azuma Karage: 3 vols. 1786.
Ehon Yasu Ujigawa: Famous heroes of Japan, with poems. 3 vols. 1786.
Sanyo Dzue Ehon Takara-no-Itoguchi or *Kaiko Yachinai-gusa:* Silk culture in Japan. In collaboration with Shunshō. 1 vol. 1786. Twelve colour plates.
Ehon Biwako: 1788.
Ehon Fukuju-Sō: Illustrated legends. Signed Kitao Kōsuisai Shigemasa. 1791. Colours.
Jūni Kagura Osana Karuwaza: Unsigned. Attributed to Shigemasa and Toyokuni. 3 vols. 1793.
Miken Jaku Sanin Nawa Ye-hi: The three monstrous heads. Written by Santō Kyōden. 1 vol. 1794.
Sansai Dzue Osana Kōshaku. 1797.
Sandara Kasumi (" Fog in the Country "): An album of three coloured plates, including one signed Kōsuisai. 1797. Colours.
Ningen Issho Migaki Jōruri Kokoro-no-Kagami: 3 vols. 1798.
Otoko Toko: The mid-January festival. An album of six plates, including one signed Kitao Kōsuisai. 1798. Colours.
Kana-dehon Mune-no-Kagami: Unsigned, but attributed to Shigemasa. 3 vols. 1799.
Sore-wa Kusunoke Kyantai Heiki Muko : 3 vols. 1799.
Kana Tazuna Chūshingura: The forty-seven Ronin represented by women. Written by Santō Kyōden. Illustrated by Shigemasa. 1801.
Haru Toriki Chiye-no-Senkoku: Unsigned, but attributed to Shigemasa. 3 vols. 1802.
Shokurui Waboku-no-Kono Mono Kasen: 1802.
Momotogura Yamiyo-no-Shichiyaku: 3 vols. 1802.
Ehon Komaga-dake: Famous horses in Japan and China and their owners. 3 vols. 1802. Colours.
Kwachō Shashin Dzue: Birds and flowers. First series. Signed Kitao Kōsuisai. 3 vols. 1805. Colours.
Ehon Matsu-no-Shirabe: Attributed to Kitao Shigemasa. 1803.
Kyōka Hyakunin Isshu: Signed Kōsuisai Kitao Shigemasa. 1 vol. 1809. Colours.
Shiten-dōji Monogatari: 1 vol. Colours. Attributed to Shigemasa. No date. Rare.
Ehon Yushi Kurabe: Famous heroes. 1 vol. 1810.
Ehon Uji-no-Watashi: Historical tales. 3 vols. Colour.
Ehon Tatsu-no-Miyako (" Capital of the Dragon of the Sea "): An album containing plates of fishes, shells, etc. 1 vol.
Genji Hyakunin-Shu Nishiki Ori: One hundred poems on the Genji. 1 vol. Colours.
Kyōka Ehon Ama-no-gawa: Humorous poems. 2 vols.
Kwachō Shashin Dzue: Second series. 3 vols. 1827. Colours.

Shigemasa's most beautiful work in book illustration is found in the famous *Seirō Bijin Awase*, done in collaboration with Shunshō. It consists

[PLATE 28]

"The Kinuta". From the EHON YOTSU-NO-TOKI, by Kitao Shigemasa (1775).

of eighty-six double-page coloured plates, in which a soft rose colour is the prevailing tint, representing the inmates of the " Green Houses " at their daily occupations of writing, reading, arranging flowers, walking, etc. Each favourite has her name and the house to which she belongs inscribed on the page.

The title, meaning " Beauties of the Green Houses," had its origin in the old Chinese law which required all houses of ill-fame to be painted green, the inmates being known as " Women of the Green Houses." This book is considered by collectors to be one of the most beautiful illustrated books ever published. It vies with two works by Kitao Masanobu, the *Seirō Meikun Jihitsu Shū* and the *Yoshiwara Shin Bijin Awase*, and with the *Azuma-no-Nishiki Matsu no-Kurai* by Kōryūsai for the first place in collections of Ukiyo-ye books.

One's personal taste may not quite agree with this estimate, for less well-known books by Kiyonaga, the beautiful album called *Haru-no-Wo* by Shunman, and one or two of Utamaro's works, seem worthy of equal rank.

The book on silk culture in which Shigemasa again collaborated with Shunshō is also beautiful and perhaps even more rare than the *Seirō Bijin Awase*. The plates represent twelve different stages in the making of silk and are printed in soft and charming colours.

The *Kwachō Shashin Dzue*, containing coloured drawings of flowers and birds, is probably the most widely known of any of Shigemasa's works, since it is not so rare as to be very difficult to procure. It was intended as the first of four series of drawings of this kind, each to be made up of three volumes. The undertaking ended, however, with the second series which, although advertised to appear in 1806, the year after the first set was issued, really was not published until 1827, eight years after the artist's death. This second series is comparatively rare and much less well known than that of 1805.

Kitao MASANOBU, the famous pupil of Shigemasa, was born in 1761 of a humble Yedo family named Iwase. As a boy he worked as clerk in a tobacco shop, but later gave this up for a similar position with a chemist. He commenced to write and paint before he was fourteen years old, and finally, with the help of his employer, entered Shigemasa's studio. Here his talent developed rapidly, and by his twentieth year he was producing work which rivalled that of his master.

As a novelist and poet Masanobu was perhaps even more renowned than as an artist, and he left a number of novels in addition to several volumes of poems which won immense popularity. His author's name was Santō Kyōden, and as a poet he sometimes signed himself Migaru-no-Urisuke. He used as other artist signatures the names Rissai MASANOBU, SEI, SEIYEN,

CHAP. VII] JAPANESE BLOCK-PRINTING

SEISAI, Seisei RŌJIN, YUSEI, HAKKEI, Kyōya DENZŌ, Iwase, Haida, SANTŌ-AN, HŌSAN, Kitao SHINSAI, and KANKOKU.

His death occurred in 1816, and his tomb is in the cemetery of Eko-in Temple in Tōkyō. Among the books illustrated by him are the

Hana Shinoye Uta: Flowers of the Yoshiwara. Preface by Shunman. 3 vols. 1780.
Seirō Meikun Jihitsu Shū: Women of the Green Houses and their writing. Signed Kitao Rissai Masanobu. 1 vol. Containing seven double-page colour plates. 1782 (?).
Hishi Fukujin Daitsu-den. 1781.
Yoshiwara Shin Bijin Awase Jihitsu Kagami: New book on the women of the Yoshiwara with examples of their chirography. Signed Kitao Shinsai Masanobu. 1 large folio. 1784. Colours.
Yatsuhachi Chirabe-no-Nishiki: Music of Yatsuhachi's koto. 3 vols. 1784.
Yedo Umare Iwake-no-Kabayaki: Young life in Yedo. 1785.
Kyōka Gojū-nin Isshu: Fifty humorous poems. 1 vol. 1786. Colours.
Temmei Shinsen Gojū-nin Isshu: Supplementary to foregoing. 1 vol. 1786. Colours.
Ehon Azuma Karage: Scenes of everyday life. Signed Kitao. 3 rather small vols. 1786.
Furitsuke Miburi: Written and illustrated by Santō Kyōden " when twenty-five years old." 1 small vol.
Azuma Kyōku Kyōka Bunko: Humorous poems. Signed Kitao Denzō Seiyen. 1 vol. 1786. Colours.
Yahan-no-Chazukei: 1788.
Hako-iri Musume Menya Ningyō: 3 vols. 1791.
Eikyō-dai: 1794.
Yomo-no-Haru: Poems on spring. Plates by several different artists, including Masanobu. 1 vol. 1795. Colours.
Hyakunin Isshu Kokon Kyōka Bukuro: Fantastic poems. 1 vol. No date. Colours.
Kekkei Ryakugwa-shiki: Poems. 1 small vol. Colours.
Hitogo Koro Kagami-no-Utsushi-ye: 3 vols. 1796.
Bakemono Tsure-dzure-gusa: Ghost stories.
Kimmō Dzue: In collaboration with other artists. 1 vol. 1803.
Kwaidan Momonji-ye: Book of phantoms. 3 vols. 1803.
Kottō Shū: An encyclopædia. Signed Seisai Rōjin. Sealed Kyōden. 1 large volume with coloured frontispiece. 1804, and again in 1836.
Kyōka Gwaso Burui: Poems on artisans and their work. 1 large volume. Colours. Very fine and exceedingly rare.
Ningen Kyōgi: Good and evil spirits. Written and illustrated by Kitao Masanobu. Drawings represent people beset by spirits with heads made of circles containing the characters signifying good and bad. No date.

All of Masanobu's books have great charm and interest, his two books on the beauties of the " Green Houses," with examples of their writing, rivalling Shigemasa's and Shunshō's famous *Seirō Bijin Awase*. The colouring has less of the pink that predominates in the latter work, and the grouping of the figures is considered by many connoisseurs to be even finer. The drawings in these two books, although among the first work Kitao Masanobu is known to have done, so far surpass everything else in the way of illustration we have by him that it seems rather superfluous to speak of his other books in detail. His career as an artist, great as it was, was rather incidental to that of a writer, and the last years of his life were almost wholly given up to authorship.

CHAPTER VIII

UKIYO-YE ILLUSTRATORS OF THE UTAGAWA, KATSUGAWA, AND KITAGAWA SCHOOLS

HE third generation of Shigenaga's followers and the second of the Utagawa group begins with Utagawa TOYOKUNI, who lived between 1768 and 1825. His father, Gorobei Kurohashi, was a wood-carver of Yedo, with many friends among the actors, some of whom, including the famous Danjūrō, having had their statues carved by him. His studio was a favourite gathering-place for both the artists and actors of the city, and Toyokuni thus grew up in surroundings which not only determined his career but the channel it should follow.

The Torii artists had made prints and books of actors immensely popular long before Toyokuni's time, and the decline of their famous studio after Kiyonaga's death gave Toyokuni the opportunity of reviving this class of work. He must have entered Utagawa Toyoharu's school when hardly more than fifteen, since by the time he was eighteen he was designing prints and illustrating books himself. Utamaro, who was some fifteen years his senior, and Katsukawa Shunyei, who was almost an exact contemporary, had their share with Toyoharu, however, in forming his style, and Succo says that Ishida Gyokuzan, a well-known Ōsaka artist who had lived in Yedo, also influenced him.[1]

Toyokuni's work sprang into a great popularity, and with his large circle of friends among the actors, prints and books of portraits of these men and accounts of their lives followed as a natural consequence. He had an immense number of followers both in Yedo and Ōsaka, his influence persisting through his pupils until the Restoration in 1868.

Among the other signatures used by him were KYŌ, ICHIYŌSAI, KACHŌRŌ, ICHIŌ, KAKUTEISHA, GOSOTEI, and GYOKUZAN. In addition to countless prints, Succo lists over one hundred and eighty books illustrated by him. Those illustrated in colours have become very valuable, and with Utamaro's books of about the same time form characteristic examples of the Ukiyo-ye art of the late eighteenth and early nineteenth centuries.

The following list of Toyokuni's books is largely made up from Succo's *Toyokuni und seine Zeit*. It includes the

---

[1] See *Utagawa Toyokuni und seine Zeit*.

CHAP. VIII]　　　JAPANESE BLOCK-PRINTING

Tsugamonei Hanashi-no-Oyadama: 1 vol. 1786.
Hanashi O Yedo-ye Nagasaki Karakowa Meisho: Description of the road between Nagasaki and Yedo. 1 vol. 1787.
Intoku Ryōhō Yoikoto Bakari: 1 vol. 1787.
Tsukurinarai Sake-no-sano-Ji: 1 vol. 1787.
Yabo-no-Isshu Kwaraku-no-Motoshime: 2 vols. 1788.
Gesaku Tempitsu Ahōraku: 2 vols. 1788.
Ni-ichi Tensaku-no-Go: 2 vols. 1788.
Usode-nashi Hakone-no-Saki: 2 vols. 1789.
Ōshōshi Uwaki-no-Chokuire or *Kane-ire:* 3 vols. 1789.
Gohi-iki Tano San-shō: 2 vols. 1789.
Matekoi Mochiwa-Mochiwa: 2 vols. 1789.
Otoshi Banashi Shimai-hiki Kashiwa Mochi: Copied from pictures by Keisai Masayoshi. 3 vols. 1789.
Ehon Nioi Sensu: 1 vol. 1789.
Ikokubari Chiye-no-Tsuyadashi: 2 vols. 1790.
Bakemono Futsu Kagawari: 3 vols. 1790.
Gozonji-no-Yo-uchi Soba: 3 vols. 1790.
Chaji Kagen Yakuwari Banzuki: 3 vols. 1790.
Hakoiri Musume Menya Ningyō: 3 vols. 1791.
Hanashi-zome Kuruwa-no-Iroage: 3 vols. 1791.
Kyō Kanoko Musume Dojō Jiru: 3 vols. 1791.
Ima-mukashi Engi-no-Hakuryō: 2 vols. 1791.
Sore-wa Orogoto Gozonji Koraiya-den: 3 vols. 1791.
Te Asobi Hariko-no-Tora-no-Maki: 3 vols. 1791.
Bakemono Yofuke-no-Kaomise: 2 vols. 1791.
Baka-no-shiki Monogatari: 2 vols. 1791.
Mibu Odori Gesaku-no-Memoku: 2 vols. 1791.
Kareki ni Hana Sakusha-no-Seigwan: 3 vols. 1791.
Shinoda Azuma Jidai Moyō: 2 vols. 1791.
Yono Kotowaza Torikomi Shōfu: 2 vols. 1791.
Tata Kimaze Yarō-no-Kamaboko: 3 vols. 1791.
Hatsuka Amari ni Tsukai Hatashite Mibu Kyōgen: 2 vols. 1791.
O Chō Mazura Gaoi-no-Adanami: 2 vols. 1791.
Ukiyo Karakuri Kumen Jūmen: 3 vols. 1792.
Koi-nyobō Somewake Chaban: 3 vols. 1792.
Gozon-ji-no-Bakemono: 3 vols. 1792.
Natsu-Matsuri Dan-Shichijima: 3 vols. 1792.
Keshi-iri Kotobu-ki Takiwa Chūshingura: 2 vols. 1793.
Kyōwa Shiri Saguri-go-yō-jin: 2 vols. 1793.
Some-aishō Nanjo-no-Urayeri: 3 vols. 1793.
Toshiyori-no-Hiyamizu Soga: 3 vols. 1793.
Mongaku Ichidai-ki: 5 vols. 1793.
Saru-no-Shiri Kimpira Gobō: 2 vols. 1793.
Katakiyaku Asahina Chaban Soga: 3 vols. 1793.
Sakazuki-no-Sanoji Shichinin Jōgo: 2 vols. 1793.
Bakemono Haru Asobi: 2 vols. 1793.
Hechima-no-kawa Uta Uta-bukuro: Unsigned, but attributed to Toyokuni. 2 vols. 1793.
Ojigake Sangai Soga: 3 vols. 1793.
Ehon Seiki-no-Monokurabe: Curious customs at temple festivals in Etchū province. 1793.
Banashi Satoso-dachi Hanashi Suzume: 2 vols. 1793.
Oyadama Tengu Tsubute Hana-no-Yedoko: 3 vols. 1793.
Chana-dehon Chaban Kyōgen: 2 vols. 1793.
Mukashi Banashi Chōshū no-Hama: 3 vols. 1793.
Gushi Rokutsū Hanryaku-no-Maki: 3 vols. 1793. Attributed by some collectors to Shunyei.

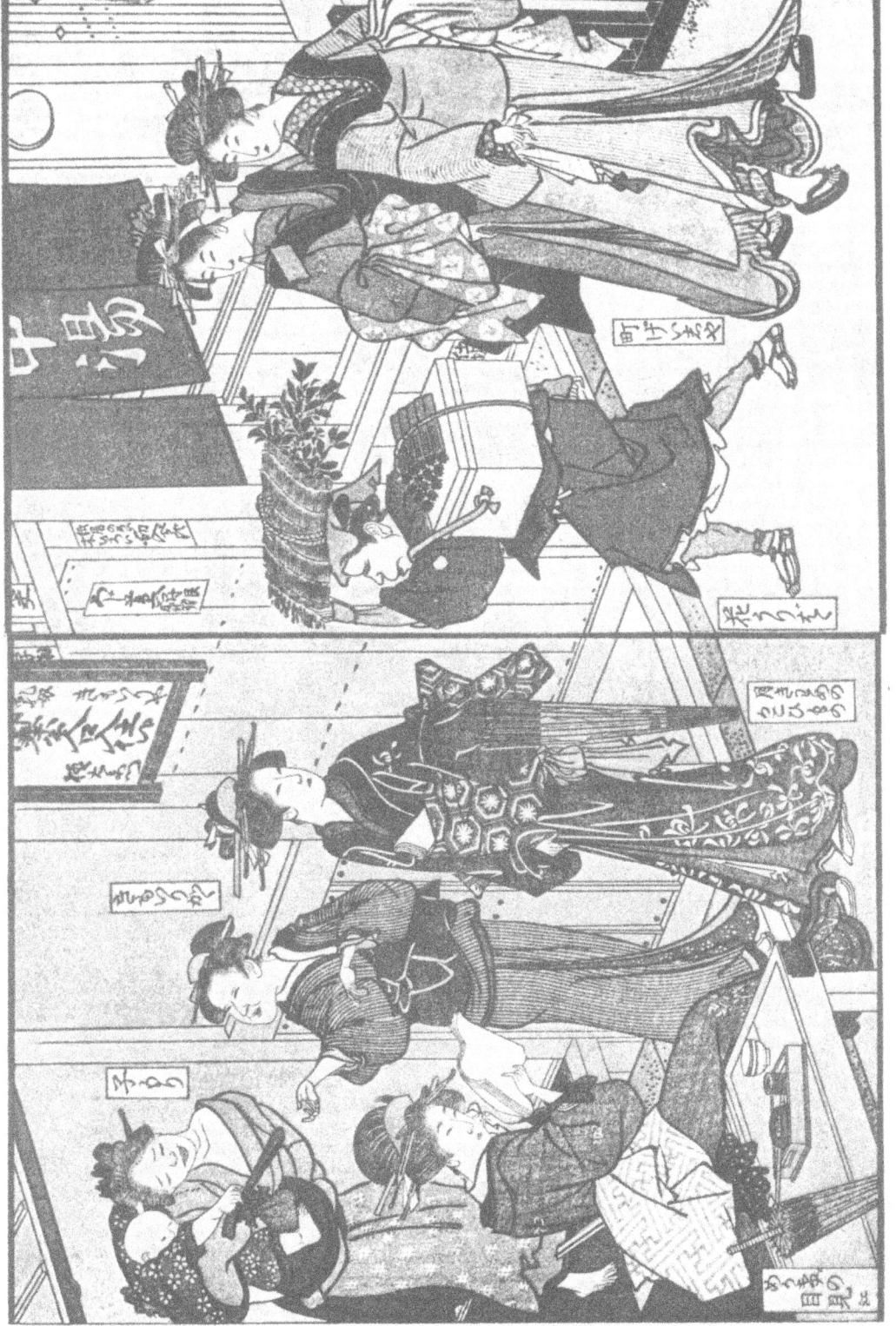

PLATE 29

From the EHON IMAYO SUGATA (1802), by Utagawa Toyokuni.

[Face p. 152

The Utagawa and Katsugawa Schools [Chap. VIII

Nezumi-no-ko Konrei-jinkōki: 3 vols. 1793.
Ōtani Dōke Hyakunin Isshu: 3 vols. 1793.
Chūshingura Ō Dogu Shachide Makunashi: 3 vols. 1793.
Onaji-mi Hanasaki Jiji: 3 vols. 1793.
Ehon Ahō-Bukuro: 2 vols. 1793.
Kamakura Tonda-ike: 2 vols. 1793.
Kataki-uchi Igo-ni-Jikan: 2 vols. 1793. With Toyohiro?
Dai-ichi Otokuyō Monogatari: 2 vols. 1793.
Hachi Kamuri Monogatari: 3 vols. 1793.
Hyakunin Isshu Odoke Kōshaku: 3 vols. 1793.
Age Yamachi Date-no-Tōfuya: 3 vols. 1793.
Tendō Ukiyo Dezukai: 3 vols. 1793.
Ningen Isshin Nozoki Karakuri: 2 vols. 1793.
Ehon Kukuri-Some: 2 vols. 1793. Colours.
Ehon Yedo-no-Mizu: 3 vols. 1793. Pleasure resorts of Yedo. Black and white.
Uchi Benkei Kanjinchō: 3 vols. 1795.
Zō Sanshō Dayu Monogatari: 2 vols. 1795.
Furutezuma Shinadama Tebako: 2 vols. 1795.
Kurote Hachijō Mukashi Ryōri Tanuki-no-Suimono: 2 vols. 1795. Republished in 1798 as the *Kurote Hachijō Tanuki-no-Kinshōsui*.
Momotarō Ōeyama-iri: 3 vols. 1795.
Komeiri Kiri-no-Nagamochi: 2 vols. 1795.
O Mukashi Bakemono Hanashi: 2 vols. 1795.
Genkurō Gitsune Ikani Benkei Onmai Ninin: 2 vols. 1795.
Kataki-uchi Gijo-no-Hanabusa: 3 vols. 1795. With Toyohiro?
Imoto wa Shinobu Go Taihei-ki Shira-ishi Banashi: 3 vols. 1795-1796.
Yedo Jiman Hana-no-Meibutsu: 1796.
Zōho Shipeitarō: 3 vols. 1796.
Tarafuku Manryō Bungen: 2 vols. 1796.
Kwaidan Kanao Kikori: 2 or 3 vols. 1796.
Akahon Mukashi Bakekurabe Hakone Shibai: An *hosoye-bon* or " small-pox book." 3 vols. 1796.
Shirai Shi-banashi Kōhen: 1796.
Kataki-uchi Ubasute-Yama: 3 vols. 1797. With Toyohiro?
Kondo wa Oni-Musoku: 2 vols. 1797.
Sanze-Sō-no-Manhasao (?): 3 vols. 1797.
Bakemono O Heiko: 2 vols. 1797.
Fuji Iro Itajime Soga: 3 vols. 1797.
Oshi-no-Tsuyoimono Nandemo Hachiman: 2 vols. 1797.
Shimpan Shinsaku Sansai Ji-e: 2 vols. 1797.
Shiouri Buntarō Monogatari: Unsigned. Attributed by some collectors to Hokusai. 3 vols. 1797.
Fukutoku Jū Goshiki Megane: 2 vols. 1797.
Kinkin Sekkai Sakate Iru Takara-no-Yamabuki: 3 vols. 1797.
Uso Yaoyorozu-no-Kami Ichiza: 2 vols. 1797.
Shiba Zenkō Yume-no-Muda-Goto: 3 vols. 1797.
Tadatanome Daihi Chiye-no-Hanashi: 3 vols. 1797.
Kokyō Tōhon-no-Negoto: 3 vols. 1797. Republished in 1802 as the *Goran Oya Kokyō*.
Kataki-uchi Ryūka Teifu: 3 vols. 1798. With Toyohiro (?).
Hito Kyōgen Kitsune-no-Kaki-iri: 2 vols. 1798.
Yuriwaka Daijin-to-no-Nemuri: 2 vols. 1798.
Naga-Uta Futatsu Mojiono-no-Tsuno Moji: Unsigned. 2 vols. 1798.
Daruma Daitsū Hanami Mosen: 3 vols. 1798.
Tenun Minonaru Kino Hachi Ne-Eigwa: 3 vols. 1798. A sequel was published in 1799 entitled *Kane-no-Naruki Tsugiho-no-Kodakara* (2 vols.).
Fuji Kenjutsu Azuma Kaidō Onna Kataki-uchi: 3 vols. 1798. With Toyohiro (?).

CHAP. VIII]   JAPANESE BLOCK-PRINTING

Yedo Murasaki Sono-ato Maku Baba Dōjōji: 3 vols. 1798.
Shōchū Kitsunebi Haruzuzumi Hesobanashi Mono: 3 vols. 1798.
Ningen Isshō Migaki Jōruri Kokoro-no-Kagami: Unsigned. Attributed by some collectors to Shigemasa. 3 vols. 1798.
Kaidan Kihachi Jō: 2 vols. 1798.
Hasu-no-Ito Botan-no-Ayatsuri: 3 vols. 1798.
Hōzuki Chōchin Oshiye-no-Chikamichi: 3 vols. 1798.
Gotai Wagō Monogatari: 3 vols. 1799.
Kataki-uchi Okitsu Shiranami: 3 vols. 1799. With Toyohiro (?).
Muzōsa Yukinari Zōshi: 3 vols. 1799.
Yomori Saiwai Tamaye Go Oku-jin: 3 vols. 1799.
Mino Kōhen Kane-no-Naruki Tsugiho-no-Kodakara: 2 vols. 1799.
Sakusha Kongen Yedo Nishiki: 2 vols. 1799.
Rokudaime Ichikawa Sanshō Yedo-no-Hana Satsuki-no-Chirigiwa. 2 vols. 1799.
Nigao Ehon Haiyū Gaku Shitsu-tsū: Portraits of actors. In collaboration with Kunimasu. Title-page by Utamaro of articles used in the *Nō* dramas. 1 vol. 1799. Colours. Rare.
Goseidai Setsuyō Gakumon: 2 vols. 1799.
Komparu Tokuwaka Inkyo: 3 vols. 1799.
Ehon Waka Murasaki: Book on the Yoshiwara. 1799.
Usono Taiboku: 3 vols. 1800.
Musume Kataki-uchi Ōgi-no-Gimmen: 3 vols. With Toyohiro (?). 1800.
Nijū Donsu Santoku Hira: 3 vols. 1800.
Shirogana Chōja Nifukutsui Yeiga Haru Bukuro: 3 vols. 1800.
Hanami Banashi Shirame Seisuiki: 3 vols. 1800.
Otoko Ichi-Kagami Kaminuki-Kagami: 2 vols. 1800.
Ko Wo Umu Kogane Shichiya-no-Iwai: 2 vols. 1800.
Gotai Fugu Dokukeshi Gusuri: 3 vols. 1800.
Yakusha Meisho Dzue: A comparison of the theatre with famous places in Japan. A humorous work written by Bakin. Illustrations by Ichiyōsai Uta Toyokuni. 2 vols. 1800. Colours.
Tōsei Banashi Suikoden: 1 vol. 1800.
Kataki-uchi Fuse Rishōki: 3 vols. 1801. With Toyohiro (?).
Sakuragawa Hanashi-no-Chōjime: 2 vols. 1801.
Kurabe Goshi Nari Hiragata: 3 vols. 1801.
Oya-no-Kataki Utsunomiya Monogatari: 3 vols. 1801.
Utsunomiya Godan Jōruri Sakamise: 2 vols. 1801.
Ehon Hōshū-roku: 3 vols. 1801.
Tamizu Shinzaemon Kataki-uchi Nezasa-no-Yuki: 3 vols. 1801.
Yoho Fuki Jizai Kogane-no-Toshidama: 3 vols. 1801.
Jinshin Ryōmen-zuri: Attributed to Jippensha Ikku by some collectors. 3 vols. 1801.
Yōhō (or Gwazu) Yakusha Shashin Sangai Kyō: Theatrical scenes and actors. Sometimes called Recreations of Actors. 2 vols. 1801. Colours. Rare.
Aki Kengu-no-Minato Sento Shinwa: 3 vols. 1802.
Ehon Imayō Sugata: Women of different classes at various occupations. 2 vols. 1802. Colours.
Ehon Tokiyo Yosoöi: Fashions of the day. 1802.
Sanjūni-sō: Thirty-two types of faces. 1 small vol. Colours. Very rare.
Yakusha Kono Tei Kashiwa: Portrait busts of actors. On the right-hand pages the actors are represented in their most famous rôles; on the opposite pages as in everyday life. 2 vols. 1803. Colours. Rare.
Otogi Kanoko: Stories illustrated by Toyokuni and Toyohiro in collaboration. 1803. Colours.
Kataki-uchi Sesshu Gappo-no-Tsuji: 5 vols. 1803. With Toyohiro (?).
Kokkei Shiro-to Shibai: 1 vol. 1803.
Shibai Kimmō Dzue: An encyclopædia of the theatre. Drawings by Toyokuni and Kutokusai Katsukawa Shunyei. 8 vols. 1803. Black and white and colours. Rare and interesting.
Sugata Zempen Onnai Saru-no-Adachi: By Toyokuni and Hokusai. 3 vols. 1804.
Ryōmen Shushi-no-Sugata Kagami: Second series of above. By Toyokuni and Hokusai. 5 vols. 1804.

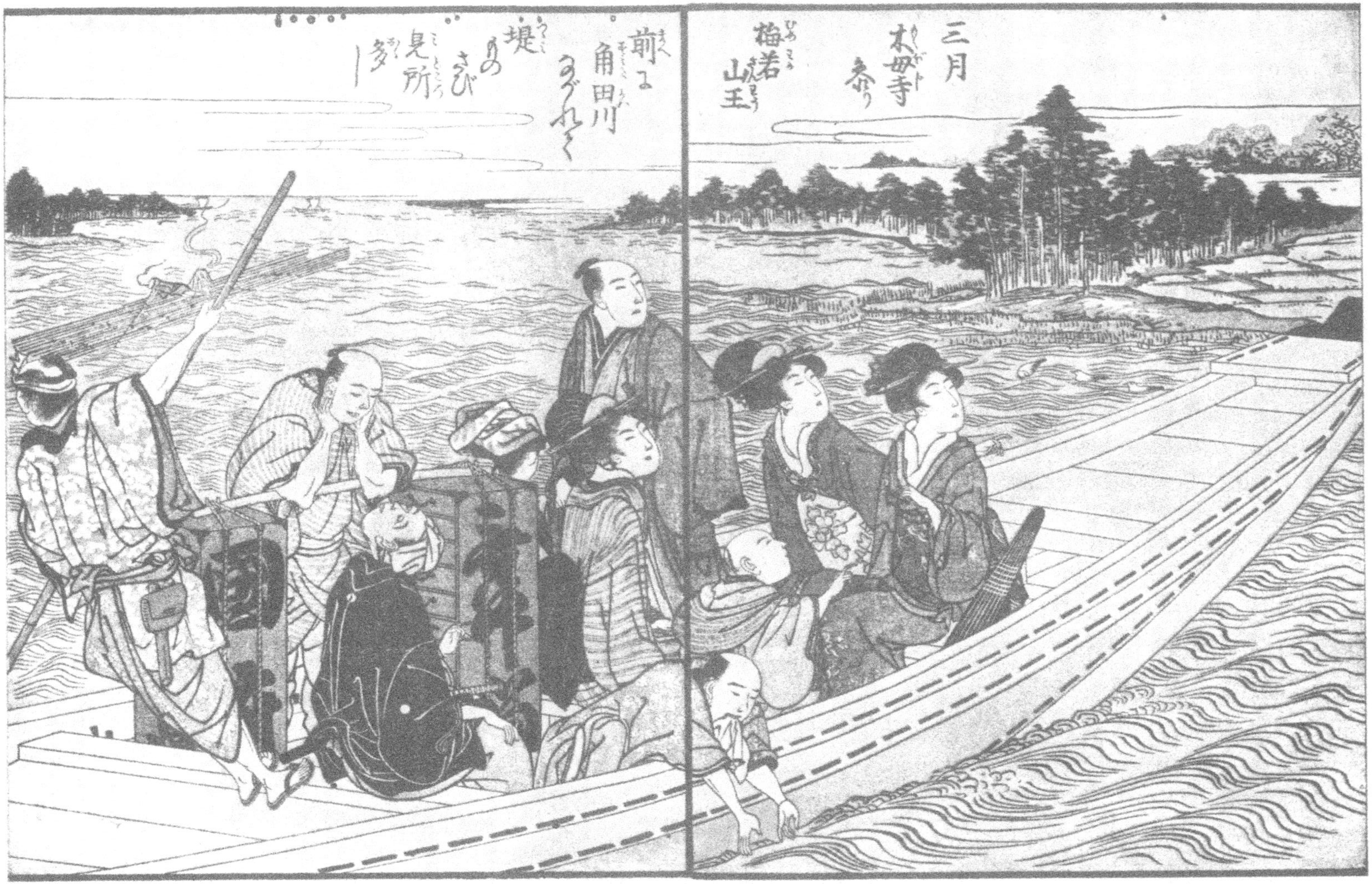

PLATE 30] From the Ehon Azuma Warawa (1804), by Utagawa Toyohiro.

THE UTAGAWA AND KATSUGAWA SCHOOLS [CHAP. VIII

Shinobu-zuri Nishiki-no-Date Zome: 3 vols. 1804.
Haiyū Nigao (or *Sobo*) *Kagami:* Portraits of actors with poems above. 2 folios. 1804. Colours. One of Toyokuni's most famous books.
Yakusha Awase Kagami: Portraits of actors. 1804. Colours.
Yedo Jiman Meisan Dzue: 3 vols. 1805.
Sakura Hime Zenden Akebono Zōshi: History of the Princess Sakura. 1805.
Eiri Zakura Hime: Another version of the foregoing. Written by Santō Kyōden. 5 vols. 1806.
Orokushi Kiso-no-Adachi: 7 vols. 1807.
Kataki-uchi Mie Chukotei: Toyokuni and Toyohiro in collaboration. 9 vols. 1807.
Kataki-uchi Katami-no-Osafune: 2 vols. 1807. With Toyohiro (?).
Iwaikushi Kumeno-no-Adachi: Written by Santō Kyōden. 7 vols. 1808.
Kagamiyama Homare-no-Adachi: Illustrated by Toyokuni and Kunisada. 5 vols. 1808.
Uto-no-Omokage: Written by Santō Kyōden. 6 vols. 1810.
Zensei-no-Tsurebushi Itsui Otoko Hayari: Portraits of different artists of the Utagawa school. By Toyokuni and Kunisada. 2 vols. 1810.
Karei-zaki Hanagawa Monogatari: Novel by Bakin. 4 vols. 1816. Signed Utagawa Toyokuni. Black and white.
Yakusha Nigao Haya Gei-ko: Portraits of actors. 1 vol. 1817. Colours.
Ehon Zembon Zakura: 1 vol. 1818.
Ippai Kigen: Stories of drunkards. By Samba. 2 vols. 1822.
Sugoroku-ye Zakura Tsugiho-no-Hachine: By Toyokuni and Keisai Eisen in collaboration. 6 vols. 1822.
Yakusha Hitori Tebiki: 1 vol. No date.
Toyokuni Toshidama Fude: The New Year festivities. 1 vol. No date. Small coloured drawings.
Kunizu-kushi Yamato-no-Homare: Actors of different provinces. By Toyokuni and his pupils. No date.
Yedo Meisho: Second edition of the *Ehon Weke Murasaki*. Colours.

Toyokuni's younger brother, Utagawa TOYOHIRO, has never received the recognition he deserves, because in comparison with Toyokuni's immense amount of work his own output was small. In quality, however, in many respects it was finer. Ficke in his *Chats on Japanese Prints* gives an understanding appreciation of Toyohiro and says " . . . that this difference in fame [between Toyokuni and Toyohiro] is due less to difference in merit than to the fact that Toyokuni was enormously prolific while Toyohiro's work was scanty. The contemporaneous popularity may be ascribed to the ability of Toyokuni to shift and veer with every change in public taste, while Toyohiro was unable or unwilling to move with these fluctuating winds."

Toyohiro lived between 1773 and 1828, and was also known as TŌJIRŌ (when young), ICHIYŪSAI, and ICHIRYŪSAI. He refused to make actor prints, his favourite work apparently having been landscapes. His sheets of this kind are very charming, and with their *surimono*-like printing are treasures which print collectors are more and more seeking. The series of prints known as the *Yedo Hakkei* (Eight Views of Yedo) is especially remarkable in showing Toyohiro's ability to express space and distance. The plate in this set called *Homing Geese at Yoshiwara*, representing pale, distant rice-fields beyond a brown-roofed village in the foreground, with a flock of wild geese falling through the middle of the sheet from the clouds to the far-off misty edge of the picture, is marvellous in its expression of these qualities.

Hiroshige chose a worthy teacher in Toyohiro, who must have exerted a wholesome and restraining influence upon many artists of this time, for his work has a simplicity and delicacy of colouring entirely untouched by the degeneration which was beginning to ruin the Ukiyo-ye school.

Toyohiro illustrated a number of books in addition to designing prints, and collaborated with Toyokuni occasionally. A list of his books includes the

O-Ukeai Gesaku-no-Gaso-Uri: 1791.
Kokinshū: Humorous verses. 1 vol. 1793.
Kataki-uchi Ume-no-Tsugiho: 3 vols. 1800. With Toyokuni (?).
Wata on Jaku: 1 vol. 1802.
Goriyaku Moshigo-no-Yasa Otoko: Festival at Otoko. Unsigned. 2 vols. 1802.
Shichi Fuku Konen Banashi: Unsigned, but attributed by Succo to Toyohiro. 2 vols. 1802.
Otogi Kanoka: With Toyokuni. 1 vol. 1803. Six double-page colour plates.
Kataki-uchi Kinuta-no-Uchita: 3 vols. 1803. With Toyokuni (?).
Kataki-uchi Hari-no-Tamakura: 2 vols. 1804. With Toyokuni (?).
Banchu Maiko-no-Hana: A dramatic romance. 2 vols. 1804. Colours.
Ehon Tōto Jūni Tsuki: Twelve months in Yedo. 2 vols. 1804. Colours. Signed Utagawa Ichiryūsai Toyohiro.
Fuku Nezumi Shirio-no-Futozawa: The lucky rat. 2 vols. 1804. Colours.
Ehon Azuma Warawa: Outings of the Twelve Months. Signed Utagawa Ichiryūsai Toyohiro. 2 vols. 1804. In two editions, one printed in black and white and grey, and the other in colours.
Kataki-uchi Iwate-no-Tsutsuji: 3 vols. 1804. With Toyokuni (?).
Kataki-uchi Hasu Wakaba: 1804. With Toyokuni (?).
Kataki-uchi Kinshi-no-Tsumeni: 2 vols. 1805. With Toyokuni (?).
Asakanuma Go-nichi-no-Adachi: The vengeance of Asaka-numa. A novel written by Santō Kyōden. 2 vols. 1807.
Matsura Sayohime Sekikon-roku: A novel by Bakin.
Kataki-uchi Mie Chukotei: By Toyohiro and Toyokuni in collaboration. 9 vols. 1807.
Kataki-uchi Shima Meguri Kosuke-no-Fune: 6 vols. 1807. With Toyokuni (?).
Sundan Jitsu-Jitsuke: Novel by Bakin. 5 vols. 1808.
Hidari Jingoro Yabuchi-no-Adachi: Novel by Kyōden. Illustrations unsigned, but attributed to Toyohiro by Succo. 1808.
Kataki-uchi Sembon Zakura: 1809. With Toyokuni (?).
Uta Yasukata Ichidai-ki: Biographies of great men.
Musō Byōye Kōchō Monogatari: Novel by Bakin. First series 5 vols. 1809. Second series 4 vols. 1810. Black and white. Signed Ichiryūsai Toyohiro.
Tosei Shōryū Ika-bon Ezu: Drawings of flower arrangements.
Jūsan-ban Kyōka Awase: Thirteen humorous poems. 1 vol. Colours.
Zen Myōkan Sayo Tsuke: Novel by Bakin. 5 vols.
Asahina Shima Meguri-noki: Novel by Bakin. 1819.

The books whose titles begin with *Kataki-uchi* are nearly all unsigned, but Succo attributes them to Toyokuni and Toyohiro working in collaboration. The *Ehon Azuma Asobi* with its drawings of holiday crowds is much like Toyokuni's best work in illustration, both editions, that printed in black and white and grey as well as that in colours, being charming.

It is also rare and commands a high price when offered for sale. There is, however, a beautiful modern edition of this book published by Yoshikawa Kobunkan of Tōkyō (1916).

Of Toyokuni's pupils, Utagawa KUNISADA achieved the greatest fame, although this renown was founded rather on the quantity than the quality of his work.

Kunisada was born in 1787 in the province of Bōshū. While still a child his family moved to Yedo, where as soon as he was old enough he became his father's assistant in the ferry-boat business on the Sumida river. His spare time was so entirely given to drawing that eventually his father, doubtless with as much of an appreciation of the money-making possibilities of the talent as any love for art, took the boy to Toyokuni, who agreed to teach him. His progress was rapid and his drawings appealed to the people. By the first years of the nineteenth century he was fully launched and was designing prints and illustrating books in great numbers, even rivalling Toyokuni in the amount of work produced.

Other signatures used by him were KACHŌRŌ, KOCHŌRŌ, GOTOTEI, KYŌ, JUYEN, TO-JUYEN, KOKUTEISHA, ICHIYŪSAI, HOKUBAIDŌ, BAIDŌ, GEPPARŌ, CHOKARA, Fubō SANJIN, Hanabusa ITTAI, and after 1844, Ichiyōsai TOYOKUNI or TOYOKUNI II.

Although the decline of the Ukiyo-ye art had commenced with Toyokuni, this artist was still a great enough man to impress what he did with a tremendous force and his colour sense remained fine. With Kunisada, however, the deterioration was rapid and pronounced. His drawing became greatly exaggerated, his colour crude, and before middle age he had become a victim to the hysteria which at recurring intervals attacks the world's art, and sweeps beauty aside for a dalliance with strange and ugly gods.

Notwithstanding this degeneration, Kunisada undoubtedly had great natural ability, and it was probably because the demand of the time was for this exaggerated work that he produced it. The fault lay rather with his character than in his talent—he was not great enough to " refuse the whole world " that he might " keep his own soul."

Kunisada's death occurred in 1864 and his tomb is in the cemetery of Komyō-ji temple in Tōkyō. In addition to the enormous quantity of prints which he designed, he also illustrated a number of books, among which are the

Shogwatsu Yaoko-no-Kado: About 1810.
Otoko-no-Nakano-no-Otoko Kagami: A novelette. 1816.
Yakusha (or *Haiyo*) *Sugao Natsu-no-Fuji :* A work by Santō Kyōden on actors in private life. Illustrated by Kunisada. 2 vols. 1827 or 1828. Colours. Signed Kōchōrō Utagawa Kunisada.
Santo Yakusha Suiko-den: Actors of three capitals (Kyōto, Ōsaka, and Yedo). Signed Gototei Kunisada. 1829. Partly printed in colours.

Geki-jō Ikkwan Mushime-gana: Guide to the theatre. 2 vols. 1830.
Kowairo Haya Gwaten: Selections from the drama with portraits of actors. Signed Kachōrō Kunisada. 1831.
Shibai Saiken Mitsuba-gusa: Dramas with the names and portraits of actors who had appeared in them. 1832. Colours.
Te-Suisen Segawa Boshi: Collection of poems in honour of the poet Segawa. Illustrated by Kunisada and other artists. 1 vol. 1832. Colours. A *kubari-hon*.
Kaikwan Ryōki Kyōka Kuden: Written by Bakin. 1833.
Haiyū Kigen-den : Lives of celebrated comedians. 2 vols. 1833.
Godai Soshi Meita Hatsu Uri: Written by Jippensha Ikku. Comical illustrations by Kunisada. 1 small vol. 1833. Black and white and grey.
Taitokai Kabuki Suiko-den: 1 vol.
Haiyū Sanjū-rok-kasen: The Thirty-six Poets. Kunisada in collaboration with Hokkei. 1835.
San Baso : A play in three acts. 1836. Colours.
Toyokuni Toshidama-no-fude: Drawings from Toyokuni by Kunisada. 1 vol.
Kimbei-bai : Novel by Bakin. Several vols. 1841–1842.
Miyamoto Mansoshi: 124 coloured plates. 1 folio.
Hana-no-Sugata Mi: Dramas with portraits of actors. 1 folio. Colours.
Nihon Genji Kagami: Drama founded on the story of the Genji. 2 vols.
Gwanjaku Tesuisen Hanashi Tori: Collection of poems in honour of the comedian Kwanjaku (Hirano Masu-umi). Charming impressionistic illustrations by Kunisada and other artists. 2 vols. 1852. A rare *kubari-hon*. Colours.
Katsushika Monogatari: Tales by Tanehiko. 1865.
Kamigata Koi Shugyō: Signed Gototei Kunisada.
Inaka Genji.
Meisho Makkei: Album of nine colour-plates.
Uta-no-Tomobune: Poems illustrated in colours by Kunisada and Gakutei. Excessively rare.

Utagawa KUNIYOSHI was, after Kunisada, the most prolific and the most famous of Toyokuni's pupils. His work is superior to Kunisada's, however, the latter artist never approaching in anything that he ever did some of the landscape prints by Kuniyoshi.

This artist was the son of a dyer of Yedo and lived between 1800 and 1861. He used as other signatures the names ICHIYŪSAI, ISSHU, and CHŌ-Ō-RO, and later in life, when he had come under the influence of Zeshin, the famous lacquer artist, he occasionally used the name SENSHIN.

The poet Umeya Kakuju, whose comic poems he sometimes illustrated, probably also influenced him to a considerable extent, and is said to have inspired the extremely clever caricatures which Kuniyoshi was given to drawing. Among the books illustrated by Kuniyoshi were the

Ichiyū Gwafu: Warriors. 1 vol. (Bermond Catalogue gives date as 1820.) Also an edition of 1831.
Kuniyoshi Zatsuga: No date.
Wakan Eiyū Gwaden: Heroes of China and Japan. 2 vols. No date.
Uwo Kagami: Different fishes and the methods used in catching them. Signed Ichiyūsai Kuniyoshi. 2 vols. 1831. Seven coloured plates. Rare.
Fuzoku Ko Meidan: Anecdotes of celebrated personages. 2 vols. 1840.
Ichiyūsai Gwafu: Various drawings. Signed Ichiyūsai Kuniyoshi. 1 vol. 1846.
Hakkenden: 14 vols. 1847–1851.
—— *Chushingura:* Story of the Forty-seven Ronin. 1 small vol. 1848. Colours.
Tsushin Meimei Gwaden: The Forty-seven Ronin. First vol. by Kuniyoshi; second vol. by Sadahide. 2 vols. 1848.

THE UTAGAWA AND KATSUGAWA SCHOOLS [CHAP. VIII

Ichiyūsai Mangwa: Sequel to the *Uchiyūsai Gwafu.* 1 vol. 1855.
Jinji Andon (Vol. II.): Sketches for decorating the lanterns used at the Bon festival. Colours.
Kyōka Dzushiki: Humorous poems on the One Hundred and Eight Heroes. Signed Ichiyūsai Kuniyoshi.
Dai Nippon Koku Kaibyaku Yuraiki: Ancient legends of Japan. 6 vols. 1856.
Tosei Suiko-den.
Hō-edzu Bisei.
Dai Nippon Koku Kaibyaku Yuraiki: Supplementary series to that of 1856. 4 vols. 1860.

Utagawa KUNINAO, the friend and possibly the teacher of Kuniyoshi, was born in Shinano, the son of Kichigawa Utsura. Most of his life was spent in Yedo, however, where after experimenting in the Chinese manner of work he finally joined Toyokuni's school. His work, although rare, shows him to have been one of the best of Toyokuni's pupils.

Kuninao's real name was Kichigawa Taizō, but as an artist he used the signatures ICHISAI, RYŪYENDŌ, RYŪYENRŌ, SHARAKU-Ō, UKIYO-AN, ICHIYŌSAI, ICHIYENSAI, SHIROBEI, and Kosoyen KUNINAO. He illustrated the fourth volume of the well-known set of books called *Jinji Andon* in addition to the following.

Bijin Imayō Nishiki: Women at different occupations. 2 medium-sized vols. Very charming and rare. Colours.
Bijin Shokunin Dzukushi: Beautiful women at various tasks. Colours.
Ehon Chushingura: The Forty-seven Ronin. Illustrated by Kuninao and Shunsen in collaboration. 1 vol. 11 coloured plates.
Tatsumi-no-Sono: Customs of the Yedo geisha. Signed Utagawa Kuninao. No date.
Ukiyo-Ede-hon: A charming little *gwajō* of sketches of people, flowers, animals, landscapes, etc. Signed Utagawa Kuninao. No date. Colours. Rare.
Bijin Kasen-shū: Beautiful women poets. Written by Rokujūyen Sensei. Illustrated by Utagawa Kuninao and Keisai Eisen. In two series of one and two rather small volumes. 1825. Very charming coloured plates. Rare.
Bijin Momo-chidori: A *gwajō* of beautifully printed plates of beautiful women. Variously attributed to Kuninao and Keisai Eisen.

Utagawa KUNIMASA, one of Toyokuni's early pupils, was born in Somedo in the province of Ōshū of a family named Jinsuke. He lived between 1772 and 1810, thus being only four years the junior of his master and dying fifteen years earlier. His early life was spent as a workman in a dyeing establishment in Yedo, but his talent for painting won the attention of Toyokuni, and it ended by this famous artist offering him a training in his studio. Kunimasa's actor prints attained a great popularity and drew to him students of his own. As other signatures he used the names ICHIYŪSAI and BAIDŌ. In addition to print designing he illustrated a few books, among which are the

Nigao Ehon Haiyū Gaku Shitsu Tsu: Portraits of Yedo actors. In collaboration with Toyokuni. Title-page by Utamaro represents the articles used in the *Nō* drama. 1799.
Ezō-shi: Signed Utagawa Kunimasa.

A second KUNIMASA, who studied under Kunisada, worked a little later. He was also known as YUGO, CHŌBUNSAI, and YAMASHITA.

Hundreds of other artists of the Utagawa school, pupils of either Toyokuni or Kunisada, worked in Yedo and Ōsaka at this time, but with few exceptions their drawings had so deteriorated in quality that they hardly merit recognition. The very popularity of this work spelled the doom of the whole Ukiyo-ye movement. Hokusai, the first Hiroshige, and a few other men who retained their sanity, delayed it to some extent, but the decay was there, and before the Restoration it had eaten its way through all the Yedo studios. No wonder that the educated classes, who had been bred to the fine simplicity and dignity of the Tosa and Kanō art, despised these Yedo pictures, and no wonder that to-day they still look with suspicion and ill favour upon a style which these debased Ukiyo-ye sheets had grown to represent.

It is with a sense of relief, therefore, that one leaves the late work of the Utagawa group and goes back to the beginnings of still another branch of the Ukiyo-ye movement. This branch, which is known as the Katsukawa school, had its real origin in Miyagawa CHŌSHUN, who lived in Yedo between 1680 and 1752, and is said to have been a pupil of Moronobu's.

Chōshun was also known as NAGAHARU,[1] SHUNKYOKUDŌ, CHŌZAEMON, and KIHEI, and was the teacher of Miyagawa or, as he became known toward 1750, Katsukawa SHUNSUI, who is generally regarded as the first leader of the school and was the artist from whom it took its name.[2]

Like most of the Yedo artists of the time, Shunsui was greatly influenced by Okumura Masanobu and followed his leadings in the choice and treatment of subjects almost exclusively. Although Shunsui was a painter rather than a print designer, he left at least one beautiful and excessively rare book. This is the *Ehon Tomochidori*, containing drawings in black and white of beautiful women, signed Muyagawa Shunsui and published in three volumes in 1762.

Katsukawa SHUNSHŌ, one of Shunsui's early pupils, became very famous, and both his prints and illustrated books are among the best work of the Ukiyo-ye school. He was born in 1725 in the province of Owari of a family named Katsu Miyakawa. After going to Yedo he first studied under Sūkoku, who had been trained by Hanabusa Itchō, and entered Shunsui's studio a year or two later.

Shunshō's reputation was of slow growth, and at the age of forty he is said to have still been so poor that he was obliged to accept lodgings with the publisher Hayashi Hichiyemon of Yedo, and the well-known jar-shaped seal which caused him to be nicknamed Tsubo and Tsubo Shunshō was a receiving seal borrowed of Hayashi, Shunshō not possessing one of his own.

He used a number of other signatures, however, among which were the

---

[1] Another reading of the characters forming his name.
[2] See *Masters of the Ukiyo-ye*, by Fenollosa.

names Yūsuke, Yūji, Jugasei, Rokuroku-an, Riren, Shuntei, Kyokurō, Kyokurōsei, Kirosei, Katsu Miyagawa, Shiren Shunshō, and Katsukawa. His death occurred in 1793, and his tomb is in the cemetery of the Hongwan-ji temple in Tōkyō.

Shunshō's subjects were not of great variety, consisting principally of actors and beautiful women, and a number of renditions of the Thirty-six and the Hundred Poets. He left many pupils, some of whom became very famous. Among these men were Shunchō, Shunyei, Shunkō, Shunman, Shunzan, Ippitsusai Bunchō, Hokusai, and Gakutei, and a number of artists in Ōsaka who, if not Shunshō's personal pupils, had studied his method through men who had come under his direct influence. Most of these Ōsaka followers used as signatures names of which the first character is *Shun*, " Spring."

Shunshō illustrated some very interesting and beautiful books which have become exceedingly rare and valuable. Among them are the

Ehon Butai-no-Ōgi: Portraits of Yedo actors on fans. Illustrated by Shunshō in collaboration with Ippitsusai Bunchō. Published by Kariganeya Jihei of Yedo. 3 folios. 1770. In two editions, one printed in black and white and the other in colours. Rare in either set.
Kobi-no-Tsubo: Portraits of actors. 1770. A second edition in 1790.
Kanoko Mochi: 1772.
Nishiki Hyakunin Isshu Azuma Ori: The Hundred Poets. 1 large vol. 1774. Colours. One of Shunshō's best-known works. Signed Ririn Katsukawa Yūsuke Fuji Shunshō.
Sanjū-rok-kasen: The Thirty-six Poets. 1 vol. 1775. Colours.
Nishiki Hyakunin Isshu: Another rendering of the Hundred Poets. With a poem above each drawing. 1 vol. 1775. Colours.
Seirō Bijin Awase Sugata Kagami: Beautiful women of the Green Houses. Illustrated by Shunshō and Kitao Shigemasa in collaboration. 3 vols. 1776. Contains 86 double-page colour-plates.
Ehon Zoku Butai-no-Ōgi: A smaller supplementary series to the set of 1770. Published by Kariganeya Jihei of Yedo and Kikuya Yasube of Kyōto. 2 vols. 1778. Printed in both black and white and colours. Both sets very rare.
Ehon Ibukiyama: 3 vols. 1778. Colours.
Nō-Daiki: Tales written by Samba. 1 vol. 1779.
Yakusha Natsu-no-Fuji: Private life of famous actors. 1 vol. 1780.
Iroha Uta: Illustrated poems. 1 vol. About 1780. 41 coloured illustrations.
Ehon Takara-no-Chiribune: Symbols of good fortune. 1 vol. 1786. Colours.
Sanyō Dzue Ehon Takara-no-Itoguchi or *Kaiko Yashinai-gusa:* Silk culture in Japan. Illustrated by Shunshō and Shigemasa in collaboration. 1 vol. 1786. Twelve square colour-plates.
Yoshitsune Ichidai-ki: Life of Yoshitsune. 1787.
San Shibai Yakusha Ehon: Actors of three cities (Yedo, Kyōto, and Ōsaka). 1 vol. Colours.
Sanjū-rok-kasen: The Thirty-six Poets. 1 folio. 1789. Beautifully printed on paper which is decorated in colours across tops of pages and under poems. In this book each right-hand page has poems by the poet represented on left-hand page. Colours. Published by Nishimuraya Denbei, Yedo. Signed Kiro-e Kakukawa Shunshō.
Kasen Kimmō-ino Hana: 1 vol. 1789.
Ehon Sakaye-gusa: Scenes at a marriage ceremony. 2 vols. 1790. Eight coloured illustrations.
Ehon Tsugiho-no-Hana: 4 vols.
Yakusha Kuni-no-Hana: Theatre scenes and actors. 1 vol. Colours.
Ko-Dakara Yama: An *hosoye-bon*. Printed entirely in red.
Ise Monogatari: An *hosoye-bon*.

CHAP. VIII] JAPANESE BLOCK-PRINTING

Kwaidan Hyaku Dzue: One hundred monsters. By Katsukawa Shunshō and Shunyei in collaboration. 3 vols.
Fūryū Nishikiye Ise Monogatari: Tales of Ise. 1 vol., in colours. No date. Plates signed Katsukawa Shunshō or Shunshō.

Ippitsusai BUNCHŌ, a contemporary and friend of Katsukawa Shunshō, was born of a *samurai* family and studied under Ishikawa Kōgen,[1] a painter of the Kanō school. His fame as a painter had won him the title of Hokkyō from the Shōgunate, but notwithstanding this, the work of the Ukiyo-ye artists had become too popular for him to resist, and about 1763 or 1764 he threw off the allegiance to classical methods and joined the more popular school. His prints are chiefly of theatrical subjects. They are extremely rare and good examples are usually to be found only when fine private collections are broken up and sold.

Bunchō was also known as Kishi Uyemon and Tsuburi-no-Hikaru (a pen-name). He died in 1796. His work in book illustration was incidental to print designing and painting, although, as we have seen, he collaborated with Shunshō in some of that artist's books.

Von Seidlitz speaks of the *Bunchō Sensei Gwafu* of 1816 as containing reproductions of his work. (See *A History of Japanese Colour Prints*, p. 115.)[2]

Shimokōbe[3] JŪSUI was one of the few Kyōto artists who worked in the Ukiyo-ye manner. He studied first with a teacher of the Kanō school and then went to Yedo, where he was a contemporary with Shunshō in Shunsui's studio. A number of interesting illustrated books were left by him, among which were the

Iro Uta Eshō: Poems for children on morals. 3 vols. 1775.
Ehon Amaya-dori: Temporary lodgings, a moral tale. 3 vols. 1780.
Ehon Yashinai-gusa: 1783.
Zōho Kashira Gaki Kimmō Dzue Taisei: An encyclopædia. By Shimokawabe Jūsui. 21 vols. 1789. Kyōto.
Kyō-no-Mizu Fukuo Chijime: Kyōto fashions. 2 vols.
Ebiki Setsu Yōshū: An encyclopædia.
Mime Fumidari Miyako-no-Nishiki.
Ehon Fuku Zenpen: 2 vols.
Takana Kagami.
Hyakunin Isshu.
Kyōtei Kun.

[1] Also known as Ishikawa Takamoto and Yukimoto.
[2] I have never seen a copy of such a book by Ippitsusai Bunchō, and I feel certain that von Seidlitz is confusing the famous *Bunchō Gwafu* by Tani Bunchō with supposed work by the far less renowned print designer. It would seem that even amateurs need not be warned about mistaking the identity of these two men, and yet in one of the museum collections in America I found that the *Shazanrō Gwahon* had been listed as by Ippitsusai Bunchō. Shazanrō was one of the artist names used by Tani Bunchō— a much more famous artist than Ippitsusai Bunchō—being painter to the Tokugawa Court in the first quarter of the nineteenth century.—L. N. B.
[3] Or " Shimokawabe."

PLATE 31   From the EHON EIGADANE (1790), by Chūrinsha Shunchō.

Katsukawa SHUNCHŌ, who first studied under Shunshō and later became a devoted follower of Kiyonaga, was working in Yedo between 1786 and 1820. His work shows the influence of both men. At best Shunchō was hardly more than an imitator of greater artists, and although he produced some charming works, very few of them were wholly original. He used as other signatures the names SHUNKEN, SANKŌ, CHŪRINSHA, CHŪRIN, TOSHIYEN, Kissadō SHUNCHŌ, and Ushida SHUNCHŌ.

He illustrated a number of the little yellow-covered novelettes called *ki-byōshi*, in addition to his more important books. Among the latter are the

Temman-gu Yengi: History of Temman-gu. 3 vols. 1786.
Ehon Momiji-no-Hashi (" Bridge of the Maples "): 1 vol. About 1790. 40 colour-plates.
Ehon Chiyo-no-Aki: Poems on the pleasures of autumn in Yedo. Signed Katsukawa Shunchō Sankō. 1 vol. About 1790.
Ehon Sakaye-gusa or *Ehon Eigadane* (" Growing Herbs "): Scenes in the lives of women from childhood to motherhood. Signed Chūrinsha Katsukawa Shunchō. 2 folios. 1790. Colours. Rare. At least one plate in this book is an exact copy of a book-page by Kiyonaga.
Ehon Eka-shū or *Ehon Tani*: Book on the Yoshiwara. Kwansei period.

In the *Ehon Eigadane* Shunchō not only imitated Kiyonaga, but actually plagiarized from him in the most flagrant manner. The first double-page plate, representing a woman with an infant on her back while she is giving a lesson in writing to five other children, is an exact copy, except that it is a very little larger, of a signed colour-plate by Kiyonaga, which was originally probably the page of a book, since it is the size of an ordinary book page, and has been cut along a margin. Whether the other plates in the *Ehon Eigadane* are also copies of earlier work by Kiyonaga is uncertain. In any case the book is beautiful in both composition and colour, and forms one of the great treasures of a collection of *ehon*.

Another pupil of Shunchō's who achieved considerable fame was Katsukawa SHUNYEI, who lived between 1768 and 1819. Shunyei was a musician as well as an artist, and is said to have been something of a poet. He was chiefly noted for his actor prints, in which the influence of Shunshō is easily seen. Other signatures used by him were Kinjirō ISODA, KINTOKUSAI, KUTOKUSAI, and probably SHUNJŌ. Among the books illustrated by him are the

Usokawa Mukashi Banashi: Ancient tales. Signed Katsukawa Shunjō. About 1780.
Jūnichi Daitsu Banashi: The twelve animals of the zodiac represented by actors. Signed Katsukawa Shunjō. 1 vol. 1782.
Konden Sumo Daizen: A history of war. 1 vol. About 1789. This was followed by a supplement by Rantokusai Shundō in 2 vols. in 1790.
Komai-gusa Taihei Banashi: 3 vols. 1793.
Kore-wa Kuno Komachi Baka-no-Isaoshi: 2 vols. 1793.
Gushi Rokutsū Hanryaku-no-Maki: 3 vols. 1793.

Chap. VIII]　　JAPANESE BLOCK-PRINTING

Ukiyo-on Chazuki Jūni Innen: Attributed to Shunyei and Toyokuni working in collaboration. 3 vols. 1793.
Ehon Yumi (or *Isai*) *Bukuro:* Anecdotes of Chinese and Japanese heroes. 2 vols. 1801. Colours.
Shibai-ye Kimmō Dzue: A history of the theatre. Written by Shikitei Samba. First six volumes illustrated by Shunyei; last two by Toyokuni. 8 vols. 1806. Part of the illustrations are in colours. A rare set of books.
Hyakunin Isshu: The Hundred Poets. Signed Katsukawa Shunjō. 1 vol.
Kwaidan Hyaku Dzue: One hundred monsters. By Katsukawa Shunyei and Shunshō working together. 3 vols. Colours. No date.

Katsukawa SHUNKŌ, also known as SHUN-Ō and KO-TSUBO (Little Jar), is thought by some collectors to have been Shunshō's son. He was certainly a pupil, and used a jar-shaped seal like Shunshō's, from which he took one of his signatures. Strange says that his work was interrupted before middle age by a severe attack of palsy, which left him without the use of his right arm. During the latter part of his life Shunkō made his home at Zembuku-ji Temple in Yedo, where his death occurred in 1829. He left prints of actors and wrestlers chiefly and several illustrated books. Among the latter were the

Hyakunin Isshu: The Hundred Poets. 1 folio. 1795. Very fine coloured plates.
Nakamura Utaemon Jūni-baki Shosagoto: The actor Nakamura representing the Twelve Months. 1 small *gwajō* containing twelve little portraits in colours. Rare.

A second SHUNKŌ (written with different characters), also known as Katsukawa SHUNSEN, SHUNBENI, SHUNRIN, KICHŌSAI, and KASHŌSAI, was a contemporary of Hokusai and a fellow-pupil with him under Tsutsumi Tōrin, later joining Shunyei's classes. Strange gives an account of his life and says that after having been a print designer and an illustrator he abandoned this work for the decoration of porcelain. His work bears considerable resemblance to that of Keisai Eisen. Among a few books illustrated by him were the

Gengora Bunna: A novel written by Tōsai-an Namboku.
Gekkai Dzue: Signed Katsukawa Shunsen. 2 or 3 vols.

Still another SHUNKŌ, known as Odagiri or Tadachika SHUNKŌ, lived in Nagoya toward the middle of the nineteenth century. He was a pupil of Mori Kogan and illustrated some delightful books on celebrated spots in Ōmi province. These were the

Owari Meisho Dzue: A guide to famous places in Owari. 7 vols. 1844. Nagoya. Colours.
Meiku Shōkei: Small oblong colour-plates of places in Owari. Two series of 2 vols. each. 1847. Charming and uncommon.
Narumi-gata: A well-known collection of designs from ancient brocades, porcelains, bronzes, etc. 5 vols. Black and white.

The charming miniature colour-prints representing places in Owari and about Lake Biwa in the first two of the foregoing sets by Shunkō are models of composition and soft colour and are additions to a collection which in time to come will be rare and valuable.

Kubo SHUNMAN, who was one of the best of Shunshō's pupils, although his work is rare, lived in Yedo between 1757 and 1820. He came of a family named Ihei, and studied first with Takebe Ryōtai, a well-known painter of the Chinese school, but soon abandoned the classical manner for the Ukiyo-ye and joined Shigemasa's studio. Later he worked under Shunshō.

Like all the Ukiyo-ye men of his time, he fell under the spell of Kiyonaga's work, and this artist's influence upon him was, perhaps, the most potent of all. Fenollosa calls Shunman Shigenaga's greatest pupil,[1] but except in an indirect way this was impossible, since Shigenaga died the year before Shunman was born.

Considerable confusion has existed in regard to some of Shunman's work on account of the different ways in which he signed his name, the first syllable *shun* not always being written with the same character. It is said that he found himself being taken as one of Shunshō's pupils if he used the character " Spring " in his signatures, so after he had thrown off his allegiance to that artist he adopted another manner of writing his name, which while read in the same way would not cause him to be regarded as belonging to the Katsukawa group.

Other signatures used by him were Nadaka SHIRAN (as a poet), YASUBEI, SHŌSADŌ (from using his left hand), CHŌKADA, HARUMITSU (another reading of Shunman), and Tosada TOSHIMITSU. Shunman was well known as a writer of humorous verses in addition to being an artist. His chief work, however, was the designing of prints and *surimono*, which are characterized by a charming delicacy of colour and a half-mystical quality that almost baffles description. Perhaps it is because of this peculiar fascination that Japanese collectors place Shunman among the very greatest of all the Ukiyo-ye artists, being quicker than the European to feel " the touch of fantasy " in so much of his work.

Shunman, in addition to his print designing, illustrated some beautiful books, all of which are excessively rare. Among them are the

Fukujū-ko: Illustrated poems. Two colour-plates. 1 vol. 1795.
Ehon Uta Yomi Dori: 2 *orihon*. 1795. Containing full-sized oblong colour-plates by Shunman, Tsutsumi Tōrin, Suzuki Rinshō, and other well-known artists. The subjects are beautiful women, a ferry-boat scene, the well-known plate of an ox carrying bundles through a forest, etc.
Yema Awase Onna Kana-de-hon: A rendering of the Forty-seven Ronin. 1 vol. 1796.
Gojūni-ni-shū: Famous poets. 1 vol. 1801. Colours.
Tsuki-no-Ye Tsuki-no-To: Illustrated poems. Signed Tosada Shunman. 1 vol. 1802. Two colour-plates. A *kubari-hon*.
Kyōka Hidare Domoye: Humorous poems. Written and illustrated by Tosada Shunman. 3 vols. 1802.
Kyōka Hidare Domoye Kōhen: Supplement to foregoing. 2 vols. Between 1805 and 1810.
Kyōka Kotobana Takimizu: Humorous poems written and illustrated by Shōsadō Shunman. 1810.

---

[1] See *Epochs of Chinese and Japanese Art*, vol. ii., p. 196.

CHAP. VIII]   JAPANESE BLOCK-PRINTING

Tamano Ikago: Illustrated poems. 1 vol. 1815.
Ehon Haru-no-Wo: Album of six colour-plates by Shunman. Printed in *surimono* style with delicate colours and gaufrage. Very rare and valuable.
Shiki Ogi E-Awase: Pictures representing the Four Seasons for fan decorations. Signed Kubo Shunman. Temmei period.

Katsukawa SHUNTEI, also known as SHŌKŌSAI, Katsunami KANA-I, SUIHŌ, ITSUJIN, MATSUTAKASAI, and Yamaguchi CHŌJŪRŌ, lived between 1769 and 1820. Although more or less of an invalid himself, his principal work was the making of colour-prints of the men who were renowned for their size and physical strength—namely, the wrestlers. He left many sheets and also some prints and book illustrations of historical subjects. Among his books were the

Kabuki Nendai-ki: A history of the drama.
Kurai Yama Homare-no-Yoko Tsuna: A novel written by Jippensha Ikku. 1812.
Hatsuyume Fujimi Soga: Written by Tanshuro Emba. Illustrations signed Matsutakasai Shuntei. 2 vols. 1813.
Nanko Seichiu Gwaden: History of Kusunoki Masashige. 1815.
Ito Guruma Tengu Baikai: A novel. 6 vols. About 1815.

Katsukawa SHUNZAN was a pupil of Shunshō who worked through the last twenty years of the eighteenth century and well into the nineteenth. Like most artists of his time, he was much influenced by Kiyonaga. Little is known of his life and his work is not common. What we have of it shows force and a good feeling for colour. He occasionally used the signature Ryōdōsai. Two small but interesting sets of the *Ōmi Hakkei* (Eight Views of Lake Biwa) were left by him. In one the drawings are printed in white on a black ground, with a poem accompanying each cut. The work is signed Shunzan, but the seal reads Ryōdōsai. It is undated. The other set is much better known, and consists of circles with drawings within them printed chiefly in pink and green, placed upon an almost square black background.

There were many other pupils of Shunshō, but until we come to Hokusai their work is not of especial interest. They may be recognized by their use of the name Katsukawa and the syllable *shun* (" Spring ") in the second parts of their names. Of these men were Katsukawa SHUNDO, also known as RANTOKUSAI; Katsukawa SHUNSEN, who illustrated the *Gekkai Dzue*, containing curious bird's-eye views of people, street scenes, etc. (2 vols.); Kashōsai SHUNSEN (who may have been the same man), who left an *hosoye-bon* entitled *Ehon Kodomo Asobi*.

In addition to the schools of Ukiyo-ye painting which have already been mentioned, still another group, of which Utamaro became the most noted representative, was founded by Toriyama SEKIYEN. The latter artist lived between 1712 and 1788 and obtained his early training under the Kanō painter, Kokuyen Chikanobu.

Sekiyen and Ishikawa Toyonobu were almost exact contemporaries, Toyonobu being a year older and dying a year after Sekiyen. Fenollosa thought that Sekiyen and Toyoharu may have studied together under Toyonobu, but it seems more probable that he and Toyonobu worked together in Shigenaga's studio.

Sekiyen was a well-born man and occupied a far higher place in Yedo life than most of the Ukiyo-ye painters. He is said to have had a beautiful house and garden, where he was fond of entertaining friends at the ceremonial tea, at which he was considered an adept. Other signatures used by him were TOYOFUSA, SANO, and ROKU (" Old Fox ").

At the temple of Sensō-ji in Asakusa there is a famous painting of the actor Nakamura Kiyosaburō by Sekiyen, which was presented to the temple as a votive offering. In addition to his paintings, for which he was chiefly known, he also wrote and illustrated a number of books on supernatural matters, and Henri Joly has used these works as references in his studies of Japanese ghost stories.

A list of Sekiyen's books includes the

Ehon Hyaku Yagyō: Supernatural phenomena. Five series of books, of 3 vols. each.[1] About 1770–1781.
Toriyama Biken.
Ehon Hiken.
Sekiyen Gwafu: Various drawings by Sekiyen and his pupils Shiko, Sekichō, and Guesha. 2 large folios. Colours. Rare.
Toriyama Sekiyen Gwa-shiki (*Gwafu?*): A similar work to the foregoing. 1 large folio. 1774. Colours.
Yezu Hyakki Yagyō: Eight monsters of Yezu. Sekiyen in collaboration with other artists. 3 vols. 1776. Black and white and grey. (One of the sets of the series of fifteen volumes mentioned by Joly?)
Konjaku Hyakki Shū: Eight forgotten monsters.
Konjaku Zoku Hyakki Shū: Supplement to foregoing.
Jizi Hiken: Celebrated characters. Illustrated by Toriyama Sekiyen. 1778. Tints. (Listed in Bermond Catalogue.)
Gwato Hyakki Tsure-dzure Bukuro: Book on monsters. (Of series first listed?) Illustrated by Sekiyen with Shiko, Yenchi, and Sekichō. 3 vols. 1784. A second edition in 1805.
Suiko Gwasen-ran.
Tozen Bukuro: Book on ghosts. Signed Toriyama Sekiyen. 3 vols. 1784. Black and white and grey. (Of series first listed?)
Hyakki Yagyō Shū: Of the series of fifteen?
Toriyama Saishiki Dzuri.

All of Sekiyen's books are excessively rare, and the foregoing list has been made from old catalogues and such articles as Joly's alluded to in the note below. It is probable that all the books on ghosts go to make up the series which Joly speaks of, and that the *Ehon Hyaku Yagyō* is simply a collective title used for convenience.

[1] See article "Bakemono" by Henri Joly in vol. ix. of *Transactions of the Japan Society*.

CHAP. VIII]   JAPANESE BLOCK-PRINTING

Among the early pupils of Sekiyen were the following artists:

Toriyama YENCHI, also known as ANGYŪSAI, is said by Von Seidlitz to have been an early follower of Shunshō. He took his name from Sekiyen, however, under whom he worked at a later period. He left an interesting book on the celebrities of Yedo entitled the *Ukiyo Meitai-ki*, published in one volume in 1770.

Suzuki FUYŌ, also known as FUYŌBOKU, YOKO, BUNKI, and HOKOKU-JIN, was a native of Shinano, and lived between 1748 and 1816. He became a pupil of Sekiyen's toward 1765 and later was made painter to the Daimyō of Awa. He left at least one illustrated book in the *Kaiyo Hiso*, containing coloured plates of horses, signed Ko-Fuyō and published in 1791. The Nanki Bunko in Tōkyō owns a copy of this rare book.

Seki NARUTO was Fuyō's son-in-law, also an artist, who lived until 1899.

It was Kitagawa UTAMARO, the dissolute but talented pupil of Sekiyen, who best represents the group, however, and from whom the name of the school was taken. Utamaro was born in the province of Musashi in 1753, of a branch of the famous Minamoto family. By some collectors he is said to have been Sekiyen's son, but probably was the latter's nephew and was adopted by him. His first training was obtained under Sekiyen, although Kiyonaga's work was also a strong factor in determining his style.

Talented to a degree, Utamaro was, nevertheless, ill-balanced, and his low habits resulted in Sekiyen's disinheriting him when he was about twenty-five and refusing to allow him in his house any longer. The publisher Tsutaya Jūsaburō took him into his shop and Utamaro lived there until Tsutaya's death, in 1797, compelled him to find new lodgings. Utamaro never reformed, and his extremes of dissipation resulted in his death in 1806—at only fifty-three years of age.

As a pupil of Sekiyen he had used the signature Toriyama TOYOAKI, Hosho TOYOAKI, TOYO-AKIRA, and TOYO-KIRA, but later, after he went to live with Tsutaya, he changed his name to Kitagawa UTAMARO, occasionally also using the names HITAGAWA, YENTAISAI, YENBOKU, YENTOKU, NOBU-YOSHI, MURASAKIYA, KARAMARO, ICHITARŌ, YŪSUKE, and Shōmei UTAMARO.

His work was of great variety and included, in addition to paintings, prints of beautiful women, landscapes, figures in landscape settings, and even a few actor prints as well as some very rare and beautiful illustrated books. Among the latter the earliest were the small yellow-covered *ki-byōshi* in which his pupils Mitamao and Yukimaro collaborated. They date from about 1770-1775. Other books were the

Kana-dehon Chūshingura: The Forty-seven Ronin. 1 vol. 1777.
Uso Ha-byaku Mempachi-den: The adventures of Mempachi. Signed Utamaro. 3 vols. 1780.
Minari Daitsu-jin Ryaku Yenge: A book of warriors. A *ki-byōshi*. 3 vols. 1781.
Gantori Chō: A *ki-byōshi*. 3 vols. 1783.

PLATE 32]

From the Shiki-no-Hana (1801), by Kitagawa Utamaro.

[Face p. 168

Daizen Sekai Kaki-no-Soto: A *ki-byōshi.* 2 vols. 1784.
Sore-kara Irai-ki: A *ki-byōshi.* 1784.
Kajiwara Saiken Nido-no-ō: A *ki-byōshi.* Written by Shiho Sanjin. 2 vols. 1784.
Hito Shirazu Omoi Fukai: A *ki-byōshi.* 2 vols. 1784.
Nitta Tsu Senki: Military tales. A *ki-byōshi.* 2 vols. 1784.
Ehon Waka Ebisu: Album of five colour-plates representing Ebisu and the festivities of the New Year. Contains the well-known plate of a man with a trick monkey entertaining a group of people in a charming interior. Published by Tsutaya Jūsaburō, Yedo. 1 *gwajō.* About 1786. Colour, gold, silver and gaufrage.
Ehon Yedo Suzume (" Yedo sparrows "): 3 vols. 1786. Black and white. Preface by Yadoya Meshimori. A second edition in 1788 and a third in 1797.
Ehon Mina Mezame: An erotic work. Written by Rankokusai. Drawings by Utamaro and Shundō Rantokusai. 1786.
Ehon Kotoba-no-Hana: 2 vols. 1787. A second edition in 1797.
Sue-hiro: A *ki-byōshi.* Signed Utamaro. 3 vols. 1788.
Uta Makura: An erotic work. Large album of twelve plates. 1788. Colours.
Shiohi-no-Tsuto: Shells at ebb-tide. Known as the " Shell Book." Preface by Akara Sagaye. No date, but between 1780 and 1788. Eight double-page colour-plates. Rare and beautiful.
Ehon Mushi Erabe: Book of insects. Preface by Toriyama Toyofusa (Sekiyen), in which he speaks of Utamaro as his " pupil " and describes his fondness for catching and studying insects even when a child. 2 folios. 1788. Contains fifteen double-page colour-plates and title-page. Very rare in this edition. Was published again in 1823 under the title of *Ehon Goku Saishiki Mushi Awase,* in which the printing and colours are poor.
Kamuri Kotoba Nanatsume Jūni Hishi-ki: A *ki-byōshi.* 3 vols. 1789.
Ro Biraki Hanashi Kuchi-kiri: Winter festivals. A *ki-byōshi.* 2 vols. 1789.
Ehon Tatoye-no-Bushi: Illustrated poems. Signed Kitagawa Utamaro. 3 vols. 1789. Printed in an edition with colours and also one in black and white.
Ehon Kogetsu-bo: Festival scenes. Signed Kitagawa Utamaro Toyoakira. 1 *gwajō.* 1789. Five double-page colour-plates.
Ehon Tama Kushige: An erotic work. 1789.
Ehon Kimigata-te Makura: An erotic work. No signature. 1789. Twelve colour-plates.
Kurui Tsuki Machi: Poems to the moon. 1 vol. 1789. Colours.
Gesaku Gedai Kagami: Signed Toyoaki. About 1789.
Ehon Azuma Asobi: Walks around the Eastern capital. 3 vols. 1790.
Ehon Suruga-no-Mai: Festival scenes at Suruga. Signed Kitagawa Utamaro. 3 vols. 1790. Black and white.
Kyōka Ehon Ama-no-Gawa: Humorous poems. 2 vols. 1790.
Ehon Yomogi-no-Shima: Everyday scenes. Signed Kitagawa Utamaro. 3 vols. 1790.
Tama Migaku Aoto Gazeni: A *ki-byōshi.* 3 vols. 1790.
Yujoro Kotobuki Banashi: A *ki-byōshi.* Signed Utamaro. 3 vols. 1790.
Chuko Asobi Shi Goto: A *ki-byōshi.* 1790.
Sakushiki Mimigaku-mon: A *ki-byōshi.* 1790.
Uwaki Banashi: A *ki-byōshi.* 3 vols. 1790.
Yuki Onna Kuruwa (" The Snow woman of the Yoshiwara "): A *ki-byōshi.* About 1790.
Ehon Gin-seki (" The Silver World "): Poems on snow with five double-page colour-plates of snowy landscapes. Signed Kitagawa Utamaro Toyoakira. 1 *gwajō.* 1790. One of the rarest and most charming of Utamaro's works.
Fuken-zō: Promenades in the season of spring flowers. Signed Kitagawa Utamaro. 1 *gwajō.* 1790. Compiled by Ippitsusai Bunchō under the pen-name of Tsuburi-no-Hikaru. Five colour-plates.
Ehon Momo-chidori Kyōka Awase: Birds and flowers. Signed Kitagawa Utamaro. 1 *gwajō.* No date. Eight double-page colour-plates. Very beautiful and rare. First series. Probably published about 1791.

CHAP. VIII]   JAPANESE BLOCK-PRINTING

Ehon Momo-chidori Kyōka Awase Kōhen: Supplement to foregoing. 2 *gwajō*. No date, but probably about 1791. Contains seven double-page colour-plates of birds. Said by Kurth to be the last of Utamaro's works on natural history.[1] On each plate are two humorous poems.
Kyōka Haru-no-Iro: Poems on Spring. Plates by different artists, including one by Utamaro. 1 *gwajō*. 1794. Colours.
Ehon Matsu-no-Shirabe ("Testing of the Pines"): Signed Karamaro. 4 (?) vols. 1795. Colours.
Ehon Musha Waraji: 2 vols. 1795. Colours.
Ehon Shiki-no-Hana ("Flowers of the Four Seasons"): Beautiful women. Signed Kitagawa Utamaro. 2 vols. 1801. Colours.
Akureba Hana-no-Haruto Keshi Tari: Romance of the Yoshiwara. 1 vol. 1802.
Aki-no-Haru: A *ki-byōshi*. 1 vol. 1802.
Toko-no-Mume: An erotic work. 1 *gwajō*. 1802. Twelve colour-plates.
Seirō Ehon Nenju Gyō-ji ("Annual of the Green Houses"): A description of life in the Yoshiwara during the four seasons. Signed Yedo Eshi Kitagawasha Murasaki Utamarofude (assisted by his pupils Kikumaro, Hidemaro, and Takemaro). The text was written by Jippensha Ikku, an eccentric writer of the time, who at the end of the second volume promises the early appearance of a supplementary series. A quarrel between Utamaro and himself arose, however, as to the comparative merits of the illustrations and text, each contending that his part was the more valuable. This difference stopped the project for another series.

The border of the index represents the main gate of the Yoshiwara. The blue covers of the books are printed with a design of checker-boards in gaufrage taken from the lanterns used in the Yoshiwara processions. The less well-known edition of this famous work, printed in black and white, is thought by Kurth to have preceded the one in colours. De Goncourt thinks this black-and-white edition was printed to be used in experiments with the colours chosen for the books. Both editions published in 2 vols. 1804. One of Utamaro's most famous works.

Other books by Utamaro without dates were the

Ehon Hana-no-Kumo ("Flowers of the Sky"): Customs of women of different classes. Colours. Small.
Michiyuki Koi-no-Futosao: Marionettes. Not signed, but attributed by Kurth to Utamaro or Utamaro and Kikumaro working in collaboration. 3 small volumes. Coloured illustrations of marionettes. Rare.
Ehon Waraji Jogo: An erotic work. 3 vols. Colours.
Seiten Toki Uta Shū: Illustrated poems.

The following are placed among the erotic works by Kurth:

Ehon Isa-oshi Dori: 3 vols.
Ehon Yomitsu Fune: 3 vols.
Ehon Chigusa-no-Iro: 3 vols.
Ehon Masu Kagami: 3 vols.
Tsu Manabe: 3 vols.
Ehon Hime Haji Uri: 3 vols.
Ehon Koi Ebi Kata: 3 vols.
Ehon Yedo Nishiki: 3 vols.

In addition to his books Utamaro made many colour-plates for the popular albums of the time. Among these most charming works were the

Haru-no-Nagami: Poems and two colour-plates. One by Utamaro and the other by Sōrin. No date.
Otoko Fumi Uta: Poems with colour-plates by several artists. One plate by Utamaro. No date.
Otoko Toka: Colour-plates representing the festival of mid-January. One by Utamaro. 1798.
Shunkyō-jo ("Spring Thoughts"): Album with three colour-plates, the first by Utamaro.

[1] See *Utamaro*, by Dr. Julius Kurth, p. 81, and also Major O'Brien Sexton's article on Utamaro in one of the numbers of the *Burlington Magazine* in 1919.

THE UTAGAWA AND KATSUGAWA SCHOOLS [CHAP. VIII

Kitagawa HARUMACHI, sometimes called Shunchō (a different reading of the characters), was another pupil of Sekiyen's. After Utamaro's death in 1806 he married that artist's widow and went cheerfully on in Utamaro's house filling the demands for his predecessor's prints. He is said not only to have finished work left incomplete by Utamaro, but to have signed much of his own work with Utamaro's name. He afterwards changed his signature to Kitagawa TETSUGORŌ and is also known as UTAMARO II.

Nagayoshi CHŌKI, who lived between 1773 and 1805,[1] is said to have been Utamaro's fellow-pupil under Sekiyen,[2] but as Utamaro was twenty years his senior, and Sekiyen died when Chōki was only fifteen years of age, this seems improbable. His work is so strikingly like Utamaro's that it is more than possible that he was that artist's pupil rather than Sekiyen's. Kiyonaga's work also was a decided influence with him.

It must be remembered that there was an earlier Chōki (Miyagawa), the son of Katsukawa Shunsui, who was a contemporary of Sekiyen's, and references to Chōki in connection with Sekiyen may refer to this artist.

Other signatures used by Nagayoshi Chōki were SHIKŌ, Shikō MOMOKAWA, YEISHŌSAI, and Yeishōsai CHŌKI. His death occurred when he was only thirty-two years old, which accounts for the small amount of work left by him. In beauty and charm, however, it makes up for the small quantity, and examples of it are eagerly sought by collectors.

Only a few books are known to have been illustrated by him. They include the

Ehon Matsu-no-Shirabe: Music of the Pines. 1795. A second edition in 1803.
Ryōken: Novelette by Bakin. Illustrations signed Chōki. No date.

Chōbunsai EISHI, who should be classed with Utamaro and Chōki from the resemblance his work bears to theirs, seems to have had no especial training in the Ukiyo-ye style, but began his career as a painter of the Kanō school. He left this to study under Okumura Bunkaku, an exponent of the classical old Tosa art, but still later, the popularity of the prints proving too great a temptation, he abandoned the older schools and gave himself up to designing colour-sheets.

Eishi was born in 1760 of a family much higher in Yedo life than the majority of the artists of the Ukiyo-ye school, and his desertion of the classical painting for work considered so undignified as print designing brought him the condemnation of family and friends alike.

His real name was Hosoda Tokitomi, but as artist signatures he used the names CHŌBUNSAI, HOSOI, JIBUKYŌ, and Hosada TERAYUKI. His death occurred in 1829.

[1] Dates taken from the *Kokkwa Magazine*.
[2] See *History of Japanese Colour Prints*, by W. von Seidlitz, p. 155.

CHAP. VIII]   JAPANESE BLOCK-PRINTING

Both in drawing and colour Eishi's work is charming and his prints are rapidly winning a high place in the estimation of collectors. He also illustrated some delightful books and left plates in a number of the albums of the time. Among the books containing drawings by him are the

Momonga Ima-Kwaiden: Tales of supernatural beings. 5 vols. 1788.
Yanagi-no-Ito ("Willow Silk"): Poems on spring. Contains colour-plates by several artists including Eishi. 1 *gwajō*. 1797. Rare and charming.
Nishiki Zuri Onna Sanjū-rok-kasen Edzukushi: Thirty-six women poets. Signed Hosoi Chōbunsai. Double-page title plate by Hokusai. 1 vol. 1798. Very rare and beautiful. A second edition in 1801.
Otoko Toka: Festival of mid-January. Eishi and other artists (Hakuho, Yekishi, Tōrin, Shigemasa, Utamaro and Hokusai). 1 *gwajō*. 1798. Colours.
Ehon Kasen Shū: Famous poets. 1 large folio. 1799. Thirty-four colour-plates.
Anata Yomo-no-Haru: Album with coloured plates by Eishi, Tsunegaki, and Hokusai. No date.

A pupil of Eishi's, known as EISHŌ, illustrated the

Hate Mezura Chiki Futatsu-no-Utsuwa: 3 vols. 1798.

YUKIMARO was an early pupil of Utamaro's, and collaborated with him as early as 1785 in the illustration of the little yellow-covered novelettes called *ki-byōshi*. Strange places Yukimaro as the son of Kikumaro, but if any relationship existed between them it is more probable that it was reversed, for Kikumaro was a much later man. Yukimaro gave up painting toward middle age and became a writer. He illustrated the

Bumbu Nido Mango Kusu: 3 vols. 1788.

KIKUMARO, also known as TSUKIMARO and Kitagawa ROKUSABURŌ, worked much in Utamaro's manner, but toward middle age abandoned the Ukiyo-ye school and took to painting under the name of KWANSETSU. He died in 1829. Books illustrated by him were the

Hana Momiji Futari Anko: 3 vols. 1805.
Kane-no-Waraji: Sight-seeing in Yedo.
Yedo Meisho: Twelve coloured plates of Yedo.

SHIKIMARO illustrated a book called *Zensei Tagu-no-Kurabe*, representing a gathering of beautiful women.

TOYOMARO, whose name indicates that Toyokuni as well as Utamaro had influenced him, was working toward the beginning of the nineteenth century. He left the

Kurawa Suga-Shō: 1796.
Fukutoku Irimon Mitsubiki: 2 vols. 1798.

Kitagawa EIZAN, a late follower of Utamaro, was the son of Kanō Eiri of Yedo, under whom he first studied. His ordinary name was Gyokusai

Mangorō, but as other artist signatures he used the names TAMEGORŌ and TOSHINOBU. He was a good deal of an eclectic and was affiliated with the Hokusai group, as well as doing work in the manner of Utamaro. He is said to have forged Utamaro's name on prints of his own after that master's death. Eizan was known as a writer in addition to being an artist, and wrote many of the books which he illustrated.

Keisai Eisen, a contemporary of Hiroshige's and one of the well-known nineteenth-century print designers, was his pupil.

CHAPTER IX

LATE UKIYO-YE ILLUSTRATORS

HE late Ukiyo-ye school is, of course, chiefly represented by HOKUSAI and his followers, but before speaking of these artists one should mention Tawaraya SŌRI and Tsutsumi TŌRIN, both of whom were well-known Yedo painters in the latter part of the eighteenth century. These two men exerted a considerable influence upon the art life of Yedo, and Hokusai, as well as several other noted men, was among their pupils.

Sōri (*c.* 1764–1781) was the son of Tawaraya Sōrin and was familiar with both the Tosa and Kanō methods. It was owing to his admiration for the work of Tawaraya Sōtatsu of the preceding century as much as to the fact that he was Sōrin's son that he used the syllable *Sō* in his own artist's name. Other signatures used by him were Genshi RYŪRYŪKYŌ, HYAKURIN, and Hishikawa SŌRI. Kōrin's work was also a large factor in forming his style, and paintings by Sōri, sealed with a large round seal much like Kōrin's, have sometimes been mistaken for that artist's work. Sōri did very little in wood engraving, although he left one book entitled the *Segan Shū*, a collection of illustrated proverbs, published in 1758.

Among his pupils were SŌRIN II., who established a school in Akita; SŌRI II.; and Ryūryūkyo SHINSAI, also known as Hanjirō MASAYUKI, who was a contemporary of Hokusai. Shinsai made *surimono* and worked to some extent at illustrating, making the drawings in the

Kyōka Isso-no-Kami or *Kyōka Gojū-nin Isshu:* A collection of humorous poems. Illustrations signed Ryūryūkyō Shinsai. 1 vol. 1803. Colours.
Shinsen Kyōka Gojū-nin Isshu: 1 vol. Colours. Rare.
Ōmi Hakkei: Eight views of Lake Biwa.

SŌRI II., also known as HYAKURIN and HISHIKAWA, has sometimes been confounded with Hokusai. He was a contemporary and friend of that artist and a fellow-pupil with him under Tawaraya Sōri. He illustrated several charming books in colours much in Hokusai's manner, among which were the

Kyōka Ehon Chūshingura Kagami: A version of the Forty-seven Rōnin. 1 vol. 1803. Colours.
Kyōka Ehon Shokunin Kagami: Artisans and their work. Humorous poems. Signed Hishikawa Sōri. 1 vol. 1803. Colours.
Akebono: A *gwajō* by Sōri II. and Utamaro.

PLATE 33]   Poetess: from the SHINSEN KYŌKA GOJŪ-NIN
ISSHU, by Ryūryūkyo Shinsai. Kyōwa period.

Hokusai was an intense admirer of Sōri, and used that name in combination with others for a considerable period, sometimes being called, according to Revon, Sōri III.[1]

Sōri IV., also called Hashimoto Sōji and Shōbei, studied under Sōri I. and later with Hokusai. He left a book entitled *Kusabana Koromono* (" Flowers to perfume Garments "), which appeared in 1801.

Tsutsumi Tōrin, the other artist under whose influence Hokusai fell after leaving Shunshō's and Sōri's studios, was working in Yedo from about 1770 until the end of the century. He was born between 1742 and 1745, and is said to have been a descendant of the fifteenth-century artist Sesshū. His real name was Ginji Tsukioka, but as artist signatures he used the names Sessan, Teino, Tei, and Tsumbo, in addition to Tsumi and Tsutsumi. He first studied under a painter of the Chinese school, but abandoned this style of work for the Ukiyo-ye, and eventually opened a studio of his own in Yedo called the Tei *Ryū*.

Tōrin's early work was chiefly devoted to large lacquer paintings on wood intended for votive offerings to temples. Later, when he took up the designing of *surimono* and book illustration, his drawings were characterized by a delightful humour and a much more impressionistic technique than was common with the Ukiyo-ye men.

Fenollosa speaks of Sōri and Tōrin as having a " coarse, broad, loose style,"[2] but in reality both men had formed their manner on classical Chinese and Japanese models, which was much more in accord with the best Japanese traditions than the style of the Ukiyo-ye artists. Tōrin's death occurred in 1820. A number of the popular albums of the day contain delightful colour-plates by him, their technique bearing a strong resemblance to that in work by Toriyama Sekiyen, suggesting a possible connection between the two men.

Among the albums containing work by Tōrin were the

Ehon Uta Yomi Dori: Poems with full-sized oblong colour-plates by Tōrin, Rinsho, Shunman, Shōho, and other artists. 2 *gwajō*. 1795. Very beautiful and rare.
Yanagi-no-Ito (" Willow-silk "): Poems on spring, with colour-plates by Tōrin, Rinsho, Kwaran, Eishi, and Hokusai Sōri. 1 *gwajō*. 1797.
Ehon Kyōka-Shū: Gwajō with five colour-plates by Tōrin, Eishi, Rinsho, and Kwaran. 1797.
Otoko Toka: The festival of mid-January. Colour-plates by Tōrin, Kitao Kōsuisai (Shigemasa), Hakuho Ekigi, Eishi, Utamaro, and Hokusai Sōri. 1 *gwajō*. 1798.

Tōrin left a number of pupils who worked in his style and adopted the first syllable of his name.

Tōsen, also known as Yuyūsai, and Kimura, was working in the first quarter of the nineteenth century. He illustrated the

---

[1] See *Hoksai*, by M. Revon, p. 63.
[2] See *Epochs of Chinese and Japanese Art*, vol. ii., p. 201.

CHAP. IX] JAPANESE BLOCK-PRINTING

Yakko-no-Koman: A novel. Illustrations signed Yuyūsai Tōsen. 5 vols. 1807.
Ui Manabe Gwafu: Drawings of horses and other animals. With a frontispiece much in Hokusai's manner. Three very small volumes. No date. Interesting and uncommon.
Shogaku Ede-hon: Supplementary series to the foregoing containing drawings of flowers and plants. 3 vols.

SEISAI was one of Tōrin's best pupils. Late reproductions of his work are found in the *Syun (?) Shū Kinga*, birds, flowers, etc., in the Chinese style (1 vol. 1822. Colours).

Other followers were Sansei TŌRIN, probably the same as Tōrin II.; AKITSUKI or TŌRIN III.;[1] Sawa SEKKYŌ; Kobayashi UMPO; Ryūsai MASAZUMI, perhaps the son of the Ryūsai Sakai who was illustrating in the Hōreki period; ITTO; Ekigi HAKUHO; Tsutsumi TŌSHIN; Tsutsumi SHŪGETSU; and Tsutsumi SHŪYEI, who established a studio in Ōsaka, where Gakutei studied for a time.

There was another Tōrin of Yedo who is not to be confused with Tsutsumi Tōrin. This was Hasegawa or Ono TŌRIN, the adopted son of Tōhaku and who painted in his style. He belonged to the Unkoku school, and was noted for his pictures of birds and flowers. He was also known as YOSETSU and Abe HAYATARŌ.

It is with the famous Hokusai, however, that we come to the artist whose work is perhaps more widely known and appreciated in Europe and America than that of any other Japanese painter, and it is safe to say that the amateur collector of Japanese prints and illustrated books will begin by buying something bearing his signature, for if no other Japanese artist is known to him, the name of Hokusai, at least, will be familiar. This is partly because of the enormous output of the man, and its greater or less resemblance to a form of art understood by the Occidental collector; partly because much of it is really beautiful and interesting; and also, sad to say, very largely probably because the power of suggestion is so potent and the very name of Hokusai seems to be in the air.

No newcomer to Japan can enter a curio shop and ask for prints without having something by this artist shown him first, last, and inevitably, and the dealers must reap immense annual harvests from Hokusai prints alone.

That Hokusai was a great artist no one would deny, but that he deserves the exalted place in Japanese art accorded him by most foreigners one would hesitate very decidedly in agreeing to. In point of variety and quantity of work done, however, he stands supreme, for there was nothing that he did not attempt and nothing he failed to do well. His energy and industry were phenomenal, and his work is imbued with a rugged sincerity which certainly endears him to us. Although hardships and disappointments

[1] Strictly speaking Akitsuki was the fifth Tōrin, his grandfather, who worked in the Genroku period, being the first Tōrin.

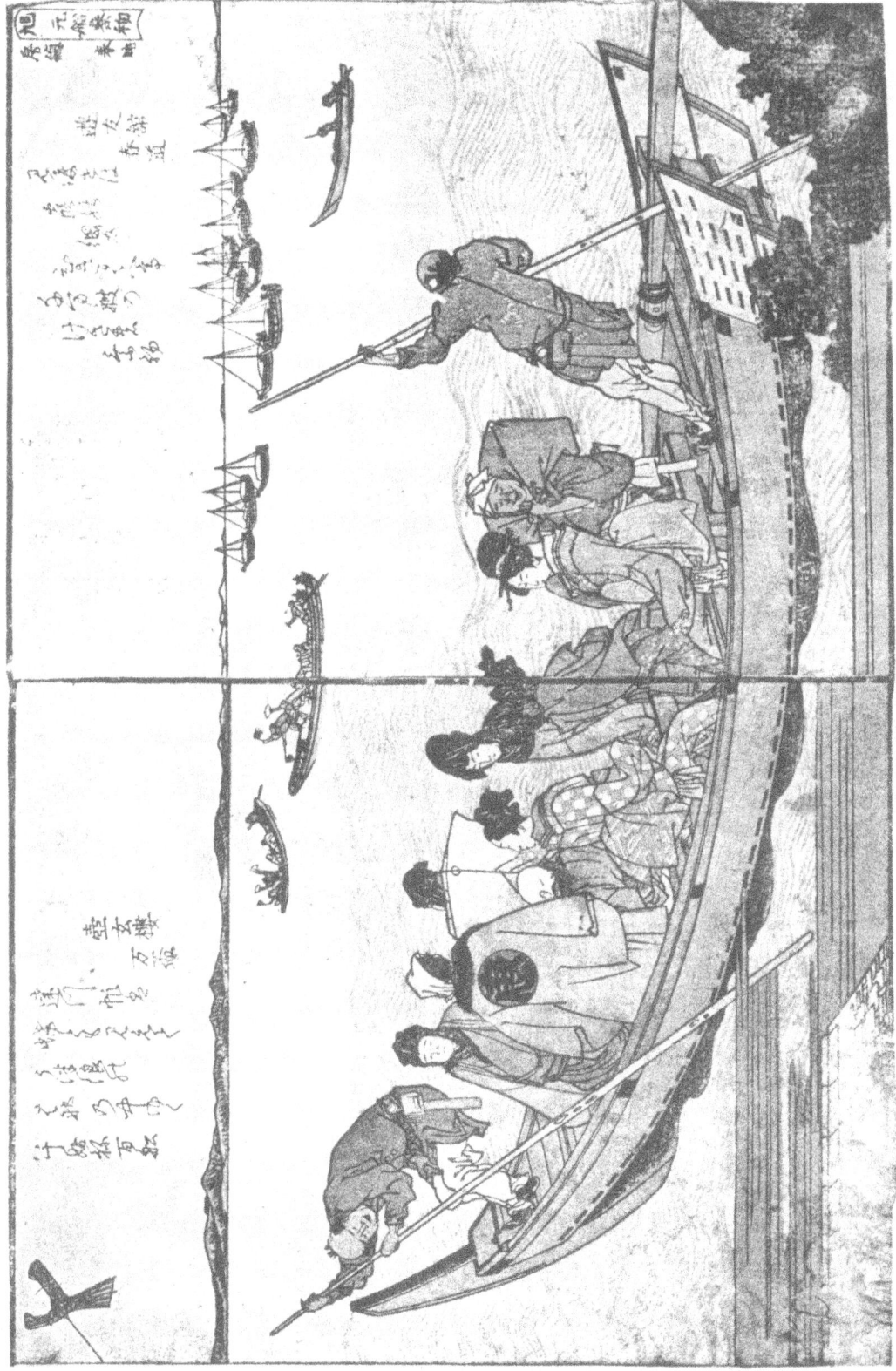

From the Sumidagawa Ryōgan Ichiran (C. 1804). By Hokusai.

filled his life, his simplicity, his carelessness about material things, his pride, and the kindness of his nature endured. He refused to worship the false gods that the late Utagawa artists were following, and the wholesomeness of his work was the leaven which kept the declining Ukiyo-ye art at least passably healthy for years.

It still remains uncertain whether the ides of March of 1760 or the autumn of that year welcomed Hokusai into this workaday world, where his father, Nakajima Ise, was mirror-maker to the Tokugawa Court, and had his metal-casting establishment as well as his dwelling-house in the Honjō quarter of Yedo, across the Sumidagawa. Here Hokusai spent his childhood. In his twelfth year he went to work in a publishing house. This doubtless had its effect in determining his career, for the natural talent he possessed must have been quickened by the constant handling of books and pictures, and it is easy to imagine him on the *tatami*-covered floor of the shop poring over books and prints in his idle hours and making youthful artistic attempts of his own. Two years later (1772) it was decided that he should study for wood-engraving, and by the time he was fifteen he had begun to illustrate small novelettes and make prints in the style of Shunshō, who had been chosen as his master. By his twentieth year he seems to have been fully launched in his profession, using the signature SHUNRŌ for his early productions.

Other periods of study were interspersed with his work, however, and he was a pupil at different times of Tawaraya Sōri, Tsutsumi Tōrin, Kanō Yusen, Hiroyuki, and even attempted oil painting under Shiba Kōkan, who had returned to Yedo from Nagasaki and was inflicting his " Western art " upon the receptive souls of the capital.

As was natural under these various influences, Hokusai's style went through many changes, the eighties of the eighteenth century witnessing his allegiance to extremely tall and graceful figures, very charming and full of fascination, while later his work took on a different character and a looser technique, probably acquired from the painter Tōrin, who was his teacher toward 1790–1795. The different influences in his career may be traced to some extent by his signatures, which are bewildering in number and possibly not all known yet. His early work is variously signed TOKITARŌ (" First-born Son "), Katsukawa SHUNRŌ, Mugura SHUNRŌ, and Sono SHUNRŌ, in remembrance of Shunshō; TAWARAYA, HYAKUNIN, and Hokusai SŌRI, after the painter Sōri; and TŌSHU and TEI-ITSU, in honour of Tsutsumi Tōrin. Other signatures were GUMMATEI (about 1786–1788) and Katsushika HOKUSAI. After the beginning of the nineteenth century he used the names Gwakyō Rōjin HOKUSAI, I-ITSU (TAMEKAZU), Haku Sanjin KAKŌ, Hokui SHINSEI, Sakino Hokusai MANJI, Katsushika Manji Rōjin HACHIYEMON, RAISHIN, RAITO, Muraya HACHIYEMON, Umemaru YUSEN, Genryūsa

TAITO, SAITO, Tokitarō SOROBEIKU, Hokusai TATSUMASA, Tengudō NETTETSU, and various other combinations of these names.

Hokusai had a life of ups and downs, even in his student days being subject to occasional trouble with whom ever he for the time being was studying under. He was obliged to leave Shunshō's studio because of his experiments in the classical Kanō manner; his criticism of a drawing by Kanō Yusen resulted in his being dismissed from work which that artist had engaged him for in the Nikkō temples; and frequent quarrels seem to have taken place between him and other students, all caused by a splendid independence he had of any one method, and a catholic tolerance for them all. Periods of great poverty also marked his life which at one time compelled him to resort to street peddling.

In spite of all these vicissitudes, however, his fame grew, until at last the curiosity of the Shōgun was aroused. An appointment was made through Tani Bunchō for Hokusai to exhibit his skill at a temple in the Honjō quarter one day as the Shōgun passed through that part of Yedo on a hunting trip. The result was an amazing success, and the notoriety it brought him, added to that made by his gigantic drawing of Daruma before a throng of Yedo spectators, caused him to become the most talked of artist of the day, orders pouring in from all quarters until at last popularity and prosperity seemed permanently his.

In 1817, unhappily, trouble with his son-in-law, Yanagawa Shigenobu, interrupted this peace and drove him away from Yedo. For nearly five years he took refuge in Nagoya, Ōsaka, and Kyōto, and even travelled through the remote provinces south and west.

It was during this absence from Yedo while visiting the artist Bokusen of Nagoya that the idea for the famous Mangwa set of books took form, and Bokusen collaborated with him in much of the work. Later Hokusai went to Ōsaka, where his influence over certain Ōsaka artists became paramount, the work of Akatsuki Kanenari, Hishikawa Kiyoharu, and Matsukawa Hanzan in particular, proclaiming them as among the closest of all his followers. From Ōsaka Hokusai went to Kyōto, the ancient city, where the old traditions were living in a new-old art movement expressed in the Shijō and Maruyama work. Here he lived quietly under an assumed name, realizing that the contempt of these more aristocratic artists for the Ukiyo-ye productions would be too great for him to meet.[1] It was not until Tani Bunchō's arrival there from Yedo that his identity was discovered, and that famous artist's friendship for him—for Bunchō was painter to the Tokugawa Court—gave Hokusai the *cachet* which made him welcome.

In 1832 Hokusai returned to Yedo from his second absence, but soon left again on a year's visit to Takai Sankurō, a pupil who had left Ganku's

[1] See *Hoksai*, by M. Revon, pp. 92, 93.

studio in Kyōto to put himself under Hokusai's instruction, and who lived in a luxurious home in Shinano.

In 1835 his third exodus took place, and for two years he lived in Uraga under the name of Muraya Hachiyemon. It is said that these absences from Yedo were caused by the disgrace brought upon him by his disreputable son-in-law and grandson. One hopes that these visits brought him satisfaction, for happiness and prosperity lacked permanence for him in the capital, where he returned a last time in 1836 to find that a terrible famine had laid its hand on the people and that they were too poor to buy pictures.

Hokusai and his daughter Ōyei lived in the greatest need, resorting to all sorts of expedients to bring in enough money for the bare necessities of life. Fortunately, by this time one trial was lessened, for Shigenobu had left his wife and gone to Ōsaka, where he made dolls in the intervals of his painting.

The next three years seem to have been rather uneventful. Some degree of prosperity was again attained, but in 1839 came the worst blow of all, a veritable calamity, for Hokusai's house was burned and with it, except a few brushes, all his possessions, including clothes, painting materials, and hundreds of pictures and unfinished sketches. Hokusai lived for ten years after this, beginning in a small way in the poorest of quarters, but with his spirit unbroken and his ardour unabated. Up to the year of his death, in 1849, he worked incessantly, producing paintings, prints, and book illustrations in enormous quantities.

He left a large number of followers who worked much in his style, several of whom had collaborated with him in special pieces of work.

Although Hokusai's paintings and prints are much more widely known than his books, the latter are equally interesting. He commenced his work in illustration with the little yellow-covered novelettes called *ki-byōshi* in 1775, some of which he is said to have also written, and continued to produce great numbers of books for the next seventy years. Many of Bakin's novels were illustrated by him, as well as stories, translations from the Chinese, works on drawing, moral tales, proverbs, and poems. It is his books printed in colours which are most sought after, although some of those printed in black and white are extremely rare and valuable. Among the latter are the Falcon's Feather edition of the *Fugaku Hyakkei* and the *Azuma Asobi Miyako-no-Teburi*. The *Azuma Asobi* was first published in 1799 in one volume containing black-and-white drawings of scenes in and around "the Eastern Capital" (Yedo), with poems by Sensō-an on the pages between the illustrations. The original cover is blue and bears a design in gaufrage. The book is exceedingly rare and eagerly sought by collectors. In 1802 it was published again with coloured illustrations and bound in three volumes. The poems are omitted. This edition also is rare and valuable.

JAPANESE BLOCK-PRINTING

The *Yama Mata Yama* is one of Hokusai's rarest colour-printed books and is generally considered the finest, although just why it should be so ranked is puzzling, for neither in composition, colour, nor printing does it compare with the three volumes of the Sumidagawa set, in which some of Hokusai's very best work appears.

The *Tōto Shōkei Ichiran* of 1800 is another of his well-known works, in which the illustrations represent various aspects of life in Yedo.

The *Hokusai Shashin Gwafu*, a *gwajō* containing charming oblong double-page colour plates of animals, birds, people, etc., published in 1814, is almost impossible to find now, and even the reprint of 1819 is exceedingly rare and when found is usually sold as the original edition.

The famous *Mangwa* is, of course, his best-known work, and its fifteen volumes form an epitome of pretty much all of Japanese life. The idea for it originated, according to Revon, during Hokusai's visit to Bokusen of Nagoya in 1817, and during the next ten years numbers of it appeared at intervals until in 1827,[1] after ten volumes had been published, the blocks were bought by Yerakuya Tōshirō of Nagoya. Four more volumes were issued by this publisher between 1834 and 1849, and after Hokusai's death still another, made up of drawings collected by his friends and students.

In the first ten volumes of the *Mangwa*, Bokusen, Hoku-un, Hokkei, and Hokusen collaborated with him, but the last five volumes seem to have been mostly his own work.

A complete set of the original edition of the *Mangwa* in good order can now hardly be obtained. By virtue of patience and continued search, however, one may sometimes form a full set by finding single volumes here and there and uniting them; a set thus collected engendering a greater affection perhaps in the heart of the collector than one found complete in a curio shop. One feels that he has been the means of bringing the lost members of a family together, and that the books recognize him as a flock knows its shepherd.

Hokusai's daughter, Ōyei Eijō, illustrated a book written by Takai Ranzan called the *Onna Chōchōki*, a work on the education of women (5 vols. 1847), which Hokusai is said to have thought contained better drawings of women's figures than any he had ever made himself.

The list of books[2] illustrated by Hokusai is a long one and includes the

Buchōho Sokuseki Ryōri: The awkward cook. Written and illustrated by Tokitarō Kakō (Hokusai). 3 small vols. No date.
Yedo Murasaki: History of Gompachi and Murasaki. Signed Tokitarō. 1 vol. 1780.
Honchō Meisho Arigataki Tsuno Ichiji: Stories of Japan. 1781.
Kamakura Tsu Shin-den: Signed Shunrō. 2 vols. 1782.

---

[1] Both Strange and Dickins say in Bunsei 10, which would have been 1827.
[2] I have taken many of these books from the list in Revon's *Hoksai*.

PLATE 35]

From the Hokusai Gwashiki (1819), by Hokusai.

[Face p. 180

Shi Tennō Daitsu Jitate: Four kings of Heaven. Signed Shunrō. 2 vols. 1782.
Umbiraki Ogi-no-Hanaka: Perfumed fans. Signed Shunrō. 2 vols. 1784.
Ehon Onaga Mochi: Various tales. Signed Katsukawa Shunrō. 1 vol. 1784.
Nozo-ki Karakuri Yoshitsune Yama Eiri: Yoshitsune and his valorous deeds. Signed Shunrō. 2 vols. 1784.
Oya Yuzuri Hana-no-Komyō: A work on filial piety. Signed Shunrō. 3 vols. About 1785.
Honen Uji Hotarubi: The revenge of the River Uji. Signed Shunrō. 2 vols. 1785.
Nichi Tensaku Nishinga Isshu: Lesson book. Signed Shunrō. 3 vols. 1786.
Mae-mae Taiheki: Peaceful reigns of past sovereigns. Signed Katsu Shunrō. 4 vols. 1786.
Yabara Mombara-no-Nakana Chō: A novel. Signed Shunrō. 3 vols. 1786.
Jinkōki Nishiki Mutshi (?): History of two wars. Signed Gummatei. 1788.
Fukitaru Uraigao Kadomatsu: The pursuit of Happiness. 2 vols. 1789.
Kusa-kimo Nabiku Hiri Kuraye: Days of good fortune. Signed Shunrō. 2 vols. 1789.
Rok-kasen Kyōjitsu Tensaku: Corrections of mistakes by the poets. Signed Shunrō. 3 vols. 1789.
Mitata Chūshingura: Comparison of contemporary men with the Rōnin. Signed Hokusai. 1 vol. 1790.
Ringu Sentaku Banashi: Story of the Ringu Palace. Signed Shunrō. 2 vols. 1791.
Nuye Yorimasa Meika Shiba: Yorimasa's song. Signed Shunrō. 2 vols. 1791.
Mukashi Mukashi Momotarō Hōtan Unsetsu: The legend of Momotaro. Signed Shunrō. 3 vols. 1792.
Bimpoku Ryōdochi Unoki: Lives of the rich and poor. Signed Shunrō. 3 vols. 1793.
Chiye Shidai Hakone Dzumi: Siege of Hakone. A game. Signed Shunrō. 1793.
Tōdaibutsu Momiji Meisho: Site of the great Daibutsu. Signed Haku Sanjin Kakō. 1793.
Fukujūkai Muryō Skinadama: A novel by Bakin. Signed Shunrō. 3 vols. 1794.
Nozo-kimi Tatoye Fushiyama: Signed Shunrō. 2 vols. 1794.
Asahina O Hige-no-Shiri: Arrows of Asahina. Signed Hokusai. 1796.
Yamato Honzo: Monsters of Japan. Signed Tokitarō. 3 vols. 1797.
Nishiki Zuri Onna Sanjū-rok-kasen: The Thirty-six Women Poets. Coloured frontispiece signed Gwakyō Jin Hokusai. 1 vol. 1798.
Bakemono Iwa-no-So: History of phantoms. Signed Kakō. 2 vols. 1798.
Azuma Asobi Miyako-no-Teburi ("Walks around the Eastern Capital"): With poems by Sensōan. 1 vol. 1799.
Tōto Meisho Shōkei Ichiran: The environs of Yedo. Signed Hokusai Tatsumasa. 2 vols. 1800. Colours.
Kamada Shōgun Kanryaku-no-Maki: Historical work. Signed Tokitaro Kakō. 3 vols. 1800.
Jido Bunshu Chikyō-kun: Instructions for children. Signed Kakō. 3 vols. 1801.
Furyū Gojū-nin Isshu Izukawa Kyōka Guruna: Humorous poems and poets. Signed Hokusai Tatsumasa. 1 vol. 1802. Colours. Rare.
Itako Zekku Shū: Songs of Itako. Signed Hokusai. 1 vol. 1802.
Ehon Tōto Asobi ("Walks in the Eastern Capital"): 3 vols. 1802. Colours.
Ehon Chūshingura: The Forty-seven Rōnin. Signed Hokusai Tatsumasa. 1 vol. of two parts. 1802. Colours.
Chūshingura Hyaku Ari Kyōka: 100 poems on the Forty-seven Rōnin. Signed Hokui Shinsei. 2 vols. 1802.
Azuma Asobi ("Walks around the Eastern Capital"): 3 vols. 1802. Colours. A second edition of the work of 1799 with poems omitted.
Ehon Kyōka Yama Mata Yama: Verses on "mountains upon mountains." 3 vols. 1803 or 1804. Colours.
Fuchiuho Sokusetsu Ryōri: Signed Kakō. 1803.
Ogura Hyaku Donsaku Kusen: One hundred parodies on the Hundred Poets. Signed Hokusai Tatsumasa. 1 vol. 1803.
Sangoku Wakan Ran Satsuga: Stories of China, Japan, and Holland. Signed Kakō. 2 vols. 1803.
Kyōgu Jūnen Ashinkiro: Signed Kakō. 3 vols. 1803.
Jinkōki Urai Sango-Jūgo Kangirimono Sanyo: Signed Kakō. 1803.

JAPANESE BLOCK-PRINTING

Ehon Sumidagawa Ryōgan Ichiran: The banks of the Sumida river. 3 vols. About 1804–1806. Colours. One of Hokusai's finest books.
Ryōmen Shūshi Sugata Kagami Onnai Saru Kataki-uchi: The vengeance of a monkey. 2 vols. First volume illustrated by Toyokuni; second by Tokitaro Kakō. 1804.
Shōsetsu Hyaku-mu: Signed Hokusai Tatsumasa. 2 vols. 1804.
Tamashige Ishidomaru Monogatari: Signed Sakino Hokusai. 3 vols. 1804–1818.
Asa Kinhiro: Shell-headed men. 3 vols. 1804.
Fukushu Ehon Futabano Nishiki: A story of vengeance. 1805.
Azuma Nishiki: 1 vol. 1805.
Nitta Yoshimune Koshinroku: The loyal followers of Yoshimune. Signed Katsushika Hokusai. 5 vols. 1806.
Waki Dzushi: Different tales. Signed Hokusai. 3 vols. 1806.
Chuko Ita Kobushi: Moral teachings. Signed Katsushika Hokusai. 5 vols. 1807.
Sumidagawa Bairyū Shinsho: The trees along the Sumida river. Signed Katsushika Hokusai. 5 vols. 1807.
Shin Kasane Gedatsu Monogatari: Novel by Bakin. Signed Katsushika Hokusai. 1807.
Shinpen Suiko Gwaden: Chinese heroes. Translated from the Chinese by Bakin and Takai Ranzan. Illustrations signed Katsushika Hokusai. 9 vols. 1807.
Yuryū Akanui Iru-Taka: The falcons of Yuryū Akanui. Signed Katsushika Hokusai. 5 vols. 1807.
Hyōchu Sono-no-Yuki: Snow in the garden. Novel by Bakin. Signed Katsushika Hokusai. 5 vols. 1807.
Yuku-no-Misao Renrino Mochibana: Signed Hokusai. 10 vols. 1807.
Sanshichi Zenden Nanka-no-Yume: Dream of Sanshichi. Novel by Bakin. Signed Katsushika Hokusai. 7 vols. 1808.
Raigō Kaisō-den: Signed Katsushika Hokusai. 5 vols. 1808.
Kana-dehon Gojitsu-no-Bunko: The Forty-seven Rōnin. Signed Katsushika Hokusai. 1808.
Shimo-Yo-Boshi: Signed Katsushika Hokusai. 5 vols. 1808.
Kataki-uchi Shindai Rimego: Old tales. Signed Hokusai. 6 vols. 1808.
Kataki-uchi Migawari Myōgo: Novel by Bakin. Signed Katsushika Hokusai. 1 vol. 1808.
Ryūryaku Jōkyō-kun: Instructions for women. Signed Gwakyōjin Hokusai. 5 vols. 1808.
Kataki-uchi Mukui-no-Ja-yanagi: Novel. Signed Hokusai. 6 vols. 1808.
Ehon Tama-no-Ochibo: History of a devout family. Signed Katsushika Hokusai. 6 vols. 1808.
Yume-no-Ukibashi: Bridge of dreams. Signed Katsushika Hokusai. 3 vols. 1809.
Hokuyetsu Ki-den: Curious tales of Hokuyetsu. Signed Hokusai. 1809.
Chūkō Itako-bushi: 5 vols. 1809. Black and white. Signed Katsushika Hokusai.
Eiri Sanchō Taiyu: A romance. Signed Katsushika Hokusai. 5 vols. 1809.
Shoki-ocho Shiraito Sashi: History of Shiraito. Signed Katsushika Hokusai Shinsei. 5 vols. 1810.
In-nyō Imoseyama: Book on marriage. Signed Hokusai. 1810.
Chinsetsu Yumihari Dzuki: Novel by Bakin. A celebrated work which has gone through many editions. 29 vols. 1810.
Nanka Koki: Signed Katsushika Hokusai. 1811.
Aoto Fuji Moryō-an: Novel by Bakin. Signed Katsushika Hokusai. 5 vols. 1812.
Matsuo Monogatari: Signed Hokusai. 6 vols. 1811.
Shimpen Toki-no-Kumasaka Banashi: History of the brigand Kumasaki. Signed Tokitaro Kakō. 1811.
Hyakugwa Haya Oshiye: Drawing book. Signed Hokusai. 1 vol. 1812.
Hokusai E-Kagami: Signed Katsushika Hokusai. 1813.
Hokusai Gwakyō: In collaboration with Gakutei, Bokusen, and Hokuyo. 2 vols. 1813. A second edition in colours.
Hokusai Gwakan: Various drawings. 3 vols. 1813.
Ryakugwa Haya-Shinan: Drawing book. 3 vols. 1814.
Hokusai Shashin Gwafu: Double-page colour-plates of animals, birds, flowers, etc. 1 *gwajō*. 1814. A second edition in 1819, less well printed. Excessively rare in first edition.

PLATE 36]   From EHON TŌSHISEN. Illustration to a poem by Wang Wei, Chinese poet of the 8th century; by Hokusai.

[Face p. 182

Santai Gwafu: Drawings done by three methods. In collaboration with Hokkei, Hokusen, Gakutei, Bokusen, and Utamasa. Signed Hokusai. 1 vol. 1815. Colours.
Ehon Jōruri Zekku: Poems. Signed Katsushika Hokusai. In collaboration with Hokutei and Bokusen. 1 vol. 1815. Colours. (This is a second edition of the *Chōsei-den*.) Rare.
Beibei Kyōdan: Signed Sakino Hokusai Taito. 8 vols. 1815.
Hashi Kuyō: Bridge building. Signed Hokusai. 1815.
Odori Hotori Geiko: Instructions in dancing. Signed Katsushika Hokusai. 1 vol. 1817.
Ehon Haya-biki: Drawing lessons. 2 vols. 1817–1819.
Denshin Gwakyō: Various drawings. (From the *Hokusai Gwakyō*.) 1 vol. 1818.
Hyōsui Kigwa or (in a later issue) *Ehon Ryūhitsu* ("Aquatic Plants"): Fanciful title referring to the harmonious union of Ryūkōsai and Hokusai in the drawings which go to make up the book. Landscapes by Ryūkōsai and figures by Hokusai. 2 vols. 1818. In two editions—one in black and white, and one in colours. Rare.
Hokusai Gwa-shiki: Various drawings. Signed Katsushika Taito. 1 vol. 1819. Tints.
Hokusai Gwafu: A supplementary set to foregoing. 2 vols. 1820. Tints. (The drawings in the *Hokusai Gwa-shiki* and the *Gwafu* were reproduced in a set of three smaller books in 1849 in which the colours are more pronounced.)
Teitsu Sensei Keijō Gwafu: Various drawings. 1819.
Hokusai Sogwa: Hokusai in collaboration with Bokusen, Taiso, Hokuyo, and Utamasa. 1 vol. 1820.
Nijūshi-kō: Twenty-four examples of filial piety. 1822.
Zokuetsu Ki-dan: Stories of the province of Echigo. Signed Katsushika Hokusai. 6 vols. 1823.
Imayō Kushi Kogai Hinagata: Drawings of combs and hair-pins. Signed Katsushika Tamekazu. 2 vols. 1823.
Ippitsu Gwafu: Drawings made with one stroke of the brush. From a collection of sketches left by Fukuzensai. Hokusai in collaboration with Hoku-un, Hokutei, and Bokusen. 1 vol. 1823. Colours.
Shinagata Komonsho: Decorative designs. Signed Sakino Hokusai Tamekazu. 1 vol. 1824.
Aki-no-Hana Tori Shū: Poems illustrated by Hokusai, Hokkei, and Gyōku-kei. 1 vol. 1826.
Ehon Teikun Warai: Work on education. Signed Sakino Hokusai Tamekazu. 3 vols. 1828.
Suiko-den Yushi-no-Edzukushi: One hundred and eight heroes. Signed Katsushika Sakino Hokusai Teitsu Rōjin. 1 vol. 1829.
Waka Inshitsu Bun Esho: Translation of a Chinese work on famous historical characters. 2 vols. 1829.
Banshoku Dzuko: Designs for artisans. Signed Katsushika Taito. 5 vols. 1829–1835. Colours.
Ehon Tōshisen Gogon Zekku: Poems of the T'ang dynasty. Signed Sakino Hokusai Manji. 5 vols. 1833.
Ehon Chūkyō: Book on Confucius. Signed Sakino Hokusai Tamekazu Rōjin. 1 vol. 1834.
Fugaku Hyakkei: One hundred views of Mount Fuji. In the first edition (Yedo) this work was published in two volumes and bound in gaufraged salmon-pink covers with title slips printed in blue representing a falcon's feather. This edition is known as the "Falcon's Feather Edition." It was beautifully printed in black and white and grey, and dates from 1834 (first volume) and 1835 (second volume). There is a preface by Ryūtei Tanehiko, a *samurai* of the Tokugawa, who was an artist and writer of the early and middle nineteenth century. The books are signed Gwakyō Rōjin Manji. A third volume was added afterwards, published by Yerakuya Tōshirō of Nagoya, who bought the blocks of the original set from the Yedo publisher Nishimura.
Fugaku Hyakkei: A later printing of the same book. 3 vols. in plain yellow covers. Still another edition of this famous work appeared with a blue tint added to the cuts. Nagoya.
Wakan Ehon Sakigaki: Historical tales. Signed Sakino Hokusai Teitsu. 1 vol. 1836.
Ehon Musashi Abumi: The great fire of Yedo. Signed Sakino Hokusai Teitsu. 1836.
Katsushika Shin Hinagata: New designs. Signed Katsushika Sakino Hokusai. 1836.
Dōchu Gwafu: Sketches made on a journey. 2 vols. 1836. Colours.
Ehon Tsuzoku Sango Kushi: A romance. Signed Katsushika Taito. 1836.
Nikkō-San-Shi: Description of Nikkō. 6 vols. 1836.
Gwahon Musashi Yoroi: Ancient warriors. 1836.

CHAP. IX]   JAPANESE BLOCK-PRINTING

Hyakunin Isshu Ubagawa Yetoki: One hundred poems explained by the nurse. 1 vol. 1839. Colours. Rare.
Shaka Suson Go-ichi-Dai-ki Dzue: Illustrated life of Shaka. 6 vols. 1839.
Jingō Kōgō Sankan Tai-ji: Conquest of Korea by the Empress Jingō. Signed Katsushika Taito. 5 vols. 1840.
Gempei Nagashira Ehon Musha Buroi: The wars between the Minamoto and Taira clans. Signed Katsushika Tamekazu. 1 vol. 1841.
Manwō Sohitsu Gwafu: Miscellaneous drawings. Signed Sakino Hokusai Manji. 2 vols. 1843.
Hokusai Gwaken: Signed Sakino Rōjin Manji. 3 vols. 1843.
Ehon Saishikitsu: 2 vols. 1848.
Shinga Hyakunin Isshu: One hundred Chinese poems and poets. Signed Hokusai Manji Rōjin. 1 vol. 1848.
Kwachō Gwafu: Birds and flowers. Signed Katsushika Taito. 1 vol. 1848. Colours.
Kwachō Gwaden: Supplement to foregoing. 1 vol. 1849. Colours.
Hokusai Gwafu: A smaller edition of the *Hokusai Gwashiki* and the original *Hokusai Gwafu*. 3 vols. 1849. Colours.
Ehon Waka-no-Homare: Celebrities of China and Japan. Signed Sakino Hokusai. 1850.

UNDATED BOOKS BY HOKUSAI

Chōsei-den: From an old *Jōruri-bon*. Early work with very tall figures. Published again in 1815 as the *Ehon Jōruri Zekku*. Colours. Extremely rare.
Eiyu Dzue: Pictures of warriors. Signed Katsushika Genryūsai. 1 vol. Colours.
Hokusai Gwasetsu: Theory of drawings. 1 vol.
Hokusai Ringwa: Drawing book. 1 vol.
Ehon Ryōfude: Drawings by Hokusai Taito and Rikkōsai of Ōsaka. 1 vol.
Chibun Hinagata: Signed Hokusai.
Teitsu Gwafu: Various drawings. Signed Teitsu.
Shōnin Kagami: Types of men. 3 vols.
Meizan Shokei Shinzu: Views of different mountains. 1 vol.
Azuma Hyakunin Isshu Tamoza: One hundred poems on Yedo. 1 vol.
Saifu-no-Himo Shirami Use Gusuri: History of a miser. Written by Hokusai under the name of Tenbohiro. Illustrations signed Hokusai. 1 vol.
Yorozu Hyakunin Isshu Sobunshō: One hundred poems. 1 vol.
Taisei Hyakunin Chiye Kagami: Sayings of one hundred wise men. 1 vol.
Yuigahama Chūya Monogatari: Signed Hokusai. 1 vol.
Ehon Onna Imagawa: Book on women. 2 vols. Black and white and colours.
Anata Yomo-no-Haru: Poems on spring. Album containing three oblong colour-plates by Hokusai, Tsunegaki, and Eishi.
Ryōsan-dō Ichiran: Mountain roads. 3 vols.
Chūshingura Jūni-dan: The Forty-seven Rōnin.
Asagawa Shū: Poems illustrated by Hokusai and his pupils. 1 vol.
Boso Ichiran Dzue: Views in the north and south.
Kataki-uchi Urami Kusunoha: Novel by Bakin. Illustrations signed Katsushika Hokusai. 5 vols.
Ehon Kan-so Gundan: A tale of feudal wars. Signed Katsushika Manji Rōjin Hachiyemon.
Tema Ezuki Akaho-no-Shiokara: Humorous version of the Forty-seven Rōnin. An *hōsōye-bon*. 1 vol.
Kyōka Ressen Gwaso Shū: Poems illustrated by Zen Hokusai Tamekazu. Compiled by Goshōtei Kizan. 3 vols. Rare.
Tsuki-no-Kumasaka: Signed Tokitarō. 1 vol.
Ehon Katsushika Buroi: Method of drawing.
Hokusai Bijin Kyōka Shū: Verses on beautiful women. Hokusai and other artists.
Hokusai Jimbutsu Ehon: Drawings of people.

PLATE 37] [Face p. 184

From the HOKUSAI GWAFU (1820).

Ehon Saiyu Zenden Saiyuki: History of a voyage to the west. An account of the journey of the Chinese priest Hsüan-tsang, of the seventh century, from China to India. Signed Katsushika Taito. 12 vols. (Illustrations to the Chinese novel *Hsi Yu Chi?*)
Nihon Meibutsu Gwasen Shū: Poems. Signed Taito. 1 vol. Tints.
Hitori Hokku: Short poems. Hokusai and other artists.
Shunju-an Yomihatsu Mushiro: Signed Getchi Rōjin Tamekazu. 1 vol.
Hokusai Mangwa Haya Shinan: Drawing book. Signed Sakino Tamekatsu Rōjin. In two series of two volumes each. First edition in black and white, later reissued in colours.
Iihitsu Gwafu: Drawings made from Chinese characters. Small.
Ryūhitsu Gwafu: The second edition of the *Hyōsai Kigwa* of 1818.

In regard to the famous *Mangwa* set there is still some dispute as to the date of the first volume. The preface, written by Hanshū Sanjin (or Keijin) of Owari, is dated Mizu-no-e, Saru year, which Mr. F. Victor Dickins figures out to be December of 1812 by European chronology. Nevertheless, Revon had very good authority for putting the year of *publication* at 1817.[1] Moreover, in the preface to Volume V. it is stated[2] that " these random sketches, as the master calls them, have for some time past, owing to the favour with which the earlier ones were received, been engraved and published year after year, and the present one is the fifth of the series." Strange takes this to actually mean that each year up to the publication of the tenth volume one volume was added to the set. He says:[3] " . . . The date of the tenth volume, tenth month of Bunsei 10 (A.D. 1819), has never been questioned and bears on its face every impress of truth, in the characteristic appropriation of a series of tens for a notable and auspicious achievement." Now if Strange is correct in this assumption that one volume a year was added after the appearance of the first volume, it proves rather than discredits Revon's date for the first volume (1817), for Strange makes the mistake of giving 1819 as the equivalent of Bunsei 10, whereas it should be 1827, the Bunsei period beginning in 1818 and lasting until 1830; the tenth year thus having been 1827 and not 1817, as both Dickins and Strange give it.

The date of the *Bokusen Sogwa* (1815) Strange gives as an added proof that the *Mangwa* must have appeared earlier than this, and he says of the former book that it is " a fairly close imitation of the early volumes of the *Mangwa*, both in style, execution, and selection of subject." In style, of course, it bears the stamp of Hokusai's influence, since Bokusen had been Hokusai's pupil, but in other respects it is more easy to imagine it as an imitation of the *Hi-Kangen Gwashiki* (1787), a set of books containing drawings of various subjects by the Chinese artist Hi-Kangen; or of the two charming books by the Kyōto artist Kawamura Bumpō, the *Bumpō Sogwa* and the

---

[1] See *Hoksai*, by M. Revon, pp. 92, 93.

[2] See " The Mangwa of Hokusai," by F. Victor Dickins in the *Transactions of the Japan Society*, London, vol. vi., pp. 293-297.

[3] See *Hokusai*, by Edward F. Strange, p. 17.

CHAP. IX]   JAPANESE BLOCK-PRINTING

Bumpō Kangwa, published respectively in 1800 and 1803, both of which are made up of dashing little coloured sketches representing people at various tasks and pastimes.[1]

All this, however, is rather unimportant, for after all " the book's the thing," and it is enough to know that the first thirteen volumes were published at intervals before 1849, and that afterwards the publishers added Volumes XIV. and XV., the latter dated 1878 and made up of reproductions of work by Hokusai and added to at the request of the publishers by Ota Kyōsai and Numada Gessai, who made some drawings especially for this last volume.[2]

The whole series of the *Mangwa* is as follows:[3]

VOL. I.: Preface by Hanshū Sanjin (or Keijin). Various drawings signed Hokusai, in which Bokusen and Hoku-un collaborated.

VOL. II.: Preface by Rokujuyen. Drawings of men and women, plants, trees, birds, animals, fishes, etc. Signed Katsushika Taito. With Hokkei, Hokusen, Bokusen, and Hoku-un collaborating.

VOL. III.: Preface by Shoku Sanjin. Drawings of various things. Signed Katsushika Taito, with Hokkei, Hokusen, Bokusen and Hoku-un collaborating.

VOL. IV.: Preface by Hōzan Gyo-ō. Drawings of acrobats, etc. Signed Katsushika Hokusai, with Bokusen, and Hoku-un collaborating.

VOL. V.: Preface by Rokujuyen. Drawings of *torii*, pagodas, temples, galleries, etc. Signed Katsushika Taito, with Hokkei, Hokusen, Bokusen, and Hoku-un collaborating.

VOL. VI.: Preface by Shoku Sanjin. Drawings representing athletic games, fencing, archery, gunnery, etc. Signed Katsushika Taito, with Bokusen, Hokusen, Hokkei, and Hoku-un collaborating.

VOL. VII.: Preface by Shikitei Samba. Drawings of landscapes in different provinces and other various aspects. Signed Katsushika Hokusai, with Bokusen and Hoku-un collaborating.

VOL. VIII.: Preface by Hōzan. Drawings representing different industries. Signed Katsushika Hokusai, with Hokkei, Hokusen, Bokusen, and Hoku-un collaborating.

VOL. IX. Preface signed Rokujuyen. Drawings of Chinese and Japanese heroes, famous characters, etc.

VOL. X.: Preface by Shurōdai. (Dated the 10th month of the 10th year of Bunsei, or 1827.) Drawings of shrines, monasteries, magicians, types of men and women, etc. Signed Katsushika Hokusai, with Bokusen and Hoku-un in collaboration.

VOL. XI.: Preface by Ryūtei Tanehiko. Drawings of miscellaneous subjects. Unsigned.

VOL. XII.: Preface by Bunrakutei. Miscellaneous drawings. Unsigned.

VOL. XIII.: Preface by Sankin Gwaishi Ogasa. Drawings of flowers, birds, etc., which are compared with Kaishiyen's and Juchikusai's work. Signed Katsushika Tamekazu Rōjin. Nagoya. 1849.

VOL. XIV.: Preface by Hyakusu. Drawings unsigned. Nagoya. 1875.

VOL. XV.: Preface by Katano Tōshirō and dated the 7th month of the 11th year of Meiji, or 1877. Compiled by the editor from sketches left by Hokusai and drawings by Ota Kyōsai and Numada Gessai made at his request to fill an otherwise too small volume. Nagoya. 1878.

---

[1] Note from the Duret Catalogue (p. 274):

" Ces croquis de Boumpô sont du gendre de ceux nous devons à Kitao Masayoshi, et à Hokousai, dans le premier volume de la Mangoua. Ils donnent la réprésentation, sous une forme minuscule, des scènes du monde vivant et montrent les gens dans les attitudes et les occupations les plus variées."

[2] See *Hoksai*, by M. Revon, p. 92.

[3] From " The Mangwa of Hokusai," by F. Victor Dickins in vol. vi. of the *Transactions and Proceedings of the Japan Society*, London, 1905.

PLATE 38] From the Hokkei Mangwa Shōhen. By Uwoya Hokkei (About 1814).

[Face p. 186

Among Hokusai's followers Uoya HOKKEI was hardly inferior in ability to Hokusai himself. This artist was born in Yedo in 1780. In early life he is said to have been a fish-dealer, his ordinary name being Hatsugawa Kinyemon. Later he moved to the Akasuka quarter of Yedo and took up the study of painting under Kanō Yōsen.[1] Eventually, however, he placed himself under Hokusai's instruction and collaborated with that artist in much of his work.

Hokkei is chiefly noted for his beautiful *surimono*, but he also designed some charming prints and illustrated a number of books. Other signatures used by him were HATSUGORŌ, SAI-EN, KYŌSAI, UOGA, SHINYŌSAI, TODŌYA, KIYEN, AYEOKA, AYEGAOKA, and Omoriya HOKKEI. His death occurred in 1850 and his tomb is in the cemetery of Ribō-ji at Aoyama in Tōkyō.

Among his books are the

Fujin Gwaso Shū: Women poets of Japan. 1 vol. 1806.
Kyōka Banka Shū: Humorous poems with illustrations signed Kyōsai Hokkei. (Afterwards these drawings were republished as part of the *Hokkei Mangwa*.) 2 vols. 1810. Colours. Exceedingly rare.
Hokkei Mangwa: Drawings taken in part from the foregoing. 1 vol. 1814. Colours. Also an edition in black and white.
Hokkei Mangwa Shōhen: Supplement to the *Hokkei Mangwa*.
Kyōka Gojū-nin Isshu: Fifty humorous poems. 1 vol. 1819.
Shinsen Kyōka Gojū-nin Isshu: Supplement to foregoing. 1 vol. 1819.
Kyōka Tōto Jūni Kei: Humorous poems with twelve views of Yedo. 1 vol. 1819.
Yoshiwara Hokuri Jūni Toka: Twelve hours in the Yoshiwara. 1 vol. 1820.
Suiko Gwaden: The One Hundred and Eight Chinese Heroes. 3 vols. 1820. Colours. A reprint in 1828. Colours.
Fusō Meisho Kyōka Shū: Poems on celebrated places. 3 vols. 1824. Colours. Rare.
Renge-dai ("Water Plants"): Hokkei with other artists. 1 vol. 1826.
Aki-no-Hana Tori Shū: Poems illustrated by Hokusai, Hokkei, and Gyōkukei. 1 vol. 1826. Tints. Rare.
Yuki Hyaku Shū: Poems on snow. 1 vol. 1829. Three double-page colour-plates. Very beautiful and rare. A *kubari-hon*.
Kyōka Keika Shū: Illustrated poems. 1 vol. 1829.
Kinsetsu Bishonen Roku: Novel by Bakin. 5 vols. 1830.
Poems on Famous Waterfalls: Illustrated by Hokkei and Chiharu. 1 vol. 1833.
Sansui Gwayo: Landscapes. 1 vol. 1835. Colours.
Yomo-no-Haru: Album containing two colour-plates. Signed Hokkei. 1836.
Kyōka Sanjū-roku Shū: Thirty-six humorous poems by the Thirty-six Poets. Illustrated by Hokkei and Hiroshige. 1 vol. 1840.
Haikai Hyaku Shū: One hundred poems and portraits of the poets. 1 vol. 1848.
Kyōka Dōchu Gwafu: Poems on places along the Tōkaidō. 1 vol.
Shokoku Meisho.
Kwachō Dzue: Birds and flowers. 1 vol.
Hokkei Zuko: Sketches in three tones. 2 vols.
Tokiwa-no-Taki: Story of Tokiwa. Hokkei with Chiharu. 1 vol.
Shikiku Awase: Poems on the Four Seasons. Hokkei and Geppo. 1 vol.
Yamato Meisho Ichiran: Celebrated places in Yedo, Ōsaka, and Kyōto. 1 vol. The coloured illustrations in the book appeared originally in the *Fuso Meisho Kyōka Shū*.
Asahi-no-Kage: Poems to the dawn. 1 vol.

---
[1] 1748–1808.

CHAP. IX] JAPANESE BLOCK-PRINTING

Kyōka Awase Ryōgan Dzue: Humorous poems describing the banks of the Sumida river. 1 vol.
Hokuki Jūni-ji: Daily occupations.
Gosen Shunkyō Shū: Poems with drawings of landscapes and flowers. Hokkei with Gakutei and other artists. No date. Colours.
Kyōka Mutsu Tamagawa: Humorous poems with six coloured drawings of the Tama river. No date. A *kubari-hon*.
Tōshi Gwafu: Chinese poems. Illustrated by Hokkei. No date.

Of Hokkei's books the *Kyōka Banka Shū* is perhaps the rarest. In 1814 other drawings were added and it was republished as the *Hokkei Mangwa*. The colours used are delicate and the drawings very charming.

The *Yuki Hyaku Shū* is both rare and beautiful. The double-page colour plates represent a hunting party returning through a wintry landscape, people engaged in making great snowballs, shovelling snow, and other winter scenes.

The *Gosen Shunkyō Shū*, a rare little *kubari-hon*, contains one charming plate by Hokkei representing a *samurai* and his servants on a trip to Mount Fuji. It is beautifully printed with gold and gaufrage added to the colour.

Gekkōtei BOKUSEN, also known as HOKUTEI, TOENRŌ, and HYAKUSAI, was the artist to whom Hokusai is said to have been indebted for the idea of the *Mangwa* set of books, and it was at his house in Nagoya that the drawings for the first volume were made; Bokusen himself collaborating in much of the work. In addition to often working with Hokusai, Bokusen illustrated the

Bokusen Gwafu: A sketch book. 2 vols. 1809. Colours.
Shashin Gakuhitsu Bokusen Sogwa: Various sketches. 1 vol. 1815. Colours. (There is also an edition of the same year in black and white.)
Kyō Gwayen: A book of caricatures.

HOKUSEN, also known as TAIGAKU, left the

Banshoku Dzuku: Designs for artisans. 5 vols. 1835. Ōsaka. Colours. In imitation of Hokusai's well-known books (?).
Kwachō Gwaden: Birds and flowers. 2 vols. 1848–1849. Colours.

Teisai HOKUBA, a left-handed artist whose ordinary name was Gorohachi Arisaka, was one of Hokusai's earliest pupils. He lived in Yedo between 1770 and 1844 and at one time was associated with Tani Bunchō in some of the latter's work. Hokuba was more of a painter than a print designer, and was also well known for his delightful miniature paintings. He entered the priesthood toward middle life, although continuing his art work. Other signatures used by him were HOSHINŌ, SHUNSHUNSAI, and OKUBA. He illustrated the

Ikyōku Kwachō Shū: Poems with drawings of birds and flowers. 1 vol. 1798.
Poems: 1804.
Sanshitsuzen Denran Kanō Ume: Romance by Bakin. 3 vols. 1808.
Tamura Monogatari: Story of the Daimyō Tamura. 6 vols. 1809.

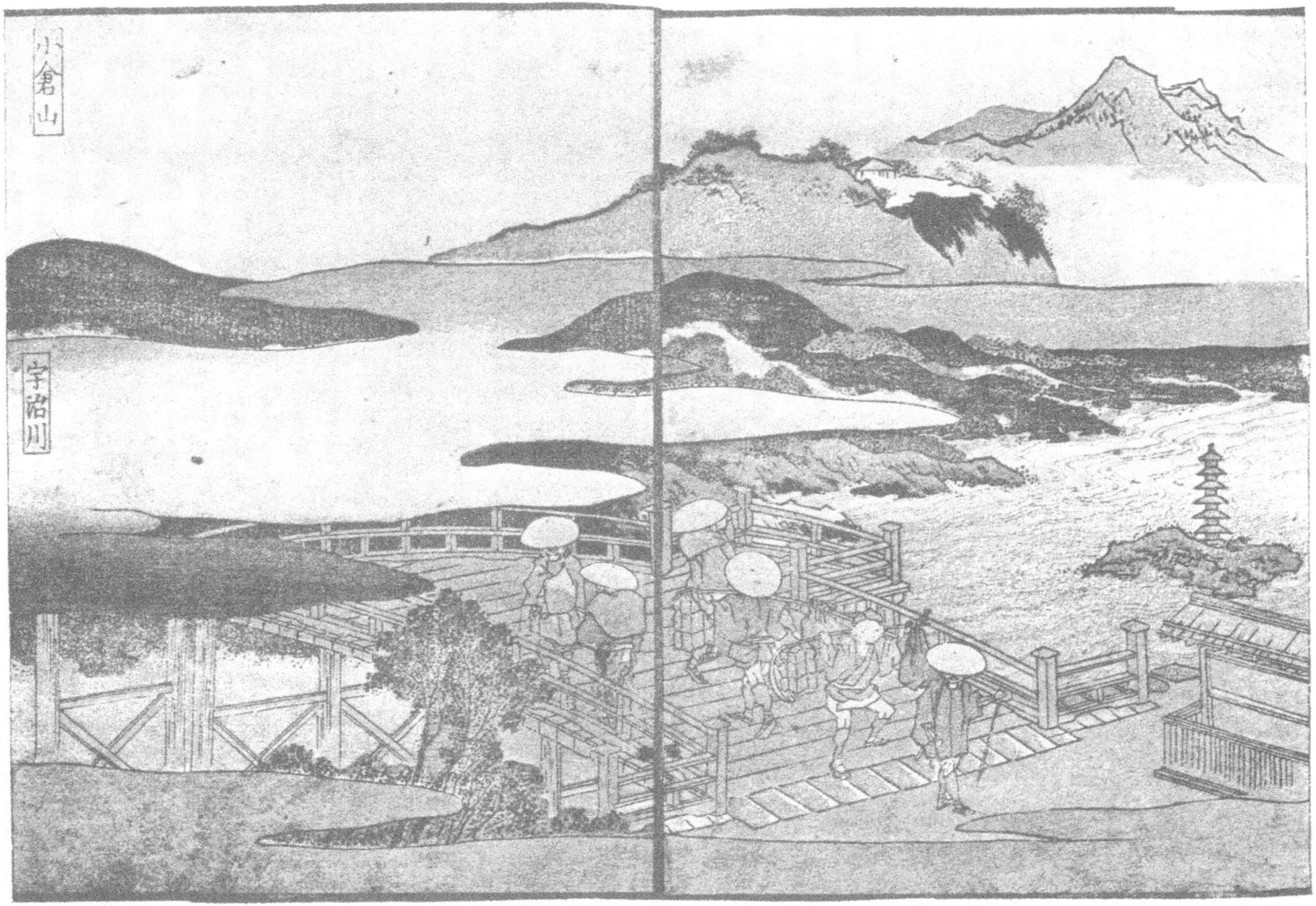

PLATE 39] Mount Ogura and the Uji River. From the Fusō Meisho Kyōka Shu, by Uwoya Hokkei (1824).

Toshitsu Yogen Kwairoku: A romance. 28 vols. 1809.
Denka Chawa: A romance. 5 vols. 1829.
Seikutsu-roku: The manufacture of starch. 1 vol. 1830.
Teisai Gwafu: 2 oblong vols.
Hokuba Fude Shōkei Jo: Album with fifteen landscapes and figures in landscape settings.
Wakaki: The evils of infidelity. Signed Okuba. 1 vol.

Taiga HOKU-UN, a follower of Hokusai who became an architect and settled in Nagoya, is said to have made the greater part of the drawings in the fifth volume of the *Mangwa* representing *torii*, temples, pagodas, and various architectural details. In collaboration with Hokuga and Hokuju he also illustrated the *Hoku-un Mangwa*, published in 1818 by Yerakuya, the Nagoya publisher who issued part of the *Hokusai Mangwa*; and with Hokusai, Hokutei, and Bokusen compiled the famous *Ippitsu Gwafu* made up of drawings done by one stroke of the brush by Fukuzensai, an artist of the Chinese school, whose work Hokusai is said to have greatly admired. Hoku-un used as other signatures the names KINGORŌ, BUNGORŌ, TŌZAINAN, and TŌNANSEI; the last two suggesting Tsutsumi Tōrin's influence.

Hotei HOKUGA, also known as GOSA and Nanyōsai HOKUGA, was rather an obscure follower of Hokusai, who is said to have been the best colour mixer in Yedo, and whose colours were in great demand by the artists there. Like all of Hokusai's pupils he made *surimono* in addition to designing prints and illustrating books.

Among the books left by him are the

Kyōka Ressen Gwaso Shū: Humorous poems on the sages. Illustrated in collaboration with Hokusai. 1 vol. 1820.
Kyōka Kasen Hyaku Shū: Humorous poems on the poets. 2 vols. About 1820.

There was also, according to Revon, a Katsushika Hokuga who was another rather obscure follower of Hokusai.

Shōtei HOKUJU was a fellow-pupil with Hokkei under Hokusai. His work also shows foreign influence. Among the books illustrated by him were the

Kyōka Tōkaidō Dōchu Gwafu: Humorous poems on the stations along the Tōkaidō. 1 vol. 1813.
Hokuju Gwafu: Sketch book. 2 or 3 vols. Colours. Small.
Kwachō Sansui Hokuju Gwafu: A very curious and interesting set of two *gwajō* of landscapes, flowers, birds, etc. Printed in crude greens, blues, and purples, with great white cloud masses in the landscapes in deep gaufrage. Extremely rare.

Kameya SABURA, a descendant of the Ōsaka Kondō family whose Yedo branch formed the famous Torii school of Ukiyo-ye painting, was the artist to whom Hokusai, in 1816, gave the name of Taito, and it was this man who settled in Ōsaka and endeavoured to pass as Hokusai himself, signing that artist's name to many of his pictures.

While in Yedo he had kept a tea-house near the main gate of the Yoshiwara and had been a pupil of Hokusai's. He used as other signatures the names Kondō Endō HANYEMON, Nidaimei HOKUSAI (HOKUSAI II.) and was called by those who knew his tendency to plagiarize, " Inu Hokusai," or " Hokusai's dog." Among the books left by him are the

Meisho Kagami.
Saito Gwafu.
Kōmin Hinagata.

Takai SANKURŌ, also known as Kodōye, was the son of a rich wine merchant of Shinano. He commenced his studies under Ganku in Kyōto, but one day in giving an informal talk to his pupils, Ganku said that although he felt himself to be the equal of any of the famous Kyōto or Ōsaka artists of the time, he feared the great renown that the Yedo artist, Hokusai had won. This tribute to Hokusai's talent, together with the fact that shortly before this Tani Bunchō and Hokusai had been in Kyōto together and Hokusai had done some work there, induced Sankurō to leave Kyōto and take up his residence in Yedo, where he became one of Hokusai's most ardent disciples. An intimate friendship sprang up between the two men, and in 1831 or 1832, after renewed trouble with his grandson, Hokusai accepted an invitation from Sankurō to visit him in the country, where he remained a year.

Sankurō was chiefly known as a painter, his work for wood-engraving apparently having been confined to a few unimportant drawings in compilations of the time.

The best of the second generation of the Hokusai group was Yashima GAKUTEI, who, although he had studied under Hokusai for a time as well as in the Katsukawa Shunshō school, was really a disciple of Hokkei's. He was born in Yedo but spent some years while a young man in Ōsaka, where he studied under Tsutsumi Tōrin's pupil, Tsutsumi Shūyei.

Gakutei became well known as a poet and writer as well as an artist, using as signatures for his literary work the names HORIKAWA-NO-TARŌ, SHINKADŌ, and ICHIRŌ, while as artist names he used KYŪZAN, HARUNOBU II., Gakutei HARUNOBU, GOGAKU, ICHINO, SHINSADŌ, TAIKŌ, TEIKOKYŌ, and SADAOKA. His chief work for wood-engraving was the designing of *surimono*. He became famous for this, and although he made some prints and illustrated a few charming books they remain rather incidental to the better known *surimono*.

Gakutei left a son, Gokei, who achieved a reputation hardly inferior to his own.

Among the books illustrated by him were the

Kyōka Suikoden: Humorous poems on the One Hundred and Eight Chinese heroes. 1 vol. 1822.
Ichirō Gwafu: Landscapes and other drawings, including a beautiful night scene. 1 vol. 1823. Colours.
Kyōka Kijin-den: Anecdotes of the comic poets. 2 vols. 1824.
Inaki: Poems on artisans. 1826.

PLATE 40]   From the Kyōka Meishu Gwaso Shū,
       illustrated by Gakutei Yashima Sadaoka.

[Face p. 190

Murasaki-gusa: Book on the Yoshiwara women. 2 vols. 1827. Twelve coloured plates. Very beautiful.
Hyaku Kiya-kyō: Stories of ghosts and monsters. Illustrated in collaboration with Seiyo. 1 vol. 1829.
Kyōka Ryakugwa Sanjin Rok-kasen: Comic poems by the Thirty-six Poets. Signed Kyūzan Gakutei. 1 vol. 1830.
Kyōka Nihon or *Nippon Fūdoki:* Humorous verses on famous places in Japan. 2 vols. 1831. Colours.
Tempō Yama Haikai Kusha Hashikaki: Short poems with charming landscape and figure illustrations. Signed Yashima Gogaku. 2 small vols. 1836. Colours. Rare.
Ryakugwa Shokunin Dzukushi: Craftsmen and their work. 1 vol. in 1826 and second in 1841. Colours. Signed Gakutei Teiko.
Gosen Shunkyō Shū: Poems illustrated by Gakutei in collaboration with Kiyozumi, Danjūrō VII., and Hokkei. 1 vol. No date. A *kubari-hon*. Rare and charming.
Sansui Kikwan Kyōkwachō: Landscapes, flowers, birds, etc. Signed Kyūzan Gakutei. 1 vol.
Kyōka Meishu Gwaso Shū: Comic poems with portraits of the poets. 1 vol. Signed Gakutei Yashima Sadaoka. Colours.
Uta-no-Tomobune: Poems illustrated by Gakutei Yashima Sadaoka and Kunisada. 1 vol. Tempō period. Colours. Rare and charming.
Hyakunin Isshu Kyōka: Humorous poems. Landscapes and figures of the poets. Colours.

Katsushika ISSAI, also known as Shimizu SHŌJI and SUIYOKEN, was a Yedo artist of the second generation of Hokusai's pupils. He illustrated the

Soto Hyakunin Isshu: The Hundred Poets. Issai with Kunisada, Sadahide, Kuniyoshi, and Yoshitora. 1 vol. 1853. Two plates in colours, other illustrations in black and white.
Sanji-Kyō Esho: Moral stories for children. 1 vol. 1853.
Nichiren Shōnin Ichidai-Dzue: Life of Nichiren. 6 vols. 1858. In two editions, one printed in black and white and one in colours.
Bambutsu Dzue Issai Gwashiki: Designs for artisans. 2 vols. 1864.
Issai Gwa-shiki: Various drawings. 1864.
Kwachō Sansui Dzushiki: Birds, landscapes, flowers, etc. 5 oblong vols. 1866.
Kwachō Sansui Mangwa Hyabiki: Birds, flowers, landscapes, etc. 1 vol. 1867.

Yanagawa SHIGENOBU, the troublesome son-in-law of Hokusai, was born in Yedo in 1780. He was known in ordinary life as Suzuki Jūbei. After some time spent in studying in the Utagawa school, he left that studio to work under Hokusai. Here he met Hokusai's eldest daughter, Omiya, whom he finally married. After various disgraceful escapades he left his wife and settled in Ōsaka, where he worked under Nanrei and Gyokuzan, producing eventually some very creditable work both in prints and book illustrations. Later he gave up painting and took to making dolls.

Both Shigenobu and his son were great trials to Hokusai, their debts being a terrible burden to him, and their propensity for forging his name to inferior work a source of embarrassment and worry. Shigenobu was talented, however, and left some interesting work. As other signatures he used the name Ryūsen, and, after 1820, the name Taito, which had been used earlier by Hokusai. At the time of his death, in 1832, Shigenobu was engaged in illustrating a novel by Bakin which was afterwards finished by his pupil, Jūsen.

CHAP. IX]　　　JAPANESE BLOCK-PRINTING

Among the books left by Shigenobu were the

Yanagawa Gwajo: Various drawings printed chiefly in red and black. 1 vol. 1821.
Ryūsen Gwajo: Various drawings. 2 vols. No date.
Kyōka Gojū-nin Isshu: Humorous poems by fifty poets. 1 large folio with double-page frontispiece in colours and other illustrations in black and white and tints. 1823.
Kyōka Meisho Dzue: Humorous poems on famous places in Japan. 1 vol. 1826. Tints.
Satomi Hakken-den: Historical incidents. Shigenobu with Sadahide and Keisai Eisen.
Kyōka Imayō Genji: Humorous poems on the Genji. 1 vol. 1832.
Sansui Gwajo: Landscapes. Unsigned and sometimes attributed to Gakutei. 1 vol. 1835. Colours.
Ehon Fuji Bakawa: History of noble women. With Yanagawa Jūsen. 2 vols. 1823 and 1836. Colours.
Meishu Kyōka Shū: Humorous verses on destiny. 1 vol. 1839.
Kyōka Shukin Shū: Humorous poems. 1 vol.
Ryūsen Suiko Gwaden-den: The One Hundred and Eight Chinese Heroes. 2 vols.
Michi-no-Shiori: Copies of work by Hokusai done by Shigenobu and the former's daughter, Ōyei.
Yanagawa Mangwa: Various small sketches. 2 vols. Colours.
Yanagawa Shigenobu Gwafu: Sketch book. 2 vols. 1855. Colours.
Yanagawa Gwajin (listed in Catalogue of Japanese Books at the South Kensington Museum).

Hasegawa SETTAN, also known as GENGAKUSAI and SHŌSHU, should not, strictly speaking, be placed among the Ukiyo-ye artists, although he was a Yedo man and a contemporary of Eisen and Hiroshige. He lived between 1778 and 1843 and was a descendant of Hasegawa Tōhaku.[1] The rank of Hokkyō was conferred upon him by the Shōgunate, and he became well known for his beautiful *meisho-ki* for Yedo and its environs. These were as comprehensive for the latter city as Shunshōsai's guide-books had been many years earlier for Kyōto.

Books left by Settan were the

Yedo Meisho Hana Koyomi: The flower festivals of Yedo. 3 vols. 1827.
Yedo Meisho Dzue: Description of Yedo. 20 vols. 1836.
Tōto Sai-shiki: The annual festivals of Yedo. 5 vols. 1838.

Settan was survived by a son, Hasegawa Settei, who collaborated with him in some of his work.

Leaving the Hokusai school, one finds a slightly later group of artists who were still doing good work, not yet greatly affected by the extravagance and deterioration which had become so manifest in the work of the Utagawa school. Of this group Keisai EISEN and HIROSHIGE were the chief figures.

Keisai Eisen was slightly the elder of the two men, having been born in 1792, the son of Ikedo Yoshikiyo, a Kanō painter of Yedo, a writer and a well-known *cha-jin* or tea ceremony expert. Eisen thus had a much higher social position than most of the Ukiyo-ye artists and was familiar with both the Tosa and Kanō methods of work. Later he abandoned the classic art

[1] See *Painters of Japan*, by Arthur Morrison, which gives a very complete study of the Hasegawa school.

and with it, unhappily, a good many other restraining influences, becoming an exponent of the popular school and adopting the loose manners and morals of many of its members. His ability was undoubted, however, and he was probably the best of Eizan's pupils.

Eisen designed prints, *surimono*, book illustrations, was something of a writer and at one time took to making kites and toys. After about 1830 he ceased working to any extent, but lived on until 1848. Other signatures used by him were IKEDA, YOSHINOBU, IPPITSU-AN, KŌSO, KAKŌ, ZENJIRŌ, RISUKE, and MUMEI-Ō.

Much of his work has great charm. He was an exceedingly clever draughtsman, and used colour with considerable feeling and taste. Among the books illustrated by him were the

Teinitsu Taki-no-Yogatari: History of a virtuous couple. 3 vols. 1824.
Kintai Gwaso: Designs for artisans. 1 vol. 1828. Colours.
Gwahon Nishiki-no-Fukuro: Various drawings. 2 small vols. 1829. Colours.
Kogane-no-Suzu Sachibana Sōshi: A novel. 1829.
Bijin Kasen Shū: Poems on beautiful women. Illustrated by Keisai Eisen and Kuninao in collaboration. 3 small vols. No date. Colours. Charming and rare.
Kōso Gwafu: Various drawings. 2 vols. 1832. In two editions—black-and-white and coloured illustrations.
Kyōka Guruma Hyaku Shū: Humorous poems on the Yoshiwara. Not signed, but attributed to Keisai Eisen. 2 vols. 1832. Colours.
Sanryō Tōgwa Keisai Sogwa: Charming impressionistic sketches in colour. 5 vols. Last volume issued in 1832. Although this work has generally been attributed to Keisai Eisen as a whole, in reality only vols. iii. and v. are by him, the others being by Keisai Masayoshi (vol. i.), Baitei Kahei (vol. ii.), and Rai-an Genki (vol. iv.).
Buyū Sakigake Dzue: Famous heroes. 3 vols. 1835. A second edition in 1838.
Keisai Gwafu: Various sketches.
Yeiyū Teiyu Gwashiki: Book of heroes. 1 vol. 1836. In two editions, one printed in black and white and one in colours.
Jin-ji Andon: Vols. iii. and v. Sketches designed for the decorations of the lanterns used in the Bon festival. Colours. A well-known set of books.
Ryūsai Gwafu and *Keisai Ukiyo Gwafu:* Various sketches. By Hiroshige and Keisai Eisen in collaboration. No date. About 1836. Colours.
Genji Monogatari: Story of the Genji. 3 vols. 1841–1843. Black and white and colours.
Meisho Hoku Shū: Poems on famous places. Small. No date. Colours.
Makura Bunko.
Kodakara Yama: Story of Kintoki. An *hōsōye-bon*, or "small-pox book." Printed entirely in red.
Kakuzen Zuko: An illustrated account of decorated leather work. Written and illustrated by Ikeda Yoshinobu (Eisen). 1845. Colours.
Eisen Meisho: 2 vols. No date. Colours.
Sogwa Shashin Shiki-no-Hana Zono: ("Flowers of the Four Seasons"): 4 vols. 1848. Tints.
Satomi Hakken-den: A novel by Bakin. Illustrated by Eisen in collaboration with Shigenobu and Sadahide.

Andō Hiroshige, whose name is hardly less well known in Europe and America than Hokusai's, was born in 1797 and died of cholera in 1858. He first studied under Okajima Rinsai, an obscure Kanō artist, then under Toyohiro, and finally with Ōoka Umpo, a teacher of the Chinese school. He was one of the last of the great print designers and one of the few

CHAP. IX]   JAPANESE BLOCK-PRINTING

Ukiyo-ye artists of his time who was not influenced by the unwholesome and extravagant tendencies which were ruining the Yedo men's work. His teacher, Utagawa Toyohiro, was probably partly responsible for this, for he too had remained true to higher ideals and refused to follow in the steps of his brother Toyokuni.

Although one can trace a resemblance to Toyohiro in much that Hiroshige did, the latter artist worked with much richer colour and abandoned to a greater extent the use of intervening clouds which had been such a marked characteristic of Toyohiro's landscape work. Hiroshige is said to have had considerable ability as a poet and composed many of the verses which he was fond of illustrating. Other signatures used by him were Andō TOKUTARŌ, RYŪSAI (before 1832), RISSAI, RITSUSAI, and ICHIRYŪSAI.

The confusion in regard to the badly coloured and uninteresting later prints signed Hiroshige seemed at one time to have been satisfactorily cleared up by Edward Strange, who succeeded in disentangling the personalities of three different artists, Hiroshige I., II., and III. Judging from the prints themselves, one certainly must agree with Strange, for both in composition and colouring these later sheets are distinctly inferior. The present tendency to go back to the one-man theory one suspects to have arisen among the dealers, and the recent prices which prints in crude greens, purples, and blues have brought because they have borne the charmed name of Hiroshige bear out this suspicion.

The first Hiroshige is said to have left several adopted sons who followed his methods and doubtless did much of this poorly coloured later work. One of these adopted sons was the grandson of his teacher Toyohiro, known as Toyokuma. Another was Andō Tokubei, who sometimes used the signature Shigemasa and probably was identical with Tokubei Sadanobu, whose work so closely resembles that of Hiroshige. A third adopted son became known as Hiroshige III.

Although Hiroshige's fame was founded upon his charming prints, he also illustrated a number of no less delightful books. These include the

Kyōka Hyakunin Isshu: Humorous poems on the Hundred Poets. Signed Ritsusai Hiroshige. Tints.
Kyōka Yamato Jimbutsu: Poems on street scenes in Yedo. Seven volumes. Privately printed between 1843 and 1848. Signed Ryūsai Hiroshige Sensei. Very charming colour work. Excessively rare.
Yedo Meisho Hyakkei: 2 folios. 120 colour-plates. 1820.
Hyakunin Isshu Jō-kun Shō: One hundred poems for women. Hiroshige and other artists. 1 vol. 1831.
Ryūsai Gwafu and *Ukiyo Gwafu:* Various sketches by Ryūsai (Hiroshige) and Keisai Eisen. 3 vols. About 1836. Colours. Nagoya.
Kyōka Sanjū-roku Shū: Humorous poems by the Thirty-six Poets. Hiroshige and Hokkei. 1 vol. 1840.

Tōkaidō Meisho Dzue: Views along the Tōkaidō. Signed Ichiryūsai Hiroshige. 1848. Colours.
Kyōka Sokon Shū: Illustrated poems. 5 vols. Colours. Rare and charming.
Ehon Tebiki-gusa: Drawings of flowers and fishes. Signed Ichiryūsai Hiroshige. Several volumes. 1848. Colours.
Ryūsai Sohitsu Gwafu: Various sketches. 3 small vols. 1848–1852.
Yedo Miyage (" Souvenir of Yedo "): A series of ten small guide-books for Yedo. Colours. 1850–1867. (Vols. ix. and x. are by the second Hiroshige.)
Fuji Mi Hyaku Dzue: One hundred views of Fuji. Signed Hiroshige. 1 vol. 1857. Colours.
Ryakugwa Kōrin-fu Rissai Hyaku Dzue: One hundred drawings after Kōrin. Signed Rissai. 1 vol. 1851. Afterwards reprinted as vol. iv. of the *Sohitsu Gwafu*.
Tōkaidō Fukei Dzue: Views along the Tōkaidō. Signed Ichiryūsai Hiroshige. 2 vols. 1851. Tints. A supplement to the *Tōkaidō Meisho Dzue*.
Kyōka Cha-kisai Kashū: Illustrated poems on the ceremonial tea. Portraits of celebrated *Cha-jin* by Hiroshige and Yoshitora. 1 vol. 1855.
Tōkaidō Harimaze Dzue: Views along the Tōkaidō. Originally in *gwajō* form. Colours. 1856. Large.
Kyōka Koto Meisho Dzue: Poems on famous places around Yedo. By Temmei Rojin Takumi. Illustrated by Hiroshige. 14 vols. 1856.
Kyōka Momo-chidori: Hiroshige with other artists. 1 *gwajō*. 1857.
Hiroshige Gwafu: Small *gwajō* of twenty colour-plates. 1862.
Shōshoku Gwatsu: Designs. Several vols. Signed Ryūsai Hiroshige. By Hiroshige and his sons. 1863.
Kinka Shū: Views along the Tōkaidō with figures. 1858.
Ryōchū Kokoro-oboe: Sketch-book with daily notes.
Yoshitsune Ichidai Dzue: Life of Yoshitsune. Colours. Signed Ichiryūsai Hiroshige. 1 vol. 1856.

Ichiyusai SHIGENOBU (not to be confused with Yanagawa Shigenobu) became known as HIROSHIGE II., and also used the name Ichiryūsai HIROSHIGE. He did some very charming work, one little *gwajō* of Tōkaidō views with figures being especially delightful. Among other books illustrated by him and Hiroshige III. are three of the volumes of the *Shoshoku Gwatsu*, 1863.

A late follower of the Utagawa school was Gyokuransai SADAHIDE of Yedo, who lived between 1820 and 1867. His ordinary name was Hashimoto Kanejirō, but as an artist he used the signatures GOUNTEI, UTAGAWA, GOKURANSAI, GOKURAN, and Gofūtei SADAHIDE. His work consisted chiefly of landscape-prints with figures, and book illustrations, including some extremely curious drawings of foreigners as they appeared to Japanese eyes when they were first allowed in the country. Among the books left by him are the

Saijiki Dzue: Festivals of the year. 1 vol. 1846.
Eiju Hyakunin Isshu and *Wakan Eiju Hyakunin Isshu:* The Hundred Poets. 2 vols. 1858.
Chūshin Meimei Gwaden: The Forty-seven Rōnin. 2 vols., one by Kuniyoshi and the second by Sadahide. 1848–1859.
Hakken-den: A version of Bakin's famous work for children. Illustrated by Sadahide in collaboration with Kunisada and other artists. 1849.
Kasen Buke Zoroi: Celebrated warriors, with poems. In two editions, one printed in black and white and the other in colours.
Banshō Shashin Zufu (?): Drawings of plants, birds, animals, etc. Signed Gyokuransai. 2 vols. Colours.

CHAP. IX]   JAPANESE BLOCK-PRINTING

Kobu-kuyo Kasen: Book on warriors. 1 vol. of four parts. Black and white and colours. 1850.
Yokohama Kaikō Kenbunshi: Incidents in the opening of Yokohama port. Signed Gountei Sadahide. Two series of 3 vols. each. 1862–1865. Very curious and amusing drawings representing the life of foreigners in Yokohama after the visit of Commodore Perry (including portraits of Perry and his staff). Excessively rare.

Shōfu KYŌSAI, the last of the important Ukiyo-ye artists, was born in 1831 in Kōga, in the province of Shimotsuke. While still a boy he went to Yedo, where he entered the studio of Kuniyoshi, whose influence remained with him in spite of a later period of study under Kanō Dōhaku. The greater freedom of the Ukiyo-ye work seemed to suit his temperament, for he was among the gayest and wildest of the gay Ukiyo-ye group in Yedo, and is said to have been imprisoned three times for caricaturing the Shōgun. Much of his work in both prints and books is of a humorous character and resembles Kuniyoshi's comic sheets. Other signatures used by him were CHIKAMARO, Shōjō CHIKAMARO, Kawanabe KYŌSAI, TŌ-IKU, TŌYUKO, and Shōjō KYŌSAI.

With all his vagaries and dissipations Kyōsai was an artist of great originality and talent, and his serious work as seen in his paintings is very beautiful. Here the Kanō influence predominated, and many of his *kakemono* are worthy of the most famous of the classic painters.

His work in book illustration was rather incidental to his painting and print designing, although it included some very interesting books. Among them are the

Kyōsai Gwafu: Various comic drawings. 1 vol. 1860. Colours. A second edition in 1880.
Ehon Takagami: Drawings of hawks. 5 vols. 1870. Colours.
Kyōsai Mangwa: Sketch book. Signed Shōjō Kyōsai. 1 vol. 1881. Colours.
Kyōsai Ryakugwa: Drawings of fruit, flowers, animals, etc. 2 *gwajō*. 1881. Colours.
Kyōsai Dongwa: Caricatures and comic drawings. Signed Kyōsai Kawanabe Tō-iku. 1 vol. 1881. Colours.
Kyōsai Suigwa ("Drunken Sketches"): 3 small vols. 1882. Colours.
Kyōsai Gwaden: A history of Japanese art, with illustrations of the styles of different artists, and an autobiography of Kyōsai himself. 4 vols. 1884. Some colour. Printed partly in very amusing English.
Hōnen Gōkoku Matsuri: The harvest festival. 3 small vols.
Hyaku Gaden: The One Hundred Monsters of the Night. 1 *gwajō*. 1889. Colours.
No-Kuwa (?): Sketches of everyday scenes. 2 vols. Colours.

The *Kyōsai Ryakugwa* and the *Hyaku Gaden* are the rarest of Kyōsai's books, although they can generally be found by searching. The *Kyōsai Gwaden* is not difficult to find even in the first edition, and it is very interesting. To the student of Japanese art it is also of considerable value, for the first two volumes contain drawings copied from the work of famous painters with descriptions in English. The two last volumes are given up to an autobiography, and contain some very interesting drawings, including one of great spirit representing Hokusai making his famous gigantic sketch of Daruma.

With Kyōsai's death in 1889 the Ukiyo-ye art had run its course.

It was one of the great art movements of the world, and its beginnings, its development, its culmination, and finally its decline, are open to the student. It began with a naïve simplicity, culminated in the rich dignity of Kiyonaga's work, and then, top-heavy, fell from the vulgarity of too great wealth of colour and ornamentation. Its renaissance is unlikely and undesirable, since in art, as in literature, simplicity and sincerity are gone with the sophistication and self-consciousness which a renaissance always presupposes and of which it is the outcome.

CHAPTER X

MODERN ILLUSTRATORS OF JAPAN

IN this age of machinery the modern methods of printing and the use of collotypes, which are made so beautifully in Japan, have largely superseded the early processes in printing books there. Nevertheless, there are still a few publishers who from time to time issue delightful volumes of block-made pictures.

The Shimbi Shoin of Tōkyō, whose publications form probably the most beautiful work of this kind done anywhere in the world, has printed superb collections of Japanese and Chinese work done in the old manner, and this company may be relied upon to keep vital the knowledge of block cutting and printing. Yamada Unsōdō of Kyōto, Watanabe of Tōkyō, and a few other firms, also, from time to time, publish very charming new books of design and colour-plates of landscapes, birds, flowers, etc., printed in the old way, while in 1915 and 1916 many of the famous books by the Ukiyo-ye artists were published again in beautiful editions by Yoshikawa Kobunkan and Zuga Keikokan of Tōkyō.

These modern editions of old time favourites are wholly charming, even the wax-like quality in the colours apparently having been rediscovered and put to use again. The hope is thus warranted that a revival of Japanese *ehon* may take place, since the reason for their decline was partly that the best artists became unwilling to have their work appear in badly printed and crudely coloured illustrations.

The art never really died, however—it ebbed; but ever since the Restoration examples have occasionally appeared which have proved that it still maintained its hold upon the people's interest.

Shujin SŪGAKUDŌ, an Ōsaka artist born in the first quarter of the nineteenth century, produced several most beautiful folios of birds and flowers even considerably before this time, and his *Sho Utsushi Shijū-hachi Taka* of 1848,[1] made up of forty-eight colour-plates of birds and flowers, is one of the most charming works of its kind in existence. This was followed by a supplementary folio which appeared about 1860. The upright colour-plates are printed on a very finely gaufraged paper with each page margined in canary yellow. Hardly less beautiful is his *Shiki-no-Kwachō* made up of coloured plates of birds and flowers of the four seasons, which was published in 1861.

[1] See Happer Catalogue.

HINE-NO-TAIZAN (1810–1867), also known as Nichi SHŌNEN, SEI, SEIGEN, NARIYUKI, CHŌ, and KINRINSHI, was an early nineteenth-century artist who went to Kyōto from Sakai in the province of Idzumi. He was a follower of the Chinese school and known as a painter, his work for wood-engraving being incidental to his painting and teaching. After his death his pupils collected a number of his sketches and published them in the *Taizan Gwafu* (2 vols. 1879. Tints).

Ikeda UNSHO (1824–1886) was the son of a *samurai* family in the service of the Daimyō of Tsu in Ise province. After a period of study in Kyōto under Nakanichi Koseki and Yamada Chōdo, he opened a studio of his own there, where he taught the Chinese method of painting. Other signatures used by him were SEIKEI, KOI, and HANSEN. He achieved considerable renown as a painter, and reproductions of his work are often found in compilations of about 1880–1885.

Suzuki HYAKUNEN (1823–1891), also known as SEIJU, SHIKO, ZUSHO, and TAICHINRŌ, was a well-known painter and teacher in Kyōto during the last half of the nineteenth century. His work for wood-engraving was rather incidental to his painting, and the *Yamato Nishiki* (5 vols.), containing reproductions of some of his principal works, and the *Gwaho Sensei*, two small volumes of charming sketches published in 1879, are among the few books left by him.

Hyakunin was survived by a son, Suzuki SHŌNEN, who was born in 1881 and who lives in Kyōto in a very beautiful house near Chion-in Temple. Shōnen is ranked among the great painters of modern Japan, his work for wood-engraving being limited to the beautiful *Shōnen Sansui Gwafu*, made up of twelve upright colour-plates of landscapes; the *Shōnen-Keinen Gwafu*, work by Shōnen and Keinen in collaboration; and the *Shōnen Sogwa Shū*, consisting of various sketches in one volume.

Of the next generation of artists, Kōno BAIREI (1843–1895) of Kyōto was one of the most famous. He studied under Nakajima Raishō[1] and Shiokawa Bunrin[2] and left a large number of followers himself, many of whom are well-known painters of to-day.

Bairei used as other signatures the names CHOKUHO and SHIJUN. His books of flowers and birds are among the most beautiful of the modern *ehon* and are known among art-lovers the world over. They include the

Bairei Hyaku-chō Gwafu: One hundred pictures of flowers and birds. 3 vols. 1881. Colours.
Bairei Hyaku-chō Gwafu: A supplementary series. 3 vols. 1884. Colours.
Bairei Gwafu: Vols. 1 and 2, birds and flowers; vol. 3, insects. 1886. Colours.

---

[1] A follower of the Maruyama school. Died in 1871.
[2] A landscape painter of Shijō school. Died 1877. Left a set of four folios of birds and flowers, the *Bunrin Kwachō Gwafu*, which has become very rare.

CHAP. X]   JAPANESE BLOCK-PRINTING

Inaka-no-Tsuki ("Moonlight in the Country"): Birds, animals, and fish at night. 1 vol. 1889. Colours.
Bairei Kiku Hyaku Shū: One hundred varieties of chrysanthemums. 3 vols. 1891, 1892, 1896. Colours.
Bairei Kwachō Gwafu: Birds and flowers. 4 large folios, designated as Spring, Summer, Autumn, and Winter. 1883 and 1899. Colours. (Bairei's most famous book.)
Shiki Kwachō-no-Dzue: Birds and flowers of the Four Seasons. Bairei in collaboration with Gyōkusen, Suzuki Shōnen, and Keinen: Vol. i., *Spring*, by Suzuki Shōnen; vol. ii., *Summer*, by Gyōkusen; vol. iii., *Autumn*, by Bairei; vol. iv., *Winter*, by Imao Keinen. Colours.
Bairei Gwakan: Method of drawing. 7 vols.
Kwachō Natsu-no-Dzue: Birds and flowers of Summer. Colours.
Sogwa Hyaku Shū: Various drawings. 2 vols. Colours.
Sogwa Hyaku Shū Nihen: Supplementary series to foregoing. 2 vols. Colours.
Chikusa-no-Hana: Different flowers from Nature. 4 vols. Colours.

Imao KEINEN, also known as YOSŌSAI, RYŌJI, and RAKYŌ, is the *doyen* of present-day Japanese painters. He was born in Kyōto on August 12th, 1845, the third son of Imao Senka. When eleven years old he commenced his artistic education and entered the studio of Umesawa in Tōkyō. Three years later he joined the classes in painting and chirography under Suzuki Hyakunen and took up the study of the Chinese classics with Yumin Sangoku. In 1871 he established a private art school in Kyōto, which became one of the famous Japanese studios. It is safe to say that two-thirds of the modern painters of Japan have been Keinen's pupils, and the absolute sincerity of his teachings has flowered in some very wonderful work.

There are many anecdotes of the absorbed study which Keinen bestowed upon his art, and study of his paintings impresses one deeply with the immense amount of close nature-study to which he must have devoted himself.

Like all great artists, Keinen never became a slave to any one school. From his early method he turned to the more impressionistic work of Goshun and Keibun. Following this was a period when the ancient Chinese art of Liyusen appealed strongly to him, and then by various steps along the pathway in which Chin Nampin, Bai-itsu, and Shunkin had trod he took his way. He is especially noted, however, for his studies of birds and flowers, even the work of Kōno Bairei and Sugakudo, of this kind, beautiful, as it is, yielding to the superior grace of composition in Keinen's paintings.

Even Occidental art had its influence upon him and he made a large collection of European printed pictures.

Gardening has been Keinen's chief hobby, aside from his profession, however, and he is known among the old school garden makers as an expert cultivator of *bonsai*, or trained pot plants.

His house on Sakai-machi in Kyōto is a most beautiful example of a purely Japanese home. A stone-paved passage leads in from the street, and one enters a small ante-room before reaching the main part of the house. The visitor is then ushered into a room, the *fusuma* of which are gleaming with golden mountains, through which a silver stream winds across three sides of the apartment to finally lose itself in a cataract and mist of silver spray. The screen before the entrance to this room has a silver moon rising over mountain peaks on the side facing east, while on that toward the entrance a glorious red-gold sun is setting. The exquisite woodwork in ceilings, alcoves, and above the *fusuma*, was done with rare woods brought especially from Formosa. Everything about the house was designed by Keinen himself, and in the classic room for ceremonial tea one is shown a complete set of " tea furniture," every piece of which was designed by this artist and worked out in metal, pottery, and lacquer by artisans working under his immediate supervision. Three charming gardens bound the house, and upstairs the studios and sleeping rooms look down upon these quiet, richly green spots, all seemingly as far removed from the turmoil of modern life as any Japanese home could have been a century ago.

An atmosphere of peace pervades these purely Japanese houses belonging to the artists and old scholars that is indescribable. Almost upon entering, the sense of worry and hurry suddenly drops away and one finds oneself at ease—the ease in which one need not talk, need do nothing forced or insincere. They breathe beauty and peace and harmony—perhaps because conserved in them is the old, beautiful spirit of Japan.

Although Keinen is chiefly known as a painter, he has also illustrated some most charming books. Among them the *Keinen Kwachō Gwafu*, published by Nishimura Sozaemon of Kyōto in 1885, made up of four large folios (*Spring*, *Summer*, *Autumn*, and *Winter*), is perhaps the most beautiful work of this kind ever printed in Japan. In the first edition tiny drops of lacquer were used to paint the eyes of the different birds, giving an extraordinarily brilliant effect. Unfortunately this edition is not to be found, most of the books having been given by the artist to his friends immediately after its publication. It has gone through many other printings however, and although the colours in the later issues are less soft and harmonious, even these more modern copies are very beautiful.

Other illustrated books by Keinen are the

Keinen Kwachō Gwakan: Twelve sheets of flowers and birds.
Keinen Shū Gwajo: A manual of drawing.
Yosōsai Gwafu: Album of flowers and birds. 2 vols.
Shiki Kwachō-no-Dzue: In collaboration with Suzuki Shōnen, Gyokusen, and Kōno Bairei. 4 folios. Colours.

Another well-known artist of the Meiji period and a fellow-pupil of Keinen's under Nakajima Raishō was Kawabata GYOKUSHŌ, who lived between 1842 and 1914. Although a Kyōto man, he eventually established himself in Tōkyō, where he became one of the capital's most noted painters. Among the books illustrated by him are the

Shugwa Hyakudai: One hundred sketches. 5 *gwajō*. 1898. Very impressionistic and charmingly coloured.
Mohitsugwa Hitori Keiko: A book on drawing. 2 vols.

Numada KASHŪ, who became noted for his paintings of flowers and birds, left the *Kashū Kwachō Shū*, a most beautiful collection of coloured plates of birds and flowers which is also a very fine example of modern wood-block printing (1890).

Kikuchi HŌBUN (born 1862), also known as TSUNEJIRŌ, studied under Kanō Hōyen and became affiliated with the Kyōto art school. He was well known as a painter and left the

Hōbun Gwafu: Various drawings. 1 vol. Very fine.
Kotori-no-Negura: Studies of different kinds of birds'-nests. 1 vol.

Watanabe SHŌTEI, also known as SEITEI, GIFUKU, and RYŌSUKE, was born in 1851. His training was obtained under the famous Kikuchi Yōsai. Although devoting most of his time to painting and teaching in his Tōkyō studio, Shōtei has also illustrated from time to time some delightful books. Among them are the

Kwachō-jo: An album of flowers and birds. 1 vol. Colours.
Meika Shogwa Zuroku: Copies of famous Chinese paintings.
Shōtei Kwachō Gwafu: Flowers and birds. 3 vols. 1891. Colours. First edition out of print. Very beautiful.
Kwachō: Birds and flowers. 1 vol. 1903.

A series of charmingly coloured sheets of landscapes, birds, flowers, insects, etc., was issued in wrappers in 1915.

Takeuchi SEIHŌ (born in 1864) is not only one of the great painters of Japan, but one of the great artists of the world. He lives in Kyōto and was a pupil of Tsuchida Eirin and Kōno Bairei. His work shows that he is master of many styles, some of his early productions even indicating foreign influence. He has returned, however, to a purely Japanese expression, and all lovers of Japanese painting must be happy that his really great genius is saved for native art rather than being devoted to the more clumsy Western methods. His work for wood-engraving has been entirely incidental to his painting, although it embraces some very beautiful books. Among them are the

Jūnishi-Chō: The twelve animals of the Zodiac. Twelve large coloured plates. Very beautiful, and wonderful examples of modern block-printing.
Eisho Hyaku-chō Gwafu: One hundred birds reproduced from work by Eisho. 2 vols.
Jūni Fuji: Twelve views of Mount Fuji. 1 vol.
Churin Gwafu: Book of insects. In collaboration with Hōbun. 1 vol.
Seihō Shū Gwajo: Manual of drawing. 4 vols.

PLATE 41] From a drawing by Seiko, a famous woman artist, in the Meiji Gwafu, a compilation of sketches and poems by artists of the Meiji period (1883).

[Face p. 202

Yofu Gwafu: Views in and around Kyōto. Seihō with other artists. 3 vols.
Chiomi-gusa: Book of designs.
Seihō Gwafu: Reproductions of Seihō's most famous paintings in a series of very fine collotypes. 6 folios.
Seihō Sakuhin-shū: 3 series (of which the last is still in the hands of the printers) of twenty-four colour-plates each. Published by Benrido, Kyōto. 1921. A most beautiful work.

Of the modern designers of Japan, Tomioka Tessai (born in 1836), a Kyōto artist also known as Hyakuren and Gakko Shō-in, is one of the most famous. His pupils embrace many of the well-known younger designers, and there are many charming books from their brushes. Among these late books of design, which are, without exception, models of colour-printing, are the

Meika Hyakusan Gwafu: Designs for fans by famous artists. 1895.
Tennen Moyō Kan: Designs for *kimono*. Signed Kaigwai Tennen. 5 large folios. 1899. Colours.
Tennen Moyō Kan: Designs for the linings of *haori*, or the outer *kimono* worn as a European wears an overcoat or cloak. 1 large oblong volume. 1899. Colours.
Tennen Hyaku: One hundred designs for various purposes. By Kaigwai Tennen. 1 vol. 1900. Colours.
Take Dzukushi, Matsu Dzukushi, Ume Dzukushi: Designs from the bamboo, pine, and plum blossom. By Furuya Kōrin. 3 *orihon*. 1905. Colours.
Hinagata: Ceremonial *kimono*. By Yamashita Kōrin. 1 vol. 1900. Colours.
Haregata: A supplementary series. 1901. Colours.
Keika Zu-an: Designs by Hasegawa Keika. 2 vols. 1905. Colours.
Azuma Nishiki: Designs by Yamamoto Hyōsai. 1 vol. 1901. Colours.
Moyō-ye: Designs by Kobayashi Gyokunen. 1 vol. 1901. Colours.

One might further elaborate this list of modern books of design until it would fill a volume in itself. These books may be found in all the second-hand book shops of Japan, and perhaps if the foreigners who flock to Kyōto and Tōkyō every spring and autumn only knew of them, the art schools of America and Europe would be the richer. They are utterly charming, comparatively inexpensive, and although out of print now, are picked up without great difficulty. A collection made up of such works alone would be well worth forming and would not involve the disappointments that collecting the rarer books is certain to bring at times.

One should remember also that what is new now and not difficult to obtain will, before many years, by no means be found at every corner.

In addition to the foregoing works there are also a large number of delightful compilations of poems and sketches by artists of the Meiji period, Among these books are the

Ho-un Kyō Shiga Shōnin: Poems illustrated by early Meiji artists. 2 vols. Colours.
Meiji Shinsen Shogwa Jin-meishi: Poems illustrated by artists of the early Meiji period. 1 *gwajō*. 1872. Colours.
Meiji Shogwa-jō: A delightful collection of poems and coloured sketches by famous painters of the Meiji period. 1 *gwajō*. 1881.

Kinsei Shidari Ika Gwafu: Famous places in Japan. By Takahiya Aigai, Chinzan, Watanabe Kwazan, Ryūko, and other artists. 2 vols. 1881. Colours.
Meiji Gwafu: Drawings by artists of the Meiji period. 1 *gwajō*. 1883. Colours.
Shotaikwa Sansui Gwafu: Reproductions of landscapes by different artists. 2 oblong *gwajō*. 1896–1897. Very beautiful.
Chō Shishū Gwafu: Flowers, fish, insects, etc., by Chō Shishū, of the Chinese school. 2 vols. 1897. Colours.

The above list, like that of the books of design, gives but a few of many such compilations, all of which are charming and well worth adding to a collection.

As has been said, a revival of the delightful block-printed *ehon*, now that better colours are used, is to be expected, and it is wise for collectors of a catholic taste to keep in touch with the publishers of these modern works in order to obtain copies of the first printings.

CHAPTER XI

MISCELLANEOUS BOOKS

N every large collection of these old books there will be a number which might be easily enough classified if there were sufficient of the same kind to make this worth doing. But as a collector picks up volumes here and there, there are bound to be some that do not fit into any of his special boxes. This does not mean that they are less valuable or less interesting than the others, for often the box or shelf marked *Miscellaneous* may contain some of the most curious works in the whole collection.

It might include, for instance, old calendars and books on magic; books on gardens, flower arrangement and the tea ceremony; drawing books; collections of copies of old pictures; collections of illustrated poems; odd works on etiquette and morals (subjects closely connected in the Japanese mind); books of design; *Jōruri-bon* ; queer old works on military tactics; ancient maps; *hōsōye-bon* or " small-pox books "; works on botany, astronomy, and natural history; and most amusing of all, books relating to the " foreign devils " and their strange habits, who, willy-nilly—welcome or unwelcome—insisted upon coming to the country.

Such a box or shelf has possibilities, one must admit, and this chapter will be devoted to these fascinating odds and ends.

If age is to be given preference, perhaps the old books on magic and military tactics should be spoken of first, for both these subjects were treated of in very early times.

Crudely illustrated calendars containing rules for divination are said to have been printed in the fifteenth century, and at least one work on military matters preceded the Fushimi edition of the *Seven Rules in Military Tactics* of the Keichō period.

Of the old calendars, the *Kotei Zeikyō* is one of the earliest known. This was published in *gwajō* form in Genva 10 (1624), and contains diagrams to be used in choosing auspicious days for important undertakings as well as some very curious drawings of animals, figures, etc. Later in the century, during the Keian period (1648–1652), the same naïve illustrations were used in another book on divination entitled *Inyō Hakke-no-Ho*.

The *Nyūhaku Dzusetsu*, also an early work on divination, appeared in two large folios in 1626, and contains very amusing drawings showing the effect of different planetary conditions on the human body and gives rules and diagrams to be used in bringing about good fortune.

The *San Ze Sō* is the copy of a very ancient Chinese calendar, published in Japan by Nakano Shozaemon of Kyōto in 1635. It consists of two large folios containing numerous primitive but very interesting wood-engravings representing the animals of the zodiac, the means of foretelling and averting misfortune, methods of divination for determining the destiny of a child born under special astronomical conditions, etc.

Among the books on military matters, the earliest is probably the *Bijingusa*,[1] which according to the colophon is made up of notes on the secret military tactics of different feudal lords transmitted by the great Ogasawara *daimyō* to his son Mochikiyo. These notes cover the period from Kōken to Ōyei (1256–1428) and were kept in written form until published (privately) in Kwanshō 5, or 1464.[2] The two volumes are $7\frac{1}{2}$ by $11\frac{1}{4}$ inches, and are bound in the dark, leather-like covers which are characteristic of the old *gozan-ban* and other fifteenth-century works. They contain four very simple wood-cuts representing quivers, arrows, and spear-heads.

In 1606 the well-known Fushimi set of military books, said to contain a few simple drawings, was published.

Many others followed in succeeding years, of which the *Kishi-ki Dzue* or *On Sashi Mono Zoroi*, three large folios containing engravings of flags, banners, and other war paraphernalia, were published in 1637. This was evidently a book *de luxe*, for it was gotten up in the richest manner—the paper, bindings, and printing all being of the finest quality.

The *Jiyo Shū*, published in twelve volumes in 1653, is also very interesting. It describes the secret military methods of the famous Ogasawara clan, and according to the colophon was written in Genwa 4 (1618) and printed by Kato Shojiro " whose printing-house is on Teramachi opposite Honnō-ji Temple in Kyōto."

Both of these works contain many most curious wood-engravings representing fortifications and the disposition of troops, the best manner of making signal fires, means of determining fortunate days for assaults on the enemy, the making and setting up of the curtains which were used to enclose the commanding *daimyō's* tent, war banners, swords, bows and arrows, shields, military gloves, the conch shells which were used as war trumpets, war drums, scaling ladders, catapults, and the most effective manner of applying blazing torches to buildings to set them quickly on fire.

Another queer old work of the Manji period was the *Kōyō Gunkwan*, describing the wars between the Takeda and Uesumigi families. It was

---
[1] A fanciful title meaning " Gathering of Beautiful Women."
[2] These works on military tactics existed in written form long before they were printed, as knowledge of " secret tactics " would not be spread broadcast at the time they were in use.

printed from a manuscript copy of 1575, and contains wood-cuts of weapons and fighting paraphernalia used during the struggle, copied from drawings in the more ancient written volume.

A book of instructions for military men called the *Buke Chiyo Hoki*, published in five volumes by Yoshinaga Shichirōbei of Kyōto in 1694, contains a large number of very interesting illustrations of arrows, spears, shields, helmets, and armour. It also gives instruction in the proper procedure to be observed at war councils, the presentation of swords, the etiquette of *samurai* when in attendance upon their *daimyō*, and ends with a double-page drawing of a lesson in cannon firing, apparently taking place in the *daimyō's* garden with the *daimyō* himself, sitting on the narrow balcony of the house, watching the operations. The illustrations are not signed, but are probably by Yoshida Hanbei. The book is rare and it is a special bit of good fortune if the collector picks up a complete set.

The story of the Forty-seven Rōnin has gone through hundreds of versions and editions, with illustrations good, bad, and indifferent, but the *Fuso Gishi-den* published in 1719, dealing with this subject, is rare and unique. The first volume of the set of fifteen is almost entirely given up to very powerful drawings of the Rōnin, which are evidently the work of some early follower of Moronobu. In many details they are like early illustrations by Okumura Masanobu, but unfortunately bear no signature.

Of instructive works of other kinds there is almost literally no end. One might make a large collection of books dealing with the tea ceremony and flower arrangement alone, or books of instructions for women, all full of fascinating illustrations and published in every year period from the early Kwanyei.

One of the first of the printed works on flower arrangement to contain wood-cuts was the *Ikebana Hiden Senden Sho*, which appeared in one volume in 1643. The drawings represent floral arrangements in the proper receptacles for use in a *cha-no-yu* room. Other early works on this subject were the *Rikkwa*[1] *Hiden Shō*, published in two folios in 1677, with a preface written by Gyokusen in 1537.[2]

This was followed in 1681 by the *Rikkwa Shōshin Shō*, the secrets of flower arrangement as practised by the Ike-no-bo school of floral art, and in 1682 a similar work entitled *Kokon Rikkwa Daizen*, issued in five volumes, appeared.

The *Rikkwa Jisei Yosoōi*, written by Nishimura, a physician of Kyōto during the Genroku period who was noted for his flower arrangements, was published in 1688 in seven large and beautiful folios, printed on heavy

---

[1] The word *rikkwa* may also be read *tatabana* or *tachibana*.
[2] In the manuscript copy of that date.

cream paper and bound in covers bearing a design in grey and silver. It is a very rare and valuable book.

The *Rikkwa Kimmō Dzue*, an illustrated encyclopædia of flower arrangement, appeared in five volumes in 1695, followed by a supplementary volume, the *Zōho Rikkwa Kimmō Dzue*, in 1696. These works also are rare and greatly prized by Japanese collectors.

All the books on this subject contain numerous illustrations showing the method of bending and making supple the branches; the best manner of cutting the stems and roots; the proportions in height and width to the vase in which they are to be placed; all the tools used in the art; the receptacles of various shapes and sizes with the appropriate arrangement for each one, and finally the proper disposition in the room itself of the result, with the correct *kakemono* and incense burner to accompany it.

Early books on the tea ceremony were also numerous; and some charming old works on gardens and garden-making exist. Among the latter is the *Tsukiyama Niwa Tsukuri* written by Fuji Shinsai, which appeared in three volumes in 1723. It is regarded by the Japanese as a classic on the subject and contains numerous large wood-engravings representing the proper placing of rocks, lanterns, pagodas, and bridges, with text explaining the relation of these accessories to the garden itself.

Coming down to more recent times, there are several delightful books containing colour-plates of the miniature bowl landscapes which are so well known in Japan. One of the best-known works of this kind is the *Senkeiban Dzushiki*, by Kangin and Kōchoku, published in two folios in 1826.

Equally well known and even more charming is the *Hachiyama Gwafu*, containing instructions for making miniature views of the stations along the Tōkaidō. The colour-plates are the work of Nanyusai Yoshishige and represent the fifty-three stations in bowls and flat dishes of different kinds of pottery. The set is in two volumes, bearing a colour design on the covers of snow-capped Fuji with two pine trees in the foreground. It was published in 1848. Both of the foregoing sets have become very rare in the original editions and are valuable and interesting additions to a collection.

Collecting old maps is a favourite hobby with many an educated Japanese, and some of these collections are immensely valuable. Map-making has always been a rather special *forte* of the Japanese and represents, as perhaps nothing else does, the unusual combination of a fondness for exactitude and a willingness to give to work the most painstaking care, with a love of beauty which always redeems such work from being merely mechanical.

Many of the ancient maps should be spoken of among the wood-engravings, for the old map-makers had far too much of the artist about them to be satisfied with mere diagrams and geometrical precision. If the populous centre of a city must be represented by squares and lines and rectangles, the outlying districts could be suggested by something nearer beauty, so we find the edges of the maps softening off into pictures of mountains, with temples and pagodas among the trees, winding rivers bearing sampans sculled by big-hatted boatmen, and bordering seas with gallant fishing craft setting out in full-sailed pride to their work miles away in the deep waters.

Among the early maps is one of the city of Kyōto, dating from Keichō 5 or 1595. It belongs to Dr. Saiki of Kyōto, and to one who loves the charming old Japanese city it is of great interest, for it shows the streets as they were before the widening and improvements of modern days.

The *Shū Kaisho*, published in five large folios in 1642, consists of notes on the early history of Japan and the Imperial House, with maps of Kyōto showing the palace, the *yashiki* of the nobles, old walls, gates, etc., as they were in very ancient times.

Not all the map-makers have remained unknown however, and several famous artists have left examples of this work. The set of five *gwajō* containing maps of the route between Yedo and Kyōto, by Moronobu, is well known to collectors. It is a combination of map and picture and represents (Vol. I.) the road from Yedo to Odawara; (Vol. II.) from Odawara to Fuchu; (Vol. III.) from Fuchu to Yoshida; (Vol. IV.) from Yoshida to Kamiyama; and (Vol. V.) from Kamiyama to Kyōto. The text is by Enkindō, and the interesting maps themselves by Moronobu under the name of Hishikawa Kichibei. The work was published by Hichirōbei of Yedo in 1690.

Tachibana Morikuni also condescended to map-making and left a map of the Arima district, published in *gwajō* form.

If the collector has been fortunate enough to find many of the old *Jōruri-bon* they will be the stars among his miscellaneous books, for they are among the rarest of all the old *ehon*. Their origin has already been spoken of. Few of them are signed, but after their appearance in the Keichō period, and later when the first theatres were established in Kyōto and Ōsaka, they became very popular and were made by nearly all the men who worked for wood-engraving.

Among the early books of this kind those published at the Saga Press have been described under the *Saga-bon*. In 1634 a work called *Hanaya* appeared in two volumes, describing the adventures and battles of a *samurai* of that name, which contained crudely drawn illustrations. Three years later, in 1637, the *Akuchi*, describing the adventures of the nobleman Akuchi, was published, in which the illustrations, although primitive, are exceedingly interesting and the placing of blacks very effective. The *Akashi*, of two parts of two or three volumes each, appeared in 1645, the drawings representing the events in the life of the Daimyō Akashi, and showing much better workmanship, bearing considerable resemblance to Moronobu's early work.

From the Meiriki period (1655–1658), the technique in these books is of the big, dashing style which one associates with all the *Jōruri-bon*, probably settled upon by the artists as being the most appropriate for pictures representing heroic deeds—although, as a matter of fact, the earliest of these books were not distinguished by any special manner of drawing. Many of the late seventeenth-century *Jōruri-bon* were by Moronobu and this school.

Among the most famous of these rare and interesting books are the

Momiji Gari: The description of a *daimyō's* picnic in the maple season interrupted by an attack from his enemies. Unsigned, but attributed to Moronobu. 1658.
Kuwateki Fune Ikuse: A *Jōruri-bon* of 1660.
Kimpira Hōmon Arasoi: 1661.
Hogwan Yoshino Gassen: Battles of Yoshitsune. 1661.
Hana-mono Guroi ("Flower Madness"): Kwanbun period.
Tengu Ha-uchi: Battle of the Tengu. 1661.
Oishi Yama Maru : The deeds of the giant Kimpira. 1661.
Gwatsukai Chōja: History of an Indian nabob. 1662.
Chinzei Hachirō Tametomo: The heroes of the Minamoto clan. Signed Moronobu. 1670.
Raikō Atome-Ron: Dispute as to the successor to the Daimyō Raikō of the Minamoto clan. Meiriki-Manji period.
Fuki-age ("The Fountain"): Attributed to Moronobu. About Manji.
Jimmu Tennō: The brave deeds of Jimmu Tennō. 1676.
Tameyoshi Ubusuna Mondo: Visit of the Minamota *daimyō*, Tameyoshi, to Hachiman Temple. 1674.
Kimpei Sennin-giri: A rare *Jōruri-bon* of 1691.

From about 1670 many of the *Jōruri-bon* contain drawings which, although unsigned, may with reasonable certainty be attributed to Yoshida Hanbei, Ishikawa Ryūsen, and Naomura Johaku, while through the early years of the eighteenth century others appeared which must have been the work of Morofusa, Moroshige, and other followers of the Moronobu school. Okumura Masanobu also illustrated some of these striking books, and the *Sanshō Dayu* of 1711, the history of the abduction of some beautiful women, is probably early work by this artist.

A collector, if he is ever so fortunate as to find any of them, will easily learn to recognize the early *Jōruri-bon* by their peculiar bindings and size. They were usually thin, medium-sized books and broad for their length, while the covers were almost invariably of coarse black paper with a rather striking title-slip in heavy black *hirakana* characters. The publication of these popular books continued through the entire eighteenth century, although the powerful drawings of the early books made those in later volumes seem far less interesting.

A complete list of the *Jōruri-bon* would require a volume in itself, and even the valuable and comprehensive work by Midzutani Futo[1] on the subject of these books treats only of the most famous and valuable examples.

---
[1] See the *Eiri Jōruri Shi.* 3 vols. 1915.

A collector might easily devote most of his energies, and incidentally the contents of his purse, to these books. They are extremely fascinating, extremely rare, and most extremely high in price, even single volumes in very poor condition selling at the book auctions in Japan for fifteen, twenty, and thirty *yen*.

Of all the books marked *Miscellaneous*, the ones containing *kimono* and other designs are perhaps the most charming. Some of them date back to the seventeenth century, and are greatly sought after by the modern painters of Japan, who find in them valuable suggestions for their own work, since a knowledge of the designs used in dress and other decoration at different periods is necessary in painting historical pictures, and these delightful books furnish this in addition to giving pleasure because of their beauty.

Among the works of this kind, the *On Hinagata* is one of the earliest known. The designs are for *kimono* used in the Meiriki period (1655–1658), and the set of three volumes was published in 1667. The books are unsigned, although attributed by some Japanese collectors to Moronobu.

Yoshida Hanbei in 1688 left a series of four volumes of delightful designs of this kind called the *Onna Yō Kimmō Dzue*, which includes drawings of beautiful women dressed in the *kimono* represented.

In 1690 Takagi Sadatake's famous book of designs, called the *Gofuku Moyō Utai Hinagata*, in two volumes, was published, containing some of the most charming drawings in any of these delightful works. Many other similar books followed, among which are the

Yojō Hinagata: Kimono designs by Yūsen, a noted designer of Kyōto. 1 vol. 1691.
Yaro Yakusha: Kimono worn by actors. 2 vols. 1691.
Shinsen Somimono Hinagata: Kimono designs by Otoyama Jūhichi. 1 vol. About 1700.
Tōryū Hinagata Kyō-no-Mizu: Kyōto fashions in *kimono*. 3 vols. Kyōto. 1705. (Illustrated in the Duret Catalogue.) Very charming.
Fūryū Hinagata Taisei: Ancient *kimono* designs. By Imura Katsukichi. 2 vols. 1712.
Hinagata Gion Banashi: Kimono designs by Matsune Takatsu. 2 vols. 1714.
Kyōhō Hinagata: Kimono worn during the Kyōho period. By Nishigawa Sukenobu. 1 vol. 1716.
Hinagata Tsuru-no-Koye: 3 vols. 1725.
Kōrin Hinagata Suso Moyō: Designs for *kimono* after Kōrin. 2 vols. 1727. Exceedingly rare.
Hinagata Akebono Zakura: Kimono for courtesans. By Tachibana Morikuni and Hasegawa Mitsunobu. 3 vols. 1727. Rare.
Hinagata Yado-no-Ume: Kimono designs by Nakajima Tanjirō. 3 vols. 1727.
Tokiwa Hinagata: Designs by Takagi Kosuke. 1732.
Hinagata Some-iro-no-Yama: Kimono designs by Kōrin, compiled by Nonomura Chubei, a famous designer of Ōsaka. 3 vols. 1732. Very rare and charming.
Shin Hinagata Natorigawa: Designs by Kwanzan. 1 vol. 1733.
Tama Mizu: Kimono designs by Nonomura Chubei. 3 vols. 1739.
Hinagata Miyako-no-Haru (" Spring Kimono for the Capital "): By Ebishiya Chushigi. 1747.
Hinagata Miyako Shōnin: Attributed to Okumura Masanobu, with a full-page frontispiece of figures. 3 (?) vols. Very rare and beautiful.
Kwaiyo Hinagata: Kimono designs by Shita Eshi Kiyotsune. 3 vols.

CHAP. XI]   JAPANESE BLOCK-PRINTING

In addition to the foregoing works there is an extremely interesting book called the *Shōzoku Dzushiki*, which describes the customs and fashions of the Court during the sixteenth century, written by Ryūsaku (one of the Court chamberlains) in Genki 2, or 1571, to be transmitted to his son at his death but not to be read or circulated outside the Court. In 1692 this request was swept aside and the work was published in two volumes by Tomikura Tohei of Kyōto. It contains many illustrations of Court *kimono*, *hakama*, swords and sword-belts, various decorations, fans of different kinds, etc.

The foregoing list is of but a few of these delightful volumes, and if one comes down to modern days it might be increased indefinitely, for there is no end to the modern books of design printed in colours. As said in Chapter X., these later works are altogether charming and show little of the deteriorating effect which Occidental design has been responsible for in much other Japanese work. The set of five large folios by Kwagwai Tennen, a modern artist of Kyōto, contains designs for *kimono* printed in colours and gaufrage, and is a treasure which in years to come will rank high in a collection. Many of these modern books are the work of famous men, for the Japanese painters have never hesitated to give their genius to design, and this explains in part the beauty possessed by the commonest articles in their country.

In every particular—design, colour, and printing—these charming books put our Western " fashion magazines," with their hideous vulgarity, to utter shame, and one has a feeling of hopeless inferiority in comparing them.

In the spring and autumn of each year, when the cotton and silk factories change the patterns used on their fabrics, great numbers of these books of design may be found in the second-hand shops and the street markets. Often they are scarcely soiled and for a mere song one may pick up works of this kind that will always be a delight to the eye.

Among other odd volumes to be found with the miscellaneous books might be a stray *hōsōye-bon*[1] or two. In English they are known as " red books " or " small-pox books." They were printed and bound entirely in red, it being an ancient idea in Japan that a patient kept in a room hung in this colour and having everything about him also in red would get through the disease more quickly and easily than without this treatment. Kaempher, in his *History of Japan*, quotes from a book which was ancient even in his time, saying that Japanese physicians " think it very material in the cure of small-pox to wrap up the patient in red cloth, and everything in the room and the clothes of the attendants must be red." It is said that *hōsōye-bon* were first printed in the Genroku period, but they are all so extremely rare that it has not been possible to get a detailed account of many of them. Japanese

---

[1] Also called *Yōkōye-bon* and *aka-hon* (cochineal or red books).

physicians explain the rarity of these books by saying that they were destroyed along with the other things used by a small-pox patient as soon as he had recovered.

During the Kwan-en period (1748–1751) a number of these " red books " were printed, and if a collector finds a copy it is apt to date from that time.

Okumura Masanobu illustrated a book of this kind called the *Hana-saki Jiji Tanoshima-no-Eiga*, published in two volumes, but bearing no date.

Nishimura Shigenobu (Toyonobu) also left one of these books, entitled *Aka-hon Sarukani Gassen*, but undated.

Shunchō and Keisai Eisen each left one bearing the title *Kodakara Yama*. Other *hōsōye-bon* were the

Dai Shinpan Tenjin-ki: The history of Tenjin. 10 vols. 1749.
Tsunokuni Nayotoga Ike: 3 vols. 1749.
Higashi-yama San Buku Tsui: 3 vols. 1749.
Kochi-ho-in: 3 vols. 1749.

A collector might be in Japan a year or two and spend most of his time in the old bookshops without finding a single copy of these rare sets, and when a volume does turn up it bears every appearance of hard usage, so if small-pox germs maintain their vigour into old age these books are probably not wholly desirable additions to a collection, curious and unusual though they are.

Collecting *sugoroku* is a popular fad with many Japanese, and some of these sheets are exceedingly interesting. *Sugoroku* is a game for two people something like *parcheesi*, the board being either a round or large oblong sheet of small printed pictures (usually coloured) arranged around one slightly larger in the centre. It is played with dice, the number thrown indicating the number of steps, each step being one of these little pictures, to take in the progress toward the centre drawing, which is the goal.

The game is of Chinese origin and very ancient. Many of the well-known Japanese artists designed these *sugoroku*, and there are some charming colour-printed sheets in colours by the Ukiyo-ye men. Hokusai and Hiroshige both made delightful sheets of this kind; one by Hiroshige of the *Fifty-three Stations along the Tōkaidō*, with a little print of Sanjō bridge in Kyōto for the goal, being especially interesting. The artists of the Utagawa school also designed a large number of *sugoroku*.

Still other books in the boxes of odds and ends might be memorial books of famous pageants and processions Many of these works are valuable to historians, giving as they do the details of costume, procedure, etc.

An early and remarkable work of this kind, the *Kwanyei Gyoku-ki*, has already been spoken of in Chapter II. under the seventeenth-century books.

Other later books of this kind were the *Ryūryūjin Gyōretsu*, published in 1748, illustrating the procession of an envoy from the Loo Choo islands to Yedo. The first engravings represent the high-decked ships which brought the envoy and his suite to Japan, and are followed by drawings of the procession itself taking its way with gifts and flags and banners to do honour to the Shōgun.

About 1831 another envoy came from these islands to Japan, and the *Ryūryū Gyōretsu Dzue*, describing and illustrating the event, was printed as a souvenir of the occasion.

The *Kasuga Taigū Gosairei Ryakkei*, a description of the temple festival held in Nara in March each year, was first published probably in the Kyōhō period, since the preface was written in 1718. The only set available for inspection, however, has been one of 1780. The spirited drawings represent the procession making its way through the avenue of great cryptomerias to the shrine, the midnight torch-light procession up the steps and along the galleries of the Nigwatsudō, and finally the winding line as it makes its way to the religious service following. It is very interesting and the first edition almost impossible to obtain.

The *Ehon Nori-no-Suihiro*, representing a religious festival with drawings unsigned, but much in Shigemasa's style, appeared in 1798. Hundreds of other books illustrating Imperial processions—the procession of the Shōgun and his retinue on his annual visit to the Emperor in Kyōto, as well as civic pageants and fêtes—appeared from time to time, all extremely interesting and well worth adding to a collection.

In 1831 a beautiful book entitled *Konshi-jo-no-Roku* was published, describing the great religious festival at the Hongwan-ji Temple in Ōsaka in August of that year. Very fine coloured plates representing gifts to the temple, made of the large oval ten *yen* gold pieces then in use, form the greater part of the book. Great masses of flowers, screens, ornaments, and various other things, all either made of or ornamented with thousands of these coins, are pictured, while the procession itself on its way from the Kyōto Temple to that in Ōsaka winds across the first four pages of the book. Unfortunately the artist's name is not given, but the plates are so beautiful both in drawing and colour that they must have been the work of some well-known man—possibly Akatsuki Kanenari, who was living in Ōsaka and doing his best work about that time.

Finally in this lot of miscellaneous books we come to some very amusing volumes.

Intentionally humorous as many of the Japanese books are, none of them are more comical than the serious works on foreign countries and foreigners. These books began to appear as early as the seventeenth

PLATE 42]

From the KAIGWAI SHINWA SHŪEI (War in Foreign Countries), by Minedo Fuko. (1849).

[Face p. 214

century. Among the earliest of these curious publications are the *Kwaitsu Shōko* and the *Zōho Kwaitsu Shōko*, published by Nishikawa Kurinsai of Nagasaki in five volumes. Unfortunately the only set that I have ever been able to see is incomplete, and the last volume, which would have borne the date of publication, if the year were given, is missing. From the paper, bindings, etc., however, it is probable that it appeared about 1680–1690. The illustrations show a highly imaginative map of China, drawings of Chinese mandarins and ladies with suspiciously Moronobu-like countenances, amazing Chinese war vessels, maps of North and South America with their relative positions in regard to a most superior Europe, Africa, and Asia, cuts of natives of Annam, Siam, Holland, and other countries, and engravings of foreign sailing vessels. The set is extremely rare and only to be found by the greatest good fortune.

Another important work of this sort, the *Bankoku Jimbutsu Dzue* was published in two large folios beautifully printed on rich paper in 1720. It contains delightfully amusing drawings of the natives of different foreign countries, with the names taken from the Dutch and Latin. There are engravings of people from different parts of China, India, the Malay Peninsula, the South Sea Islands, Australia, and all the different countries of Europe, and North and South America. This also is a very rare book for which a collector may search for months without finding.

The *Bankoku Ichiran Dzusetsu* is a history of foreign countries, with drawings representing the customs of the inhabitants, the houses, utensils, etc., used by them. It was written by Furuyama Genrin and illustrated by Ōoka Naokata of Ōsaka, appearing in two volumes in 1810.

Toward the middle of the nineteenth century, when Japan was called to face the admittance of foreigners to the country, a large number of these quaint works were printed.

In 1849 the five volumes of the *Kaigwai Shinwa Shuei*, on war in foreign countries, appeared. The illustrations represent foreign soldiers, their arms, cannon, etc., as the Japanese artist imagined them to be. The results are extraordinarily curious and not highly flattering to the Occidentals. A supplementary series to this work, also in five volumes, appeared later in the same year. In both sets some of the drawings are tinted.

The *Kaigwai Jimbutsu Shoden*, a history of foreign military matters, with illustrations in both black and white and tints, was published in five volumes in 1853.

The *Gwaiban Yōbo Dzuga*, on the inhabitants of different foreign countries, is very interesting and amusing. It was published in two folios in 1854 and is printed on heavy paper. It contains numerous most ugly but probably well intentioned colour-plates representing types of people in various remote lands. The set is extremely rare and in good condition easily brings thirty or forty *yen* when offered for sale at the Tōkyō and Kyōto book auctions.

The *Kaigwai Ibun* is the story of thirteen Japanese fishermen whose boat was blown out to sea as they were going from Uraga to Izu in September, 1841. After some three months they sighted a big Spanish sailing vessel, which rescued them and took them to her destination on the west Mexican coast. Here they remained several years and upon their return to Japan by another Spanish ship bound for Canton this book was written and illustrated from their account of their adventures. It contains a Japanese-Spanish vocabulary, and the curious coloured drawings represent different incidents in their life in Mexico, as well as the cities there, street scenes, houses, house-interiors, furniture, utensils for various purposes, and articles of clothing. The set was published in five volumes in 1854 and is one of the most amusing and interesting of these books on foreigners.

The *Seiyō Ishokujū* contains highly amusing drawings of foreign furniture, clothing, utensils, etc., and was issued in 1867.

Although undated, the two *gwajō* entitled *Bansen Dzue* and the *Ifu Shashin Kagami*, containing curious but beautifully printed coloured plates, probably appeared about the Bunkwa period. The former is a small oblong book with pictures of foreign ships and a frontispiece representing a globe and a map of the world. It was published by Shiundo of Nagasaki, and is a wonderful example of colour printing—the technical excellence being beyond praise. Later the drawings were copied in larger size and republished about the Ansei period.

The *Ifu Shashin Kagami* contains seven double-page colour-plates of English ships, troops, officers, etc., and was issued by Bunsaidō Yamatoya of Nagasaki. Both books are extremely rare and command high prices when found.

Perhaps the most amusing of any of these *bankoku* books, however, is the *Yokohama Kaikō Kenbunshi*, illustrated by Gountei Sadahide and published in two series of three volumes each in 1862 and 1865. The clever and highly satirical drawings represent incidents in the opening of Yokohama port, and the customs and activities of the foreigners there at that time, including engravings of Commodore Perry and the officers of his staff.

It was a kind providence that kept the foreign strangers from seeing themselves as others saw them, else they never would have had the assurance to put themselves in the position of mentors to the Japanese. Since those days we have learned ourselves that early Victorian architecture, spreading hoops, coal-scuttle bonnets, and ringlets, have elements about them not of beauty; but probably by no effort of the imagination can we get at the absurd and grotesque aspect of it all that the Japanese saw, accustomed as they

PLATE 43] "American Woman Bathing her Children." From the YOKOHAMA KAIKŌ KENBUNSHI (Incidents in the Opening of Yokohama Port) by Gountei Sadahide. A very rare set of books, 1862—1865.

[Face p. 216

had always been to gentle manners and to beauty in the slightest and commonest things they ever used.

With the books on foreign peoples and their customs go the curious text-books which were published about the time the country was opened to foreigners. These books might form an interesting and unique collection in themselves. They are not, however, by any means easy to find, as one might expect them to be, for the second-hand shops all over Japan have orders for them from the Government, which is buying them and putting them into public libraries and museums in different cities as curious mementoes of an important epoch in the country's history.

During the agitation which preceded the Restoration, when the necessity for an understanding of European languages arose, the printing of these quaint text-books was commenced. The numerous illustrations, often printed in colours, representing foreign wearing apparel, furniture, little things in everyday use, houses, public libraries, and other public buildings, bridges, railways and their equipment, military paraphernalia, etc., have the accompanying text in Japanese with the equivalent in English, and often in French and German as well.

Even though one smiles at the amusing spelling, the strange use of capitals, and the queer use of words in naïve composition, one is also filled with sincere admiration for the pluck and magnificent audacity of the men who made books. For although they knew but little—and that often not very well—of the foreigners' languages, they put that little to the best use they could in helping others of their countrymen who knew less, and they compiled these books of whatever seemed most necessary for people to immediately know in order to meet the new conditions which the year 1868 ushered in.

The foregoing notes are merely to suggest what might stray into a collection in the way of odds and ends. Collecting any one kind of such books would be interesting and distinctly worth doing. To be successful, however, one would have to prowl about Japan and hunt them up oneself, for the curio men and print dealers who sell old *ehon* still pin their faith largely to the Ukiyo-ye art.

CHAPTER XII

SUGGESTIONS TO COLLECTORS

O amateurs courageous enough to subject themselves to the contagion of book-collecting in Japan there are offered here a few suggestions. The beginner is warned, however, that the hobby may develop into a malignant even if a not wholly unpleasant fever to have—and as far as can be determined it is incurable. One's temperature falls at times, to be sure, but seemingly only to mount again—often to a mild form of delirium.[1]

There is a lesser form of this malady which manifests itself as mere book-buying, and although this entails a more costly treatment, it is not so chronic and not given to such wild pulse variations, for there is a great difference between buying and collecting these fascinating old volumes.

One may buy them at a pleasant shop, seated in a comfortable chair at a convenient table, while the suave and English-speaking proprietor hovers about and graciously charges from six to ten times what he should. If one goes in a motor-car with a guide, the prices may be twenty times too great, for the guide gets at least 10 per cent. of the amount charged, and if he is an autocrat and popular with tourists the percentage which he demands of the shopkeeper may be much greater than this.

In coming to Japan, therefore, with the idea of collecting, it is better to prowl about for a time, asking questions, buying little or nothing at first, and to wait until one has collected one's wits before embarking upon making a collection of anything else, for to the foreigner who is in the country for the first time the first few weeks are dream-like and unreal. He goes about not certain that he will not shortly come to himself again and find the familiar streets of Boston, New York, or London bounding his days. Everything around him is fascinating and delightful, but unreal to the point of impossibility. During this period he can only buy at shops where English is spoken or through a guide who can interpret for him. To begin to really collect anything intelligently while in this helpless condition is impossible. His first necessity is to buckle down to the language sufficiently to make himself independent of the doubtful services of a guide.

This is much easier than it sounds, and in two or three weeks, at most, one should achieve enough of a vocabulary to ask for books and to understand—with the aid of considerable intuition—what the dealer says about

---

[1] This condition usually follows the discovery of some rare book for an infinitesimal sum.

them, and to buy them, if one wishes, at the numerous old-book shops where only Japanese is spoken. There is no difficulty whatever about the money—that is, the understanding of it—for it is on a decimal system; a *yen* (fifty cents in U.S. money) corresponding (although worth about half as much) whether in a silver piece or a *yen* note to an English two-shilling piece or the American dollar; the twenty-five and fifty *sen* pieces (twelve and twenty-five cents) to the American " quarters " and fifty cent pieces; while copper one and two *sen* pieces, nickle five *sen* pieces, and silver ten *sen* pieces take the places of pennies, five cent pieces and " dimes." Paper notes of two, five, ten, twenty, and larger denominations in *yen* correspond to American notes of the same number of dollars.

With an understanding of the money, therefore, and a slight but growing vocabulary, one may begin to investigate the second-hand book shops for oneself. If the collector travels with a guide the chances are that he will never hear of these delightful shops, piled to the roofs though many of them are with all sorts and descriptions of venerable books, manuscripts, and old rolls, and with prices a mere fraction of those charged at the curio shops where his guide and mentor takes him. These shops are the places where the curio dealers themselves buy many of their books and prints, and naturally they prefer the foreigner not to know of them.

Just at first, in trying to find books at these purely Japanese shops, the new-comer may experience some difficulty apart from the language and have the feeling that he is unwelcome and his patronage not greatly desired. He asks for *ehon*—picture books—and if the dealer is not wrapped in a too impenetrable dignity or too prejudiced to deal with a European, perhaps he will bring out something by Hokusai or Hiroshige if he happens to have it, for to his mind it is inconceivable that the foreigner may wish for anything else. Never, by any chance, will be bring out some quaint old seventeenth-century *meisho-ki*, an ancient religious book with delightful, primitive wood-engravings, or some old history or *monogatari* full of fascinating illustrations. *Ehon* does not mean such works, and to get them one must increase one's vocabulary by as many different words as stand for these different kinds of books.

The effort and study spent in learning a little of the spoken language and enough of the Chinese characters to read signatures and dates is so small in proportion to the immense interest and delight one will gain by having this knowledge, that the time given to acquiring it is more than well spent. Gradually too, if one is persistent and unfailingly courteous, the cold dignity of the book-dealers—many of them old men and scholars—softens, and the inherent kindness in the Japanese nature comes to the surface. Then will they begin to bring out their treasures and finally the visitor himself may be allowed to penetrate the inner recesses of the premises.

By the end of my first year in Japan I had wheedled nearly all the old-book dealers in Kyōto into letting me prowl around dimly lighted precincts and had explored the depths of antique go-downs in Nagoya, Ōsaka, Tōkyō, and a half-dozen other cities.

In doing this the collector learns the thrill of finding rare old books among bushels of dusty possibilities that he himself has pulled down from ancient shelves of low-ceiled upper rooms, or unearthed from the depths of tomb-like go-downs. And by handling thousands of these books, small facts in regard to bindings, title-slips, paper, and printing, marshall themselves in his subconsciousness, until at last a sixth sense develops and the student knows, without knowing just *how* he knows, whether a book is a genuine " find " or only something of moderate importance.

One comes upon wonderful old volumes of which one has never heard before, and which none of the foreign books or auction catalogues have ever listed—full of the most delightful drawings—and with finding them comes an added respect and admiration for a people who so manifestly for hundreds of years have had scholarship and art for their handmaids.

In these purely Japanese shops one is not likely to find modern copies posing as originals, and the constant handling of truly old books makes it comparatively easy to detect the former then found in other places. Modern copies do exist, however, in large numbers and one must be on one's guard against them. Although it is much more difficult to manufacture " old books " than " original prints," it is being done to a large extent, and the illustrations, text, bindings, and dates are all copied as exactly as possible.

It is chiefly in the paper and the bindings where the enterprising imitators of first editions fail, for the paper can always with a little experience and comparison be detected, while the discoloration made by a hot iron passed over the shining newness of a binding, no matter how skilfully or hopefully done, resembles the wear and stains of time so little that to meet these books ingenuously masquerading as venerable and valuable originals is rather pleasantly amusing than otherwise.

One is sometimes deceived, however, by new books stained to a creamy brown by the judicious use of tea, with the right number of thumb marks on the first few pages, being bound in genuinely old covers which in happier days covered other books, but now, cut down to the proper size and with strange title-slips, are playing their part in passing off modern copies as century-old originals.

True reprints, on the other hand, are not copies. They are later editions printed from the original blocks, and many times are very beautiful and well worth having. The date of the second printing usually appears by the side of that for the first, and the publisher, at least, intended no deceit.

It is almost indispensable, however, that the amateur collector should see a few good collections before commencing to buy extensively himself, especially if his time in the country is limited. He will gain in this way some knowledge of the old bindings which is very important and learn something about the paper which was used at different periods.

The earliest Buddhist books were almost invariably printed on a thick paper which is uneven in texture and rather coarse in quality. A few books of the very early seventeenth century were printed on rich, heavy paper of great beauty, but these volumes are so rare and valuable that they are not to be " picked up " except by the most extraordinary good fortune, for they formed the famous *Kōyetsu-bon* and *Saga-bon* published at the Saga Press by Suminokura Soan during the early years of the seventeenth century.

From the Kwanyei period through the following century books were usually printed on fine and extremely thin paper, which was only suitable for the line drawings which illustrations at that time were. As soon as colour commenced to be used to any extent the paper changed to a heavier absorbent quality which took the tints better.[1]

As to bindings, the very early sacred books for temple use were mounted in *orihon* form and in rolls, and not in true book form. Other kinds of literature and Buddhist books not intended for temple services were often bound in regular book form, generally in covers of a dark mahogany-coloured paper of a tough and very heavy texture. These dark, leather-like bindings form an almost distinguishing characteristic of the fifteenth and sixteenth century books, and once seen are easily recognized.

On the books published between the Keichō and Kwanbun year periods bindings made of paper bearing a stamped design were generally used, often in bright scarlet, but also in brown, black, dark blue, and occasionally a dark green. Moronobu's earliest works were all bound in these stamped covers, while later, after transferring his studio to Yedo, his books usually appeared in plain, light brown bindings with the title-slips in the middle of the covers instead of on the upper left-hand side.

This placing of the title-slip in the middle of the cover is rather characteristic of most of the books just before and during the Genroku era and into the first quarter of the next century, although it was not a fixed rule.

In the early books there was rarely a preface, its place being taken by a colophon on the last page which usually contained the place and date of publication. Later, prefaces commenced to be used, sometimes written by the author or artist, but more often by a friend, and usually containing a brief comment on the book, how it came to be written, and other interesting and sometimes very valuable facts which establish bits of knowledge and dates, and make their translation well worth undertaking. Although there was

[1] Probably the earliest experiments in colour work in books were made upon the thin paper, as was the case in the *Jinkō-ki* in Mr. Kobayashi's collection. See Chapter II., p. 21.

sometimes a considerable period intervening between the date of the preface and that of the publication of a book, it was usually the same or the previous year, and in buying books it is always well to compare the year given in the preface with that on the lining of the back cover.[1]

As to signatures, one grows to know the more important rather easily, but since all the artists were given to using many different names, the foreign collector will often at first have to go to some Japanese friend for help, and the latter should be a scholar or he may easily give an incorrect reading of the characters. This fact should perhaps be emphasized. It is exceptional when a man of the shopkeeping class or a student of the mission schools can give assistance of this kind which can be relied upon. I found that it was necessary to go over again the entire work of months because I had depended upon a Japanese who had been educated in one of the mission schools in Japan. He had a very slight and a very poor knowledge of the Japanese classics and the *hirakana* characters used in printing them, and read names very often as no educated Japanese would think of doing. His training, I regret to say, did not prevent him from calling pretence to his aid, and I was imposed upon for months and wasted both time and energy in making notes from his translations.

To go back to the signatures of books, however. As has already been said, the better-known names of the most important men can be learned without great difficulty, and with proper help their other signatures will also gradually become familiar. Many extremely interesting books are unsigned, however, and what is more important to know than signatures is the work itself, and whether a book is signed or unsigned to know from the style of the drawings who made them. As had been said, Moronobu's work is unmistakable; and the drawings by Morofusa, Moroshige, and others of Moronobu's followers can always be placed as by an illustrator of the Moronobu school, even if one is uncertain as to the precise artist whose work they may be. This is true of most of the books down to the Meiji period, and with experience one has only to glance at illustrations by any of the well-known artists to know, without looking at the signatures, who drew them.

It is well, anyway, not to place too much value upon signatures, otherwise one's horizon will always be limited to as narrow a circle as that in which the admirers of the Ukiyo-ye work have shut themselves. If one has any true feeling for art one does not need a signature to make it certain that he is making no mistake. He buys a book because it is interesting and beautiful, and if incidentally it turns out to be by some famous man, so much the better. If not, he still has something beautiful.

[1] It is understood, of course, that all Japanese books are printed and bound in exactly the opposite manner from that in European works—the first page being what would be the last page in an English book.

It is undoubtedly a satisfaction, however, when a book bought only because it is beautiful turns out to be by some renowned artist, and in this connection collectors are advised to familiarize themselves as rapidly as possible with the different names used by the illustrators. This is much more difficult than learning to speak and understand enough Japanese to get about with, or to learn the Chinese characters for dates, numbers, and the signatures commonly used. The bewildering number of names taken by the Japanese artists at different steps in their careers is very confusing and forms another reason for depending largely upon one's sense of beauty in buying books.

I once picked up, in the early days of my malady, two charming volumes of poems containing coloured landscapes of much beauty. They were signed Gogaku, and the shopkeeper, looking at the name and not finding it familiar, let me have them for a mere nothing. I did not know myself at the time that I had some very beautiful examples of Gakutei's work.

The same thing is true of the Kyōto impressionists. They all used many different names, so that it is much wiser to buy a book because it pleases, and then perhaps, after all, find that the unfamiliar signature was one used by a famous man.

In regard to the publishers of various books, unless for some special reason a collector wishes to make a study of them, it seems rather unnecessary to speak at length.

I have purposely refrained from giving the names of the publishers of the works listed in this book because to do so would many times be confusing and misleading. From Moronobu's time on, it was often the custom for a book illustrated by a popular artist to be issued simultaneously by allied printing houses in Kyōto, Ōsaka, and Yedo, and occasionally also in Nagoya. If one gives one name of a publishing house only and the date of the first edition, it throws a discredit, often not deserved, on the same volume issued by one of the other houses, although the latter book also is just as truly a "first edition," and except in a few well-known works and for especial reasons just as valuable.

When one considers the primitive and delightfully ingenuous drawings in the early seventeenth-century books, the noble work done by the early eighteenth-century Ōsaka artists, and the utterly charming coloured illustrations in the books by the men of the Impressionistic schools, the narrow horizon of the print collectors becomes incomprehensible. There was such a multitude of illustrated books printed in Japan that unless one has a catholic taste one loses a great deal of enjoyment and gains but the most superficial knowledge of what wood-engraving in Japan included—an art by no means limited to the men whose names have become familiar to Europeans from their prints. Even a few months spent in book-collecting in Japan will dispel forever the idea that the prints and books of the Ukiyo-ye artists, beautiful as many of them are, represent in any adequate way the tremendous thing that Japanese illustration was, or that they form anything but an infinitesimal part of the delightful volumes full of interesting drawings both in colours and in black and white.

The titles of these books are so often purely fanciful that in cataloguing a collection it seems better to give what they stand for than the literal translations. Several artists illustrated books called *Yedo Suzumi* and *Naniwa Suzumi*, literally meaning "Yedo Swallows" and "Naniwa (Ōsaka) Swallows," but in reality referring to the people and life of these cities and forming *meisho-ki* for these districts.

The *Kyō Warabe*, a rare and delightful *meisho-ki* for Kyōto published in 1658, and containing charmingly quaint drawings by Moronobu, really, when literally translated, means, "Kyōto Children."

The *Shiki-no-Hana*, Utamaro's famous book, if searched for in the belief that it was actually a book on the "flowers of the four seasons," would hardly be recognized when found to be made up of drawings of beautiful women.

The *Yedo Murasaki*, a title used by a number of artists for different books, refers to the women of the Yoshiwara, although one would translate it as "Yedo Violets."

And so with hundreds of others. The names, when translated, being entirely misleading unless one understands this characteristic Japanese tendency to escape the obvious and put the fanciful and imaginative in its place.

In book-collecting one often comes upon single volumes of sets which can generally be had for very little. It is interesting and wise to buy them, for it is more than possible that sooner or later the other volumes will turn up somewhere. This is always intensely exciting, and a series of books, one bought in Nagoya, one in Kyōto, one in Wakayama, and one in Ōsaka, forming the complete set of the *Ariwara Bunko* (1802), a rare and delightful collection of poems illustrated by Baitei, Bumpō, Kihō, Kwazan, Soken, Rosetsu, and many other famous artists of the Kyōto movement, is among the best beloved of my flock, shepherded as it has been through such widely divergent fields.

Sometimes the volumes of sets made up in this irregular way will not be exactly the same size. This can easily be remedied by any Japanese bookbinder or *kakemono*-mounter, who, by cutting them all down to the size of the smallest volume and making over the backs and lower edges of the other books, will produce a set of uniform size which will be entirely satisfactory. Even if the books are not equally clean and perfect, much can be done in the way of washing and mending, and although to have this done by a good man is expensive, often costing as much or more than the books themselves, it is often very well worth having done.

By getting a proper board one can do a good deal in cleaning books oneself. Cut the threads of the bindings and immerse the separate sheets in water for a moment, then spread them smoothly on the wet board. If very much soiled, one may even rub a piece of pure soap lightly over the pages. Rinse them thoroughly and let dry on the board, removing them when they have become only damp and putting them between large sheets of blotting paper under some weight larger than the sheets of illustrations themselves. In the books printed before the use of aniline colours—and the latter with few exceptions are not worth the trouble of cleaning—the colours are almost perfectly fast, and will scarcely run at all, although care must be taken, of course, in the amount of rubbing as the surface of the paper is easily damaged. In any case the first experiments would better be made with a few pages of some duplicate book of slight value.

The volumes of a set of books are marked in different ways. Four-volume editions are often designated by the names of the seasons, as Haru (Spring), Natsu (Summer), Aki (Autumn), and Fuyu (Winter); and also by the points of the compass, Kita (North), Minami (South), Higashi (East), and Nishi (West). Three-volume sets are marked Ten (Heaven), Chi (Earth), and Jin (People); and also Jō (Top), Chū (Middle), and Ge (Bottom). Two-volume editions are found marked either Ken (Above or Up) and Kon (Below or Down); or Jō and Ge; while the sets made up of more than three or four volumes have the number of each marked below the *hashira* on the dividing lines of the pages.

As to places in which to hunt for old books, I have found Kyōto, Ōsaka, and Tōkyō the best, and there are a large number of shops in each of these cities dealing only in these old volumes. Tōkyō is naturally the best place to look for works by the Ukiyo-ye artists, although of course, one comes upon their books elsewhere as well. A trip of a week or two made to remote places in the country will also often yield surprising results, and in these smaller towns one sometimes makes wonderful finds for absurdly small sums. Such book-hunting trips into the provinces are exceedingly interesting in every way. You may travel by train or *kuruma*, spending the nights in Japanese inns, where amusing and curious experiences multiply, and even if you are not rewarded by finding a great number of books, you are certain to find some; and many other things about these unique jaunts will more than repay you. The old cities that in feudal days were the seats of different *daimyō* nearly always yield a good harvest, the north especially being full of treasures.

In regard to prices, they are rapidly and continually rising. The Japanese themselves are very keen about old books, and book-collecting is no new fad among them. The seventeenth-century books have not all been gleaned yet and many interesting early works may still be found. This, of course, does not apply to signed work by Moronobu or the men of his school, or to books like the *Ise Monogatari* or other *Saga-bon* and *Kōyetsu-bon*, which are all so rare as to bring very high prices. Moronobu's signed books bring from twenty to three hundred *yen* and more each, Okumura Masanobu's are still higher, while some of Harunobu's books containing coloured plates may bring over one thousand *yen*. Kitao Masanobu's books also command high prices, and certain rare works by Kiyonaga, Shunman, and Koryūsai, are hardly to be found at all.

During 1916 two sets of Utamaro's *Shiki-no-Hana* sold in Kyōto for two hundred and fifty *yen* each, a set of Hokusai's *Sumidagawa Ryōgan Ichiran* for the same sum, and the second edition (1819) of the *Hokusai Shashin Gwafu* for two hundred *yen*. It goes without saying that Americans bought them, and all true collectors condemned them to blackest hell for paying such prices.

It depends largely upon whether one is buying or collecting what prices one will have to pay. Books by the Shijō and Maruyama artists, which one would give from ten to fifteen *yen* for at the shops dealing only in old books, will be sold by the curio and print dealers for probably six times as much. A set of the *Meika Gwafu*, which one would pay from twelve to fifteen *yen* for at one of these purely Japanese shops, was sold during the summer of 1916, by a curio dealer of Kyōto, to an American and his guide and motor-car for something like fifty *yen*, and three volumes of another set of books which the curio dealer bought at one of the second-hand book shops in the morning for four and one-half *yen* became the property of the American in the afternoon for twenty-two *yen*, who, although he ended by possessing the books, had never had the keen delight in hunting for them or known the thrill of running home fearing that the police might be after him for inveigling the old shopkeeper into parting with them for too small a sum.

There is a catalogue of " market prices " for all the well-known books which is issued every few months. The dealers in old books go by this, but the curio and print-sellers soar high above it, and their customers never find out that such a catalogue exists.

Perhaps the most practical information I could add to this chapter would be the names of the shops where I picked up my chief treasures. I have found the proprietors of most of these places perfectly reliable, and the prices usually about right, although some reduction will always be made if one buys a number of books.

In addition to these shops there are the morning and evening street markets which are held every day in Kyōto, and two or three times a month in Ōsaka, where one may sometimes pick up a book worth having. The big fairs in Kyōto are at Tōji and Kitano Temples on the 21st and 25th of each month, and on the 9th and 15th at the Danno Temple there are also markets where occasionally something worth while will be found; while in Ōsaka the fairs on the 21st and the 25th of each month near Tennō-ji are interesting, and about the middle of each month there is a great evening market on Hirano-machi.

Among the shops in Kyōto dealing in old books, Wakabayashi's on Tera-machi-Oike near the Kyōto Hotel is the most interesting. From the street one sees nothing but an ordinary Japanese book-shop, but upstairs there are two immense rooms containing thousands of old Chinese, Korean, and Japanese works. I had been in Japan for nearly two years before the wealth of these upper rooms was disclosed to me. Two or three times I had gone into the shop only to meet with such an icy reception that I resolved never to go there again. One of the professors up at the University softened the old proprietor's heart toward me finally, however, and on a never-to-be-forgotten morning, when I made what I determined would be my last attempt, I received permission—a most unusual favour, I found afterwards—to go up to the second floor. My shoes were off so quickly that the buttons never recovered from the shock, and I followed the dignified, non-committal proprietor up the steep and narrow stairs.

Never, never, can I describe the wonders of those two enormous, low-ceiled upper rooms. Piles, stacks, shelves, and great chests of old books, manuscripts, rolls, prints, maps, and *kakemono*, as well as rare old pieces of lacquer and other curios, filled the rooms almost to the ceiling, and in the back room opening above the garden, just in front of the *shōji*, was a huge pile of unassorted books, rolls, and prints. For the next month I practically lived on the floor near that diminishing pile of ancient books, unearthing from it from time to time some treasure which set my pulses going at such a rate that I half feared an attack of apoplexy might forever put an end to my book-collecting. Every day I dug out dusty jewels that sent me back to the hotel at night with my heart beating up into my throat, to wait impatiently for the next morning. By measure and weight I should say that several bushels and several hundred pounds of books were speedily removed to the Kyōto Hotel, where evening after evening I went over them, arranging, sorting, and making notes. Those quiet, wonderful days spent in that silent room above the little garden with the *amado* and *shōji* all flung open to the light and air are not to be repeated I am afraid, and although the rooms are still piled high with treasures, for me the experience is at an end, for the piles and shelves have been too thoroughly gone over to yield to my own collection anything more than duplicates.

Another interesting shop in Kyōto is Hosogawa's on Sanjō-dōri, close to the corner of Tera-machi. This also is a very good hunting-ground, and is patronized by Japanese collectors all over Japan. Each month the proprietors get out a catalogue of their stock and frequently have orders by telegram from cities as far away as Nagasaki and Sendai. At both Wakabayashi's and Hosogawa's some English is spoken, although at neither place is the slightest effort made to win foreign customers, the owners seemingly preferring to sell to the big curio and print dealers and to Japanese connoisseurs.

Sazaki's shop on Tera-machi, before one gets to Sanjō-dōri, is one of the oldest book-shops in Kyōto, the business having been handed down from father to son for three hundred years. Although they make no special effort to keep illustrated books and deal chiefly in old Chinese and Japanese classics, one may still very often find there something interesting containing engravings.

Yamada's shop is still further down on Tera-machi and will occasionally yield something worth having. The old proprietor is considered a very good authority on ancient Chinese and Buddhist works.

Kichūdō's shop is far south on Tera-machi, not far from Gojō-dōri, and there is often an interesting volume or two to be found there, although the prices are too high.

Just south of Kichūdō's is another place which deals almost exclusively in old religious books, and occasionally one may pick up some rare old *kyōmon* or *shōgyō* there.

On Shijō-dōri, not far from the famous Gion shrine, Konohana's tiny shop often yields something well worth having and the proprietor is reliable and his prices reasonable.

In addition to these well-known shops there are any number of smaller ones in various parts of the city, and on Tera-machi, north of Oike, and on Maruta-machi, on both sides of the street toward and across the river, there are dozens of second-hand book shops which deal chiefly in used copies of modern French, German, and English works, but where one may also occasionally pick up something very interesting in old illustrated books for a mere fraction of their value.

In Ōsaka the best shops are Kimura's, Shikata's, and Hashimoto Tokubei's, but one may also often find something worth having at Kumago's, Ishikawa's, Tori's, Itō's, and Yanagi's little places.

In Nagoya, Asahina has two curio shops where one may sometimes find something valuable, although his prices are far too high.

Todoya's in Nagoya is a small shop which deals only in old books, and the old proprietor is very reliable and often has works which are very rare and valuable.

In Tōkyō also there are many fascinating shops which deal only in old books. Of these Murako's near the Shimbashi station is undoubtedly the best, although his prices are rather high. Sakai's place in Kanda is also very good and the proprietor very accommodating and helpful.

Up near the University on Jimbō-chō, and several other streets in that district, there are literally hundreds of second-hand book shops, which, although dealing chiefly in used books printed in Europe and America, also nearly always have a few—and sometimes very valuable—illustrated Japanese books. Other Tōkyō shops with the street addresses will be given further on in a list of such places that I have made from my note-book. They are all decidedly worth investigating, and I have bought books in all of them—many of which are treasures that I prize highly.

In addition to the old-book shops there are big book auctions once or twice a year in both Tōkyō and Kyōto. These are usually held at the Nihombashi Club in Tōkyō and at the Kyōto Club in Kyōto. The important sales in Tōkyō are always advertised in the English papers, and there is generally someone present who speaks English. In Kyōto, on the other hand, these sales are never advertised except in the Japanese paper, and there is no effort made to induce foreigners to attend them. On the 12th of each month the Kyōto dealers meet at Hosogawa's house on Goko-machi, near Ebisugawa, to exchange and sell to each other, and on the 20th there is always a sale at the Book Auction Company at Butokuden-Nishi, Rikuseikai, in Kyōto, where used foreign books change hands, but where also occasionally one may come across some interesting *ehon*. In Ōsaka there is a small auction (usually at Shikata's) on the 8th of each month.

The collector will find these sales extremely interesting apart from the books for which he is searching. The latter are spread in long double rows on the floors of the rooms where they are exhibited, and the visitors kneel or squat in front of them as they look them over. The foreigner will probably require the services of a good masseur after a day spent at one of these sales, but in spite of aching joints the experience is as well worth having as the books he may find there.

Of the private collections of old books in Japan I do not feel at liberty to speak except in a few cases. There are many of the greatest interest and of immense value. With proper letters of introduction, the foreign collector will probably have no difficulty about seeing some of them, and after he has been in the country long enough to have made friends there, all this will be arranged for him. Let him be on his guard, however, about " private collections " owned by the friends of dealers and guides. These are usually " arranged," and by " special favour " sometimes the foreigner is allowed to purchase something at an absurd price. The owners of the really valuable collections are aristocrats—although this in Japan does not necessarily mean that they are all men of wealth—and they are not pining to show and sell their treasures to foreigners, no matter how fat the purses of the latter may be.

The books in the Imperial Museum in Tōkyō, although not a large collection, may be seen by making arrangements with the curator. The Imperial University Libraries in both Tōkyō and Kyōto own some very valuable books, and the librarians will show them to anyone who is truly interested. Mr. Wada, the Librarian of the Imperial University Library in Tōkyō, is one of the best authorities in Japan on old books, and has written a very important work on the old Japanese *meisho-ki*. The Nanki Bunko, also known as the Cabinet or Shōgun's Library, belongs to the Tokugawa family and may be seen by making arrangements through one's Embassy. The immense collection contains many extremely old books, rolls, and paintings of the greatest interest.

North-west of Tōkyō, in the city of Ashikaga, not far from Maebashi, is an old school of classics founded by Ono Takamura in the ninth century. The original buildings are no longer in existence, but early in the fifteenth century new ones were put up and many valuable old Chinese books imported to increase the already large collection. Although these books are by no means all illustrated, the library is a fascinating place and well worth visiting.

Not the least interesting thing about a collection is the arrangement of it. This is something in regard to which one may change one's mind several times, and therein lies one of its charms. The precious volumes may be kept in boxes or baskets, drawers, or on shelves, but in any case the collector will find the stiff folding covers for them, which are so well and cheaply made at the places where screens and *kakemono* are mounted, very desirable. At the street fairs beautiful old *obi* are always to be found and one of these sashes is enough for ten or twelve cases, the making of which the mounter will charge from sixty *sen* to one *yen* fifty each for. These covers add so much to the appearance as well as to the safe-keeping of the books that the very slight trouble and expense involved in having them made are well worth assuming.

Book-collecting, fascinating as it is, is not without its reactions and disappointments, but in spite of this it continually lures one on, and incidental to it are many unique and delightful as well as amusing experiences.

Although the books are becoming rarer and more valuable every year, there is still time for a collector to make an interesting and large collection. In a few years there will be nothing of any value left outside the private collections, and to obtain them one will have to wait for such collections to be broken up and sold.

Incidentally the hobby may have other results than are apparent or expected, for it leads one through Japanese history, literature, and art, and after treading these wonderful paths the collector would be blind indeed not to realize that Japanese civilization has wealth undreamed of to give, if the Occidental will only see and accept it.

The collector learns also, notwithstanding much foreign testimony to the contrary, that in big work—great screens and panels—the art soul of Japan still lives, strong and virile, and the modern painters who have had the wisdom to let Western art alone and remain true to their own traditions are doing splendid things. Every autumn exhibition of the Mumbushō shows this. Whether in a smaller way something in pictorial work will evolve which will correspond to the prints and charming illustrated books of an earlier day remains to be seen. That there is a healthy reaction in favour of a purely Japanese expression is certain, and it is probable that when the world recovers from the hysteria in poetry and painting which has marked this decade in Occidental literature and art, and of which the echoes have sounded in Japan, Nippon will again completely find herself, for life there, beneath the surface, is still sane and beautiful.

OLD-BOOK SHOPS IN JAPAN

Kyōto

B. Hosogawa	Sanjō Tera-machi.
Hayashi	Nijō-dōri near Karasumaro.
Konohana	Shijō-dōri near the Gion shrine.
Kichūdō	Tera-machi north of Gojō-dōri.
Sazaki	Tera-machi south of Oike.
Wakabayashi	Tera-machi-Oike.
Yamada	Tera-machi south of Sanjō-dōri.
Yuwabuchi	Rokuhara-dōri.

Ōsaka

Ishikawa	Karamono-chō. 4 chōme, Higashi-ku.
Itō	Shima-machi, 20.
S. Kumura	25 Minami Sunyachō, Minami-ku.
Hasegawa Kumago	Awaji-machi, Higashi-ku.
S. Shikata	Andō-machi. 4 chōme.
Hashimoto Tokubei	Shinsai-bashi-dōri, Kitakutaro-machi, Minamura.
Tori	Minami-Watanabe-chō. 1.
Yanagi-ya	Hirano-machi, Higashi-ku.

Nagoya

Asahina	Near Nagoya Hotel.
Tōyōdō	
Yuwata	

Tōkyō

Asakura-ya	Naka-chō, Kitashigashi, Asakusa.
K. Ishii	65 Tansu-chō, Azabu.
Katō	Ginza, short distance below the Museum.
Yoshida Kichigorō	Okachi-machi, Shitaya.
Komura	9 2 chōme, Kakigara-chō.
Murako	Higake-chō, Shiba. Near Shimbashi station.
S. Sakai	4 2 chōme, Awaji-chō, Kanda.
Saitō	Naka-chō, Kitashigashi, Asakusa.
Shōsandō	Nishiki-chō, near Ogawa-machi tram station, Kanda.
Katō Shōten	9 Tashirō-chō, near Sueshiro tram station, Kanda.
Shimidzu	Ginza, below the Museum.
M. Suwa	2 Tatami-chō, near Kyōbashi.

Kanazawa

Zembei Ike	35 Minami-chō.
K. Ishii	Kata-machi.

GLOSSARY

ABACUS (also SOROBAN): Instrument for making arithmetical calculations.
AKA-HON: "Red book." Books printed entirely in red for the use of small-pox patients.
AKI: Autumn.
AMADO: Sliding outside panels, serving the purpose of doors.
AZUMA: The name of an early Japanese princess whose death occurred on a visit to Yedo. Afterwards the name came to mean the Eastern Capital—Yedo.

BAKEMONO: Ghost, monster.
BAN: Block (when referring to books).
BIWA: Japanese musical instrument, a four-stringed lute.
BON: Reading of the character for *book*. Sometimes used instead of *hon*.
BONSAI: Pot-grown plants.
BONSEKI: "Bowl landscapes."
BUNJINGWA: An extremely impressionistic style of painting used by literary men; the term was first employed to describe the method of the Confucian or Southern Chinese school.
BUSSHŌ: Buddhist books of a descriptive character. Also called *shōgyō*.
BUTSU-YE: Buddhist picture.
BYŌBU: A folding screen.

CHA-JIN: A ceremonial tea expert.
CHA-NO-YU: The ceremonial tea.
CHI: The earth.
CHŪ: Middle, between.

DAIMOKU: The prayer of the Nichiren-shū or Hokke-shū.
DAIMYŌ: The feudal lord of a province.
DERA (or TERA): A temple.
DHÂRANÎ: Sacred Buddhist text.

E (or YE): Picture.
EDORI-BON (or YEDORI-BON): Ancient printed books in which the engravings are coloured by hand.
EHON (or YEHON): Picture book.

FUKUSA: A square silk cloth used for wrapping up parcels.
FUSUMA: The sliding panels between the rooms in a Japanese house.

GAUFRAGE: "Blind printing." A term applied to printing by heavy pressure, producing an indentation of the paper.
GE: Bottom, low.
GO: The Japanese chess, number five.
GOZAN-BAN: "Five-mountain Block," a name given to the books published at five famous Zen monasteries during the fourteenth and fifteenth centuries.
GWA: A drawing, sketch.
GWAFU: Sketch book, brush drawing.
GWAJŌ: A folding album of drawings.

JAPANESE BLOCK-PRINTING

HAIGWA: Illustrated *haikai*.
HAIKAI, HAIKU, HOKKU: Seventeen-syllable poems.
HAKKEI: A set of eight views.
HAORI: An over-*kimono*, worn as a cloak or overcoat.
HASHIRA: The mark on the outer edges of the pages of a book, sometimes containing its title. Occasionally the *hashira* is placed at the top of the page, indicating that the sheets were intended to be mounted in a roll or *orihon*.
HIBACHI: The jar-shaped pottery or metal charcoal stoves used in Japan.
HIRAKANA: Writing or printing in which the Chinese characters are made to flow together. A very cursive and difficult style to read.
HŌIN, HŌGEN, HOKKYŌ: Originally clerical titles, but under the Togugawas given as honorifics to be used by artists (chiefly of the Kanō school) and physicians affiliated with the priesthood.
HŌSŌYE-BON: "Small-pox books," printed entirely in red.
HOTOKE-BON: Sacred books.
HYAKU: One hundred.
HYAKUMAN-TŌ: Term applied to the small wooden pagodas made in the eighth century for the *dhârani* printed by order of the Empress Kōken. Literally "million towers."

ICHIMAI-YE: Single sheet pictures.

JI: Temple.
JIN: Man, men, people.
JŌ and JO: Top, woman, women, preface to a book.
JŌRURI-BON: Books of ballad dramas and heroic deeds.

KAKEMONO: A hanging picture.
KASUGA-BON or KASUGA-BAN (Kasuga blocks): Books printed at Nara under the auspices of the Kasuga shrine, during the twelfth, thirteenth, and following centuries.
KATAKANA: A simplified form of writing the Chinese characters.
KEN: First, up, or above, top (when applied to sets of books).
KI-BYŌSHI: Small yellow-covered novelettes of the late eighteenth and early nineteenth centuries.
KIMPIRA-BON: Books in the style of the *Jōruri-bon* relating the adventures of the giant Kimpira.
KŌHEN: Supplement, second series.
KON: Down, below, last (when applied to a set of books).
KONDŌ: Main building of a temple.
KOTO: A Japanese musical instrument.
KŌYETSU-BON: Books printed from Kōyetsu's chirography or from the movable wooden types invented by him.
KUBARI-HON: Books printed as souvenirs of special occasions and not intended for sale.
KURUMA: A jinrikisha.
KWACHŌ: Collections of drawings of birds and flowers.
KWANBAKU: An official of the Court who receives messages before their transmission to the Emperor, a regent, a prime minister.
KYŌGEN: Short comedies played in the intervals of the Nō drama.
KYŌKA: Comic poems, humorous poems.
KYŌMON: Sacred Buddhist books, scriptures.

MAKEMONO: A rolled picture or text.
MAKURA-BON: Oblong books, so named because when placed one above another they resemble and can be used as a pillow (*makura*).

Glossary

MANDARA: Picture of the Buddhist paradise.
MATSURI: A festival.
MEISHO or MEISHO-KI: A descriptive guide book.
MOKUROKU: A list or catalogue.
MON: The crest used on a family's clothing, furniture, ornaments, etc.
MONOGATARI: A story, tale.

NAN-GWA: Southern pictures—*i.e.*, the *bunjingwa* paintings.
NARA-E-BON: Ancient books with pictures painted by hand (usually in the Tosa manner).
NETSUKE: A carved button or toggle used to suspend a tobacco pouch or medicine case from the *obi*.
NISHIKI-YE: "Brocade pictures," prints.
NŌTAN: "The actual spotting of the dark and light in pictures."

OBI: A sash, girdle.
OIRAN: A courtesan.
ORIHON: A folding book.
ŌTSU-YE: Small rough paintings which preceded the single sheets.

RAMMA: Panels above the *fusuma* in Japanese houses.
RIKKWA: Pertaining to flower arrangement. (The characters may also be read Tatabana or Tachibana.)
RYŌMEN-GWAJŌ: A folding album with pictures on both sides, a double *gwajō*.

SAGA-BON: Books published during the seventeenth century at the Saga Press west of Kyōto.
SAGA UTA-BON: Collections of *uta*, or poems, published at the Saga Press.
SAMISEN: A stringed musical instrument.
SHAKA: Shākyamuni Buddha.
SHIKISHI: Decorated writing paper.
SHŌGYŌ: Buddhist books of a descriptive character.
SHŌJI: Sliding, paper-covered panels between the rooms in a Japanese house and the street or garden.
SHOMOTSU-BON: Regular sewed books.
SHŌSŌ-IN: An ancient storehouse of imperial treasures at Nara.
SHOZURI: Earliest edition (when applied to books).
SŌJŌ, SŌDZU, SHŌNIN: Priestly titles.
SUMI-YE: "Ink picture," usually applied to prints where no colour has been used.
SURI-HON: Printed book.
SURI-MONO: Literally "printed thing," cards and sheets used as souvenirs of special occasions.
SŪTRA: Sacred books supposed to record the sayings of Buddha. In Sanscrit the word means *thread*, and is a term applied to certain texts which consist of aphorisms and part aphorisms, and are necessarily obscure because of their conciseness. They belong to the old system of memorizing and are really a series of suggestions covering the whole ground of an argument, in which each sentence is intended to revive the memory of certain steps. The corresponding word in Chinese is *warp*, that which is to be woven upon. (From *Ideals of the East*, by Okakura Kakuzo, p. 161.)

TAKARA-BUNE: Treasure boat.
TAKARA-MONO: Precious things, emblems of good fortune.
TATAMI: Straw mats used for floor coverings in Japan.
TEN: Heaven.
TŌ: Tower, pagoda.

Japanese Block-Printing

Toba-ye: Comical pictures and caricatures named from Toba Sōjō.

Tokoniwa: A miniature garden or landscape in a bowl to be placed in the alcove of a Japanese house.

Tōri: Gate, street, passage.

Torii: Arch or gate before a Shintō temple.

Uchiwa: A folding fan.

Ukiyo-ye: "Pictures of the floating world," a term applied to the art of the print designers.

Ukiyo-ye Ryū: Ukiyo-ye school.

Urushi: Lacquer.

Uta: A song, ballad, poem.

Warabe: A child, a boy.

Waraji: Straw sandals.

Yamato-ye: Early Japanese pictures.

Yashiki: Mansion, large house, palace.

Yedori-bon: See *Edori-bon*.

Yedo-ye: Yedo pictures.

Yōkō-ye bon: Cochineal or carmine books, also called "red books" and "small-pox books."

Zōho: A supplement, a second series.

BIBLIOGRAPHY

ANDERSON, W.: " A History of Japanese Art," *Transactions of the Asiatic Society*, vol. vii., 1879.
    Descriptive and Historical Catalogue of a Collection of Japanese and Chinese Paintings in the British Museum. London. 1886.
    " Japanese Wood Engraving," *The Portfolio*. 1895.
    The Pictorial Arts of Japan. 1886.
    Prints and Books Illustrating Engraving in Japan exhibited at the Burlington Fine Arts Club. London. 1888.
ASTON, W. G.: *Japanese Literature*. London. 1898 and 1907.
    " Early Japanese History," *Transactions of the Asiatic Society of Japan*, vol. xvi., part 1. Yokohama. 1888.

BARBOUTAU: See Catalogues.
BING, S.: *Le Japon Artistique*. Paris. 1889–1891.
    Le Gravure Japonaise. Paris. 1897.
    " The Art of Utamaro," *The Studio*, No. 4, 1895.
BINYON, L.: *Painting in the Far East*. London. 1908.
    Catalogue of Japanese and Chinese Woodcuts in the British Museum. 1916.
BRINKLEY, CAPTAIN F.: *Japan, Its History, Art, and Literature*. 1901.

CATALOGUES:
    Appleton Catalogue. London.
    Descriptive and Historical Catalogue of a Collection of Japanese and Chinese Paintings in the British Museum. By W. ANDERSON. London. 1886.
    Burlington. See ANDERSON.
    Collection P. Barboutau. Paris. 1904.
    Collection de M. Ch. Bermond. Estampes Japonaises des 18 et 19 Siècles. Paris. 1913.
    Collection Ph. Burty. Peintures et d'Estampes Japonaises, de Kakemonos, de Miniatures Indo-Persanes, et de Livres Relatifs à l'Orient et au Japon. Paris. 1891.
    Livres et Albums Illustrés du Japon Réunis et Catalogués par Théodore Duret. Paris. 1900.
    Dessins, Estampes, Livres Illustrés du Japon Réunis par T. Hayashi. Paris. 1902.
    Collection Ch. Gillot. Estampes Japonaises et Livres Illustrés. Paris. 1904.
    Gookin Collection. Loan Exhibition of Japanese Colour Prints. Chicago. 1908.
    Happer Collection of Japanese Prints and Illustrated Books. London. 1909.
    Guide to an Exhibition of Japanese and Chinese Paintings in the British Museum, principally from the Arthur Morrison Collection. London. 1914.
    Guide to the Exhibition of Chinese and Japanese Paintings in the Print and Drawing Gallery of the British Museum. London. 1888.
    A Guide to the Chinese and Japanese Illustrated Books Exhibited in the King's Library of the British Museum. London. 1887.
    Descriptive Account of the Collection of Chinese, Tibetan, Mongol, and Japanese Books in the Newberry Library. By B. LAUFER. Chicago. 1913.
    Japanese Colour Prints. Collection of James Orange, Esq., and Dr. T. C. Thornicraft. London. 1912.
CHAMBERLAIN, B. H.: *Things Japanese*.

DE VINNE, THEODORE L.: *The Invention of Printing*.
DICK, STEWART.: " The Kanō School of Painting," *Transactions of the Japan Society*, vol. x., part 1. London. 1912.

JAPANESE BLOCK-PRINTING

DICKINS, F. V.: *Fugaku Hyaku-kei: A Hundred Views of Fuji by Hokusai.* London. 1880.
"The Mangwa of Hokusai," *Transactions of the Japan Society*, vol. vi., part 3. London. 1905.
"The Beginnings of Ancient Japanese Literature," *Transactions of the Japan Society*, vol. vii., part 3. London. 1907.

DILLON, EDWARD.: *The Arts of Japan.* London. 1906.
DU HALDE: *Description de l'Empire de la Chine.* 1736.

FENOLLOSA, ERNEST, F.: *Masters of the Ukiyo-ye.* 1896.
Epochs of Chinese and Japanese Art. London. 1912.
An Outline History of the Ukiyo-ye. Tokyo. 1911.

FICKE, A. D.: *Chats on Japanese Prints.* London. 1915.

GONCOURT, E. DE: *Outamaro: Le Peintre des Maisons Vertes.* Paris. 1891.
Hokousai. Paris. 1896.

GONZE, L.: *L'Art Japonaise.* Paris. 1883.
GORDON, E. A.: *The Lotus Gospel.* Tōkyō. 1911.
Temples of the Orient and their Message. 1902.

GUIMET, ÉMILE: *Promenades Japonaises.* Paris. 1880.

HAPPER: See Catalogues.
HAYASHI: See Catalogues.

ICHIHARA, M.: *Kyōto and the Allied Prefectures.* Nara. 1895.

JOLY, HENRI: "Bakemono (Japanese Ghosts and Goblins)," *Transactions of the Japan Society*, vol. ix., part 1. London. 1910.

Kokkwa: Magazine of Japanese and other Oriental Art. Tōkyō. 1889 sqq.
KURTH, JULIUS. *Harunobu.* 1910.
Utamaro. Leipzig. 1907.

MORRISON, ARTHUR: *Painters of Japan.* 1911.
MUNRO, NEIL GORDON: *Prehistoric Japan.* 1908.
"Primitive Culture in Japan," *Transactions of Asiatic Society*, vol. xxxiv., part 2.
"Some Origins and Survivals," *Transactions of Asiatic Society*, vol. xxxviii., part 3.

NETTO, C. and G. WAGENER: *Japanischer Humor.* 1888.

OKAKURA, KAKUZO: *The Ideals of the East.* London. 1903.

PAPILLON: *Traité historique de la Gravure en Bois.* Paris. 1766.
PARKER, E. H.: "Ma Twan-Lin's Account of Japan up to A.D. 1200," *Transactions of the Asiatic Society of Japan*, vol. xxii., part 1. Yokohama. 1894.
PERZYNSKI, FRIEDRICH: *Hokusai.* Leipzig. 1908.

REVON, M.: *Hoksai.* Paris. 1896.

SATOW, SIR ERNEST: "On the Early History of Printing in Japan," *Transactions of the Asiatic Society of Japan*, vol. x., part 1. Yokohama. 1882.
"Further Notes on Movable Types in Korea and Early Japanese Books," *Transactions of the Asiatic Society of Japan*, vol. x., part 2. Yokohama. 1882.

SEIDLITZ, W. VON: *A History of Japanese Colour Prints.* London. 1910.
SEXTON, MAJOR J. J. O'BRIEN: "Illustrated Books of Japan," in *Burlington Magazine* for November, 1917. Also an article on Utamaro in a number of the *Burlington Magazine* for 1919.

Bibliography

STEIN, SIR AUREL: *Ruins of Desert Cathay.* 1912.

STEWART, BASIL: *On Collecting Japanese Colour Prints.* 8vo. Kegan Paul, London. 1917.
    Japanese Colour Prints and the Subjects they Illustrate. 4to. Kegan Paul, London (Dutton, New York). 1920.
    Subjects Portrayed by Japanese Colour Prints. Folio. Kegan Paul, London (Dutton, New York). 1922.

STRANGE, EDWARD: *Catalogue of the Japanese Books and Albums of Prints in Colour in the National Art Library, South Kensington.* London. 1893.
    Japanese Colour Prints. London. 1896.
    Japanese Illustration. London. 1897.
    Colour Prints of Japan. London. 1910.
    " Colour Prints by Hiroshige and other Landscape Artists of Japan," *Transactions of the Japan Society*, vol. ix., part 1. London. 1910.
    Hokusai. London. 1906.

SUCCO, FRIEDRICH: *Utagawa Toyokuni und seine Zeit.* 1914.

TAJIMA, S.: *Selected Relics of Japanese Art.* Kyōto. 1899.

WALEY, ARTHUR.: " Note on the Invention of Printing," *New China Review.* 1919.

East Asia Official Guide Book: Vols. ii. and iii. Imperial Japanese Government Railways. Tōkyō. 1914.

Handbook for Japan: By BASIL HALL CHAMBERLAIN and W. B. MASON.

History of the Empire of Japan. Compiled by the Imperial Japanese Commission of the World's Columbian Exposition, Chicago, U.S.A. Tōkyō. 1893.

BIBLIOGRAPHY OF JAPANESE WORKS

Buchōhōki: By SHIKITEI SAMBA.
Eiri Jōruri Shi: An illustrated book on the *jōruri-bon*. By MIZUTANI FUTO. 3 vols. 1915.
Enseki Jishu: A miscellany. 1836.
Enseki Shūshi: By TAKISAWA SŌRITSU. 5 vols. 1809.
Fusō Gwajinden: By KOHITSU RYŌCHŪ. 1884.
Gwajō Yōryaku: By SHIRAI KWAZAN. 1831.
Honchō Gwashi: By KANŌ EINŌ. 1693.
Honchō Ukiyo Gwajin-den: 1899.
Hyaku Meika Shogwa Jō: One hundred writers and artists of the *samurai* class. 2 vols. 1832.
Kinsei Itsujin Gwashi: By ISEYA HEIJIRŌ.
Kinsei Kiseki-kō: By SANTŌ KYŌDEN. 1805.
Kogwa Bikō: Reprint. 1912.
Kohan Chishi Kaidai: A bibliographical work on the old *meisho-ki*, by MANKICHI WADA, the chief librarian of the Imperial University Library, Tōkyō. 1 vol. 1915.
Mumei-ō Zuhitsu: By IKEDA YOSHINOBU (Keisai Eisen). 1808.
Nihon Bijutsu Gwahō: Current periodical.
Nihon Shoga Rakkan Impu: Seals and signatures of famous Japanese artists and writers. 5 vols. 1914.
Nikkō-zan Shi: A guide to Nikkō. By UEDA MOSHIN. 5 vols. 1837.
Nippon Shōsetsu Nempyō: By ASAKURA MUSEI. 1806.
Rekidai Nengō: Japanese year periods.
Ukiyo-e Bikō: Second edition. 1909.
Ukiyo-e Hennenshi: 1891.
Ukiyo-e Ruikō: Enlarged edition. 1899.
Ukiyo-eshi Benran: 1893.
Zoku Haigwa Kijin-den: Famous artist-poets. 1832.

GENERAL INDEX

Aizen-Myō-ō, 7
Akahori, Professor M., 6
Akitsuki, 176
Amida, 11
Anderson, Dr. W., 5, 54, 73 (n), 112
Ariyoshi, Kondō, 107, 138
Aston, W. G., 27 (n), 34 (n), 76

Bai-itsu, Yamamoto, 117
Baidō, 159
Bairei, Kōno, 199
Baitei, Kino, 92
Bakin's novels, 179
Bansui, Furuyama, 50
Bermond Catalogue, 58 (n), 61, 67 (n)
Binyon, Laurence, 7
Bokusen, Gekkōtei, 178, 186, 188
Bruyer, 84
Bumpō, Kawamura, 84, 103, 106, 185
Bunchō, Ippitsusai, 113, 119, 162
Bunchō, Tani, 117, 162 (n), 178
Bunchōmei, 70
Bunrei, Katō, 117
Bunrin, Shiokawa, 107, 113
Bunsen, Seki, 80
Bunshin, Tai, 70
Burty Catalogue, 84, 106 (n), 112 (n)
Busei, 119
Buson, 86, 96

Chikuden, Tanomura, 119
Chikudō, Kino, 103
Chikudō, Kishi, 78 (n), 103
Chikutō, Nakabayashi, 107
Chin Nampin, 85, 86, 89, 98, 102, 103, 111, 113
Chinchō, Hanegawa, 137, 138
Chinnen, Ōnishi, 106, 107
Chinzan, Tsubaki, 120
Chō-ō-rō, 158
Chōki, Miyagawa, 171
Chōki, Nagayoshi, 171
Chokunyu, 119
Choshoshi, Kinoshita, 88 (n)
Chōshun, Miyagawa, 160
Chūbei, Nonomura, 59
Crewdson Catalogue, 137 (n)

De Goncourt, 125, 170
Dengyō Daishi, 112 (n)
dhâranî, 4
Dickins, F. Victor, 180 (n), 185 (n), 186 (n)
Dillon, Edward, 43 (n), 73 (n), 96 (n)
Dōgen Zenshi, of Ehei-ji, 10
Donkō, 99
Donkyō, Ōhara, 95
Donshū, Ōhara, 95
Dōun, Ikenaga, 57
Duret Catalogue, 84, 125, 186 (n)

Eiken, Hokkyō, 8
Einō, Kanō, 77
Eishi, Chōbunsai, 171
Eishin, Kanō, 77
Eishō, 172
Eishun, 19
Eizan, Kitagawa, 172
Ekwa, 11
Enkō Daishi, 11

Fenollosa, E. F., 25, 44 (n), 70, 88, 98, 145, 167, 175
Ficke, A. D., 155
flower arrangement, 207
Fukū, 11
Fusanobu, Yamamoto, 145
Fushimi press, 28
Futō, Midzutani, 27
Fuyō, Suzuki, 168

Ganku, Utanosuke, 86, 102
Gembei, Iwasa, 43
Genki, Komai, 98
Gentai, Watanabe, 120
Genzaburō, Maki-eshi, 51
Geppo, 89
Gessai, Numada, 110
Gessen, Shaku, 97
Gesshō, Chō, 108
Gessō, Taniguchi, 98
Gillot Catalogue, 22, 75 (n), 78 (n), 141 (n)
Gitō, Shibata, 91, 95
Gombei, Yamaguchiya, 38
Goshun, Matsumura, 89, 90, 91
Gyōdai, 93
Gyokuzan, Ishida, 69, 151
Gyokuzan, Okada, 69

Hakuho, Ekigi, 176
Hakuyei, Keichūrō, 100
Hana, Orizomi, 51
Hanbei, Yoshida, 37, 39, 52, 53, 207, 211
Hanzan, Matsukara, 80
Happer Catalogue, 125, 126 (n), 198 (n)
Harumachi, Kitagawa, 171
Harunari, Kitagawa, 107
Harunobu, 143, 226
Harunobu II, 146
Hayashi Catalogue, 58, 75, 125, 136
Hi-Kangen, 103
Hidetada, Shōgun, 31
Hideyoshi, 40
Hiroshige, 81, 193, 194, 213
Hiroshige II and III, 194
Hōbun, Kikuchi, 202
Hōitsu, Sakai, 60, 61
Hokkei, 186, 188
Hoku-un, Taiga, 189
Hokuba, Teisai, 188
Hokuga, Hotei, 189
Hokuga, Katsushika, 189
Hokuju, Shōtei, 189
Hokumei, Togetsu, 79
Hokusai, 116, 174, 176, 213
Hokusen, 188
Hokusō-ō, 55
Hokuyei, Shunkōsai, 78
Hokyūshi, Katsushika, 30 (n)
Hōnen Shōnin, 11
Hōni, Tanaka, 61
Hōsaiyen, 111, 112 (n)
Hosogawa, Mr, 93
Hōyen, Nishiyama, 83, 95
Hozan, Tsuji, 93
Hyakunen, Suzuki, 199

Ichigyō, 11
Ichiyūsai, 146, 158
Ida-Ten, 16
I-fukyū, 88, 111
Iemitsu, Shōgun, 41
Ikkei, Hanabusa, 57
Ikkyō, Hanabusa, 57
Ikku, Jippensha, 76, 77
Ingen, 111
Ippō, Hanabusa, 56, 57
Ippō, Kawamura, 105
Ippō, Mori, 82, 105 (n)
Issai, Katsushika, 191
Isshū, 57

Itchō, Hanabusa, 43, 49, 55, 56, 96
Itteisei, Suisatei, 57
Itto, 176
Izumi-no-jō, Hayashi, 37

Jakuchū, Itō, 115
Jakusai, 19
Jihei, Sugimura, 52
Jingō, Queen, 40
Jōchō, 8
Jōhaku, Naemura, 52
Joly, H. L., 78, 167 (*n*)
Jōruri, 42
Jūroku-Zenjin, 16
Jūsui, Shimokōbe, 162

Kachōrō, 157
Kaempfer, Engelbert, 212
Kagen, Niwa, 116
Kaidō, 114
Kaisen, Oda, 95
Kanenari, Akatsuki, 79
Kangin, 208
Kanrin, Okada, 121
Kanyōsai, Takebe, 115
Kanzai, Mori, 82
Karamaro, 168
Kashū, Numada, 202
Katsumasa, Kishigawa, 134
Keibun, Matsumura, 91
Keiho, Takata, 77
Keinen, Imao, 200
Keisai Eisen, 173, 192
Keisai Masayoshi, 58, 105, 122, 126
Keisai, Ōnishi, 113, 121
Kengaku, 17
Kenzan, Ogata, 59, 61
Ki-itchi, 61
Ki-itsu, Suzuki, 61, 62
Kien, Yanagisawa, 113
Kihō, Kawamura, 105
Kikaku, Takarai, 57
Kikumaro, 172
Kinsui, 103
Kiun, Nakagawa, 34
Kiyoaki, 140
Kiyofusa, Torii, 140
Kiyoharu, Hishikawa, 138
Kiyoharu, Kondō, 79, 137, 138, 140
Kiyohide I and II, 141
Kiyohiro, 141
Kiyokuni, 141
Kiyomasa, 141
Kiyomasu, 137
Kiyomatsu, 141
Kiyomine, Torii, 140
Kiyomitsu, Torii, 138
Kiyomitsu III, 140
Kiyomoto, 141
Kiyonaga, 139, 149, 171, 226
Kiyonobu I, 63, 129, 136

Kiyosada, 141
Kiyosato, 141
Kiyoshige, 140
Kiyosomo, 140
Kiyotada, 137, 140
Kiyotoshi, 141
Kiyotsune, Torii, 141
Kiyoyasu, 141
Kō Sūkei, 57
Kō Sūkoku, 57
Kobayashi, Mr, 19
Kōbō, Daishi, 11, 39
Kōchō, Ueda, 94
Kōchōku, 208
Kochōrō, 157
Kōgaku, 106
Kōho (Kūchūsai), Honnami, 59
Kōitsu, 61
Kokan, Meiyo, 77
Kōkan, Shiba, 146
Kōkei, Ueda, 94
Kokkō, 70
Kongōchi, 11
Kōrin, Ogata, 44, 49, 58, 59, 96, 122, 174
Koryūsai, Isoda, 145, 149, 226
Kosa, Urakawa, 80
Kōsetsu, 38
Koshū, Hatta, 100
Kōson, Ikeda, 61
Kōyetsu, Honnami, 23, 24, 26, 36, 122
Kozan, Ogo, 21
Kuho, Yorita (?), 110
Kumashirō, Yūhi, 113
Kunimasa, Utagawa, 159
Kunimasa II, 159
Kuninao, Utagawa, 159
Kunisada, Utagawa, 157
Kuniyoshi, Utagawa, 158
Kunkei, Ichikawa, 108
Kurth, Dr Julius, 125, 170 (and *n*)
Kwaigetsudō, 136
Kwangetsu, Shitomi, 68, 81
Kwansetsu, Mr Hashimoto, 8
Kwannon, Jūichi-men, 10
Kwanzan, Mori, 82
Kwazan, Watanabe, 119
Kyōsai, Shōfu, 196
Kyūemon press, 32

Magosaburō, Nishimura, 143
Masafusa, Okumura Bunshi, 134
Masami, Hayano, 93
Masanobu, Kitao, 148, 149, 226
Masanobu, Okumura, 123, 160, 207,
Masanobu, Tsukioka, 57, 67, 68, 77
Masanojō, Hishikawa, 49

Masataka, Sugimura, 50
Masayoshi, Keisai; *v*. Keisai Masayoshi
Masazumi, Ryūsai, 176
Masunobu, Tanaka, 140
Matabei, Iwasa, 41, 44, 128
Matabei, Kanō, 43
Matora, Ōishi, 109
Matsunaga, Shorin, 50
meisho-ki, 31, 33
Michinobu, Ōōka, 73
Michiomi-no-Mikoto, 39
Midzutani Futo, 210
Minkō, Tachibana, 66
Minosuke, Takekawa, 30 (*n*)
Minwa, Aikawa, 107
Mitsuhiro, Karasumaru, 36
Mitsukuni, 19
Mitsunobu, Fujiwara, 60
Mitsunobu, Hasegawa, 72, 74
Mitsunobu, Kanō, 25, 73
Mitsuyoshi, Yoshida, 29
Moku-an, 111
Mōkyō, 115
Monju-Bosatsu, 15
Morikuni, Tachibana, 64, 209
Morinori, Sekichusai, 65
Morita, Mr, 5
Morofusa, 136
Morofusa, Furuyana, 49, 50
Morohira, Hishikawa, 50
Morohisa, 50
Moromasa, Furuyama, 50
Moromori, Hishikawa, 50
Moronaga, Hishikawa, 49
Moronobu, Harukawa, 34, 35, 36, 39, 50, 53, 55, 63
Moronobu, Hishikawa, 41
Moroshige, Hishikawa, 49, 50
Morotani, Furuyama, 50
Morotsugu, 50
Morrison, Arthur, 44 (*n*), 58 (*n*), 70, 89 (*n*), 112, 192 (*n*)
Myōchin, Mr T., 8, 9
Nambara, Keisho, 108
Nangaku, Watanabe, 104, 106
Nanko, Haruki, 121
Nanrei, Suzuki, 106
Nantei, Nishimura, 99
Naofusa, Terai, 67
Narihira, 25
Naruto, Seki, 168
Nichiren, 9
Nichōsai, 72, 75
Niho, Kawamura, 105
Niho, Mori, 82, 105 (*n*)
Nijō Castle, 43
Nikkō, 6
Nikkwa, Tanaka, 95
Nobutada, Prince Konoe (Sammyaku-in), 23

Ogata Kōrin, 55
Ohō, 61

General Index

Ōju, 97
Okakura Kakuzo, 36 (n)
Ōkyo, 86, 95, 106
Oōka, 30, 65
Orange-Thornicroft Catalogue, 144 (n)
ori-hon, 13, 14
Ōshin, 97
Ōyei Eijō, 180
Ōzui, Maryuama, 97

Petrucci, Raphael, 7

Raishō, Nakajima, 101
Rakuya, printing-house, 39
Rankō, Nakai, 81, 82
Renzan, Aoki, 102
Revon, M., 77 (n), 100 (n), 175 (n), 178 (n), 185 (n), 186 (n), 189
Rinsai, Okajima, 193
Rippo, 36 (n)
Rokubei, Yamamori, 34
Rosetsu, Nagasawa, 98
Rōshu, Hasegawa, 75
Roshū, Nagasawa, 99
Rosui, Tsuruoka, 99
Ryōi, Asai, 34
Ryūchi, 11
Ryūho, Hinaya, 30, 35, 36, 41
Ryūmō, 11
Ryūryūkyō, Genshi, 174
Ryūsai, Chikamatsu, 30 (n)
Ryūsen, Ishikawa, 52, 53
Ryūshū, Ishikawa, 54
Ryūsui, Katsuma, 57, 58, 124 (n)

Sabura, Kameya, 189
Sadahide, Gountei, 216
Sadahide, Gyokuransai, 195
Sadahiro, Utagawa, 81
Sadanobu, Hasegawa, 81
Sadatake, Takagi, 51, 211
Saikaku, Ihara, 52
Sankurō, Takai, 190
Santō Kyōden, 49 (n), 140, 149
Sanyō, 28
Sanyō, Genkitsu, 27
Satow (Sir Ernest), 5 (n), 7, 19, 20, 112
Sawaki, 57
Seidlitz, W. von, 50, 140 (n), 162, 168, 171 (n)
Seihō, Takeuchi, 202
Seisai, 176
Sekichūsai, 65
Sekisui, Watanabe, 121
Sekiyen, Toriyama, 166, 171, 175
Sekkei, 67
Sekkōsai, Kitao, 66
Sekkyō, Sawa, 176

Senryūsai, 146
Sessai (Shūyei), 67
Sesshōsai, Ichiō, 73
Settan, Hasegawa, 68, 119, 192
Settei, Tsukioka, 68, 77
Settei Tsukioka Masanobu, 67
Sexton, Major J. J. O'Brien, 141, 143, 170 (n)
Shaka-Sanzon, 16
Shen Nan-p'in, 86 (n); v. Chin Nampin
Shigeharu, Ryūtei, 81
Shigemasa, Kitao, 147, 150
Shigenaga, Nishimura, 134, 141, 142
Shigenobu, Ichiyusai (Hiroshige II), 195
Shigenobu, Kawashima, 54
Shigenobu, Nishimura, 141, 143, 213
Shigenobu, Yanagawa, 191
Shigeyoshi, 50
Shijō, 86
Shikimaro, 172
Shikō, Mikuma, 114
Shikuya, Aoki, 89
Shimbi Shoin, 198
Shimpei, Hishikawa, 50
Shimyōbō, Hōgen, 11
Shinkō, 14
Shinsai, Ryūryūkyo, 174
shōgyō, 28
Shōkōsai, Hanbei, 68
Shōkwadō, Shōjō, 23
Shōnen, Suzuki, 199
Shoshichi, Kondō, 63
Shōtei, Watanabe, 202
Shōtoku, Prince, 2, 13
Shōzaemon, Nakano, 32
Shū-Itsu, 61
Shugetsu, Tsutsumi, 176
Shūhō, Mori, 82
Shūki, Okamoto, 121
Shunboku, 30
Shunboku, Oōka, 70, 111
Shunchō, Katsukawa, 163
Shunchō, Kitagawa, 171
Shunchōsai, Takahara, 76
Shundō, Katsukawa, 166
Shungyōsai, Hayami, 69
Shunkei, Mori, 83
Shunkō, Katsukawa, 164
Shunkō (Shunsen, Katsukawa), 164
Shunkyō, Mori, 83
Shunman, 226
Shunman, Kubo, 165
Shunparō, 147
Shunrō, Katsukawa, 177
Shunsen, Kashōsai, 166
Shunsen, Oōka, 73
Shunshō, 78, 148, 150

Shunsui (Shunshō), Katsukawa, 160
Shuntei, Katsukawa, 166
Shunyei, Katsukawa, 163
Shunzan, Katsukawa, 166
Shūsui, Shimokōbe, 162
Shūyei, Tsutsumi, 67, 176
Shūzan, Yoshimura, 73 (and n), 113
Sō-Shigan, 111
Sō-Shikō, 121
Soan, Suminokura, 24, 26, 28, 36, 221
Soden-Sunbokushi, 52
Soken, Yamaguchi, 99
Sokuhi, 111
Sōkyū, Aoi, 78
Sonchō, Prince, 36
Sōri III, 175
Sōri, Hokusai, 177
Sōri, Tawaraya, 174
Sōrin II, 174
Sōshin, Kojima, 58
Sōtatsu, Tawaraya, 23, 58
Strange, Edward F., 30 (n), 41 (n), 78, 79, 94, 110, 112, 141, 144, 180 (n), 185 (and n), 194
Succo, Friedrich, 151
Sūgakudō, Shujin, 198
Sūgetsu, Hanabusa, 57
sugoroku, 213
Suiko, Empress, 2
Suiseki, Satō, 92, 93
Sukenari, Nishikawa, 133
Sukenobu, Nishikawa, 51, 53, 65, 129
Suketada, 132
Sukeyo, Yūkōken, 133
Sun K'o-hung, 70 (n)
Sūsetsu, 57
Sushi, 57

Tai Chin, 70 (n)
Taiga II, 89
Taigadō, Ikeno, 87, 96, 116
Taigaku, 188
Taisei, Shuchō, 136
Taishaku-ten, 9
Taito, 178
Taizan, Hine-No-, 199
Takamitsu, 19
Takekiyo, Kita, 119
Tanyū, Kanō, 23, 36, 41, 43, 117, 122
Tarōbei, Furuyama, 49
Tatsunobu, Kitao, 66
Tei Gyokusen, 70
Tenkai Jigen Daishi, 11
Tennen, Kwagwai, 212
Terushige, Katsukawa, 137
Tessai, Tomioka, 203
Ting Yū-ch'uan, 70 (n)
Toba Sōjō, 84

[243]

Tōkei, Niwa, 101, 126
Tōkei, Ogura, 89
Tokifus, Shimomura, 28
Tokinobu, Kitao, 67
Tomofusa, Hishikawa, 50
Tonan, Asai, 90
Tora, Gozen, 31
Tori, Busshi, 9
Tōrin III, 176
Tōrin, Sansei, 176
Tōrin, Tsutsumi, 174
Tōsen, 175
Tōshin, Tsutsumi, 176
Tōshun, 54
Tōun, Hasegawa, 43, 54
Toyo-akira, 168
Toyokuni, Utagawa, 78, 151, 156
Toyomaro, 172

Toyonobu, Ishikawa, 143, 167
Tsunenobu, 43
Tsutsumi, Tōrin, 175

Ukiyo-ye, 42, 78
Umpo, Kobayashi, 176
Umpō, Ōoka, 121, 193
Unsho, Ikeda, 199
Utamaro, Kitagawa, 125, 168

Wa-ō, Hishikawa Inshi, 50
Wēn Chēng-ming, 70 (n)
Wên-ti, 4

Yasunobu, Kanō, 54, 55
Yenchi, Toriyama, 168
Yōsai Kikuchi, 100

Yoritomo and Yoshitsune, 32
Yosetsu, 176
Yoshikawa Kobunkan, 198
Yoshikiyo, Baikwadō, 51
Yoshikiyo, Ōmori, 51, 55
Yoshitsune, 32, 42
Yoshiwara, 37, 43, 49
Yoshiyuki, Baikadō, 51
Yukai, 11
Yukihide, 19
Yukihiro, 19
Yukimaro, 172
Yūshō, Kaihoku, 23
Yutei, 96
Yūzen, Kaihoku, 51

Zemmui, 11
Zenzai-Dōji, 17
Zuga Keikokan, 198

INDEX OF TITLES OF BOOKS RECORDED

Adzuma Nishiki-ye Yurai, 30 (n)
Age Yamachi Date-no Tōfuya, 153
Ahō-Bukuro, 153
Aikei Sannen Daikoku Musozukin, 135
Akahon Mukashi Bakekurabe Hakone Shibai, 153
Aka-hon Sarukani Gasen, 142, 213
Akashi, 209
ake bono, 174
Ake Yasuke, 95
Aki Kengu-no-Minato-Sento Shinwa, 154
Aki-no-Hana Tori Shū, 183, 187
Aki-no-Yonaga Monogatari, 42, 49
Akuchi, 209
Ama-no-hashi-date, 48
Amaya-dori, 162
Amayo Sanbai-kigen, 53
Ameuri Dohei-den, 145
Amida-no-Munewarai, 137
Anata Yomo-no-Haru, 172, 184
Aoto Fuji Moryō-an, 182
Arashi Koroku Kwako Monogatari, 75
Arima Shigure, 35, 46
Arima Shokei-zu, 65
Ariwara Bunko, 91, 104, 224
Asa Kinhiro, 182
Asagao Hinrui Dzuko, 101
Asagawa Shū, 184
Asahina Karaku Asobi, 139
Asahina O Hige-no-Shiri, 181
Asahi-no-Kage, 187
Asahina Shima Meguri-noki, 156
Asaka-yama, 131
Asakanuma Go-nichi-no-Adachi, 156
Asakusa Reigen-ki, 69
Azuma Asobi, 143, 156, 169
Azuma Asobi Miyako-no-Teburi, 179, 181
Azuma Hyakunin Isshu Tamoza, 184
Azuma Karage, 148, 150
Azuma Kyōku Kyōka Bunko, 150
Azuma Monogatari, 33
Azuma Nishiki, 182, 203
Azuma-no-Mori, 143
Azuma-no-Nishiki Matsu-no-Kurai, 145
Azuma-no-Teburi, 106
Azuma Warawa, 156

Bai-Chiku-Ran-Kiku-Shifu, 40
Bai-oku Gwafu, 117
Bairei Gwafu, 199
Bairei Hyaku-chō Gwafu, 199
Baka-no-shiki Monogatari, 152
Bakemono Futsu Kagawari, 152
Bakemono Haru Asobi, 152
Bakemono Iwa-no-So, 181
Bakemono Kataki-Uchi, 76

Bakemono O Heiko, 153
Bakemono Tsure-dzure-gusa, 150
Bakemono Yofuke-no-Kaomise, 152
Bakemono Yutsu-nino Hachi-noki, 139
Bambutsu Dzue Issai Gwashiki, 191
Banashi Satoso-dachi Hanashi Suzume, 152
Banchu Maiko-no-Hana, 156
Bankai Setsu Yōshū, 138
Bankoku Fudoku, 147
Bankoku Ichiran Dzusetsu, 215
Bankoku Jimbutsu Dzue, 215
Bansen Dzue, 216
Banshō Shashin Zufu (?), 195
Bansho Sokugoshi, 60
Bansho Zukan, 60
Banshoku Dzuko, 183, 188
Banshū Meisho Junran Dzue, 81
Banzai Buyū E-Kagami, 73
Bashō Ichiren, 56
Beibei Kyōdan, 183
Bijin Edzukushi, 45, 47, 48
Bijin-gusa, 206
Bijin Imayō Nishiki, 159
Bijin Kasen-shū, 159, 193
Bijin Momo-chidori, 159
Bijin Ryōkwa Shū (Bijin Hishikwa Shū), 101
Bijin Shokunin Dzukushi, 159
Bimpoku Ryōdochi Unoki, 181
Bitchū Meisho-kō, 93
Biwako, 148
Biwa-no-Umi, 148
Bokusen Gwafu, 188
Bokusen Sogwa, 185
Bokuyo Kyōka-shū, 47
Bōsai, Kameda, 121
bōshimei, 3
Boso Ichiran Dzue, 184
Buchōho Sokuseki Ryōri, 180
Budo Iro Hakkei, 137
Buke Chōku Genchō, 134
Buke Hyakunin Isshu, 46
Buke Shōkugen-shō, 135
Bumbu Chiyo-no-Ume, 57
Bumbu Nido Mango Kusu, 172
Bumpō Gwafu, 104
Bumpō Kangwa, 103, 104, 186
Bumpō Sansui Gwafu, 104
Bumpō Sogwa, 103, 104, 185
Bunchō Gwafu, 118
Bunchō Sensei Gwafu, 162
Bunsho Monogatari, 48
Bunsho-no-Zōshi, 42, 48
bunjingwa, 86, 87, 90, 92, 96, 114, 116
Bunrei Gwafu, 82 (n)
Bunrei Gwasen, 117
Bunrin, Kwachō Gwafu, 199 (n)

JAPANESE BLOCK-PRINTING

Bunsen Gwafu, 81
Burlington Magazine, 141 (*n*), 143
Bushi-kun Oshiye, 48
Bussetsu Jō-Kyō, 22
Butai-no-Ōgi, 161
Buyū Homare-gusa, 51
Buyū Kongō Rishiki, 139
Buyū Nishiki-ni-Tamoto, 144
Buyū Sakigake Dzue, 193
Byōbu Kakemono E-Kagami, 44
Byōbu Kakemono Edzukushi, 47

Cha-no-yu, 52; *v.* also Tea Ceremony
Chaji Kagen Yakuwari Banzuki, 152
Chana-dehon Chaban Kyōgen, 152
Chi-ye-no-Umi, 133
Chibun Hinagata, 184
Chigusa-no-Iro, 170
Chiku Ryaku Setsu, 147
Chikuden Gwafu Kōken, 119
Chikūdo Kwachō Gwafu, 103
Chikūdo Gwafu, 103
Chikūdo Iboku, 103
Chikurin Gwafu, 77
Chikusai, 36
Chikusai Monogatari, 47
Chikutō Gwafu, 107
Chikutō Sanjin Jimbutsu, 107
Chikutō Sansui Gwakō, 107
Chikutō Shikunshi Gwafu, 107
Chinsetsu Yumihari Dzuki, 182
Chinzei Hachirō Tametomo, 46, 210
Chiomi-gusa, 203
Chitose-yama, 131
Chiwa-no-Ōyose, 50
Chiye Shidai Hakone Dzumi, 181
Chiyo-no-Aki, 163
Chiyo-no-Haru, 163
Chiyo-no-Matsu, 144
Chiyo-no-Tomozuro, 47, 49
Chiyomi-gusa, 131, 132
Chō Shishū Gwafu, 204
Chōgonka Zushō, 38
Chōjū Ryakugwa-shiki, 124
Chokei Zenta Heikei, 52
Chōnai-no-Nishiki, 14
Chōsei-den, 184
Chuko Asobi Shi Goto, 169
Chuko Ita Kobushi, 182
Chūkō Itako-bushi, 182
Chūkō Michi-no-Shiori, 94
Chūkyō, 183
Churin Gwafu, 202
Chūshin Meimei Gwaden, 195
Chūshingura, 181
Chūshingura Hyaku Ari Kyōka, 181
Chūshingura Jūni-dan, 184
Chūshingura O Dogu Shachide Makunashi, 153
Confucian Analects, 30

Dai Nippon Koku Kaibyaku Yuraiki, 159
Dai Shinpan Tenjin-ki, 213
Dai-fuku Setsuyō Mujin-Zosen, 80
Dai-itchi Otokuyō Monogatari, 153

Daihan Nehan Kyō Nyorai Seibon, 14
Daihannya Haramita, 15, 16
Daihōkō Engaku Shudari Ryōgi Kyō, 16
Daihōkōbutsu Kegon-Kyō, 20
Daimon Koshinden, 98
Daitsu Zenshi Nembutsu, 18 (*n*)
Daizen Sekai Kaki-no-Soto, 169
Danshōku Hiyoku-dori, 134
Daruma Chishōki, 139
Daruma Daitsū Hanami Mosen, 153
Dekisai Kyō Miyage, 35
Dempō Shōjū-ki, 14, 15
Denka Chawa, 189
Denshin Gwakyō, 183
Dōchu Gwafu, 183
Dōji Kyō, 69
Dōji ga Matsu, 141
Dōnō Mitsu-no-Oshie, 80
Dzue Tsumo-gusa, 143
Dzushiki Hinagata Maki-ye Daizen, 73

E-banashi Nichōsai, 75
Ebiki Setsu Yōshū, 162
Eda Sangojū, 53
edori-bon, 29, 31
Ega Yoshitsune Ezo Nishiki, 136
Ega-no-gusa, 133
Egata-Sennin Dzukushi, 48
Ehon Bunrei, 117
Ehon Chūsingura, 159
Ehon Hiken, 167
Ehon Hōkan, 54
Eigadane, 163
Eigyoku Gwakan, 110
Eihitsu Hyaku Gwa, 56
Eiju Hyakunin Isshu, 195
Eikyō-dai, 150
Eireki-Dai-Zassho, 110
Eiri Doke Hyakunin Isshu, 138
Eiri Genji Ko-Kagami, 39
Eiri Jōruri Shi, 210 (*n*)
Eiri Kamakura Monogatari, 45
Eiri Nichiren Ichidai-ki, 47
Eiri Sanchō Taiyu, 182
Eiri Shikata Banashi, 46
Eiri Waka-shū, 47
Eiri Zakura Hime, 155
Eirin Gwakyō, 56
Eisen Meisho, 193
Eishi Gwahen, 56
Eisho Hyaku-chō Gwafu, 202
Eiyū Dzue, 154
Eiyū Gwafu, 74
Eka-shū (Ehon Tani), 163
Ekuchiai Hisago-no-Tsuru, 80
Ena-oshi Gwafu, 100
Enroshi, 48
Enshū Gwafu, 118
Ezō-shi, 159

Fuchiuho Sokusetsu Ryōri, 181
Fude-no-Yama, 136
Fude Tsubana, 131
Fudzi-no-Yukari or *Eneshi*, 74

[246]

INDEX OF TITLES OF BOOKS RECORDED

Fuga Nana Komachi, 135
Fugaku Hyakkei, 179, 183
Fugyō (Fukei) Gwasō, 109
Fuji Asama Monogatari, 145
Fuji Bakawa, 192
Fuji Iro Itajime Soga, 153
Fujikawa Hyaku Shū, 47
Fuji Kenjutsu Azuma Kaidō Onna Kataki-uchi, 153
Fuji Mi Hyaku Dzue, 195
Fuji-no-Yukari, 133
Fuji-no-Yuki Mitsugi Soga, 138
Fujin Gwaso Shū, 187
Fujiwara Ishiyama Maru, 46
Fukami-gusa, 67
Fukusa Hinagata, 130
Fuken-zō, 169
Fuki-age, 210
Fukitaru Uraigao Kadomatsu, 181
Fuku Nezumi Shirio-no-Futozawa, 156
Fuku Zasshō, 48
Fuku Zenpen, 162
Fukugen Kōku-hon Kunshi Kōji, 18
Fukujō Sō, 136
Fukujū-ko, 165
Fukuju-Sō, 148
Fukujūkai Muryō Shinadama, 181
Fukujūsō, 73
Fukura Yanzei Yorimasa, 138
Fukuro-no-Kujō, 131
Fukushu Ehon Futabano Nishiki, 182
Fukutokū Ju Goshiki Megane, 153
Fukutoku Sanjūni-sō, 135
Fukuzensai Gwafu, 116
Fukuzensai Jibyō Rutoku-no-Zu, 116
Fukuzensai Seishi Roku, 116
Fumi Kotoba, 66
fumon-bon, 20
Furitsuke Miburi, 150
Furutezuma Shinadama Tebako, 153
Fūryū Bijin-no-gusa, 132
Fūryū Enshōku Maneyemon, 145
Fūryū Gojū-nin Isshu Izukawa Kyōka Guruna, 181
Fūryū Hinagata Taisei, 211
Fūryū Kagami Ga-Ike, 135
Fūryū Niwaka Tengu, 80
Fūryū Nishikiye Ise Monogatari, 162
Fūryū Tamare-gusa, 135
Fūryū Yamato Edzukushi, 132
Fūryū Yamato Edzukushi Nishikawa Fude-no-Yama, 132
Fusō Gwafu, 65
Fusō Gwajinden, 70 (n)
Fusō Gwasen-den, 56
Fusō Meisho Kyōka Shū, 187
Futaba Ao-ye, 68
Fuyo, Suzuki, 117
Fūzoku Ewaki, 56
Fūzoku Kagami Yama, 132
Fūzoku Ko Meidan, 158

Gakutei, Yashima, 190
Gakuya Dzue Shū, 68

Gantai, Uchida, 102
Gantori Chō, 168
Gasso, Seiyo, 101
Geki-jō Ehon, 138
Geki-jō Ikkwan Mushime-gana, 158
Gekkai Dzue, 164, 166
Gekkei-jō Gakuya Dzue, 68
Gempei Nagashira Ehon Musha Buroi, 184
Gempo Yokwa, 116
Gengora Bunna, 164
Gengwa-yen, 124
Genji Hyakunin Isshu, 135
Genji Hyakunin-Shu Nishiki Ori, 148
Genji Ike-bana-no-ki, 114
Genji Kumogakurei, 48
Genji Makura or *Wakan Murasaki*, 46
Genji Monogatari, 46, 193
Genji-no-Shirahata, 46
Genji-no-Yesho, 131
Genji Yamato E-Kagami, 48
Genkurō Gitsune Ikani Benkei Onmai Ninin, 153
Genpei-Hon, 32
Gensan Daishi Ōmi Kūji Shō, 134
Gentai Gwafu, 120
Gentai Sensei Gwafu, 120
Gesaku Gedai Kagami, 169
Gesaku Tempitsu Ahōraku, 152
Gessen Dzusan, 98
Gessen Gwafu, 98
Gesshō Sogwa, 109
Getcho, Yoshida, 94
Gikei-ki, 32, 33, 48
Gikun Daijo-bu, 75
Gin-seki, 169
Ginga (Mushi-no-Koye), 92
Ginka Zōshi, 79
Ginyei Bokuseki, 106
Go-Keibun Gwafu, 46
Go Mizu-no-o, Emperor and Empress, 31
Godai Soshi Meita Hatsu Uri, 158
Gofuku Moyō Utai Hinagata, 51
Gofuku Moyō Utai Hinagata, 211
Gogon Tōshi Gwafu, 40
Gohi-iki Tano San-shō, 152
Gojūni-ni-shū, 165
Gonshirō, Idzumiya, 112
Goreiko, 48
Goriyaku Moshigo-no-Yasa Otoko, 156
Goryū Ehon Zoroe, 131
Goseibei Shikimoku Esho, 50
Goseidai Setsuyō Gakumon, 154
Gosen Hyakunin Isshu, 127
Gosen Shunkyō Shū, 188, 191
Goshun Sansui Gwafu, 91
Gotai Fugu Dokukeshi Gusuri, 154
Gotai Wagō Monogatari, 154
Gototei, 157
Gozon-ji-no-Bakemono, 152
Gozonji no Yo-uchi soba, 152
Gunchō Gwayei, 56
Gunpō Goku-Hiden-sho, 113
Gusai Shachu Gwafu, 98
Gushi Rokutsū Hanryaku-no-Maki, 152, 163
Gwahin Hippo, 71

Gwahon Kōrin, 60
Gwaiban Yōbo Dzuga, 215
Gwako Hikketsu, 110
Gwakō Senran, 71
Gwanjaku Tesuisen Hanashi Tori, 158
Gwasan Tsune-no-Yama, 76
Gwashi Kwaiyō, 71
Gwashiki Shishō Shōken, 81
Gwashu Dzue, 56
Gwaten Tsūkō, 65
Gwato Hyakki Tsure-dzure Bukuro, 167
Gwato Hyak-kwachō, 65
Gwato Saiyudon, 147
Gwato Shuyei, 65
Gwato Zetsumyō, 56
Gyodai-fu, 58
Gyokai-fu, 124
Gyokushō, Kawabata, 201

Hachi Kamuri Monogatari, 153
Hachiyama Gwafu, 208
haikai, 57, 123
Haikai Futawarai, 74
Haikai Hyaku Gwasan, 98
Haikai Hyaku Shū, 187
Haikai Kato Manshu, 123
Haikai Ogura Hyaku Shū, 105
Haikai Sanjū Rok-kasen, 87
Haikai Yogoshi-no-Mono Kurabe, 145
Hairin Shōden, 56
Haiyū Kigen-den, 158
Haiyū Nigao (Sobo) Kagami, 155
Haiyū Sanjū-rok-kasen, 158
Hakkenden, 158, 195
Hakkenden Chūshingura, 158
Hako-iri Musume Menya Ningyō, 150, 152
Hakuso Sodan, 116
Hakuyen Ichidai-ki, 138
Hamochi Shōgun, 46
Hana Asobi, 145
Hana Katzura, 144
Hana Manabi, 80
Hana Momiji Futari Anko, 172
Hana Musubi Nishiki-ye Awase, 131, 132
Hana Shinoye Uta, 150
Hana-mono Guroi, 210
Hana-no-Kumo, 170
Hana-no-Midori, 143
Hana-no-Saka-dzuki, 49
Hana-no-Sugata Mi, 158
Hana-no-Yukari, 143
Hana-saki Jiji Tanoshima-no-Eiga, 135, 213
Hanabi-gusa, 37
Hanabusa Itchō Kyōgwa, 56
Hanami Banashi Shirame Seisuiki, 154
Hanashi O yedo-ye Nagasaki Karakowa Meisho, 152
Hanashi-zome Kuruwa-no-Iroage, 152
Hanaya, 209
Hankō, Okada, 121
Haregata, 203
Haru Bukuro, 141
Haru Toriki Chiye-no-Senkoku, 148
Haru-no-Nagami, 170

Haru-no-Nishiki, 144, 145
Haru-no-Tomo, 145
Haru-no-Uki, 145
Haru-no-Wo, 149, 166
Harunobu, Suzuki, 143
Harusame Goto, 50
Hashi Kuyō, 183
Hashu Gwafu, 40
Hasu-no-Ito Botan-no-Ayatsuri, 154
Hate Mezura Chiki Futatsu-no-Utsuwa, 172
Hatsu Kasei-me, 76
Hatsuharu-no-Iwai, 47
Hatsuka Amari ni Tsukai Hatashite Mibu Kyōgen, 152
Hatsuyume Fujimi Soga, 166
Haya-biki, 183
Hechima-no-kawa Uta Uta-bukuro, 152
Heigo Waka Ehon Kame-no-yama, 131
Heiji Monogatari, 29, 30, 46
Hen-gaku Kihan, 107
Henshi Gwafu, 120
Hi-Kangen Gwashiki, 185
Hi-Kangen Sansui Gwashiki, 103, 121
Hibiki-no-Taki, 133
Hidari Jingoro Yabuchi-no-Adachi, 156
Hidetada, 43
Higashiyama Meisho Dzue, 80
Higashi-yama San Buku Tsui, 213
Hiji Bukuro, 130
Hime Bunko, 67
Hime Haji Uri, 170
Hime-Kagami, 131, 137
Hime Tsubaki, 131
Hina Asobi-no-ki, 131
Hina Zuru Genji, 135
Hinagata, 203
Hinagata Akebonō Zakura, 65, 74, 211
Hinagata Gion Banashi, 211
Hinagata Mamiya-no-Yama, 59
Hinagata Miyako, Shōnin, 211
Hinagata Miyako-no-Haru, 211
Hinagata Some-iro-no-Yama, 59, 211
Hinagata Tsuru-no-Koye, 211
Hinagata Yado-no-Ume, 211
Hiroshige, 156
Hiroshige Gwafu, 195
Hishi Fukujin Daitsu-den, 150
Hissei Musha Suzuri, 71
Hitachibō Kaizon, 46
Hito Kyōgen Kitsune-no-Kaki-iri, 153
Hito Shirazu Omoi Fukai, 169
Hitogo Koro Kagami-no-Utsushi-ye, 150
Hitome Tamaboko, 35
Hitori Hokku, 185
Hitsusei Otogi Zōshi, 135
Hizakurige, 77
Hō-edzu Bisei, 159
Ho-un Kyō Shiga Shōnin, 203
Hōbun Gwafu, 202
Hōgen Ikusa Monogatari, 48
Hōgen Monogatari, 29, 30, 46
Hogwan Yoshino Gassen, 210
Hōitsu Shonin Shinseki Kagami, 61
Hōjō Go-Daiki, 45

INDEX OF TITLES OF BOOKS RECORDED

Hokke-giso (The), 16
Hokke-kyō, 7, 20
Hokke Reijoki, 35
Hokkei Mangwa, 187, 188
Hokkei Mangwa Shōhen, 187
Hokkei, Uwoya, 187
Hokkei Zuko, 187
hokku, 57
Hokku Chō, 57, 58
Hokku Shita-ye, 106
Hokuba Fude Shōkei Jo, 189
Hokuju Gwafu, 189
Hokuki Jūni-ji, 188
Hokumei Gwafu, 80
Hokumei Gwahin, 80
Hokumei, Kyūkyūshin, 79
Hokumei Mangwa, 80
Hokuri Yugi-jō, 135
Hokuri-no-Uta, 146
Hokusai Bijin Kyōka Shū, 184
Hokusai E-Kagami, 182
Hokusai Gwafu, 183, 184
Hokusai Gwakan, 182, 184
Hokusai Gwakyō, 182
Hokusai, Gwakyō Rōjin, 177
Hokusai Gwasetsu, 184
Hokusai Gwa-shiki, 184
Hokusai Jimbutsu Ehon, 184
Hokusai Mangwa Haya Shinan, 185
Hokusai Ringwa, 184
Hokusai Shashin, 226
Hokusai Shashin Gwafu, 180, 182
Hokusai Sogwa, 183
Hoku-un Mangwa, 189
Hokuyetsu Ki-den, 182
Homare-no-Taki, 133
Honchō Buke Ō Keizu, 42, 49
Honchō Gwarin, 51
Honchō Gwayei, 118
Honchō Gwayen, 65
Honchō Kokon Meijin, 25
Honchō Meika Gwafu, 101
Honchō Meisho Arigataki Tsuno Ichiji, 180
Honchō Ō-in Hiji, 53
Honchō Retsujo-den, 40
Hōnen Gōkoku Matsuri, 196
Hōnen Shōnin Shijūhachi-kwan-den, 77
Honen Uji Hotarubi, 181
Ho-ru Shū, 92
Hōrai-zan, 93
Hoshu-roku, 154
Hōsō Anzen Kodomo Karuwaza, 81
Hōzuki Chōchin Oshiye-no-Chikamichi, 154
Hyakki yagyō Shū, 167
Hyaku Bushō-den, 39
Hyaku Gaden, 196
Hyaku Kiya-kyō, 191
Hyaku Monogatari, 46
Hyaku Yagyō, 167
Hyaku-Shū Empyō, 54
Hyakugwa Haya Oshiye, 182
Hyakuman-tō, 4
Hyakunun Ikkū, 135
Hyakunin Isshu, 27, 124, 162, 164

Hyakunin Isshu Issekwa, 110
Hyakunun Isshu Jō-kun Shō, 194
Hyakunin Isshu Kyōka, 191
Hyakunin Isshu Kokon Kyōka Bukuro, 150
Hyakunin Isshu Odoke Kōshaku, 153
Hyakunin Isshu Sugata, 48
Hyakunin Isshu Ubagawa Yetoki, 184
Hyakunin Isshu Zō San Shō, 47
Hyakunin Jorō, 47
Hyakunin Jorō Shina Sadame, 130, 132
Hyakurin, 174
Hyakushō-den, 39
Hyōchu Sono-no-Yuki
Hyōkakku Kisho-no-dzu, 118
Hyōsui Kigwa, 183

Ibuki Monogatari, 79
Ibukiyama, 161
I-fukyū Gwafu, 88, 111 (and n)
Ichirō Gwafu, 190
Ichiryūsai, 146
Ichiyū Gwafu, 158
Ichiyūsai Gwafu, 158
Ichiyūsai Mangwa, 159
Idzumo Fudoki, 34
Ifu Shashin Kagami, 216
Igyō Sennin Ehon, 48
Iihitsu Gwafu, 185
Ike-no-Kawa den, 132
Ikebana Hiden Senden Sho, 207
Ikokubari Chiye Chiye-no-Tsuyadashi, 152
Ikyoku Kwachō Shū, 188
Ikyoku Tomawari Matsu, 76
Imagawa Jō, 110
Imagawa Monogatari, 46
Ima-mukashi Engi-no-Hakuryò, 152
Imamu-kachi Bakemono Oyadama, 139
Imayō Genji, 121
Imayō Kushi Kogai Hinagata, 183
Imayō Makura Byōbu, 48
Imayō Shokunin Dzukushi
Imayō Sugata, 154
Imayō Yoshiwara Makura, 48
Imoto wa Shinobu Go Taihei-ki Shira-ishi Banashi, 153
In-nyō Imoseyama, 182
Inaka Genji, 158
Inaki, 182
Ino Hagaki, 52
Intoku Ryōhō Yoikoto Bakari, 152
Inyō Hakke-no-Ho, 205
Ippai Kigen, 155
Ippitsu Gwafu, 183, 189
Iro Arasoi, 66
Iro Uta Eshō, 162
Iro Zōshi, 48
Iroha Uta, 145, 161
Irohata Yotsuya Kwaidan, 78
Isa-na-gusa, 68
Isa-oshi Dori, 170
Isaoshi-no-gusa, 119
Ise Monogatari, 22, 25, 33, 37, 39, 46, 52, 131, 162, 226

JAPANESE BLOCK-PRINTING

Ise Sangu Meisho Dzue, 68
Ishikawa Mimasu Haikai, 141
Iso-ho Monogatari, 45
Issai Gwa-shiki, 191
Itako Zekku Shū, 181
Itchō Gwafu, 56
Ito Guruma Tengu Baikai, 166
Ito Sakura Honchō Monzui, 140
Itsukushima Dzue, 110
Itsukushima Ema-Kagami, 110
Iwaikushi Kumeno-no-Adachi, 155
Iwaki Edzukushi, 45, 47
Izumi Meisho Dzue, 76

Jakuchū Gwafu, 116
Jakuchū Gwajō, 116
Jenaku Jimi Shikata Dōjō-ji, 135
Jichōsai, 75 (n)
Jido Bunchu Chikyō-kun, 181
Jihen, 56
Jikishikō, 65
Jikun Kaga-ye-no-Tato-ye, 140
Jimbutsu Gwayen, 109
Jimbutsu Kuse Dzukushi, 77
Jimbutsu Ryakugwa-shiki, 123, 124
Jimbutsu Sogwa, 77
Jimmu Tennō, 210
Jingō Kōgō Sankan Tai-ji, 184
Jin-ji Andon, 110, 193
Jinji Andon, 159
Jinkō-ki, 29, 111
Jinkōki Nishiki Mutshi, 181
Jinkōki Urai Sango-Jūgo Kangirimono Sanyo, 181
Jinrin Kimmō Dzue, 51
Jinshin Ryōmen-zuri, 154
Jishei (?) Banashi, 76
Jiyo Shū, 206
Jizan Kashū, 47
Jizi Hiken, 167
Jizō-Kyō, 20
Jo-chū Fūzoku Tsuya Kagami, 131
Jō-yuishiki-ron, 12
Jōjō Go-no-jō, 47
Jokiwa-no-Matsu, 47
Jokyō Hiden, 32, 45
Jōruri ballads, 75
Jōruri-bon, 27, 28, 33, 42, 44, 45, 90, 209
Jōruri Hime Monogatari, 27
Jōruri Jūni-dan Sōshi, 27
Jōruri Naga-uta, 139
Jōruri Zekku, 183, 184
Joyō Bunshō, 131
Joyō Hana-no-Yu, 133
Jūben Jūgi, 88
Jubutsu Mondō, 46
Juga, 56
Jūgo Hiden Nanmai Shō, 135
Jūgyū-dzu, 17, 18 (n)
Jūhachi Rakan Zusan, 38
Juhen, 56
Jūjō Genji, 36
Jūni Fuji, 202
Jūni Kagura Osana Karuwaza, 148

Jūni Kwagetsu, 135
Jūni-dan, 27
Jūni-gatsu-no Shinasadame, 47
Jūnichi Daitsu Banashi, 163
Jūnishi-Chō, 202
Jūroku Rakan Shōzō, 38
Jūsan-ban Kyōka Awase, 156
Jūshichi-Kem-pō, 13

Ka-an Gwafu, 119
Kabuki Nendai-ki, 166
Kaga-bike, 56
Kagami Hyaku-shū, 131, 133
Kagamiyama Homare-no-Adachi, 155
Kai Awase Hamaguri Genji Kasen Gai, 135
Kaidan Kihachi Jō, 154
Kaidō Kyōka Awase, 106
Kaidō Sogwa, 104, 106
Kaigwai Jimbutsu Shoden, 215
Kaigwai Shinwa Shuci, 215
Kaikaku Kongen Roku, 95
Kaiko Yachinai-gusa, 148, 161
Kaikwan Ryōki Kyōka Kuden, 158
Kaisaku Dzue, 115
Kaisei Zōho Nippon Kanoka, 35, 54
Kaishiyen Gwafu, 111
Kaitaro, 127
Kaiyo Hiso, 168
Kaji-no-ha, 52
Kajiwara Saiken Nido-no-ō, 169
Kakuchū Empu, 78
Kakuchū Kidan, 66
Kakuzen Zuko, 193
Kamada Shōgun Kanryaku-no-Maki, 181
Kamakura Monogatari, 34
Kamakura Tonda-Ike, 153
Kamakura Tsu Shin-den, 180
Kamigata Koi Shugyō, 158
Kamikuzu Minu-ye Banashi, 139
Kamo-no-Chōmei Hōjōki-sho, 45
Kamuri Kotoba Nanatsume Jūni Hishi-ki, 169
Kana Tazuna Chūshingura, 148
Kana-dehon Chūshingura, 168
Kana-dehon Gojitsu no Bunko, 182
Kana-dehon Mune-no-Kagami, 148
Kane-no-Naruki Tsugiho-no-Kodakara, 153
Kane-no-Waraji, 172
Kangan, Kitayama, 117
Kangwa Shinan, 104, 115
Kangwa Shinan Susumi-gusa, 115
Kanko Shogwa, 109
Kanoko Mochi, 191
Kanrin Gwafu, 121
Kansai Shūbi Gwafu, 83
Kan-so Gundan, 69, 184
Kanto Nagori-no-Tamoto, 134
Kanyōsai Gwafu, 115
Karaku Ichiran Dzue, 123 (n)
Karei-zaki Hanagawa Monogatari, 155
Kareki ni Hana Sakusha-no-Seigwan, 152
Karu-kuchi Eho Nadzo, 133
Kasen Buke Zoroi, 195
Kasen Kashū, 119
Kasen Kimmō-ino Hana, 161

[250]

INDEX OF TITLES OF BOOKS RECORDED

Kasen Shū, 172
Kashū Kwachō Shū, 202
Kasuga Taigū Gosairei Ryakkei, 214
Kasuga-ban, 12
Kataki-uchi Asahina Chaban Soga, 152
Kataki-uchi Fuse Rishōki, 154
Kataki-uchi Gijo-no-Hanabusa, 153
Kataki-uchi Hari-no-Tamakura, 156
Kataki-uchi Hasu Wakaba, 156
Kataki-uchi Igo-ni-Jikan, 153
Kataki-uchi Iwate-no-Tsutsuji, 156
Kataki-uchi Katami-no-Osafune, 155
Kataki-uchi Kinshi-no-Tsumeni, 156
Kataki-uchi Kinuta-no-Uchita, 156
Kataki-uchi Mie Chukotei, 155, 156
Katoki-uchi Migawari Myōgo, 182
Kataki-uchi Mukui-no-Ja-yanagi, 182
Kataki-uchi Okitsu Shiranami, 154
Kataki-uchi Ryūka Teifu, 153
Kataki-uchi Sembon Zakura, 156
Kataki-uchi Sesshu Gappo-no-Tsuji, 154
Kataki-uchi Shima Meguri Kosuke-no-Fune, 156
Kataki-uchi Shindai Rimego, 182
Kataki-uchi Ubasutei-Yama, 153
Kataki-uchi Ume-no-Tsugiho, 156
Kataki-uchi Urami Kusunoha, 184
Katsura Kasane, 75
Katsushige, 43
Katsushika Buroi, 184
Katsushika Monogatari, 158
Katsushika Shin Hinagata, 183
Kawachi Meisho Dzue, 101
Kawachi Meisho Kagami, 35
Kawa-no-gusa, 131, 132
Kazu Daizen, 47
Keibun Gwafu, 91
Keihitsu Toba Guruma, 71, 72
Keiho Gwafu, 77
Keijō Gwayen, 90, 91, 92, 105, 126, 147
Keika Zu-an, 203
Keinen Kwachō Gafu, 20
Keinen Kwachō Gwakan, 201
Keinen Shū Gwajo, 201
Keisai Gwafu, 193
Keisai Ryakugwa-shiki, 124
Keisai Sogwa, 124
Keisai Ukiyo Gwafu, 193
Kekkei Ryakugwa-shiki, 150
Kenshi Gwayen, 115
Kenzan Gwafu, 61
Kenzan Iboku, 59 (n)
Keshi-iri Kotobu-ki Takiwa Chūshingura, 152
ki-byōshi, 77, 163, 172, 179
Kihō Gwafu, 105
Kikido-kuri, 104
Kikuchi Yōsai Gwafu, 101
Kimbei-bai, 158
Kimigata-te Makura, 169
Kimmō Dzue, 150
Kimono Ehon Edzukushi, 48
Kimono-no-Moyō, 49
Kimpayen Gwafu, 104, 105
Kimpei Sennin-giri, 210

Kimpira-bon, 42
Kimpira Hōmon-Arasoi, 46, 210
Kinaga Gwafu, 127
Kinchō Gwafu, 106
Kinichō, 135
Kinka Shū, 195
Kinkin Sekkai Sakate Iru Takara-no-Yama buki, 153
Kinsei Daizen, 48
Kinsei Shidari Ika Gwafu, 204
Kinsei-kiseki-kō, 49 (n), 119
Kinsetsu Bishonen Roku, 187
Kintai Gwaso, 193
Kishi Empu, 78
Kishi-ki Dzue, 206
Kiso-Kaidō Futari Yoshinaka, 141
Kiyo-ye Sakura, 135
Kiyomasa Shinden-ki, 69
Kizuden-ki Kasen Kinkyō Shō, 47
Ko Atsumori, 137
Ko-Dakara Yama, 161
Ko-no-Kaori, 48
Kobi-no-Tsubo, 161
Kōbō Daishi Goden-ki, 39
Kōbō Daishi Gyōjō-ki, 20
Kōbō Daishi-ki, 135
Kobu-kuyo Kasen, 196
Kochi-ho-in, 213
Kōchō Gwafu, 94, 110
Kōchō Gwafu Nihen, 94
Kōchō Ryakugwa, 94
Kodakara Yama, 193, 213
Kodomo Asobi, 166
Kofū-tōfū Kakiwake Edzukushi, 47
Kogane-no-Suzu Sachibana Sōshi, 193
Kogetsu-bo, 169
Kogwa-Jō, 118
Kogwa Yōran, 117
Kohaku Genji Monogatari, 134
Kohan Chishi Kaidai, 35 (n)
Kohitsu Gwato-Jūi, 51
Kokon Yakusha Monogatari, 47
Koi Ebi Kata, 170
Koi-no-Iki Utsushi, 48
Koi-no-Mutsugoto Shijū-Hatte, 47
Koi-no-Tanoshimi, 47
Koi-no-Uwamori, 46
Koi-no-Yumihari Dzuki, 141
Koi-nyobō Somewake Chaban, 152
Koi-o-Tsuribari Narahira, 46
Kojidan, 65
Kokinran, 142
Kokinshū, 156
Kokkwa Magazine, 171 (n)
Kokon Gwasō, 114
Kokonshi Shibai Hyakunin Isshu, 137
Kokka Manyoki, 35
Kokkei Mangwa, 79
Kokkei Shiro-to Shibai, 154
Kōko-Shōkei Ichiran, 104
Kokon Bushidō Edzukushi, 48
Kokon Edzukushi, 47
Kokon Gwafu, 40
Kokon Gwasō Kōhen, 114

[251]

JAPANESE BLOCK-PRINTING

Kokon Kōsaku, 56
Kokon Rikkwa Daizen, 207
Kokon Yakusha Monogatari, 63
Kokusenya Senri-no-Hayashi Ninomaki, 138
Kokyō Tohon-no-Negoto, 153
Kokyō-ga Eiri-no-Yedo Banashi, 35
Komaga-dake, 148
Komai-gusa Taihei Banashi, 163
Komatsu Hara, 132
Komeiri Kiri-no-Nagamochi, 153
Kōmin Hinagata, 190
Komochi Nezumi Hana-no-Yama-uba, 79
Komparu Tokuwaka Inkyo, 154
Kompira Sankei Meisho Dzue, 80
Kōmyō Futaba-gusa, 67
Konden Sumo Daizen, 163
Kondo wa Oni-Musoku, 153
Konjaku Hyakki Shū, 167
Konjaku Zoku Hyakki Shū, 167
Konshi-jo-no-Roku, 214
Konzatsu Yamato Sōgwa, 146
Kore-wa Kuno Komachi Baka-no-Isaoshi, 163
Kōrin Ehon Michi Shirube, 59
Kōrin Gwafu, 59
Kōrin Gwashiki, 60, 107
Kōrin Hinagata Suso Moyō, 59, 211
Kōrin Hyaku Dzu, 59
Kōrin Hyaku Dzu Kōhen, 60
Kōrin Jūni Shu, 61
Kōrin Mangwa, 60
Korobanu-Saki-no-Dzue, 61, 69
Kōron Gwafu, 60
Kōshoko Ichidai Otoko, 48
Kōshoku Edzukushi, 53
Kōshoku Gonin Onna, 53
Kōshoku Hitomoto Zusuki, 49
Kōshoku Ise Monogatari, 53
Kōshoku Kimmō Dzue, 53
Kōshoku Tamago Zake, 135
Kōshoku Yedo Murasaki, 49
Kōshoku Yoshiwara Harugoma, 47
Koshū Hwafu, 100
Kōshū Nijūshi Shō Dzue, 71
Kōso Gwafu, 193
Kotei Zeikyō, 205
Kotoba-no-Hana, 169
Kotori Dzukai, 75
Kotori-no-Negura, 202
Kotowaza-gusa, 143, 144
Kotsu Dzue, 75
Kotsu Jikai, 75
Kottō Shū, 119, 150
Kowairo Haya Gwaten, 158
Ko Wo Umu Kogane Shichiya-no-Iwai, 154
Kōyetsu-bon, 24, 25, 221, 226
Kōyetsū-Saga-bon, 25
kubari-hon, 57, 61, 95, 106, 114, 118, 123, 124, 127, 188
Kukuri-Some, 153
Kumano-no-Honji, 31, 33, 34
Kumeido Seki, 38
Kumempeki Daruma Daitsū, 122
Kuniyoshi Zatsuga, 158
Kunizu-kushi Yamato-no-Homare, 155

Kurabe Goshi Nari Hiragata, 154
Kurai Yama Homare-no-Yoko Tsuna, 166
Kurote Hachijō Mukashi Ryōri Tanuki-no-Suimono, 153
Kurote Hachijō Tanuki-no-Kinshōsui, 153
Kurui Tsuki Machi, 169
Kusa (Sōkin) Nishiki, 66
Kusa-kimo Nabiku Hiri Kuraye, 181
Kusabana Koromono, 175
Kusumoki Nidai Gunki, 69
Kuwateki Fune Ikuse, 210
Kwa Ryakugwa-shiki, 124
Kwachō, 202
Kwachō Dzue, 187
Kwachō Gwaden, 148, 188
Kwachō Gwafu, 119, 184
Kwachō Kagami, 123
Kwachō Koretsu, 116
Kwachō Sansui Dzushiki, 191
Kwachō Sansui Hokuju Gwafu, 189
Kwachō Sansui Mangwa Hyabiki, 191
Kwachō Shashin Dzue, 148
Kwachō-jo, 202
Kwafuku Nimpitsu, 105
Kwaidan Hyaku Dzue, 164
Kwaidan Kanao Kikori, 153
Kwaidan Momonji-ye, 150
Kwaitsu Shōko, 215
Kwaiyo Hinagata, 211
Kwannon Gyō Dzue, 79
Kwanyei Gyōko-ki, 31
Kwanyei Gyoku-ki, 213
Kwanyei-bon, 29
Kwaraku Meisho Dzue, 80
Kwaraku Saiken Dzu, 54, 55
Kwashi Bukuro, 109
Kwazan Gwafu, 120
Kwazan Gwafu Issō Hyaku-tai, 120
Kyō Gwayen, 99, 188
Kyō Habutae, 35
Kyō Kanoko Musume Dojō Jiru, 152
Kyō Miyage, 80
Kyō Shimabara Yūjo Ningyō Tsukai, 51, 55
Kyō Suzume, 34
Kyō Warabe, 34, 37, 45, 224
Kyō Warabe Atooi, 34, 46
kyō-mon, 10, 11, 13
Kyō-no-Mizu Fukuo Chijime, 162
Kyō-Ōsaka Yarō Sekizumo, 53, 64
Kyōchū-no-Yama, 121 (n)
Kyōchūzan, 121
Kyōgen Dzukushi, 46
Kyōgen-ki, 46, 63
Kyōgu Jūnen Ashinkiro, 181
Kyōhō Hinagata, 130, 211
Kyōka Awase Ryōgan Dzue, 188
Kyōka Banka Shū, 187, 188
Kyōka Cha-kisai Kashū, 195
Kyōka Dōchu Gwafu, 187
Kyōka Dzushiki, 159
Kyōka Ehon Ama-no-gawa, 148, 169
Kyōka Ehon Chūshingura Kagami, 174
Kyōka Ehon Shokunin Kagami, 174
Kyōka Fusō Meisho Dzue, 101

[252]

INDEX OF TITLES OF BOOKS RECORDED

Kyōka Gojū-nin Isshu, 150, 187, 192
Kyōka Guruma Hyaku Shū, 193
Kyōka Gwaso Burui, 150
Kyōka Hidare Domoye, 165
Kyōka Hidare Domoye Kōhen, 165
Kyōka Hyakki Yakyō, 101
Kyōka Hyakunin Isshu, 148, 194
Kyōka Imayō Genji, 192
Kyōka Isso-no-Kami (Kyōka Gojū-nin Isshu), 174
Kyōka Kasen Hyaku Shū, 189
Kyōka Keika Shū, 187
Kyōka Kijin-den, 190
Kyōka Kinyō Shū, 124
Kyōka Koto Meisho Dzue, 195
Kyōka Kotobana Takimizu, 165
Kyōka Kotori Zugai, 105
Kyōka Manzai-shū, 143
Kyōka Meisho Dzue, 192
Kyōka Meishu Gwaso Shū, 191
Kyōka Momo-chidori, 195
Kyōka Mutsu Tamagawa, 188
Kyōka Naniwa Meisho Shū, 80
Kyōka Nihon (Nippon Fūdoki), 191
Kyōka Rantei Jo, 101
Kyōka Ressen Gwaso Shū, 184, 189
Kyōka Riren Gwafu, 100
Kyōka Ryakugwa Sanjin Rok-kasen, 191
Kyōka Sanjū-roku Shū, 187, 194
Kyōka-Shū, 175
Kyōka Shukin Shū, 192
Kyōka Sokon Shū, 195
Kyōka Suikoden, 190
Kyōka Tabi Makura, 47
Kyōka Tagoto-no-Hana, 126
Kyōka Tagoto-no-hana, 101
Kyōka Tōkaidō Dōchu Gwafu, 189
Kyōka Tōto Jūni Kei, 187
Kyōka Tsuki-no-Kage, 75
Kyōka Yagyō Hyaku-dai, 80
Kyōka Yama Mata Yama, 181
Kyōka Yamato Jimbutsu, 194
Kyōka Yedo Meisho Torikumi, 122
Kyokun Kokon Michi Shirube, 122
Kyōsai Dongwa, 196
Kyōsai Gwaden, 196
Kyōsai Gwafu, 196
Kyōsai Mangwa, 196
Kyōsai Ryakugwa, 196
Kyōsai Suigwa, 196
Kyōtarō, 134
Kyōtei Kun, 162
Kyōwa Shiri Saguri-go-yō-jin, 152
Kyōyei Miyako Meibutsu Shū, 101
Kyūhōdō Gwafu, 95
Kyūrō Gwafu, 92

Langkāvātāra Sutra, 15 (n)
Ling Mao Hua Hui, 112
Mae-mae Taiheki, 181
Mahāparinirvāna Sūtra, 14 (n)
Makura Bunko, 193
Makura Daizen, 47
Mamei Maki Otoko, 135

Manabe Tsu, 170
Mangwa, 186; 178, 180, 185, 188
Mangwa Hyaku Jō, 10
Manwō Sohitsu Gwafu, 184
Manzai Musha E-Kagami, 76
Maru Kagami (Impon), 138
Matsu Kagami, 131
Matekoi Mochiwa-Mochiwa, 152
Masu Kagami, 170
Matsu-no-Shirabe, 148, 170, 171
Matsuo Monogatari, 182
Matsura Sayohime Sekikon-roku, 156
Matsuri-no-ye, 136
Meien Shisen Shū, 50
Meihitsu Gwafu, 81
Meiji Gwafu, 204
Meiji Shinsen Shogwa Jin-me, 203
Meiji Shogwa-jō, 203
Meika Gwafu, 78, 82, 91, 101, 126, 226
Meika Hyakusan Gwafu, 203
Meika Jūni Shū, 71
Meika Shogwa Zuroku, 202
Meikō Sempu, 40
Meiku Shōkei, 164
Meisho Hoku Shū, 193
Meisho Kagami, 190
Meisho Makkei, 158
Meisho Miyako-dori, 35
Meishu Kyōka Shū, 192
Meisū Gwafu, 121
Meitoku Saya, 108
Meizan Shokei Shinzu, 184
Mibu Odori Gesaku-no-Memoku, 152
Michi Shirube, 60
Michi-no-Shiori, 192
Michinoku Matsushima Hakkei, 123
Michiyuki Koi-no-Futosao, 170
Mikawa, 133
Miken Jaku Sanin Nawa Ye-hi, 148
Mikenjyaku, 49
Mime Fumidari Miyako-no-Nishiki, 162
Mina Mezame, 169
Mina-no-gawa, 133
Minari Daitsu-jin Ryaku Yenge, 168
Minchō Seidō Gwayen, 30, 70, 71, 111
Minchō Shiken, 71
Mino Kagami, 46
Mino Kōhen Kane-no-Naruki Tsugiho-no kodakara, 154
Minobu Kagami, 48
Minobu-san Kongen-ki, 35
Misao, 45
Misao-gusa, 145
Mitata Chūshingura, 181
Mitsu-no-Asa, 139
Mitsunobu Gwafu, 74
Mitsuwa-gusa, 131, 132
Miura Monogatari, 42, 45
Miwaka, 74
Miyagi-nō, 48
Miyako Fūzoku Keshō-den, 69
Miyako Meisho Dzue, 76
Miyako Rinsen Dzue, 105
Miyako Zōshi, 131

JAPANESE BLOCK-PRINTING

Miyako-no-Nishiki, 123
Miyamoto Mansoshi, 158
Miyatogawa Monogatari, 48
Miyo-no-Haru, 133
Miyōshi Gun-ki, 135
Mizu-ka Sora, 75
Mohitsugwa Hitori Keiko, 202
Mokuhon Kwachō-fu, 40
Mōkyō Wakan Zatsuga, 115
Momiji Gari, 210
Momiji-no-Hashi, 163
Momo-chidori, 126
Momo-chidori Kyōka Awase, 169
Momonga Ima-Kwaiden, 172
Momotarō Oeyama-iri, 153
Momotogura Yamiyo-no-Shichiyaku, 148
Momoyo-gusa, 136
Mongaku Ichidai-ki, 152
Monomo-dori Hyakunin Isshu, 140
Moromatsu, 33
Moshiwo-gusa, 49
Moyō-ye, 203
Mukashi Banashi Chōshū no-Hama, 152
Mukashi Mukashi Momotarō Hōtan Unsetsu, 181
Muku Jōkō Dhâranî Kyō, 4
Murasaki-gusa, 191
Musashi Abumi, 37, 183
Musashi Yoroi, 183
Musashi-no-Tsuki, 136
Musha Byōshi Yoseki, 135
Musha Ehon Kongō Rikishi, 135
Musha Ehon Tsunamono Yushi-kana Meishi, 135
Musha Ehon Yedo Shisōkon, 135
Musha Tadzuna, 67
Musha Tazuma, 143
Musha Zakura, 48
Mushi Bukuro, 139
Mushi Erabe, 169
Musō Byōye Kōchō Monogatari, 156
Musume Kataki-uchi Ōgi-no-Gimmen, 154
Muzōsa Yukinari Zōshi, 154
Myōhō Renge Kyō, 16

Naga Uta, 141
Naga-Uta Futatsu Mojiono-no-Tsuno Moji, 153
Naga-uta Jōruri Shū, 139
Naga-uta-Shū, 139
Nagara Chōja Uguisu-dzuke, 69
Nagasaki Kunmonshi, 147
Nagoya Edzukushi, 48
Naka-no-Yume, 81
Nakamura Utaemon Jūni-baki Shosagoto, 164
Nakatomi Ō Harai Dzue, 80
Nami-no-Sachi, 122
Nampin, Sensei Gwafu, 103
Naniwa Meisho, 80
Naniwa Meisho Ashiwake-bune, 35
Naniwa Suzume, 35
Naniwa Suzume Atoöi, 35
Naniwa-no-Kagami, 76
Nanka Koki, 182
Nanko Seichiu Gwaden, 166
Nankō-ki, 69

Nannyō Kimmō Dzue, 47
Nantei, 84
Nantei Gwafu, 99
Nantei Gwafu Kohen, 99
Nanto Meisho Dzue, 65
Nanto Meisho Shū, 35, 53
Nara Meisho-ya E-zakura, 35
Nara Meisho Yae Zakura, 46
Narihira Honchō Noshinobu, 48
Narumi-gata, 164
Nasake-no-Uwamori, 46
Nasake-no-Yujō, 47
Nasu-no funa-Ikon, 46
Natsu Matsuri Dan-shichijima, 152
Nazame-gusa, 131
Nenjū Gyōji Taisei, 69
Nenshi, 77
Nezumi-no-ko konrei-jinkōki, 153
Ni-ichi Tensaku-no-Go, 152
Nichi Tensaku Nishinga Isshu, 181
Nichiren Shōnin Chūgwasen, 32
Nichiren Shōnin Ichidai-Dzue, 191
Nigao Ehon Haiyū Gaku Shitsu Tsū, 154, 159
Nihon Bushi Kagami, 53
Nihon Genji Kagami, 158
Nihon Meibutsu Gwasen Shū, 185
Nihon Meigwa Kagami, 91
Nihon Sankai Meibutsu Dzue, 74
Nijū Donsu Santoku Hira, 154
Nijū Gaku Dzusetsu, 31
Nijūshi-kō, 27, 141, 183
Nikkō-San-Shi, 183
Ningen Isshin Nozoki Karakuri, 153
Ningen Isshō Migaki Jōruri Kokoro-no-Kagami, 148, 154
Ningen Kyōgi, 150
Nintoku Tennō, 139
Nioi Sensu, 152
Nippon Kanoka, 35
Nippon Kanokō, 53
Nippon Kōdan Bokuga Meika, 67
Nippon Meizan Dzue, 118
Nippon Ō-Daiki, 46
Nippon Sankai Meisan Dzue, 68
Nishiki Hyakunin Isshu, 161
Nishiki Hyakunin Isshu Azuma Ori, 161
Nishiki Zuri Onna Sanjū-rok-kasen, 181
Nishiki Zuri Onna Sanjū-rok-kasen Edzukushi, 172
Nishiki-no Fukuro, 193
Nitan-no-Shirō, 46
Nitta Tsu Senki, 169
Nitta Yoshimune Koshinroku, 182
Nō-Daiki, 161
No-Kuwa, 196
Nobunaga-ki, 142
Nōka-densho, 25
Nori-no-Suihiro, 214
Nozo-ki Karakuri Yoshitsune Yama Eiri, 181
Nozo-kimi Tatoye Fushiyama, 181
Nuye Yorimasa Meika Shiba, 181
Nyoyō Bunshō Ito Guruma, 66
Nyoyō Kimmō Dzue, 53
Nyūhaku Dzusetsu, 205

INDEX OF TITLES OF BOOKS RECORDED

O Chō Masura Gaoi-no-Adanami, 152
O Mukashi Bakemono Hanashi, 153
O-Shuku-bai, 65
O-Ukeai Gesaku-no-Gaso-Uri, 156
Oboko Narihira Kyōdo-ji, 135
Odori Hotori Geiko, 183
Ogasawara Dai Shorei-shu Daizen, 116
Ogasawara Shōrei Daizen, 69
Ogata-ryū Gwafu, 60
Ogata-ryū Hyaken Dzu, 60, 61
Ogi-no-Sōshi, 25
Ogura Hyaku Donsaku Kusen, 181
Ogura Hyaku-shū Ruidai Banashi, 79
Ogura-no-Nishiki, 135
Ogura-Yama, 132
Ogura-Yama Hyakunin Isshu, 47
Oishi Yama Maru, 210
Ojigake Sangai Soga, 152
Ōjō Yōshū, 46
Okumura Musashi-ye, 136
Ōkyo, 84
Ōkyo Gwaden, 96
Ōkyo Gwafu, 96
Ōmi Hakkei, 166, 174
On Hinagata, 211
On Sashi Mono Zoroi, 206
Onaga Mochi, 181
Onaji-mi Hanasaki Jiji, 153
Ongyōku Hanage Nuki, 75
Onna Bunshō Shinan-shō, 67
Onna Buyū Kehai Kurabe, 67
Onna Buyū Yosoöi (Kurabe Kagami), 67
Onna Chōchōki, 180
Onna Chohoki, 52
Onna Chohoki Taisei, 52
Onna Dōji Kyō, 51
Onna Fūzoku Tamo Kagami, 132
Onna Geibun Sansai Dzue, 66
Onna Hyaku-fu, 107
Onna Imagawa, 65, 66, 184
Onna Imagawa Hemei Kagami, 132
Onna Kagami, 45
Onna Kasen Shinshō, 47
Onna Manyō Keiko Zōshi, 131
Onna Shisho Geimon Dzue, 116
Onna Shōgaku, 110
Onna Shorei Aya-nishiki, 99
Onna Shorei-Shu, 45
Onna Shuten Dōji Makura Kotoba, 135
Onna Takara-gura, 52
Onna Yo Kimmō Dzue, 211
Onna Yōsō Bunko, 74
Onsukuki Monogatari, 48
Orando Kiko, 147
Ori Ehon, 136
Orokushi Kiso-no-Adachi, 155
Osaka Monogatari, 46
Osana Genji, 36
Osana Najimi, 47
Oshi-no-Tsuyoimono Nandemo Hachiman, 153
Oshi-ye-gusa, 143
Oshi-ye Te-Kagami, 73
Oshōshi uwaki no chokuire, 152
Ōson Gwafu, 60

Ōtani Dōke Hyakunin Isshu, 153
Otogi Kanoka, 156
Otogi Kanoko, 154
Otoko Fumi Uta, 170
Otoko Ichi-Kagami Kaminuki-Kagami, 154
Otoko Toka, 170, 172, 175
Otoko Toko, 148
Otoko-Yama Hōjoye Dzuroku, 69
Otoko-no-Nakano-no-Otoko Kagami, 157
Otoshi Banashi Saru-no-Hitomane, 69
Otoshi Banashi Shimai-hiki Kashiwa Mochi, 152
Owari Meisho Dzue, 164
Oya Yuzuri Hana-no-Komyō, 181
Oya-no-Kataki Utsunomiya Monogatari, 154
Oyadama Tengu Tsubute Hana-no-Yedoko, 152
Oyose Hanashi-no-Shiriuma, 81

Prajnā Pāramitā Sūtra, 15 (n)

Rai Hin Dzu I., 126
Raigō Kaisō-den, 182
Raikin Dzui, 125
Raikō Atome-Ron, 46, 210
Raiko Yama Eiri, 135
Rakuyō Meisho Shū, 34, 38
Raikwō Ichidai-ki, 69
Ramma Dzushiki, 71, 72
Ranjatai, 67
Ransai Gwafu, 103
Rei Gwasen, 117
Rei-ye Gwayen, 117
Rekidai Kokkei-den, 36
Renge-dai, 187
Ressen Gwaden, 50
Ressen Zenden, 38
Rikkwa Hiden Shō, 207
Rikkwa Jisei Yosoöi, 207
Rikkwa Kimmō Dzue, 208
Rikkwa Shōshin Shō, 207
Ringu Sentaku Banashi, 181
Ritsuo (Hitsuyo?), 127
Ruyōun Chikufu, 115
Ro-ye Kyō Butai, 143
Ro Biraki Hanashi Kuchi-kiri, 169
Rok-kasen Kyōjitsu Tensaku, 181
Roku-roku Kyōka Sen, 100
Roku-Roku-sen, 93
Rokudaime Ichikawa Sansho Yedo-no-Hana Satsuki-no-Chirigwa, 154
Rokugon Tōshi Gwafu, 40
Rosetsu Gwafu, 98
Ruise Sogwa, 77
Ryaku-gwa, 65
Ryakugwa Haya-Shinan, 182
Ryakugwa Hyakunin Isshu, 101
Ryakugwa Kōrin-fu Rissai Hyaku Dzue, 195
Ryakugwa-shiki, 124
Ryakugwa Shokunin Dzukushi, 191
Ryakugwa-yen, 124
Ryōchū Kokoro-oboe, 195
Ryōfude, 184
Ryōgon-Kyō, 15
Ryōha Shigen, 137
Ryōken, 171

Ryōmen Shuhsi-no-Sugata Kagami, 154
Ryōmen Shuhsi Sugata Kagami Onnai Saru kataki-uchi, 182
Ryōsan-dō Ichiran, 184
Ryū Kwashu, 62
Ryūhitsu Gwafu, 185
Ryūryaku Jōkyō-kun, 182
Ryūryū Gyōretsu Dzue, 214
Ryūsai Gwafu, 193, 194
Ryūsai Sohitsu Gwafu, 195
Ryūsen Gwajo, 192
Ryūsen Suiko Gwaden-den, 192
Ryūzoku Kyōkasen, 124

Sadato Ikusa Edzukushi, 137
Saddharma Pundarika Sūtra, 16 (n)
Saga-bon, 25, 221, 226
Saifu-no-Himo Shirami Use Gusuri, 184
Saigwa Shokunin Burui, 66
Saigyō Waka Shugyō, 47
Saijiki Dzue, 195
Saikoku Sanjūsan-Shō Meisho Dzue, 80
Saiseiyen Gwaden, 112
Saishiki Gwaden, 66
Saishiki Gwasen, 127
Saishiki Mitsu-no-Ashita, 140
Saishikitsu, 184
Saito Gwafu, 190
Saiyu Ryōdan, 147
Saiyu Zenden Saiyuki, 185
Saji Mepokai, 75, 76
Sakaye-gusa (Eigadane), 148, 161, 163
Sakazuki-no-Sanoji Shichinin Jōgo, 152
Sakura, 122
Sakura Hime Zenden Akebono Zōshi, 155
Sakuragawa Hanashi-no-Chōjime, 154
Sakusha Kongen Yedo Nishiki, 154
Sakushiki Mimigaku-mon, 169
San Baso, 158
San Katsu-gushi Akebono Iro Gōshi, 78
San Shibai Yakusha Ehon, 161
San Ze Sō, 206
Sandara Kasumi, 148
Sangoku Wakan Ran Satsuga, 181
Sanji-Kyō Esho, 191
Sanjū-rok-kasen, 27, 48, 66, 161
Sanken Itchi Shō, 15
Sanjūni-sō, 154
Sanko Zake, 56
Sankyō Dōyu, 94
Sanryō Tōgwa Keisai Sogwa, 193
Sansai Dzue Osana Kōshaku, 135
Sanshichi Zenden Nanka-no-Yume, 182
Sanshitsuzen Denran Kanō Ume, 188
Sanshō Tayū, 148
Sansui Gwajō, 192
Sansui Gwayō, 187
Sansui Jūseki Gwafu, 88
Sansui Kikwan Kyōkwachō, 191
Sansui Ryakugwa-shiki, 124
Santai Gwafu, 183
Santo Suzume, 35
Santo Yakusha-no-Sugata-ye, 138
Santo Yakusha Suiko-den, 157

Sanuki Buri, 92
Sanyō Dzue Ehon Takara-no-Itoguchi Kaiko Yashinai-gusa), 148, 161
Sanze Aisho Makura, 49
Sanze-Sō-no-Manhasao, 153
Saru Genji, 135
Saru Hodoni Satemo Sono-nochi, 122
Saru-no-Shiri Kimpira Gobō, 152
Saryō Togwa Keisai Sogwa, 124
Sasa-ye-e Makura, 47
Sato-no-Hatsuhana, 79
Satomi Hakken-den, 192, 193
Satoshi Mondo, 143
Satsuma Tayu, 27
Sayo-goromo, 47
Sazare, Ishi, 144
Segan Shū, 174
Seihō Gwafu, 203
Seihō Shū Gwajo, 202
Seihō Sakuhin-shū, 203
Seika Jō, 106
Seiken Zu, 28
Seiki-no-Monokurabe, 152
Seikutsu-roku, 189
Seikwa Jō, 127
Seimei Tsuhensen Kiden, 48
Seimei Uta Uranai, 145
Seirō Bijin Awase, 145, 149, 150
Seirō Bijin Awase Sugata Kagami, 148, 161
Seiro Manroku, 61
Seirō Meikun Jihitsu Shū, 150
Seiroku Ruisan, 68
Seiten Toki Uta Shū, 170
Seiyo Gwaden, 147
Seiyō Ishokujū, 216
Seiyo Nampitsu, 101
Seki Gwa, 71, 73
Sekitei Gwaden, 56
Sekiyen Gwafu, 167
Sekkei Gwafu, 127
Sekkyō Karukaya, 32
Sembon Sakura, 135
Senga-no-Ura, 68
Senkei-ban Dzushiki, 208
Senmen Kosha-kyō, 7, 8
Senzai Waka-shū, 135
Serifu, 141
Settsu Meisho Dzue, 76
Settsu Meishu Shū, 101
Seven Military Classics (Seven Rules in Military Tactics), 28, 208
Sewa Edzukushi, 49
Shahō Bukuro, 65
Shaka-Hassō-ki, 46
Shaka Hassō Monogatari, 39
Shaka Suson Go-ichi-Dai-ki Dzue, 184
Shasei Kedamono Dzue, 65
Shashin Gakuhitsu Bokusen Sogwa, 188
Shazanrō Gwahon, 118, 162 (n)
Shi Tennō Daitsu Jitate, 181
Shi-Tennō Komyō Monogatari, 46
Shi-Tennō Ota-gasen, 46
Shiawase-Yoshi, 49
Shiba Zenkō Yume-no-Muda-Goto, 153

INDEX OF TITLES OF BOOKS RECORDED

Shibai Banashi, 78
Shibai Gakuya Dzue, 68
Shibai Hare Kosode, 130
Shibai Iro Kurabi, 137
Shibai Kimmō Dzue, 154
Shibai Saiken Mitsuba-gusa, 158
Shibai-ye Kimmō Dzue, 164
Shichi Fuku Konen Banashi, 156
Shichi-nan Shichi-fuku Dzue, 96
Shichigon Tōshi Gwafu, 40
Shida Monogatari, 45
Shidare Yanagi, 51
Shido-ken Yumi Monogatari, 135
Shika-no-Makifude, 49
Shikano Bunzaemon Kudan Banashi, 50
Shiki Go-shō-Sakura, 143
Shiki ku-awase, 90
Shiki Kwachō-no-Dzue, 201
Shiki Moyō Edzukushi, 47
Shiki Ogi E-Awase, 166
Shiki Onron, 33, 34
Shiki-no-Hana, 226
Shiki-no-Kwachō, 198
Shikiku Awase, 187
Shikoku Henrei Junrei-ki, 35
Shimeshi Ai-kagami, 143
Shimidzu-no-Ike, 131
Shimo-Yo-Boshi, 182
Shimpan Kwachō Edzukushi, 153
Shimpan Shinsaku Sansai-Ji-e, 47
Shimpan Wakoku Meisho Kagami, 47
Shimpen Jinkō-ki, 29
Shimpen Toki-no-Kumasaka Banashi, 182
Shin Gyoku Jo, 106
Shin Hakoya Bunko, 109
Shin Hana-tsumi, 91
Shin Hinagata Natorigawa, 211
Shin Kasane Gedatsu Monogatari, 182
Shin Otogi-bōko, 53
Shin Usuyuki Monogatari, 51
Shin Yoshiwara Sembon Sakura, 136
Shin-gaku Nannyō Kagami, 46
Shinagata Komonsho, 183
Shinga Hyakunin Isshu, 184
Shinkan Shaku Kōsei Hyōrui Mokuroku, 30
Shinki Ipputsu, 124
Shinki Isso, 124
Shinkoku Kinshi Gwafu, 111
Shinkwan Seiseki Dzu, 38
Shinobu-zuri, 66
Shinobu-gusa, 131
Shinobu-zuri Nishiki-no-Date Zome, 155
Shinoda azuma jidai Moyō, 152
Shinpen Suiko Gwaden, 182
Shinran Shōnin-ki, 47
Shinsen Kyōka Gojū-nin Isshu, 174, 187
Shinsen O Uchiwa, 135
Shinsen Somimono Hinagata, 211
Shiohi-no-Tsuto, 169
Shiouri Buntarō Monogatari, 153
Shirai Shi-banashi Kōhen, 153
Shiranui Sōshi, 69
Shirogana Chōja Nifukutsui Yeiga Haru Bukuro, 154
Shiseki, Kusumoto, 113
Shiten-dōji Monogatari, 148
Shitaya Katsura Otoko, 47
Shitori Haiku, 124, 147
Shitsuken Yume Monogatari, 135
Shiza (Yoza) Yaksuha Edzukushi, 50
Sho Utsushi Shijū-hachi Taka, 198
Shō-Chiku-Bai, 131
Shōchū Kitsunebi Haruzuzumi Hesobanashi Mono, 154
Shogaku Ede-hon, 176
Shogei Nishiki, 144
Shōgun-ki, 39, 46
Shogwatsu Yaoko-no-Kado, 157
Shoho Yaraku, 56
Shōjiki Banashi, 54
Shōjiki Banashi O-Kagami, 48
Shoki-ocho Shiraito Sashi, 182
Shokoku Meisho, 187
Shōkoku Meisho Uta Suzume, 44, 47
Shokunin, Dzukushi, 124
Shokurui Waboku-no-Kono Mono Kasen, 148
Shōnen Sansui Gwafu, 199
Shōnin Kagami, 184
Shorei-Kun, 67
Shōsetsu Hyaku-mu, 182
Shōshōku Edehon, 65
Shoshoku E-Kagami (Gwakyō), 124
Shoshōku Gwatsu, 195
Shotaikwa Sansui Gwafu, 204
Shōtei Kwachō Gwafu, 202
Shōtoku Taishi-den, 39
Shōzoku Dzushiki, 212
Shū Kaisho, 209
Shugwa Hyakudai, 202
Shūko Jisshu, 118
Shuko Meiken Gwashiki, 114
Shungwa Shohon Haru-no-Ashita, 145
Shunju-an Yomihatsu Mushiro, 185
Shunkyō, 104
Shunkyō-jo, 170
Shunparō Gwafu, 147
Shuten Dōji, 33
Shūzan Gwayei, 73
Sō-Shiseki Gwafu, 114
Sō-Shiseki Gwaso Sansui, 114
Sō-Shiseki Sansui-fu, 114
Soga Monogatari, 29, 31, 39, 46, 123
Sogwa Benran, 71
Sogwa Hyaku-Butsu, 110
Sogwa-Ho, 121
Sogwa Kokufū, 109
Sogwa Shashin Shikin-no-Hana Zono, 193
Sōgwa Tsushin Gwafu, 107
Sōhitsu Boku-gwa, 67
Sōhon Kwa Shifu, 40
Soken Gwafu, 99
Soken Gwafu Sogwa-no-bu, 99
Soken Sansui Gwafu, 99
Sōkwa Ryakugwa-shiki, 124
Some-aishō Nanjo-no-Urayeri, 152
Sonan Gwafu, 106, 107
Sonare-matsu, 131
Songs of Tomimoto, 141

JAPANESE BLOCK-PRINTING

Songwa Hyaku-butsu, 94
Sore-kara Irai-ki, 169
Sore wa Orogoto Gozonji Koraiya-den, 152
Sore-wa Kusunoke Kyantai Heiki Muko, 148
Sosen, Mori, 82
Soto Hyakunin Isshu, 191
Sue-hiro, 169
Suetsumuhana (?), 143
Sugata Zempen Onnai Saru-no-Adachi, 154
Sugata-ye Hyakunin Isshu, 45, 48
Sugoroku-ye Zakura Tsugiho-no-Hachine, 155
Sui Chōki, 46
Suigetsu Shū, 92
Suiko Gwaden, 187
Suiko Gwasen—ran, 167
Suiko-den Yushi-no-Edzukushi, 183
Suiseki, 84
Suiseki Gwafu, 93
Suiseki Gwafu Nihen, 93
Suiun Gwafu, 94
Sumidagawa Bairyū Shinsho, 182
Sumidagawa Ryōgan Ichiran, 182
Sumiyoshi Aioi Monogatari, 35
Sumiyoshi Meisho Dzue, 69
Sumiyoshi Monogatari, 46
Sundan Jutsu-Jitsuke, 156
surimono, 80
Suruga-no-Mai, 169
Suzuri-no-Chiri, 93

Tachi Bukuro, 140
Tadanori Hyaku Shū, 47
Tadatanome Daihi Chiye-no-Hanashi, 153
Taichōku Yugao Rechō-gusa, 137
Taigadō Gwafu, 88
Taigadō Gwaho, 88
Taihei Yusho, 106
Taisei Hyakunin Chiye Kagami, 184
Taisei Shin-Shafu, 108
Taisei Shōkoku Senko, 147
Taikō-ki, 69
Taitokai Kabuki Suiko-den, 158
Taizan Gwafu, 199
Taka Byōbu Kuda Monogatari, 43, 46
Takadachi, 32
Takagami, 196
Takana Kagami, 162
Takasago Tokai-eiri, 136
Takara-no-Chiribune, 161
Take Dzukushi, Matsu Dzukushi, Ume Dzukushi, 203
Take-no-Hayashi, 145
Takuan Oshō Kamakura-ki, 34, 41, 45
Tama Hiroi, 127
Tama Ho-ōki, 53
Tama Kushige, 169
Tama Migaku Aoto Gazeni, 169
Tama Mizu, 211
Tama-Kazura, 131
Tama-no-Ochibo, 182
Tamamo Monogatari, 69
Tamano Ikago, 166
Tamashige Ishidomaru Monogatari, 166
Tamatsu-shima Honji, 46

Tameyoshi Ubusuna Mondi, 210
Tamizu Shinzaemon kataki-uchi Nezasa-no-Yuki, 154
Tamura Monogatari, 188
Tanaka Shōzaemon, 28
Tani Bunchō Gwafu, 118
Tani Bunchō Honchō Gwasen Daizen, 118
Tanoshimi-gusa, 127
Tansei Kimmō, 71
Tarafuku Manryō Bungen, 153
Tata Kimaze Yarō-no-Kamaboko, 152
Tatoye-no-Bushi, 169
Tatsu-no-Miyako, 148
Tatsu-no-toshi, 94
Tatsumi-no-Sono, 159
Tayu Kurabe, 145
Te Asobi Hariko-no-Tora-no-Maki, 152
Te-Suisen Segawa Boshi, 158
Tebiki-gusa, 195
Teikan Dzusetsu, 28
Teikun Warai, 183
Teikwa, 135
Teinitsu Taki-no-Yogatari, 193
Teisai Gwafu, 189
Teito Gakei Ichiran, 104
Tesitu Gwafu, 184
Tesitu Sensei Keijō Gwafu, 183
Tema Ezuki Akaho-no-Shiokara, 184
Temare Uta, 139
Temman-gū Goshin-ji Omukai-bune Ningyō Dzu, 79, 80
Temman-gu Yengi, 163
Temmei Shinsen Gojū-nin Isshu, 150
Temmon Ryakugwa, 147
Temmon Zukai, 51
Tempō Yama Haikai Kusha Hashikaki, 191
Tendō Ukiyo Dezukai, 153
Tengu Dairi, 22
Tengu Ha-uchi, 210
Tenjin Goichi Dai-ki, 135
Tennen Hyaku, 203
Tennen Moyō Kan, 203
Tenun Minonaru Kino Hachi Ne-Eigwa, 153
Tessan, Mori, 82
Theatre programmes, 141
To-jō, 109
Toba Meihitsu Gwafu, 118
Tōbō-Saku Ku-Sensai, 145
Toba-ye Akubi-dome, 76
Toba-ye Daizan, 71
Toba-ye, Edehon, 75
Toba-ye Fude Byōshi, 74
Toba-ye Musha, 74
Toba-ye, Ōgi-no-Mato, 71, 72
Toba-ye Sango Kushi, 71, 72
Tōdaibutsu Momiji Meisho, 181
Tōdo Kimmō Dzue, 64
Tofuon Hinagata, 50
Tigen-sō, 134
Tōgoku Meisho-ki, 67
Tōkaidō, 213
Tōkaidō Buken Edzu, 48
Tōkaidō Fukei Dzue, 195
Tōkaidō Harimaze Dzue, 195

INDEX OF TITLES OF BOOKS RECORDED

Tōkaidō Meisho Dzue, 105, 125, 195
Tōkaidō Meisho-ki, 34
Tōkaidō-chū Hizakurige, 77
Tōkei Gwafu, 89
Toki Dzukase, 133
Tokiwa-gusa, 93, 131, 132
Tokiwa Hinagata, 211
Tokiwa-no-Taki, 187
Tokiyo Yosoōi, 154
Toko-no-kimono (Shiawase-Yoshi), 49
Tomodachi Banashi, 141
Tomochidori, 160
Tori Kabu-ki, Tomatsuri, 74
Tōrin, Tsutsumi, 113
Toriyama Biken, 167
Toriyama Saishiki Dzuri, 167
Toriyama Sekiyen Gwa-shiki (Gwafu?), 167
Tōryū Hinagata Kyō-no-Mizu, 211
Tōsei Banashi Suikoden, 154
Tosei Onna Danshishi, 141
Tosei Shōryū Ika-bon Ezu, 156
Tosei Suiko-den, 159
Tōshi Gwafu, 188
Tōshi, Kyūkyūshin, 79
Toshinobu, Okumura, 134
Tōshisen Gogon Zekku, 183
Toshitsu Yogen Kwairoku, 188
Toshiyori-no-Hiyamizu Soga, 152
Tōshu, Murakami, 103
Tōto Asobi, 181
Tōto Hakkei, 147
Tōto Jūni Tsuki, 156
Tōto Meisho, 145
Tōto Meisho Dzue, 69
Tōto Meisho Shōkei Ichiran, 181
Tōto Sai-shiki, 192
Tōto Saijiki, 68
Tōto Shōkei Ichiran, 80
Tōtōmi Dzufu Seiki, 114
Towa Kagami, 131
Toyoaki, Toriyama, 168
Toyohiko Kwachō Gwafu, 91
Toyohiko, Okamoto, 91
Toyohiro, Utagawa, 155, 156
Toyokuni II, Ichiyōsai, 157
Toyokuni Toshidama Fude, 155
Toyokuni Toshidama-no-fude, 158
Tozan Ran-jō, 121
Tozen Bukuro, 167
Tsubo-no-Ishibumi, 49
Tsugamonei Hanashi-no-Oyadama, 152
Tsugiho-no-Hana, 161
Tsūhōshi, 65
Tsuki-nami-no-Asobi, 48
Tsuki-no-Kumasaka, 184
Tsuki-no-Ye Tsuki-no-To, 165
Tsukinarai Sake-no-sano-Ji, 152
Tsukinu Idzumi, 69
Tsukiyama Niwa Tsukuri, 208
Tsukiyama-zu Niwa Edzukushi, 48
Tsukuba Yama, 131
Tsukurinarai Sake-no-sano-Ji, 152
Tsumawa Morokuchi Yawaragi Sogwa, 137
Tsunokuni Nayotoga Ike, 213

Tsure-dsure-gusa, 53, 131
Tsure-dsure-gusa Esho, 52
Tsure-dzure Suigwa-kawa, 75
Tsuru-take Nasakeno Akibito, 136
Tsuruga-Oka Yahazu Daimon, 80
Tsushin Meimei Gwaden, 158
Tsuzoku Sango Kushi, 183

Uchi Benkei Kanjinchō, 153
Uchiwa Edzukushi, 47
Uchiyūsai Gwafu, 159
Ui Manabe Gwafu, 176
Uji-no-Watashi, 148
Ukiyo Edzukushi, 48
Ukiyo Ehon Tsuru-no-Kuchi Bashi, 135
Ukiyo Gwafu, 194
Ukiyo Hyakunin Isshu Onna, 47
Ukiyo Karakuri Kumen Jūmen, 152
Ukiyo Meitai-ki, 168
Ukiyo Zoku Edzukushi, 47
Ukiyo Zōshi, 137
Ukiyo-Ede-hon, 159
Ukiyo-on Chazuki Jūni Innen, 164
Ukiyo-ye Bukuro, 145
Umbiraki Ōgi-no-Hanaka, 181
Ume-no-Kaori, 48
Umi-no-Sachi, 57, 58, 124 (n)
Umpitsu Sogwa, 64, 65
Urashima, 32
Uso Ha-byaku Mempachi-den, 168
Uso Yaoroyozu-no-Kami Ichiza, 153
Usode-nashi Hakone-no-Saki, 152
Usokawa Mukashi Banashi, 163
Usono Taiboku, 154
Uta Bunko, 133
Uta Makura, 169
Uta Yasukata Ichidai-ki, 156
Uta Yomi Dori, 165, 175
Uta Zakura, 49
Uta-no-Tomobune, 158, 191
Uto-no-Omokage, 155
Utsunomiya Godan Jōruri Sakamise, 154
Uwaki Banashi, 169
Uwo Kagami, 158

Wachō Meisho Gwadzu, 65
Waka Chusen-sho, 47
Waka Ebisu, 169
Waka Inshitsu Bun Esho, 183
Waka Murasaki, 154, 155
Waka Rokujū Yoshū, 47
Waka Sanjū-rok-kasen, 25
Waka-Mono-Arasoi, 52
Waka-no-Homare, 184
Waka-no-Tebiki, 48
Waka-no-Ura, 51
Waka-no-ura Kabuto, 134
Wakaki, 189
Wakakusa Genji Monogatari, 134, 136
Wakan Ehon Sakigaki, 183
Wakan Eiju Hyakunin Isshu, 195
Wakan Eiyū Gwaden, 158
Wakan Fujin Yashinai-gusa, 53
Wakan Gorui Ehon Kagami, 65

Wakan Koji Bukuyo Shingwa, 71
Wakan Meigwayen, 70, 71
Wakan Meihitsu Ehon Te-Kagami, 71, 72
Wakan Meihitsu Gwahō, 73
Wakan Meihitsu Gwayei, 73
Wakan Meihitsu Kingyoku Gwafu, 67, 73
Wakashū Asobi Makura, 47
Waki Dzushi, 182
Wakoku Hyaku-jo, 48, 132
Wakoku Meisho Kagami, 47
Warabe-no-Moto, 145
Waraji Jogo, 170
Wata on Jaku, 156
Waterfalls, Poems on Famous, 187

Ya-egaki Kumono Tayema, 50
Yabara Mombara-no-Nakana Chō, 181
Yabo-no-Isshu Kwaraku-no-Motoshime, 152
Yabo-no-Shiori, 75
Yachiyo-gusa, 145
Yahan-no-Chazukei, 150
Yakko-no-Koman, 176
Yakusha Awase Kagami, 155
Yakusha Ehon, 81
Yakusha Hitori Tebiki, 155
Yakusha Kono Tei Kashiwa, 154
Yakusha Kuni-no-Hana, 161
Yakusha Meisho Dzue, 54
Yakusha Natsu-no-Fuji, 161
Yakusha Nigao Haya Gei-ko, 155
Yakusha Sango Kushi, 81
Yakusha (or Haiyo) Sugao Natsu-no-Fuji, 157
Yakushi Engi, 77
Yama Mata Yama, 180
Yama-no-Sachi, 57, 58
Yamashiro Meisho-ki, 34
Yamashiro Shiki Monogatari, 65
Yamato Edzukushi, 47
Yamato Fūryū E-Kagami, 52
Yamato Hiji, 130
Yamato Honzo, 181
Yamato Jimbutsu Gwafu, 99
Yamato Kosaku Esho, 53
Yamato Meisho Ichiran, 187
Yamato Meisho Dzue, 76
Yamato Meisho Ehon Dzukushi, 46
Yamato Shinō Edzukushi, 47
Yamato Taiyō, 46
Yamato Utakotoba, 47
Yamato-no-Oyosei, 47
Yamato-zumi, 47
Yanagawa Gwajin, 192
Yanagawa Gwajō, 192
Yanagawa Mangwa, 192
Yanagawa Shigenobu Gwafu, 192
Yanagi Musubi, 93
Yanagi-no-Ito, 172
Yaro Yakusha, 211
Yashima Michiyuki, 33
Yashinai-gusa, 162
Yasu Ujigawa, 148
Yasunobu, 43
Yatsuhachi Chirabe-no-Nishiki, 150
Yema Awase Onna Kana-de-hon, 165

Yedo Banashi, 35
Yedo Dzu, 54
Yedo Ichiran Dzue, 123
Yedo Jiman Hana-no-Meibutsu, 153
Yedo Jiman Meisan Dzue, 155
Yedo Kanoka, 35, 49
Yedo Meisho, 77, 155, 172
Yedo Meisho Dzue, 68, 192
Yedo Meisho Dzukai, 123
Yedo Meisho Hana Koyomi, 192
Yedo Meisho Hanagoyomi, 68
Yedo Meisho Hyakkei, 194
Yedo Meisho Kinryūzan, 123
Yedo Meisho-ki, 34, 37
Yedo Miyage, 142, 145, 195
Yedo Monomi-ga-oka, 139
Yedo Murasaki, 54, 143, 180, 224
Yedo Murasaki Sono-ato Maku Baba Dōjōji, 154
Yedo Nishiki, 170
Yedo Nishiki-ye, 146
Yedo O Yama Ehon Bijin Fukutoku, 135
Yedo Sakura, 76
Yedo Sō-Kanoka, 35
Yedo Suzume, 35, 46, 169
Yedo Umare Iwake-no-Kabayaki, 150
Yedo Zukan Kōmoku, 54
Yedo-no-Mizu, 153
Yedo-ye Sudare Byōbu, 135
Yeiyu Retsujō-den, 67
Yeiyū Teiyu Gwashiki, 193
Yennō Gwafu, 96
Yezu Hyakki Yagyō, 167
Yo-Banashi-gusa, 54
Yodagawa Ryōgan Shōkei Dzue, 79
Yodogawa Ryōgan Ichiran, 80
Yofu Gwafu, 203
Yōhō (Gwazu) Yakusha Shashin Sangai Kyō, 154
Yoho Fuki Jizai Kogane-no-Toshidama, 154
Yoitoyu Hyakunin Isshu, 101
Yojo Gojū-nin Isshu, 67
Yojō Hinagata, 211
Yojo Hinagata, 52
Yokei Tsukusi no Niwa no zu, 48
Yokohama Kaikō Kenbunshi, 196, 216
Yōkyoku Gwashi, 65, 76
Yomei Iri Fukuroku, 141
Yomeiri Makura, 49
Yomitsu Fune, 170
Yomo-no-Haru, 114, 120, 150, 187
Yomogi-no-Shima, 169
Yomori Saiwai Tamaye Go Oku-jin, 154
Yono Kotowaza Torikomi Shōfu, 152
Yononaka Hyaku-shū, 54
Yorō-no-Daki, 134
Yoroi Sakura, 136
Yorozu Hyakunin Isshu Sobunshō, 184
Yōsai Rekishi Gwafu, 101
Yoshikiyo, Ōmori, 54
Yoshikono Gyokuyō Shū, 81
Yoshino-gusa, 131
Yoshino-yama Hitori Anai, 34
Yoshitsune Ichidai Dzue, 195

INDEX OF TITLES OF BOOKS RECORDED

Yoshitsune Ichidai-ki, 161
Yoshitsune-ki, 48
Yoshiwara, 170
Yoshiwara Bijin Awase, 145
Yoshiwara Daidzu Dawara Byōbu, 47
Yoshiwara Daizen, 145
Yoshiwara Genji Gojū-shi-kun, 48
Yoshiwara Hokuri Jūni Toka, 187
Yoshiwara, Homing Geese at, 155
Yoshiwara Koi-no-Michibiki, 46
Yoshiwara Makura, 46
Yoshiwara Saiken-ki, 138
Yoshiwara Shin Bijin Awase Jihitsu Kagami, 156
Yoshiwara Sode Kagami, 46
Yoshiwara Yukun Sugatami, 135
Yosōsai Gwafu, 201
Yotsu-no-Toki, 148
Yotsugi-gusa, 131
Yōyō-no-Matsu, 140
Yu Gwa-shiki, 135
Yūdzū Nembutsu Engi, 18, 19, 20, 21
Yuhi, Kumashiro, 102
Yuigahama Chūya Monogatari, 184
Yujoro Kotobuki Banashi, 169
Yuki Hyaku Shū, 187, 188
Yuki Onna Kuruwa, 169
Yukiyo Ehon Nukumei-dori, 135
Yuku-no-Misao Renrino Mochibana, 182
Yukun Ōmi Daishi, 138
Yume-no-Ukubashi, 182
Yume-no-Yojo Dzushi, 93
Yume-no-Yokozuchi, 127

Yumeigusa, 67
Yumi (Isai) Bukuro, 164
Yūmō Sanryaku-no-Maki, 67
Yuriwaka Daijin, 46
Yuriwaka Daijin-to-no-Nemuri, 153
Yuryū Akanui Isu-Taka, 182
Yūsai Gwafu, 107
Yusen, Kanō, 177
Yushi Kurabe, 148
Yūzen, Kaihoku, 51

Zembon Zakura, 155
Zen Myōkan Sayo Tsuke, 156
Zenaku Futatsu-no-Ryō-yaku, 76
Zenken Kojitsu, 101
Zensei Tagu-no-Kurabe, 172
Zensei-no-Tsurebushi Itsui Otoko Hayari, 155
Zō Sanshō Dayu Monogatari, 153
Zōho Hyakunin Isshu Esho, 53
Zōho Isaoshi-gusa, 119
Zōho Kashira Gaki Kimmō Dzue Taisei, 162
Zōho Kwaitsu Shōko, 215
Zōho Rikkwa Kimmō Dzue, 208
Zōho Shipeitarō, 153
Zoku Butai-no-Ōgi, 161
Zoku Haigwa Kijin-den, 87
Zoku Hakoya Bunko, 109
Zoku Hyaku-shū, 131
Zoku Kinsei Ki-jin-den, 56
Zoku Yedo Miyage, 145
Zokuetsu Ki-dan, 183
Zokukai Genji Monogatari, 135

ACHEVÉ D'IMPRIMER
SUR LES PRESSES OFFSET DE L'IMPRIMERIE REDA S.A.
A CHÊNE-BOURG (GENÈVE), SUISSE

SEPTEMBRE 1973

For Product Safety Concerns and Information please contact our EU
representative GPSR@taylorandfrancis.com
Taylor & Francis Verlag GmbH, Kaufingerstraße 24, 80331 München, Germany

www.ingramcontent.com/pod-product-compliance
Lightning Source LLC
Chambersburg PA
CBHW080726300426
44114CB00019B/2498